Barack Obama and African

American Empowerment

THE CRITICAL BLACK STUDIES SERIES

INSTITUTE FOR RESEARCH IN AFRICAN AMERICAN STUDIES COLUMBIA UNIVERSITY

Edited by Manning Marable

The Critical Black Studies Series features readers and anthologies examining challenging topics within the contemporary black experience—in the United States, the Caribbean, Africa, and across the African Diaspora. All readers include scholarly articles originally published in the acclaimed quarterly interdisciplinary journal *Souls*, published by the Institute for Research in African American Studies at Columbia University. Under the general editorial supervision of Manning Marable, the readers in the series are designed both for college and university course adoption, as well as for general readers and researchers. The Critical Black Studies Series seeks to provoke intellectual debate and exchange over the most critical issues confronting the political, socioeconomic, and cultural reality of black life in the United States and beyond.

Titles in this series published by Palgrave Macmillan:

Racializing Justice, Disenfranchising Lives: The Racism, Criminal Justice, and Law Reader

> Edited by Manning Marable, Keesha Middlemass, and Ian Steinberg

Seeking Higher Ground: The Hurricane Katrina Crisis, Race, and Public Policy Reader

> Edited by Manning Marable and Kristen Clarke

Transnational Blackness: Navigating the Global Color Line

> Edited by Manning Marable and Vanessa Agard-Jones

Black Routes to Islam

> Edited by Manning Marable and Hishaam D. Aidi

Barack Obama and African American Empowerment: The Rise of Black America's New Leadership

> Edited by Manning Marable and Kristen Clarke

New Social Movements in the African Diaspora: Challenging Global Apartheid

> Edited by Leith Mullings

The New Black History: The African American Experience since 1945 Reader

> Edited by Manning Marable and Peniel E. Joseph

Beyond Race: New Social Movements in the African Diaspora

> Edited by Manning Marable

The Black Women, Gender, and Sexuality Reader

> Edited by Manning Marable

Black Intellectuals: The Race, Ideology, and Power Reader

> Edited by Manning Marable

BARACK OBAMA AND AFRICAN AMERICAN EMPOWERMENT

THE RISE OF BLACK AMERICA'S NEW LEADERSHIP

Edited by Manning Marable and Kristen Clarke

First published in 2009 by PALGRAVE MACMILLAN® in the United States—a division of St. Martin's Press LLC, 175 Fifth Avenue, New York, NY 10010.

Where this book is distributed in the UK, Europe, and the rest of the world, this is by Palgrave Macmillan, a division of Macmillan Publishers Limited, registered in England, company number 785998, of Houndmills, Basingstoke, Hampshire RG21 6XS.

Palgrave Macmillan is the global academic imprint of the above companies and has companies and representatives throughout the world.

Palgrave® and Macmillan® are registered trademarks in the United States, the United Kingdom, Europe and other countries.

ISBN: 978-0-230-62050-6 (hardcover)
ISBN: 978-0-230-62052-0 (paperback)

Library of Congress Cataloging-in-Publication Data.

Barack Obama and African-American empowerment : the rise of Black America's new leadership / Manning Marable and Kristen Clarke, Editors.
    p. cm.—(The critical black studies series)
    Includes bibliographical references and index.
    ISBN 978-0-230-62050-6—ISBN 978-0-230-62052-0 1. African Americans—Politics and government 2. African American leadership. 3. Obama, Barack. 4. Presidents—United States—Election—2008. 5. United States—Race relations—Political aspects. I. Marable, Manning, 1950– II. Clarke, Kristen.

E185.615.B2855 2009
973.932092—dc22   2009010423

A catalogue record of the book is available from the British Library.

Design by Scribe Inc.

First edition: December 2009

10 9 8 7 6 5 4 3 2 1

Printed in the United States of America.

CONTENTS

RACIALIZING OBAMA

THE ENIGMA OF POSTBLACK POLITICS AND LEADERSHIP

MANNING MARABLE

THE HISTORICAL SIGNIFICANCE OF THE ELECTION OF ILLINOIS SENATOR BARACK OBAMA as president of the United States was recognized literally by the entire world. For a nation that had, only a half century earlier, refused to enforce the voting rights and constitutional liberties of people of African descent to elevate a black American to its chief executive was a stunning reversal of history. On the night of his electoral victory, spontaneous crowds of joyful celebrants rushed into streets, parks, and public establishments in thousands of venues across the country. In Harlem, over ten thousand people surrounded the Adam Clayton Powell State Office Building, cheering and crying in disbelief. To many, the impressive margin of Obama's popular-vote victory suggested the possibility that the United States had entered at long last an age of postracial politics, in which leadership and major public policy debates would not be distorted by factors of race and ethnicity. . . .

Obama's election almost overnight changed the widely held negative perceptions about America's routine abuses of power, especially those perceptions held across the Third World. One vivid example of the recognition of this new reality was represented by a petulant statement by Ayman al-Zawahri, the deputy leader of the al-Qaeda terrorist network. Al-Zawahri contemptuously dismissed Obama as the "new face of America," which only "masked a heart full of hate." Al-Qaeda also released a video in which former Bush secretaries of state Colin Powell and Condoleezza Rice, both African Americans, as well as Obama, were denigrated "[in] the words of Malcolm X (may Allah have mercy on him) [as] 'house Negroes.'" Malcolm X was favorably quoted for condemning the docile "house Negro who always looked out for his master." To al-Qaeda, Obama was nothing short of a "hypocrite and traitor to his race." America "continues to be the same as ever. . . ."[1] Despite Obama's concerted efforts to present himself as a presidential candidate "who happened to be black," both proponents and enemies like al-Qaeda were quick to freeze his identity to the reality of his blackness, for both positive and negative reasons.

To understand the main factors that contributed to Obama's spectacular but in many ways unlikely victory, it is necessary to return to the defining "racializing moment" in recent U.S. history—the tragic debacle of the Hurricane Katrina crisis of 2005, under the regime of President George W. Bush. It was not simply the deaths of over one thousand Americans and the forced relocations of hundreds of thousands of people from their homes in New Orleans and across the Gulf of Mexico states region who were disproportionately black and poor. The inevitable consequences of a natural disaster in New Orleans, a city below sea level, were not unexpected. Rather, it was the callous and contemptuous actions of the federal government—especially the Federal Emergency Management Agency (FEMA)—plagued by cronyism and corruption, that directly contributed to blacks' deaths. The world witnessed on television for days the stunning spectra of thousands of mostly black and poor people stranded in New Orleans' downtown Morial Convention Center. FEMA claimed its vehicles could not reach the center to send in medical supplies, food, and fresh water; meanwhile, media representatives and entertainers easily were able to drive to the center. States like Florida, which proposed to send in five hundred airboats to assist with Gulf Coast rescue efforts, were inexplicably turned away. Needed supplies such as electric generators, trailers, and freight cars stocked with food went undelivered to starving, desperate evacuees. The overwhelming collage of tragic images pointed to the enduring blight of racism and poverty as central themes within the arrangements of institutional power in the United States.[2] By mid-September 2005, 60 percent of all African Americans surveyed were convinced that "the federal government's delay in helping the victims in New Orleans was because the victims were black." What was striking to minorities was that the overwhelming majority of white citizens remained convinced that their government was color-blind: only 12 percent of whites surveyed agreed that the government's Katrina response was racially biased.[3]

The reality of racial injustice through governmental inaction was also reinforced among millions of black Americans by the results of the presidential elections of 2000 and 2004, both won by Republican George W. Bush. In 2000, there was substantial evidence that tens of thousands of African American voters in Florida were deliberately excluded from exercising the franchise through a variety of measures. Thousands of Florida voters with misdemeanor convictions, for example, were illegally barred from voting. Thousands of black voters in specific districts were inexplicably barred from casting ballots. Four years later, a similar process of black voter suppression occurred in Ohio, which Bush narrowly won over Democratic presidential candidate John Kerry.[4] To many African Americans, the two controversial presidential elections and the Katrina tragedy cemented the perspective that the American system was hardwired to discriminate against the interests of people of African descent. If basic political change was possible, or even conceivable, it would probably not be through frontal assaults, similar to the bold challenges of Jesse Jackson's National Rainbow Coalition presidential campaigns of 1984 and 1988. If meaningful change occurred at all, it would probably happen at the margins. Few anticipated the possibility that an African American candidate with relatively little experience at the national level could capture the Democratic Party's presidential nomination, much less win election to the presidency.

Although the overall character of national black politics was in many respects defensive and deeply pessimistic, a growing minority trend within African American leadership perceived the early years of the twenty-first century quite differently. For decades, prior to the early 1990s, there had been one ironclad rule in American racial politics: the majority of white voters in any legislative municipal or congressional district would not vote for an African American candidate, regardless of her or his ideology or partisan affiliation. There was an omnipresent glass ceiling in electoral politics limiting the rise of all black elected officials. Blacks could be elected to Congress or as mayors of major cities only if districts held high concentrations of minority voters. In the 1980s, progressive black candidates such as Harold Washington sought to circumvent this racial barrier by constructing multiracial coalitions as the base of their electoral mobilizations, reaching out to traditional liberal constituencies.[5] Other more conservative African American leaders, such as Thomas Bradley, who had been elected mayor of Los Angeles on his second try in 1972, and Philadelphia mayor Wilson Goode in the 1980s, won whites' support by deliberately downplaying their own ethnic affiliations and racial identities. They espoused a pragmatic, nonideological politics that catered to local corporate interests and promoted urban concessions. Even these moderate black officials could not depend on the electoral support of many whites, even in their own parties.

Political scientists first began observing the lack of reliability of pre-election polls for whites in races involving African American candidates nearly three decades ago. In the 1982 California gubernatorial election, pre-election polls indicated that Democratic Los Angeles Mayor Thomas Bradley would easily defeat Republican challenger George Deukmejian. After Bradley narrowly lost to Deukmejian, it became evident that a significant percentage of whites who had been predicted to support Bradley had voted for the Republican.[6] This "Bradley effect" was subsequently documented in dozens of elections. For example, in 1989, Virginia Lieutenant Governor Douglas Wilder, a Democrat, announced his candidacy for the state's governorship. In many ways Wilder ran a campaign similar to that of Obama two decades later. Wilder focused on issues largely devoid of racial overtones, such as economic development, the environment, and public health. Opinion polls in the state showed Wilder maintaining a double-digit lead over a lackluster Republican candidate, Marshall Coleman. In Virginia's gubernatorial election, which Wilder managed to win but by less than one-half of one percent of the total vote, white voters overwhelmingly had favored Coleman. Even more significantly, pollsters found that many white Virginians deliberately provided false information when revealing their voting intentions in polls. When whites were questioned about their gubernatorial preferences by a white pollster, Coleman defeated Wilder by 16 percent. But when black pollsters were used for interviews, whites favored Wilder by 10 percent over Coleman. Both the inconsistent pre-election polling information by whites and the actual election returns appear to validate the "Bradley effect."[7]

The cases of Bradley and Wilder were in many ways mirrored by the 1989 mayoral election in New York City, which was won by an African American Democrat, Manhattan Borough President David Dinkins. As noted by Andrew Kohul, the president of the Pew Research Center, the Gallup organization's polling research on New York City's voters in 1989 had indicated that Dinkins would defeat his Republican opponent, Rudolph Giuliani, by 15 percent. Instead, Dinkins only narrowly won by 2 percent. Kohul, who worked as a Gallup pollster in that election, concluded that "poorer, less well-educated [white] voters were less likely to answer our questions," so the poll didn't have the opportunity to factor in their views. As Kohul observed, "Here's the problem—these whites who do not respond to surveys tend to have more unfavorable view of blacks than respondents who do the interviews."[8]

By the twenty-first century, hundreds of race-neutral, pragmatic black officials had emerged, winning positions on city councils, state legislatures, and in the House of Representatives. Frequently they distanced themselves from traditional liberal constituencies such as unions, promoted gentrification and corporate investment in poor urban neighborhoods, and favored funding charter schools as an alternative to the failures of public school systems. A growing share of these new leaders were elected from predominately white districts. In 2001, for example, according to the Joint Center for Political and Economic Studies, roughly 16 percent of the nation's African American state legislators had won election in predominantly white districts. By 2008, out of 622 black state legislators nationally, 30 percent represented predominately white constituencies. Between 1998 and 2008, about two hundred African Americans defeated whites for municipal and state legislative races, even in states such as Iowa, Minnesota, and New Hampshire, where black populations are small.[9] In November 2006, civil rights attorney Deval Patrick, employing campaign strategies drawn from Barack Obama's successful 2004 Senate bid, easily won the gubernatorial race in Massachusetts, a state with a 79 percent white population.[10]

Ideologically, this new leadership group reflected a range of divergent views on social policy. The most prominent "moderates" within this cohort included former Tennessee Congressman Harold Ford, who is currently leader of the centrist Democratic Leadership Council, and Newark, New Jersey, Mayor Cory Booker. More ideologically "liberal" leaders in this group are Barack Obama, New York Governor David Patterson, and Massachusetts Governor Deval Patrick. This is not to suggest that these politicians possess no strong ethnic roots or identity. All of these individuals are proudly self-identified as African Americans. But strategically, none of them pursue what could be called race-based politics. None favor or would support a black agenda similar to that espoused by the Gary, Indiana, Black Political Convention in March 1972. Most probably would perceive even Jesse Jackson's Rainbow Coalition campaigns of the 1980s as too narrowly race- and ethnically based and too far to the left on economic policy.

Obama undoubtedly took most of these factors into account—the possibility of a "Bradley/Wilder effect" on whites' support of black candidates, African American grievances surrounding the 2000 and 2004 presidential campaigns, the recent debacle of the Katrina crisis, and the rise of the postracial politics of a new generation of black leaders—to construct his own image and political narrative essential for a presidential campaign. Early on in their deliberation process, the Obama precampaign group recognized that most white Americans would never vote for a *black* presidential candidate. However, they were convinced that most whites would embrace, and vote for, a remarkable, qualified presidential candidate *who happened to be black.* "Race" could be muted into an adjective, a qualifier of minimal consequence. So ethnically, Obama did not deny the reality of his African heritage; it was blended into the multicultural narrative of his uniquely "American story," which also featured white grandparents from Kansas, a white mother who studied anthropology in Hawaii, and an Indonesian stepfather. Unlike black conservatives, Obama openly acknowledged his personal debt to the sacrifices made by martyrs and activists of the civil rights movement. Yet he also spoke frequently about the need to move beyond the divisions of the sixties, to seek common ground, and a postpartisan politics of hope and reconciliation. As the Obama campaign took shape in late 2006-early 2007, the basic strategic line about "race," therefore, was to deny its enduring presence or relevance to contemporary politics. Volunteers often chanted, in Hare Krishna fashion, "Race Doesn't Matter! Race Doesn't Matter!" as if to ward off the evil spirits of America's troubled past.

Obama's strategic approach on race was indeed original, but coming at a time of hopelessness and pessimism among many African Americans, there were doubts that the young Illinois senator could actually pull it off. To some, Obama's multiracial pedigree raised questions about his loyalties to the cause of black people. Curiously, many of those with the loudest queries were African American conservatives and Republicans, whose own bona fides on racial matters were often under fire. For example, conservative writer Debra Dickerson, author of *The End of Blackness*, declared in January 2007 that "Obama would be the great black hope in the next presidential race, if he were actually black."[11] Journalist Stanley Crouch took a similarly negative approach, arguing that while Obama "has experienced some light versions of typical racial stereotypes, he cannot claim those problems as his own—nor has he lived the life of a black American."[12] Juan Williams, conservative commentator on Fox News, warned that "there are widespread questions whether this son of a white American mother and a black Kenyan father really understands the black American experience."[13]

As late as December 2007, roughly one-half of all African Americans polled still favored Hillary Clinton over Obama as their Democratic presidential candidate. Some of Obama's sharpest "racial doubters" were even from Chicago, his home base. Eddie Read, chair of Chicago's Black Independent Political Organization, for example, predicted that "nothing's going to happen" as a result of the Democratic senator's candidacy, because "he doesn't belong to us. He would not be the black president. He would be the multicultural president."[14]

Obama's ultimate victory over Hillary Clinton in the 2008 Democratic primaries began with his implacable opposition to the U.S. invasion of Iraq. Back in 2002, Obama warned that "an invasion of Iraq without a clear rationale and without strong international support will only fan the flames of the Middle East, and encourage the worst, rather than the best, impulses of the world, and strengthen the recruitment arm of al-Qaeda." Less noticed in this speech was Obama's appeal "to make sure our so-called allies in the Middle East, the Saudis and the Egyptians, stop oppressing dissent, and tolerating corruption and inequality, and mismanaging their economies so that their youth grow up without education, without prospects, without hope, the ready recruits of terrorist cells."[15] Like Malcolm X a generation earlier, Barack Obama's entry into national politics was associated with the Islamic world.

Even before the announcement of his candidacy for president, media conservatives resorted to Islamophobia to denigrate Obama. For example, on CNN's *Situation Room* on December 11, 2006, correspondent Jeanne Moos observed darkly, "Only one little consonant differentiates" Obama versus Osama, also noting that the candidate's middle name, Hussein, was shared with "a former dictator." In early 2007, Bernard McQuirk, then the executive producer of the *Don Imus Radio Show*, declared on air that Obama has "a Jew-hating name." Conservative radio commentator Rush Limbaugh repeatedly referred to the candidate as "Osama Obama."[16]

Religious bigotry and intolerance, even more than traditional racism, was the decisive weapon to delegitimize Obama. The January 17, 2007, issue of *Insight* magazine, for example, claimed that Obama "spent at least four years in a so-called madrassa, or Muslim seminary, in Indonesia." Writing in the *Chicago Sun-Times*, columnist Mark Steyn then claimed that Obama "graduated from the Sword of the Infidel grade school in Jakarta."[17] On Fox News, former liberal-turned-reactionary Juan Williams argued that Obama "comes from a father who was a Muslim and all that . . . Given that we're at war with Muslim extremists, that presents a problem."[18] The truth of Obama's background was that his biological father, while being raised as a Muslim, was an atheist like Obama's mother. Obama's stepfather was not deeply religious. The two elementary schools Obama attended—one Catholic, the other predominately Muslim—were not madrassas. In 2007, CNN correspondent John Vause traveled to Indonesia, investigated the charges, and established the truth about Obama's religious and family background. Yet despite this, the "madrassa myth" linking Obama to Islamic terrorist cells continued to be promoted on television and especially over the Internet.[19]

As the Democratic caucuses and primaries began, however, Obama quickly established the ability to win a surprisingly large share of whites' votes. He consistently won majorities among all voters under thirty, voters earning over $50,000 annually, and college-educated voters. After the South Carolina Democratic primary, where Bill Clinton's racially insensitive remarks alienated thousands of voters, the African American electorate swung decisively behind Obama.

The most damaging controversy involving race to erupt during Obama's quest for the Democratic presidential nomination involved the politics of faith: the media's rebroadcasting of provocative statements by the candidate's former minister, the Reverend Jeremiah Wright of Chicago's Trinity United Church of Christ. A major center for social justice ministry in Chicago, Trinity's activist program was not unlike that of other progressive African American churches involved in the civil rights movement in the 1960s or the antiapartheid campaign against white South Africa during the 1980s. Yet even before the controversial videos of the Reverend Wright's speeches surfaced, some white conservatives had attempted to equate Trinity Church's theological teachings with the black separatism of the Nation of Islam.[20]

Obama's response to the Reverend Wright politics of faith controversy was a masterful address, "A More Perfect Union," delivered in Philadelphia's Constitution Center on March 15, 2008. Obama began by reminding his audience that American democracy was "unfinished" at its founding in 1787, due to "this nation's original sin of slavery." Obama declared that despite his rather unusual personal history and mixed ethnic background, "seared into my genetic makeup [is] the idea that this nation is more than the sum of its parts—that out of many, we are truly one."[21]

Obama's great strength is his ability to discuss controversial and complex issues in a manner that conveys the seeking of consensus, or common ground. His Philadelphia address reminded white Americans that "so many of the disparities that exist in the African American community today can be directly traced to inequalities passed on from an earlier generation that suffered under the brutal legacy of slavery" and Jim Crow segregation. But he also acknowledged the anger and alienation of poor and working-class whites, people who do not live especially privileged lives, who feel unfairly victimized by policies like affirmative action. Obama criticized Reverend Wright's statements as "not only wrong but divisive, at a time when we need unity; racially charged at a time when we need to come together to solve a set of monumental problems . . . that are neither black or white or Latino or Asian, but rather problems that confront us all."[22]

Another astute dimension of Obama's "A More Perfect Union" speech was his repeated referencing of U.S. racial history, while simultaneously refusing to be defined or restricted by that history. For blacks, Obama asserted, the path forward "means embracing the burdens of our past without becoming victims of our past . . . it means binding our particular grievances—for better health care, and better schools, and better jobs—to the larger aspirations of all Americans."[23] In the context of electoral politics and public policy, Obama's argument makes perfect sense. In America's major cities, for example, there's no explicitly "Latino strategy" for improving public transportation, or a purely "African American strategy" to improve public health care. Obama did not deny that racial disparities in health care, education, employment, and other areas no longer existed. But by emphasizing a "politics of hope," he implied that any real solutions must depend on building multiracial, multiclass coalitions that could fight to achieve change.

Although Obama finally secured his party's presidential nomination, religious and racial stereotypes and intolerance were again deployed by many opponents to derail his campaign. In mid-September 2008, for example, a Pew Research Center survey revealed that millions of Americans held grossly erroneous views about Obama's religious and ethnic background. Despite the extensive news coverage earlier in the year concerning the Reverend Wright controversy, and Obama's repeated affirmations about his deeply held Christian beliefs, only one-half of all Americans believed the Democratic candidate was a Christian. Thirteen percent stated that Obama was a "Muslim," and another 16 percent claimed they "aren't sure about his religion because they've heard 'different things' about it." On a number of fundamentalist Christian radio stations, and conservative Christian Web sites, Obama has been described as the possible "Anti-Christ." As journalist Nicholas D. Kristol observed, "Religious prejudice is becoming a proxy for racial prejudice. In the public at least, it's not acceptable to express reservations about a candidate's skin color, so discomfort about race is sublimated into concerns about whether Mr. Obama is sufficiently Christian."[24]

What animated the fear and loathing of Obama by some terrified whites was also the recognition that America is fundamentally changing ethnically and racially. Demographically, the white majority population is rapidly vanishing. Latinos, blacks, Asians, and Native Americans combined, will outnumber Americans of European descent by 2042, earlier than predicted. By 2050, racialized groups will account for 54 percent. Already, in cities like New York, Chicago, Los Angeles, and Atlanta, whites have been a "minority group" for years, but they still have exercised decisive power, especially in government and economically. So the emergence and election of a racial minority candidate like Obama was inevitable. A majority of white Americans now recognize that the traditional racial project of "white supremacy" is no longer sustainable or even in the best interests of the nation. Nevertheless, a significant minority of whites are still dedicated proponents of both racialization and religious intolerance, as central tools in the continuing perpetuation of a racist America.

On November 4, 2008, the U.S. electorate made its decision by electing Barack Obama its first African American president by a popular vote margin of 52 percent. Obama's victory rested in part on nearly unanimous (95 percent) support provided by African Americans, who voted in record numbers. Almost as impressive, however, was the broad, multiethnic, multiclass coalition the Obama forces were able to construct from Jewish voters (78 percent), Latinos (67 percent), young voters age 18 to 29 (62 percent), and women voters (58 percent). Obama's victory sparked hundreds, perhaps even thousands, of spontaneous street demonstrations involving millions of celebrants across the nation.

Although Obama's core constituencies provided him with the essential foundations of his triumph, equally essential was his ability to attract millions of moderate Republicans and independents, many of whom had voted for George W. Bush in 2000 and/ or 2004. Throughout the 2008 campaign, Obama explicitly refused to attack the Republican Party per se, focusing his criticisms either on his presidential opponent John McCain or against the extremist right wing of the party. Obama's campaign had astutely recognized the partisan shift in voter attitudes that had taken place in the wake of disasters such as the Katrina Hurricane and the Iraq War. Obama's postblack, race-neutral rhetoric reassured millions of whites to vote for a "black candidate."

For example, according Pew Center for the People and the Press, in 2004 one-third of all registered voters (33 percent) identified themselves with the Republican Party, compared to 35 percent of registered voters favoring Democrats, and 32 percent claiming to be independents. In 2004, Republicans trailed Democrats in their support from 18 to 29 year olds, but only by four percent (29 vs. 33 percent). Republicans won pluralities over Democrats among all white registered voters (38 vs. 30 percent), voters with BA and BS degrees (38 vs. 30 percent), voters earning more than $75,000 annually (40 vs. 29 percent), white Southerners (43 vs. 28 percent), white Protestant voters (44 vs. 27 percent), and a clear majority among white evangelical Christian voters (53 vs. 22 percent).[25]

Four years later, just prior to the Democratic National Convention, the Pew Center conducted a similar national survey of registered voters and found major gains made by the Democrats in many important voter identifications. One major shift occurred among youth voters age 18 to 29, who favored Democrats over Republicans (37 vs. 23 percent), with another 40 percent identifying themselves as independents. Republican support in union households fell slightly, from 26 percent in 2004 to only 20 percent in 2008. Hispanics, who in 2004 had favored Democrats over Republicans, but only by a 44 vs. 23 percent margin, had become more partisanly Democratic (48 vs. 19 percent). But what was perhaps most striking was the growing defection of the intelligentsia and educated class from the Republicans. The 2008 Pew survey indicated that registered college graduates, who vote generally at rates above 80 percent, favored Democrats over Republicans (34 vs. 29 percent). For registered voters with postgraduate and professional degrees the partisan bias toward Democrats was even wider (38 vs. 26 percent, with 36 percent independents).[26]

The 2008 Pew survey also made clear that the United States, in terms of its political culture and civic ideology, had become a "center-left nation," rather than a "right-center nation," as it had been under Ronald Reagan. Sixty-seven percent of registered voters surveyed about their views on affirmative action, favored such policies that had been "designed to help blacks, women, and other minorities get better jobs and education." Sixty-one percent agreed that the U.S. government should guarantee "health insurance for all citizens, even if it means raising taxes." A majority of registered voters believe that abortion should be either "legal in all cases" (18 percent) or "legal in most cases" (38 percent). Over 70 percent of those surveyed believe "global warming" is either a "very serious" or "somewhat serious problem." And over 80 percent favored "increasing federal funding for research on wind, solar and hydrogen technology."[27] This was a rationale for long-overdue governmental action, along the lines proposed by Obama, not laissez-faire and the Reaganite mantra of "government-is-the-problem."

On nearly every college campus by the early fall, it became overwhelmingly clear that Obama had won the enthusiastic support of both students and faculty. In a comprehensive national survey of over 43,000 undergraduates conducted by CBS News, UWIRE, and the *Chronicle of Higher Education* in October 2008, the Obama-Biden ticket received 64 percent vs. 32 percent for McCain-Palin. When asked to describe their "feelings about your candidate," 55 percent of the Obama-backers "enthusiastically" supported him, compared to only 30 percent of McCain's supporters. By significant margins, college students described Obama as "someone you can relate to" (64 percent), someone who would "bring about real change in Washington" (70 percent), and someone who "cares about the needs and problems of people like yourself" (78 percent).[28]

Although nearly one-half (48 percent) of all students surveyed had never voted in a presidential election, a significant percentage of them had become involved in one of the national campaigns primarily through the Internet. Twenty-three percent surveyed had signed up to be a candidate's fan on a social "networking site"; 28 percent had "visited a candidate's Facebook or MySpace page"; 65 percent had browsed a candidate's official Web site; and 68 percent had seen a video of their favorite presidential candidate on YouTube. Small numbers had participated in more traditional ways. Thirteen percent had volunteered to help their candidate by canvassing or by doing voter registration. Nearly one-fourth had personally attended a rally featuring their candidate, with another 31 percent recruiting friends to join their campaign.[29]

It was the conservative British newsmagazine, the *Economist*, that identified the critical "brain gap" that contributed to McCain's electoral downfall. "Barack Obama won college graduates by two points, a group George Bush won by six points four years ago," the publication noted. "He won voters with postgraduate degrees by 18 points." The *Economist* observed that Obama even carried by six points households above $200,000 annually. McCain's core constituency, by contrast, was "among uneducated voters in Appalachia and the South." In the view of the *Economist*, "The Republicans lost the battle of ideas even more comprehensively than they lost the battle for educated votes, marching into the election armed with nothing more than slogans."[30]

On the issue of racialization, the most underreported story connected with Barack Obama's presidential victory has been the disturbing spike in racial hate crimes across the United States. On November 25, 2008, representatives of seven major civil rights groups met with the media presenting evidence of hundreds of racist incidents and hate crimes leading up to, and following, the election of Obama. These include a cross burning on the lawn of one New Jersey family, and the random beating of an African American man on Staten Island by white teenagers, who cursed him with racial epithets and "Obama." The groups involved—the Leadership Conference on Civil Rights, the National Council of La Raza, the Asian American Justice Center, the National Urban League, the National Association for the Advancement of Colored People, the Anti-Defamation League, and the Mexican American Legal Defense and Education Fund—all condemned the recent hate crimes.

"At a time when we as a nation are celebrating our demonstrated diversity" with Obama's election, NAACP Washington, D.C., Bureau Director Hilary Shelton stated, "There are unfortunately those who are still living in the past filled hatred, fear and division." Marc Morial, National Urban League Director, called upon the Justice Department to "become more aggressive in prosecuting hate crimes. . . . As a country, we've come a long way, but there is still more change needed."

What can be anticipated from an Obama administration, especially as it relates to the Middle East and, more broadly, the Islamic world? From his major speeches on international policy, Obama deeply believes in the nationalistic, world supremacist mission of the United States. In his speech "The American Moment," delivered at the Chicago Council of Global Affairs on April 23, 2007, Obama declared that "the magical place called America" was still "the last, best hope on Earth." He "reject[ed] the notion that the American moment had passed." The most disturbing line of Obama's address was his assertion that the United States had the right to launch unilateral and preemptive attacks on foreign countries, a position not unlike that of Bush and Cheney. "No president should ever hesitate to use force-unilaterally if necessary to protect ourselves and our vital interests when we are attacked or imminently threatened," Obama stated. "We must also consider using military force in circumstances beyond self-defense," Obama also argued, "in order to provide for the common security that underpins global security."[31] This is a geopolitical worldview that directly challenges the interests of both the Third World and most Islamic nations.

In fairness, Obama never claimed to be an ideologue of the Left. He promised a postpartisan government and a leadership style that incorporated the views of conservatives and liberals alike. This political pragmatism, which is also reflected in the new, postracial black leadership Obama represents, is a rejection of radical change in favor of incremental reform. As Obama explained in 2006, "Since the founding the American political tradition has been reformist, not revolutionary. What that means is that for a political leader to get things done, he or she should ideally be ahead of the curve, but not too far ahead."[32] Malcolm X at the end of his life sought to overturn capitalism, not to reform it; Obama apparently seeks to achieve Keynesian changes but within our existing, market-dominated political economy.

Such criticisms in no way are intended to minimize the significance of Obama's victory and the continuing importance of electoral politics, voting, and using all the tools of electoralism for oppressed people in the United States. The Obama victory will be of great assistance in waging the struggle for racial justice. But electoral politics is not a substitute for social protest organizing in neighborhoods and in the streets.

A new, antiracist leadership must be constructed to the left of the Obama government, one that draws upon representatives of the most oppressed and marginalized social groups within our communities: former prisoners, women activists in community-based civic organizations, youth groups, homeless coalitions, and the like. Change must occur not from the top down, as some Obama proponents would have it, but from the bottom up. The growing class stratification within African American and Latino communities has produced an opportunistic, middle-class leadership elite that in many important ways is out of touch with dire problems generated by poverty, unemployment, and mass incarceration. We must reconnect the construction of leadership by addressing and solving real-world problems of racialization that challenge everyday people's daily lives. The Obama victory has the potential for creating a positive environment for achieving dramatic reforms within public policy and improving the conditions for the truly disadvantaged—but only if it is pressured to do so. Obama may be successful in standing outside of the processes of racialization, but for millions of minorities, race and class inequality continue to define their lives, and only collective resistance will lead to their empowerment.

NOTES

1. Mark Mazzetti and Scott Shane, "Al Qaeda Offers Obama Insults and a Warning," *New York Times*, November 20, 2008.
2. See Manning Marable and Kristen Clarke, eds., *Seeking Higher Ground: The Hurricane Katrina Crisis, Race, and Public Policy Reader* (New York: Palgrave Macmillan, 2008).
3. CNN, *USA Today*, and Gallup poll on Hurricane Katrina Attitudes, September 13, 2005; and Desiree Cooper, "Outrage, Carrying Mix in Katrina Response," *Detroit Free Press*, September 15, 2005.
4. See Michael Powell and Peter Slevin, "Several Factors Contributed to 'Lost' Voters in Ohio," *Washington Post*, December 25, 2004; and Jamal Watson, "Blacks File Lawsuit in Ohio, Claim Disenfranchisement in Election," *Amsterdam News*, December 16–22, 2004.
5. See Manning Marable, "How Washington Won: The Political Economy of Race in Chicago," *Journal of Intergroup Relations* 11, no. 2 (Summer 1983): 56–81.
6. See Raphael J. Sonenshein, "Can Black Candidates Win Statewide Elections," *Political Science Quarterly*, Summer 1990.
7. See Judson Jefferies, "Douglas Wilder and the Continuing Significance of Race: An Analysis of the 1989 Gubernatorial Election," *Journal of Political Science* 23 (Summer 1995): 87–111.
8. Andrew Kohut, "Getting it Wrong," *New York Times*, January 10, 2008.
9. Rachel L. Swarns, "Quiet Political Shifts as More Blacks are Elected," *New York Times*, October 13, 2008.
10. On Deval Patrick, see Scot Lehigh, "Patrick's Stunning Victory," *Boston Globe*, September 30, 2006; and Kirk Johnson, "In Races for Governor, Party May Be Secondary," *New York Times*, November 4, 2006.
11. Debra Dickerson, "Color-blind," *Salon*, January 22, 2007, at http://www.salon.com/opinion/feature/2007/01/22/obama.
12. Stanley Crouch, "What Obama Isn't: Black Like Me," *New York Daily News*, November 2, 2006.
13. John K. Wilson, *Barack Obama: His Improbable Quest* (Boulder: Paradigm, 2008), 57–58.

14. Peter Wallsten, "Would Obama Be 'Black President'?" *Los Angeles Times*, February 10, 2007.

15. Paul Street, *Barack Obama and the Future of American Politics* (Boulder: Paradigm, 2008), 156–59.

16. Wilson, *Barack Obama*, 93–94.

17. Ibid., 95–96.

18. Ibid., 96–97.

19. Ibid., 98–99.

20. Ibid., 73–74.

21. Barack Obama, "A More Perfect Union," 18 March 2008, Philadelphia, PA.

22. Ibid.

23. Ibid.

24. Nicholas D. Kristof, "The Push to 'Otherize' Obama," *New York Times*, September 22, 2008.

25. "A Closer Look At the Parties in 2008," Report of the Pew Research Center for the People and the Press, August 22, 2008.

26. Ibid.

27. Ibid.

28. Elyse Ashburn, "Poll: Students Less Engaged Than Thought," A1, A25–A27; and CBS News, UWIRE, and the *Chronicle*, "College Students and the Presidential Election," *Chronicle of Higher Education* 55, no. 10 (October 31, 2008), A28–A29.

29. Ibid.

30. "Lexington: Ship of Fools," *Economist* 389, no. 8606 (November 15, 2008).

31. Street, *Barack Obama and the Future of American Politics*, 156–60.

32. Ken Silverstein, "Obama, Inc.: The Birth of a Washington Machine," *Harper's*, November 2006.

Part I

Background to the New Black Politics

SYSTEM VALUES AND AFRICAN AMERICAN LEADERSHIP

ROBERT C. SMITH

IN MY BOOK, *WE HAVE NO LEADERS*, PUBLISHED MORE THAN A decade ago, I concluded that African American leaders—both establishment and radical—were largely irrelevant insofar as developing policies, programs, and strategies to reconstruct and integrate black ghettos into the mainstream of American society.[1] The established black leadership—the civil rights leaders and elected and appointed government officials—were irrelevant because they had been incorporated into the system and coopted. A major result of the civil rights movement of the 1960s, in addition to the enactment of major substantive legislation, was the integration or co-optation of the leadership of the movement into systemic institutions and processes. Co-optation is understood as the process of absorbing the leadership of dissident groups into a political system in response to mass discontent and threats (or perceived threats) to system stability or legitimacy. The process of co-optation was accelerated in the late 1960s and early 1970s as a result of the radicalism of the Black Power movement and the rebellions in urban ghettos. By the 1980s, virtually all of the talented leadership of black America was incorporated or seeking incorporation into the system, contending that "working within the system" was the most important—if not the only—means to achieve the post–civil rights era objectives of the black community. However, I concluded that as a result of this process, black leaders had diminished their capacity to pressure the system to respond to the demands of the black community, the most pressing of which was the need for employment opportunities in the context of some kind of overall program of internal ghetto reconstruction and development.

While the process of co-opting establishment-leaning black leaders was accelerating in the late 1960s and early 1970s, radicals in the leadership group were becoming increasingly marginalized. This marginalization was itself partly a result of the co-optation process, but it was also the result of political repression, factionalism, and a tendency toward utopianism within certain radical leadership circles. Consequently, by the late 1980s the most influential radical, nonestablishment formation in the African American community was the Nation of Islam: the authoritarian, sectarian religious sect led by Louis Farrakhan.

We Have No Leaders was a direct, explicit critique of African American leadership. There was also an implicit, largely unrecognized critique of the political system in which they operate. As an epigram to Part III of the book (which dealt with the incorporation of blacks into legislative and executive institutions at the federal level), I used a quote from a 1971 essay by Mervyn Dymally, a former California state assemblyman, lieutenant governor, congressman, and now state senator, who is also a sophisticated student of black politics. He writes,

> When we talk about black politics we are not talking about ordinary politics. And we are not talking about ordinary politics because the American political system has not created a single social community in which the reciprocal rules of politics would apply. Conventional politics cannot solve this problem because conventional politics is a part of the problem. It is part of the problem because the political system is the major bulwark of racism in America. It is part of the problem in the sense that the political system is structured to repel fundamental social and economic change. We hear a great deal about the deficiencies, real or imagined, of certain black leaders, but not enough attention, it seems to me, is paid to the framework within which they operate. That framework prevents radical growth and innovation—as it was designed to prevent radical growth and innovation.

In this chapter I wish to engage in analysis, albeit brief, of how the values of the political system impede—indeed, always have impeded—the capabilities of African American leaders to develop policies, programs, and strategies to achieve racial justice in the United States. Before doing so, however, I would like to review the evidence that has developed on the process of co-optation since *We Have No Leaders* was published. A review of this evidence reinforces the conclusions of the study. In the past dozen years, more and more blacks have been incorporated into the system at higher and higher levels of authority. These leaders are less and less able to use their positions of authority to advance the interests of African Americans. Furthermore, the evidence increasingly suggests that not only are these leaders ineffective in pressing the system for change, but they are also increasingly less willing to try.

INSIDE THE SYSTEM

When I first started research on black leaders in Washington in the early 1970s, their numbers were small, and they held few positions of status, power, or influence in the Congress or the executive branch. The thirteen black members of the House, operating in a newly created congressional caucus, had relatively little seniority and consequently chaired only one committee (on the District of Columbia) and seven (of 137) relatively minor subcommittees. Although the Committee on the District of Columbia was a minor one in terms of national politics, for the black citizens who constituted a majority of the District's population, it was the major committee inasmuch as it exercised jurisdiction over the city's governance. For decades, a hostile southern Democrat had chaired the District committee. The ascendancy of Michigan's Congressman Charles Diggs to the committee's leadership provided District residents with a sympathetic person in a position of power. Diggs ultimately used that power to enact legislation granting "Home Rule" to the District, with the right to elect a mayor and city council. Yet, overall the black caucus in Congress was a small body with few formal positions of power or influence.[2]

A similar situation existed for blacks in the executive branch. There were no blacks in the cabinet in the Nixon administration, and although President Nixon appointed blacks to 4 percent of executive-branch positions, they were junior-level assistant and deputy assistant secretaries concentrated in the social-welfare departments.[3] In these departments, many of the officials were responsible for administering equal-opportunity programs rather than substantive policymaking. Although blacks in the Nixon administration were small in number and held minor positions, they did organize a caucus (the Council of Black Appointees) to try to influence administration civil-rights policy collectively, at one point threatening mass resignations to protest Nixon's policies on school desegregation.

Nearly forty years later, the progress of black incorporation into legislative and executive branches has been remarkable. The Congressional Black Caucus (CBC) has quadrupled in size, and its members in the 110th Congress (2007–2009) chaired five committees and seventeen subcommittees. The committees chaired by African American members include Ways and Means—the oldest and most powerful committee in the Congress—and Judiciary, the committee responsible for crime legislation, civil rights, civil liberties, and the Constitution. In the 1970s no black held a position in the Democratic Party leadership, whereas in the 110th Congress an African American (James Clyburn of South Carolina) holds the number-three position—majority whip—in the leadership hierarchy. (Congressman Bill Gray of Pennsylvania briefly held this position in the 1980s.)

Similarly, the percentage of blacks in the executive during this period tripled, rising from 4 percent in the Nixon administration to 12 percent in the Carter administration, 13 percent under Clinton, and 10 percent in the George W. Bush administration. The positions held by blacks are not obscure, inconsequential positions like assistant and deputy assistant secretaries in Health, Education and Welfare (HEW) or Housing and Urban Development (HUD). On the contrary, in the Clinton administration African Americans held four of thirteen cabinet posts, including agriculture, energy, commerce, and the Office of Management and Budget. In the George W. Bush administration, African Americans twice held the senior cabinet post—secretary of state—as well as such important posts as deputy attorney general, vice chair of the Federal Reserve, and head of the White House Domestic Policy Council.

Inevitably, as members of the caucus have achieved seniority and power in the House, they have tended to prioritize the interests of the Democratic Party over those of the black community. The process of co-optation or institutionalization necessarily involves the embrace of the values of the system or the institution. Arthur Stinchcombe observes, "The institutionalization of a value or practice can be fruitfully defined as the correlation of power with commitment to that value or practice; so that the more powerful a man is the more likely he is to hold the value."

This correlation of power with commitment to institutional values is well illustrated by the tenure of Congressman William Gray as House Budget Committee chair. As a caucus member, Gray often helped prepare the group's alternative budgets and defended them during House debates. Once he became Chair of the Budget Committee, however, Gray declined to support the caucus budgets even with a symbolic "vote of commendation" such as was cast by Thomas Foley, the Democratic majority leader. Gray explained his position by saying,

> It's not an issue of being black. The issue is I'm Chairman of the Budget Committee, a Democrat. I build a consensus. I walk out with a budget. Now, do I vote against my own budget? . . . It's not a problem of race. It's a problem of what happens to any member of Congress who gets elevated to a position of leadership. I am not here to do the bidding of somebody just because they happen to be black. If I agree with you, I agree with you. I set my policy. I think it's a fair policy but that policy has nothing to do with being black.

Congressman John Conyers responded that he took exception to Gray's failure to cast a symbolic vote of solidarity with the caucus, saying, "I draw the line where he actively campaigns against the Black Caucus resolution."

Although Conyers was critical of Gray's tenure as budget chair, it is likely he will confront similar dilemmas as chair of the Judiciary Committee (even before he took the gavel, under pressure from Speaker Nancy Pelosi, Conyers abandoned his pledge to investigate whether there were grounds to impeach President Bush). The Judiciary Committee has jurisdiction over a range of issues touching on the interests of African Americans, including felony disenfranchisement, disparities in sentences for crack and powder cocaine, and reparations for slavery and segregation. As a senior member of the committee, Conyers has over the years introduced bills dealing with reparations and felony disenfranchisement, but he has been unable to get the committee chair to hold hearings. Now that the power to conduct hearings will rest with him, the question will be whether he will use that power to address these concerns or whether, like Chairman Gray, he will argue that "it's not a question of being black, [and that] as a Democrat I have to build a consensus"—a consensus that will result in the neglect of black issues in his committee.

From its first year, the Congressional Black Caucus was known for presenting comprehensive agendas to the president and Congress, beginning with its sixty-one recommendations to President Nixon in 1971. However, since the Clinton administration, the agendas of the CBC have become modest or nonexistent, leading William Raspberry, the veteran African American columnist at the *Washington Post*, to write in 2001 of "The Incredible Shrinking Black Agenda." The principal items on the CBC 2001 agenda were the appointment of a black to the Fourth Circuit Court and an accurate census. During the debate on the House floor shortly after Hurricane Katrina, Los Angeles Congresswoman Maxine Waters ruefully admitted that in recent years the caucus had forgotten about the problem of poverty in America, indicating that Katrina was a "wake-up call," not only for President Bush and the Republican Congress, but for the caucus as well.

None of the CBC agendas ever had a realistic chance of enactment, but they were useful in keeping before both Congress and the media some sense of what a reform agenda committed to racial equality would look like, laying the groundwork for action when the political climate might become more hospitable to activist government.

The incorporation of African American leaders into the executive branch was always more problematic than in the Congress, since presidential appointees serve at the direction and pleasure of the president. Thus, they have far fewer opportunities to advance a black agenda than members of Congress who serve largely African American electorates. However, in spite of these constraints and their relatively small numbers and minor subcabinet posts, blacks in the Nixon administration organized collectively to advance black interests. The most far-reaching post–civil rights era policy reform, namely affirmative action, was designed and implemented by Arthur Fletcher and John Wilks, lower-level functionaries in the Department of Labor. As Fletcher proudly told me in a 1972 interview, "Affirmative action was my baby."

Since the Nixon administration, activism on the part of black appointees has withered away. Not only did black appointees not form caucuses in subsequent administrations, rarely after the Nixon administration did they meet collectively to discuss issues of concern to blacks. The record of individual black appointees in administrations from Carter to George W. Bush presents a mixed picture, although on balance, black appointees during this period remained silent on issues of concern to blacks or actively worked to advance policies considered adverse to black interests.

In the Carter administration, United Nations Ambassador Andrew Young worked, without much success, to change the administration's cold war–oriented policy in southern Africa, and HUD Secretary Patricia Roberts Harris tried, also without much success, to convince President Carter to propose a comprehensive urban policy. But also in the Carter administration, Drew Days, the assistant attorney general for civil rights, and Wade McCree, the solicitor general, prepared a brief in the *Bakke* case asking the Supreme Court to declare that any consideration of race in a university's admissions decisions was "presumptively unconstitutional." It was only after protests by the Congressional Black Caucus and the intervention of Vice President Walter Mondale that President Carter directed a reluctant McCree to rewrite the brief so that it would support the principle of affirmative action.

Black appointees generally supported without reservation the conservative positions of the Reagan and two Bush administrations on race. In the Reagan administration, Clarence Pendleton, the chair of the Civil Rights Commission, and Clarence Thomas, the chair of the Equal Employment Opportunity Commission, went further, urging President Reagan to revoke the Nixon-era executive order (written by Fletcher) establishing affirmative action. In the second Bush administration, Secretary of State Colin Powell publicly urged the president to support the University of Michigan's affirmative action programs, but three administration blacks—Ralph Boyd, the assistant attorney general for civil rights; Gerald Reynolds, the assistant secretary of education for civil rights; and Brian Jones, the general counsel in the Department of Education—all argued that *Bakke* should be reversed and any consideration of race in university admissions should be declared unconstitutional. Secretary of Education Rodney Page, Deputy Attorney General Larry Thompson, and presidential advisor Condoleezza Rice, all African Americans, supported the position eventually adopted by Bush, which sidestepped the constitutional issue but argued that the Michigan programs were racial quotas and therefore prohibited by *Bakke*. Rice reportedly helped Bush make the decision and write his speech on the cases.

In the Clinton administration, most of the many black appointees were silent on issues of concern to blacks, most notably on his signing of the welfare reform bill passed by the Republican Congress. While three top-level white appointees in the administration resigned in protest and wrote op-eds and articles attacking the president, blacks in the administration accommodated a presidential decision that targeted poor black women and their children and still threatens to do enormous harm to them.

This brief review of black leaders inside the system since the late 1960s suggests that a leadership devoted wholly to working within the system is unable to produce very much in terms of benefits for its low-income constituents. This means that a major result of the incorporation of blacks into leadership within the system is that the black community has diminished capacities to press its demands on the system. To some extent, it is likely that for African Americans to realize their aspirations for full and fair inclusion in American society leadership, they must be willing to challenge the system. Incorporation into the system makes a system-challenging leadership less likely.

CORE SYSTEM VALUES AND THE AFRICAN AMERICAN QUEST FOR EQUALITY

In *We Have No Leaders*, drawing on David Easton's model for the study of political systems, I identify three core values of the U.S. system. These values define the pattern of ideational and structural relationships that characterize a political system. They are the values that elites or authorities inside the system seek to maintain. Indeed, Easton contends that "maintenance" of these values is the primary responsibility of system authorities or elites. The three core values that define the operation of the U.S. political system are capitalism, constitutionalism, and democracy. Each of these core values, I argue, to some extent constituted barriers to the realization of racial equality—values Congressman Dymally alluded to as impeding the kind of radical change and innovation necessary to overcome the legacies of slavery and segregation, and the operations of structural or institutional racism in the post–civil rights era.

Capitalism

Capitalism is perhaps more central to the system than the values of democracy and constitutionalism. Ralph Bunche identified the principal problem with capitalism for blacks in his critique of the New Deal during the 1930s. He wrote that black leadership "appears unable to realize that there is an economic system, as well as a race problem in America and that when a Negro is unemployed, it is not just because he is a Negro, but more seriously, because of the defective operation of the economy under which we live—an economy that finds it impossible to provide adequate numbers of jobs and economic security for the population."

If capitalism requires a certain level of unemployment to maintain profits and price stability—as even liberal reform economists believe that it does—and racism is a value or practice in allocating joblessness, then, axiomatically, African Americans will face disproportionately high rates of long-term joblessness. If this race-based joblessness is not ameliorated by an extensive social safety net, then a culture of poverty (or what is referred to today as the black underclass) is likely to emerge. Mack Jones states these near-axioms nicely when he argues that "the presence of the black underclass is a logical, perhaps even necessary, outgrowth of the American political economy conditioned by white racism."

In his last year, Martin Luther King, Jr., recognized this axiom and came to believe that if African Americans were to achieve genuine equality, some modifications of capitalism along the lines of the Swedish welfare state would have to be adopted in the United States. That is, King did not believe that individual initiatives and free-market capitalism would be able to integrate blacks into the economy. Nor did he believe—as Bayard Rustin, among others, argued—that the necessary reforms could be realized through the Democratic Party coalition or the democratic routines of lobbying and elections. In other words, King believed—on the basis of history and his own work—that significant racial progress in the United States could not come about without militant pressures from the black community and other reform movements. That is why during his last year he was trying to organize a poor people's march and movement.

Constitutionalism

The United States is not simply governed by a written constitution, as are many other political systems around the world. Rather, it has an ideology of constitutionalism: a belief in the Constitution, or what Louis Hartz referred to as a "cult of constitution worship." As Robert Dahl demonstrates in *How Democratic Is the American Constitution*, the Constitution is at war with democracy in America. For a people who claim to cherish democracy as a core value, the Constitution is a remarkably undemocratic document, including such features as the electoral college, an unelected, life-serving judiciary with policymaking responsibilities, and a powerful Senate in which representation is based on geography rather than the democratic principle of one person, one vote. Several of the Constitution's undemocratic features directly inhibit the representation of African American interests, and they were designed to do so. However, the major problem is constitutionalism, since ultimately what the Constitution means depends on the opinions of a few people—namely, the justices of the Supreme Court—and generally these individuals have had opinions hostile to the interests of African Americans. Because most Americans accept the opinions of these individuals as the final word on how they should be governed, the Constitution becomes a barrier to the African American quest for racial justice.

In *Dred Scott*, the Court's first decision dealing with African Americans, it declared that they had no rights "but such as those who held the power and the government might chose to grant them." Even after the Constitution was amended to confer human and civil rights on Africans, for almost a century the Court ignored the plain language and intent of the Fourteenth Amendment. For most of its history, that amendment has been more frequently used to protect the rights of persons other than blacks, including those fictitious persons called "corporations." During the brief era of the Warren Court, from the late 1940s to the 1980s, the Fourteenth Amendment was used as it was intended, but with the appointment of Justice Clarence Thomas, giving conservatives their first majority on the Court since the 1930s, the Court once again reverted to its narrow, crabbed reading of the amendment's intent.

In a series of cases, the Rehnquist Court substantially narrowed the remedial reach of affirmative action. Its successor may be poised to declare unconstitutional any use of race to achieve racial justice. In an earlier series of cases, the Court invalidated the use of race as a means to assure racial equality in legislative representation, prompting Justice John Paul Stevens to write that it was "perverse" to permit the Fourteenth Amendment to be used to assure equitable representation for Hasidic Jews, Polish Americans, and Republicans, among others, but not for "the very minority group whose history gave birth" to it in the first place.

In addition to the Court's use of the Constitution to undermine African American interests directly, since 1995, in a remarkable series of cases, the Court has sharply limited the authority of Congress to protect civil rights and the rights of persons to sue states to compel their obedience to federally granted rights and privileges. For example, the Court declared the Violence Against Women Act unconstitutional, holding that in passing it Congress exceeded its Commerce Clause powers. The Civil Rights Act of 1964 is based on the Commerce Clause, as are virtually all of the nation's civil rights and social welfare laws. In his opinion in these cases, Justice Anthony Kennedy was careful to note that the decisions did not call into question the 1964 act; however, Justice Thomas, who wished to go further, would say only that his approach "did not necessarily require a wholesale abandonment of these precedents."

Constitutionalism is thus once again a likely barrier to the aspirations of African Americans and their leaders in their quest for equality. John Noonan, a judge on the Ninth Circuit, argues that if these Commerce Clause and Eleventh Amendment precedents are not reversed, not only are civil rights in jeopardy, but so too is the capacity of the people to govern themselves through the democratic process.

Democracy

African Americans are a minority in the United States, constituting roughly 12 percent of the population. In designing the document, the framers of the Constitution—and in particular James Madison—were especially concerned to protect minority rights in order to avoid what Madison called the "tyranny of the majority." Several of the Constitution's undemocratic features are in the document to protect minority rights. However, the minorities the framers were interested in protecting were not blacks but slaveholders, men of wealth and property and persons living in states with small populations. African American legal scholar Lani Guinier has engaged in theoretical musings about how to apply some of Madison's principles to the tyranny of the white majority in relationship to the black minority. For her work, President Clinton labeled her "undemocratic" and withdrew her nomination as assistant attorney general. President Clinton's designation of Guinier's ideas as undemocratic was ironic given that Clinton was sworn to uphold and protect an undemocratic Constitution.

African Americans constitute a permanent minority in the United States, with none of the protections the American political tradition generally accords to such groups. As Ronald Walters argues, "The cost of social (permanent racial minority) status based upon an imperfect social contract for blacks is that rarely has it been possible to participate in crucial decisions such as the selection of national leadership in a manner which reflects the 'interests' of blacks . . . through what is called 'sincere' or 'straightforward' voting."

This cost is a major constraint on the capabilities of African American leaders to function efficaciously in American democracy. As Walters suggests, African Americans have distinctive ideological interests and policy preferences, locating them far to the left of the white majority. For example, on a composite index measuring six policy issues dealing with race, 63 percent of blacks were in the leftmost categories compared to 9 percent of whites, whereas only 2 percent of blacks were in the rightmost categories compared to 36 percent of whites. Seventy-three percent of blacks think the government should reduce income differences between rich and poor, whereas only 44 percent of whites think the same; 39 percent of blacks think the government should own all hospitals, whereas only 20 percent of whites take that position; and 47 percent of blacks think that banks should be government-owned, while only 18 percent of whites concur.

The African American community, therefore, has distinctive interests and policy preferences. In the American democracy, these interests and policy preferences are marginalized by a two-party system, which Clinton Rossiter describes as "the most conservative political arrangement in the Western world."

In *Uneasy Alliances: Race and Party Competition in America*, Paul Frymer argues that a two-party system was established in the United States to marginalize black interests and primarily to keep slavery off the national policy agenda.[4] Analyzing the impact of the two-party system on black interests, Frymer demonstrates that both parties have incentives to co-opt rather than mobilize blacks. This is because the two parties inevitably appeal to "median" or "swing" voters, which in the United States has tended to be racially conservative white voters. This tendency to appeal to a voter who is conceived as always white, frequently conservative, and sometimes racist, has inevitably required both of the parties to ignore or downplay issues of concern to blacks. With the election of Barack Obama to the presidency in 2008, this equation changed—which is not to say that it will not reappear in the future. On another note, comparative studies of party systems also show that multiparty systems tend to elect center-left coalition governments that adopt redistributive social policies more in line with the preferences of African Americans.

CONCLUSION

The African American community—especially its disproportionately large fraction of poor people—faced enormous difficulties as the twenty-first century opened. Its leadership was almost wholly co-opted into a system whose core values imposed severe constraints on its capacity to advance the interests of the community. Wedded ideologically, institutionally, and economically to systemic structures of power, this leadership was adverse to independent or radical thought and action, having as one of its foremost concerns quiescence in the black community and the maintenance and stability of the system. Meanwhile, the once-vibrant radical tradition in African American leadership was even more marginalized, given that much of the public space was monopolized by the leadership establishment.

The established leadership probably understands how the system's core values constrain its capabilities to deliver resources to its constituents. However, rather than engage in system-challenging behavior, black leaders have engaged in accommodationism.

Gunnar Myrdal first introduced the concept of accommodationism as a type of African American leadership based on what he described as the two extreme strategies of behavior on the part of African American leaders: protest or accommodation. Accommodation requires leaders to accept and not challenge the system and its prevailing relationships of inequality. Thus, leaders lead only in the context of seeking those changes in the conditions of blacks that do not challenge system values or upset system elites. Because of their relative lack of power, Myrdal contended that accommodation was historically the "natural," "normal," or "realistic" relationship of black leaders to the system.

Black leaders' strategy shift from protest to accommodation since the 1960s is partly the result of their co-optation. The argument might be made that because the protests of the civil rights era produced more results than accommodation, the relatively small degree of inclusion of blacks into the system, when measured against the deteriorating conditions in the ghettos, does not justify the leadership's embrace of accommodationist imperatives of the system. Nevertheless, accommodationism was paramount at the beginning of the twenty-first century. Either African American leaders were unwilling to challenge the system because they had embraced its values and prioritized them over the interests of poor blacks, or they believed they lacked the necessary power to do so.

NOTES

1. Robert Smith, *We Have No Leaders: African-Americans in the Post–Civil Rights Era* (Albany: State University of New York Press, 1996).
2. Although not a member of the Caucus, Massachusetts senator Edward Brooke served during this period as that body's lone black member.
3. Smith, *We Have No Leaders*.
4. Paul Frymer, *Uneasy Alliance: Race and Party Competition in America* (Princeton: Princeton University Press, 1999).

THE LIMITS OF BLACK PRAGMATISM

THE RISE AND FALL OF DAVID DINKINS, 1989–93

RYAN REFT

IN APRIL 1989, THE NATIONAL CONFERENCE OF BLACK MAYORS TOOK PLACE in Oakland, California. Crime, drugs, economic development, and reduced federal funding were discussed at great length, but, as one attendee noted, race emerged as a primary concern among the participants. Former Congressman Darren J. Mitchem pointed out that "within the white community, there's a group that even if you walked on water wouldn't vote for you [as a black candidate]."[1] Carl H. McCall noted that black candidates faced a unique political obstacle when compared to their white counterparts because, "if the language of black politicians is not sufficiently 'militant' . . . sections of their black base will abandon them, forcing such hopefuls to 'use sharp language' to solidify their base which in turn frighten[s] white voters."[2] The answer, according to some, was to diminish the importance of race or to "deracialize" their campaign. Others maintained that the future lay in rainbow coalitions such as the one that secured Harold Washington's 1983 victory in Chicago. Further confusing future electoral strategies, Republican and conference president Mayor James L. Usry related some advice a white political consultant had provided him in 1986 as he prepared for his race in predominantly black Atlantic City: "Do not put your foot in one white house or one white ward."[3]

Six months after the 1989 conference, machine politician David Dinkins became the first black mayor of New York City. Constructing a "Gorgeous Mosaic" consisting of blacks, liberal whites, Latinos, labor, and Jews, Dinkins defeated incumbent Ed Koch in the Democratic primary and then proceeded to ward off Republican opponent Rudy Giuliani in a tightly contested general election. Bridging the gap between Latinos and African Americans, Dinkins secured over 70 percent of the Latino vote in the general contest and 60 percent in the primary.[4] Impressively, he garnered the full support of the Harlem political community and the Brooklyn nationalists, a traditional fault line for citywide black electoral unity, receiving nearly 90 percent of the vote. However, this ethereal victory would not last. By the end of his first and only term, Dinkins's "Gorgeous Mosaic" had frayed. Writing for the *Nation* in 1993, Michael Tomasky criticized the incumbent mayor for marching in a Jewish parade that banned gays while refusing to march in the traditional St. Patrick's Day Parade for the same reason, quipping, "Dinkins figures the Irish vote is lost, but the Jews are another matter. So politically, it's smart to offend the Irish and stand up for the gays and lesbians."[5] Ultimately, Tomasky saw Dinkins's "Gorgeous Mosaic" as "the same old interest group palm greasing, just like the Irish pols used to play it, dressed up in a multicultural tuxedo."[6] Playing against a backdrop of economic stagnation, racial mistrust, and skyrocketing crime, Dinkins struggled to keep his administration above water. His pragmatic machine-based approach found success in 1989, but the same strategy enacted four years later failed to deliver the same result. What can we make of David Dinkins's watershed victory in 1989?

NEW YORK CITY, 1989

As the 1980s came to a close, New York City faced a deepening recession, a crack epidemic,[7] rising crime, a yawning budget deficit, simmering racial tension, and pervasive homelessness. Ed Koch's third term ground to an end amid recriminations concerning endemic corruption within the New York Democratic machine.[8] Compounding these difficulties was the fact many African Americans viewed Koch as hostile to their interests. The declining economy exacerbated an already contentious relationship, leading critics to "claim that he was polarizing the city along racial lines."[9] Promising to assuage the rising racial and ethnic tensions, David Dinkins emerged as the Democratic candidate for mayor. Dinkins had long served in the municipal government as city clerk in the 1970s and as Manhattan borough president from 1985 to 1989. As part of the "Gang of Four,"[10] Dinkins had distinguished himself as a loyal competent machine politician but not one of any particular dynamism. While dissatisfaction with a mayor is certainly cause for an attempt to oust the incumbent, what conditions led Dinkins and others to believe 1989 was the year New York would elect its first African American mayor?

THE JESSE JACKSON FACTOR

Jesse Jackson's 1984 and 1988 campaigns mobilized black New York politicians and activists. In 1984, Dinkins worked for Al Vann, the man who directed Jesse Jackson's New York state campaign. Under Vann's leadership, Dinkins cultivated relationships and experience, contributing to his own election as Manhattan borough president in 1985. In 1988, Dinkins organized Jackson's Rainbow Coalition through his office. Jackson emphasized improving ties with Latino elected officials over pursuing the city's black elected officials. Dinkins was closely involved in this effort, thus improving his own connections to the Latino community. Furthering this connection, Jackson placed the Rainbow Coalition's operation center at the headquarters of Local

1199, a 100,000-member, largely black and Latino hospital worker's union. In addition, both Jackson races increased black voter registration, mobilizing the community.

MUNICIPAL REFORM

While the Rainbow Coalition movement helped mobilize, register, and unite minority voters, a municipal reform to the city's charter also contributed to Dinkins's victory. The Board of Estimates (BOE) had couched power in each of the boroughs, allowing for patronage and city funding to flow through the borough presidents. Each held power over city budgets and contracts.[11] As a result, each borough developed its own unique machine dynamic. Black politicians divided along specific borough lines but had the most power in Brooklyn and Manhattan. However, Brooklyn—with its large West Indian and Caribbean populations—cultivated a black nationalist approach greatly at odds with the pragmatist "Harlem School," as it was pioneered by uptown machine politico J. Raymond Jones. The elimination of the BOE placed increased authority in the mayor's office, reduced the power of borough presidents, and encouraged political unity with a black mayoral candidate as a rallying point.

THE HARLEM SCHOOL

Though the legendary J. Raymond Jones is most associated with the Harlem accomodationist approach to electoral politics, Jones himself was less visible than another New York black political leader of the time. In 1941 Adam Clayton Powell, Jr., became the first black person to earn a seat on the New York City Council. By 1944, Powell had joined Congress, having easily earned the Democratic nomination that year. Powell chafed at the racism of the capital itself and prided himself on his opposition to white power. He referred to himself as "the first bad nigger in Congress."[12] Jones, on the other hand, chose a less militant route.

Quietly, J. Raymond Jones ascended the Democratic machine structure. By 1964, he was the first black to occupy the executive position in the organization. Jones believed black political leaders "must be militant" but at the same time believed they should operate within the party structure.[13] From his position within Tammany Hall, Jones trained two generations of New York's black political leadership, including Percy Sutton, Basil Patterson, David Dinkins, and Powell's eventual successor, Charlie Rangel. Dinkins adopted the quiet, party-oriented, pragmatic approach that Jones epitomized and slowly climbed the rungs of the machine as well.

It is from this grounding that David Dinkins emerged convinced that quiet leadership, political loyalty, and pragmatic decision making brought electoral success. Moreover, not only did the Democratic organization train Dinkins and help him establish a network of connections he would later utilize in running for mayor, but it also insulated him from criticism when he did run for office. Normally, politicians running as machine candidates are punished by "good government" forces. However, the racial climate in 1989 provided a radically different context for Dinkins. First, his race meant that even though he was a typical "clubhouse" politico, no one assumed that he was an entrenched power broker, as one pro-Dinkins pollster was quoted, "It is tough to say that anyone who is black has been any part of the power structure in

New York City."[14] Second, since many whites—especially Jewish voters—feared a black nationalist candidacy, Dinkins's membership in the Democratic organization promised their section of the electorate comfort.[15]

Thus, though historically limiting for African Americans, the Democratic organization not only enabled Dinkins to develop the skills necessary to succeed in electoral politics, but it also created a political community that could harness a movement for a black mayor, all while insulating him from charges of racial militancy.[16]

DINKINS AND THE BLACK COMMUNITY

A Dinkins supporter once said, tellingly, "I think Dave's a wonderful guy, but let me tell you three things about him running for mayor: First, he'll make a lousy candidate. Second, in the unlikely event that he does win, he'll make a terrible mayor. Third, I will support him."[17] His sentiments spoke volumes. Even though Dinkins won the 1985 Manhattan borough presidency, he failed to capture the imagination of many in the black community. In running for mayor in 1989, Dinkins placed great emphasis on campaigning in white communities and seemed uncomfortable around lower-income and poor blacks, but as the campaign attempted to mobilize greater numbers of voters, it sought to assuage black voters' reservations. One such encounter between the grassroots Industrial Areas Foundation (IAF) and the mayoral hopeful revealed this awkward dynamic. During an initial meeting with the IAF, Dinkins had both eaten his lunch and taken phone calls. In a second encounter, during a question and answer session with the group organized by his campaign director, conversation collapsed when Dinkins read from a prepared statement, sniping at the IAF membership in a moment of tension: "When we build new housing, we'll be building new communities. . . . And you ought to like that!"[18] As one organizer present commented, "We saw the depth of race and the superficiality of race—all in ten minutes."[19]

In another example of his aloofness from New York's lower-income black communities, Dinkins was accused by the more militant black newspapers like the *City Sun* and others of neglecting African American voters. Hoping to pacify his critics, Dinkins took to "the streets with a walking tour of Bedford-Stuyvesant,"[20] a move that satisfied few. Earlier that same day, Dinkins had spoken at a small East Harlem Church where he had to "prod the congregation into applause."[21]

In a late June article, the *New York Times* remarked that race had been a subverted feature of the mayoral contest up to that point but noted that "even those who would not cast a racial vote in June might do so in September, if the campaign becomes polarized along racial lines, or if some traumatic crime or other event arouses racial fears just before the primary."[22] For once, the *Times* appeared prophetic.

YUSUF HAWKINS

In August 1989, a sixteen-year-old African American was visiting Bensonhurst, Brooklyn, with three friends. As Yusuf Hawkins and his friends passed through the neighborhood, a gang of white Bensonhurst teens armed with baseball bats accosted them. One of the white youths shot Hawkins twice, killing him. Black activists reacted quickly, holding a march through Bensonhurst. Hostile residents of the neighborhood chanted, "Where's Tawana?" while holding watermelons out for the marchers to see.[23] Though he had been gaining ground on Dinkins, the incident threw Ed Koch's campaign well off course. The incumbent chastised protesters for marching, while also denying that race had anything to do with the assault. As a result, Koch had to restrain his campaign's criticism of Dinkins out of "fear of conforming to the emerging picture of him as a racially insensitive politician."[24] By contrast, Dinkins remained calm and collected, not lending himself to hyperbole but noting that Koch bore some responsibility for what had happened.[25] As numerous activists made far more denunciatory statements, the mayoral front-runner assumed the role of "conciliator" or "healer," reassuring whites that he was not radical but also comforting blacks by illustrating his concern for their community. A black population that on many occasions needed prodding to show enthusiasm for Dinkins was now exuberant.[26] Dinkins went on to defeat Koch in the primary by eight percentage points.

The general election revealed many things about David Dinkins; Rudy Giuliani, his Republican challenger; and the city's overall electorate. Despite winning the Democratic primary handily and holding a sizable lead in the campaign's initial weeks, Dinkins managed to bleed votes. Focusing on Dinkins's personal financial history, the Giuliani campaign brought to light the fact that the Manhattan borough president had failed to pay his income taxes from 1969 to 1972. In addition, Dinkins had sold stock to his son at greatly undervalued costs, which—though later dismissed as within legal bounds—raised concerns.[27] Coming on the heels of Koch's corrupt third term, some white voters were driven away by Dinkins's dodgy finances. His own explanations for the missing taxes were unclear and when pressed, Dinkins repeatedly responded, "I haven't committed a crime. What I did was fail to comply with the law."[28]

What role did race play in his declining numbers? Even today, the former mayor is reluctant to directly blame race for the slim victory, yet he still goes to great lengths to question Giuliani's character.[29]

RACE AS A FACTOR IN 1989

In *Changing New York City Politics*, political scientists Asher Arian, Arthur S. Goldberg, John H. Mollenkopf, and Edward T. Rogowsky analyze New York's 1989 elections. Acknowledging the importance of the Jackson campaign and noting the impressive construction of Dinkins's "Gorgeous Mosaic," they come to many of the same conclusions as have other observers. When it comes to the issue of race, though, the authors depart from conventional analyses. While they grant that race influenced voting decisions, they argue that it did so in a way that was not necessarily "racial." Instead, they argue that various issues appealed to different ethnic groups. When surveying voters for central concerns, respondents identified five main issues: drugs, crime, corruption, homelessness, and education. However, while most voters would have placed these factors within the top five, how each community prioritized issues varied.[30] Moreover, even when in agreement about a particular problem, the differences in imagined solutions revealed glaring divisions between communities. Crime emerged as an issue of concern for all voters. Certainly, the black and Latino community suffer disproportionately from crime,[31] but while whites favored "law and order" responses, blacks believed increased social services and access to education more effectively limited criminality. Thus, race itself did not determine votes, but how each group prioritized the problems and framed the solutions to them did.[32]

Some more conservative observers used the election to argue that white voters had become more tolerant. In an editorial following the Democratic primary, the *Wall Street Journal* argued that "if in fact racial animosity was as intense as some commentators suggest, Mr. Dinkins' candidacy would have been crushed in [Queens, the Bronx, and Staten Island]."[33] Even after the general election, the *Journal* emphasized Giuliani's personality and campaign style as responsible for his loss saying that "he threw mud at David Dinkins" and had not given New Yorkers anything "positive or hopeful," rather he had only "elicited . . . fear."[34]

Perhaps the most equitable explanation lay in a combination of all views. Dinkins's financial problems and his reaction to questions about them probably alienated portions of the white community unconcerned with his race. Similarly, some voters did not support Giuliani simply because Dinkins was black, but rather differed with him on how to handle various problems, such as crime. Giuliani's negative campaigning left many voters cold, as evidenced by a "white turnout that fell below historical levels."[35] Finally, though race worked against Dinkins, it also worked in his favor. Numerous media outlets promoted the idea that as a distinguished black leader with a calming demeanor, Dinkins could "cool" racial tensions, bridging the gap between the white community and blacks.[36] Thus, African Americans and Latinos believed David Dinkins would bring increased services and aid to their local communities while opening doors previously closed to them. In contrast, those whites who voted for Dinkins expected him to calm racial tensions and lower crime rates. Each based at least a portion of their beliefs on his race. However, fiscal and economic conditions limited his ability to help the former, while decades of inequality and increased racial conflict prevented him from fulfilling the hopes of the latter.

No matter the margin of victory, David Dinkins had successfully crafted a gorgeous mosaic of supporters. However, he only received a third of the white vote, entering office at the helm of a precarious alliance. Each group believed itself deserving of resources and the benefits of government largess. Dinkins had to find a way to balance competing claims while also reaching out to the business sector and the majority of whites who had opposed him. It was here that Dinkins's attempt to be a man for all seasons to all people unraveled.

The Dinkins Administration: The Difficulty of Coalitions

In a giddy January 1990 editorial, the Memphis *Tri-State Defender* heralded the dawning of the Dinkins era, pronouncing him to be "potentially the most powerful mayor in New York City's history." It went on to explain that with the elimination of the Board of Estimates' power over issues ranging from "land use" to "city budgets," the power now in the mayor's hands awarded him "a potential power base that no New York City mayor has ever had."[37] To some extent this observation rang true: the elimination of the BOE did increase the mayor's powers, but the office still remained constrained by numerous other factors, not least among them a shrinking tax revenue, declining economy, and expanding budget deficits. In addition, the mayor's power was now to be shared between his office and the expanded city council. Even with the increased power, as a former finance commissioner pleaded in a *Times* editorial, the mayor did not even have full control over the budget itself.[38]

Homelessness had exploded under the Koch administration and continued to bedevil Dinkins.[39] Crime and drugs became an omnipresent fear for many within the five boroughs. Large companies and businesses, including Morgan Stanley and Prudential, were either threatening to relocate outside of the city or had already done so. Combined with the various expectations of his diverse constituency and rising racial tensions, David Dinkins assumed office at a moment of peril rather than one easily correlated with triumphant power.

ECONOMIC DEVELOPMENT AND THE BUDGET

David Dinkins was a traditional machine politician with traditional machine support. As one liberal critic noted, much of his campaign had been funded by "the army of real estate barons, lawyers, lobbyists, and fixers who really run this city."[40] So when declining federal aid,[41] falling tax revenues, and recession[42] all intersected in 1990, Dinkins chose the path of fiscal austerity. The budget deficit was estimated conservatively at $1 billion. New York was suffering from a rapidly deteriorating infrastructure that demanded attention. Services such as day care, public health clinics, and after-school programs were drastically cut. While the business community appreciated the frugality, Dinkins's minority constituents resented the cuts because they utilized these programs at higher rates than other communities. Compounding New York's fiscal nightmare was the impending renegotiation of the city's municipal union contracts.[43]

Hardly antidevelopment or antibusiness, Dinkins continued a tradition that Koch had established by issuing tax abatements to several large companies. In many cases such tax abatements amounted to subsidies as Hardy Adasko, senior vice president of the Economic Development Corporation, related, "Most successful [tax abatement] packages included benefits to the Manhattan operations which in fact de facto deepened and obscured the [city's] subsidy."[44] In general, he said, development at the city level takes one of three routes: "lower taxes universally, lower taxes on the poorest or increased services to the poor and specific deals, more discretionary deals or programmatic deals that target companies. . . . The three are . . . always going to be in tension because the more you do of one the less you can do of the other two."[45] Following Koch's example, Dinkins gave Morgan Stanley "a tax package of over $30 million to keep its 4000 jobs in New York City."[46] Similar agreements were made with other institutions. Adasko argued that "[tax abatements were] necessary to put New York in a competitive position."

In terms of contracting, Dinkins's early policies avoided instituting set-asides out of fear of alienating any of his constituencies. However, as his tenure continued, Dinkins took notice of a discrepancy in city contracting. Though 25 percent of the city's business and construction firms were minority- or female-owned, they received only 7 percent of city contracts. The most notable field in which minorities and women seemed to suffer from discriminatory practices was construction. Acknowledging such concerns, the Dinkins administration took two major steps. First, Dinkins proposed increasing contracting to these groups to 20 percent,[47] later saying, "When we left office it was around 17 percent . . . It worked, it worked well."[48] Second, in

January 1993, Dinkins established an agreement between the city and fifteen local construction unions. Known as "Project Pathways," each union agreed to accept 250 apprentices from the city's vocational schools' graduating classes. Moreover, Dinkins instituted a policy in which any unions hoping to bid on school construction had to grant access to their apprenticeship programs to minority youth.[49] While both policies benefited his minority constituencies, each was established in the latter half of his term, meaning that by the time his reelection campaign had begun, these reforms were still unfolding.

HOMELESSNESS AND HOUSING

Throughout this time, New York City lacked affordable housing, and its homeless population seemed to be swelling to frightening proportions. Though Dinkins tried various remedies to solve the problem, most seemed to alienate the working poor and lower-middle class across racial lines, since now a significant portion of low-income housing had been reserved for the homeless. Moreover, poor communities resented the placement of shelters in their neighborhoods, since they believed that they drained resources where they were already scarce. As a result of both policy and finances, the Dinkins administration failed to increase services to these areas.[50] The cost of maintaining shelters and creating permanent housing led to skyrocketing costs.[51] Increasingly, it became an issue of credibility for the Dinkins administration from both a fiscal and public safety standpoint. Dinkins's reluctance to enforce vagrancy laws led to more visible homeless presence on the streets.[52] Many on the right complained that the homeless policy was too generous, encouraging people to "game" the system. Other critics argued that while the failed policy alienated the public and increased their resistance to future solutions to the homeless strategy, much of the pain could have been avoided had both Koch and Dinkins chosen to meet with community leaders, activists, and advocates to better determine the causes of homelessness and construct more effective measures.

In regard to housing in general, Dinkins made modest gains. However, the opposition the city government encountered from entrenched black politicians reminded Dinkins of the difficulty of his coalition. Despite tight budgets, Dinkins had secured $18.4 million in funding for the Bradhurst Redevelopment Plan. The administration had also, over the course of four years, invested $200 million in housing for central Harlem. In each case, leading black politicians and leaders viewed the developments as threats to their power and opposed them. Though the Bradhurst Plan would eventually follow through, it did so late in his mayoralty, meaning Dinkins could not campaign on its success.[53]

Again, as with economic development and the budget, many of Dinkins's housing reforms had taken shape too late to be a part of public discourse by the reelection campaign season of 1993. Many supporters were left with the impression that Dinkins had failed to mobilize the government behind the needs of their communities with respect to homelessness, housing, city budgets, and economic development.

CRIME

One of the most contentious issues of the early 1990s in many American cities, but especially in New York, was crime, though crime rates themselves are notoriously difficult to determine. For example, many crimes go unreported, while others that do get factored into the overall crime rate can be petty, having little impact on the average citizen's lives. Additionally, the public's perception of crime, heavily influenced by media reports, often matters more than the true prevalence of crime itself. Dinkins took office as the crime wave of the late 1980s reached its peak. Unfortunately, his relations with the New York City Police Department deteriorated, culminating in the notoriously racist 1992 "police riot." If whites truly saw crime through a "law and order" lens, then Dinkins's contentious relationship with the NYPD must have been politically damaging.

In regard to reducing criminality, the Dinkins administration worked with state officials to craft "Safe City, Safe Streets" legislation. It expanded the size of the police force to levels above the Koch administration's and instituted neighborhood policing, a tactic that increased community-police relations and resulted in a decline in crime rates.[54] Ironically, this approach would be more aggressively enforced under Dinkins's successor. While Rudy Giuliani seemed to benefit greatly from media coverage, Mayor Dinkins's efforts were relatively ignored. Dinkins remarks, "Everybody acknowledges that crime started to go down in '91, but during Rudy's eight years no one acknowledged that, or very few acknowledged it . . . we never got any credit for that."[55]

Two major events contributed to declining morale within the police department under Dinkins's watch. One revolved around his attempts to assuage an angry Dominican population in Washington Heights that believed that an innocent Dominican named Jose "Kiko" Garcia had been shot and killed by the police. In an effort to limit civil disorder, Dinkins met with the slain man's family and paid for his body's transportation to the Dominican Republic. Many officers took this action as an affront to the entire force, believing Dinkins to be siding with the young man who was later shown to be active in the area's drug trade.[56]

In addition, the mayor's insistence on an all-civilian Civilian Complaint Review Board ruffled many NYPD feathers.[57] Resistance to the initiative culminated in what was referred to alternately as a "police demonstration" and "police riot." An estimated 10,000 police officers blocked the Brooklyn Bridge, prevented the free flow of traffic, drank openly, and harassed African Americans passing by City Hall. The *Economist* stated sardonically that "suspiciously easily, the march got out of hand."[58] The mayor was depicted both by protestors and in the media in crude racist terms. The *New York Voice/Harlem U.S.A.* reported that "it was obvious to all that this protest stemmed from something other than the fact that the mayor wanted an all-civilian Civilian Complaint Review Board."[59] The NAACP's Benjamin Chavis, writing in the *New Pittsburgh Courier*, described the scene "as a post-modern lynch mob full of racial bigotry and hate."[60]

Dinkins was already seen by some citizens, fairly or unfairly, as "soft on crime," and his relationship with the NYPD hurt him as the reelection campaign approached. Perhaps as the ultimate irony, despite the fact the police behaved improperly, the mayor received the lion's share of the blame when the police department went beyond accepted bounds of behavior. As Richard C. Wade, an urban historian at City

University of New York, commented, "The mayor has little control over the police force, but the public holds him responsible."[61]

RACE RELATIONS

When David Dinkins became mayor, it was widely believed that his presence in the office would help dampen racial fires. This view seemed especially prevalent among his white constituents. While New York avoided rioting on the scale of Los Angeles, the city endured several moments of collective trepidation in the 1990s. In addition to the Garcia shooting, two incidents in particular aroused visceral reactions from New Yorkers: the 1990 Korean boycotts and the 1991 Crown Heights riots.

The Korean boycotts began in the fall of 1990 after an incident in which a Haitian American claimed to have been physically assaulted by a Brooklyn Korean storeowner.[62] The local African American community boycotted the store along with others, with activists aggressively picketing local markets. The chants turned racist and the pregnant wife of one storeowner lost a child after being physically attacked.[63] Though a court order had been obtained requiring protesters to remain fifty feet from targeted stores, the mayor refused to have the police enforce it. The boycotts continued until Dinkins made a symbolic statement by shopping in one of the stores, but his failure to enforce the court order eroded some of his support. This opened an early door for Rudy Giuliani and others to criticize his failed leadership.[64]

The second incident, and perhaps the defining moment of the Dinkins mayoralty, was the explosion of the Crown Heights riots in 1991. In a harrowing three-day event, a seven-year-old black child, Gavin Cato, was struck and killed by a Hasidic Jewish driver in the neighborhood. Rumors circulated that a Hasidic ambulance had picked up the injured Jewish parties but had neglected to attend to the injured child. Though this rumor was later proven false, a "mob" of African American youths killed a Jewish resident of the neighborhood. Two nights of rioting ensued, until Dinkins ordered a change in police tactics that ended the disturbances. Reminiscent of the actions of Mayor Lindsey during the Harlem Riots in the 1960s, Dinkins even went so far as to walk the streets of Crown Heights. Initially Dinkins's actions were viewed positively, but the verdicts that followed the riots compounded the situation.[65] The Jewish driver was not indicted for the child's death, and the jury ruled it an accident. The black man arrested for the stabbing of the Jewish resident, Yankel Rosenbaum, was acquitted, despite being caught with the murder weapon and confessing to the crime. Rather than protest the decision, Dinkins stated famously, "I have no doubt the criminal justice system has operated fairly and openly."[66] This, combined with Dinkins's attendance at Galvin Cato's funeral, but not Rosenbaum's, deepened Jewish resentment. Finally, a state report released in August 1993 criticized the mayor for his sluggish reaction.[67] The report reopened a wound that would plague Dinkins until the end of his tenure.

The Crown Heights riots illustrated several problematic aspects surrounding both David Dinkins and his Rainbow Coalition. First, relations between Jews and blacks had deteriorated. Economic recession and the perception that Jews held disproportionate political and social power exacerbated tensions. When Dinkins attempted to intervene, the local black community rejected his overtures.[68] Similarly, one policy expert noted, Dinkins's refusal to side with one party may have prevented further violence, but it appeared to whites that he identified with "blacks alone."[69] The *Times* remarked that Dinkins's "black skin is no magical antidote to racial tensions."[70]

Dinkins himself has acknowledged the damage that Crown Heights wrought on his term in office. When questioned about the media's coverage of the events, Dinkins states that it was "inaccurate. The police did not do a good job. It [ended] after I said, whatever you guys are doing, it's not working." As for the accusations by some journalists that Dinkins was anti-Semitic or complicit in the violence that erupted, Dinkins responded, "It was, I thought, very tough."[71]

THE "GORGEOUS MOSAIC": 1993

By 1993, the coalition that had elected Dinkins had frayed. In the African American community, the Dinkins administration reached out to the Caribbean population in Brooklyn. Though some support remained, many expressed strong reservations. When selecting the mayor for reelection, Brooklyn Democrats revealed a deep ambivalence, with nineteen voting for his nomination, ten against, and ten abstaining.[72]

Latinos echoed the concerns of blacks. An early poll published in the *New York Voice/Harlem U.S.A.* indicated that only 43 percent of those Latinos who had voted for Dinkins in 1989 were ready to do so in 1993.[73] Councilman Adam Clayton Powell, Jr., argued that "the Latino community feels betrayed by Dinkins." Bronx resident and contractor Louie Alvarez expressed a viewpoint held by a significant portion of New York's minority communities, that "he doesn't care about Latinos or blacks. . . . He only cares about white society." Others noted his perceived inability to lead in moments of crisis, stating, "The way he talked about Crown Heights and the problems with the Korean store, he messed it all up."[74]

Voter ambivalence—and in some cases hostility—toward Dinkins led many to discount programs that his administration had implemented that were meant to provide needed health, education, and social services to at-risk communities. The Communicare program expanded health care into underserved communities.[75] In terms of education and social services, the mayor instituted the Beacon School Program, which enabled some schools to stay open later for recreation, adult education, and various services. Dinkins expanded this program quickly and the Giuliani administration maintained the program despite gutting its parent organization, the Department of Youth Services. It continued to receive funding well into Giuliani's second term. Ironically, in the face of criticism from the left concerning city services, Giuliani often cited the program as one of his accomplishments.

THE 1993 ELECTION

By mid-1992, New York had rebounded from the decade's first two years, with the *Wall Street Journal* noting, "Violent crime is down, at least one bond rating is up and New Yorkers are suddenly no longer talking about whether the city will survive, but when it will emerge from recession."[76] Even the executive director of the New York State Financial Control Board noted the fiscal restraint: "This year the city managed to take control of its daily problems. It's like night and day."[77]

Voter apathy toward Dinkins's campaign emerged visibly during this time. During his tenure, the mayor had several opportunities to quell racial unrest. New York never suffered a Los Angeles-style riot, but Dinkins's actions in all of the city's controversial incidents left aggrieved constituents dissatisfied. Second, though crime had been dropping since 1991, the police riots overshadowed the mayor's achievements. His economic development efforts mirrored those of administrations prior, yet his tight fiscal budgets failed to win over a majority of the business community, who viewed the possibility of a Republican mayor as a better alternative. Four balanced budgets and fiscal austerity were not enough to outflank a probusiness GOP candidate. Similarly, Dinkins's approach to homelessness failed to deviate sharply from Koch's failed policies, while his modest successes in housing were blunted by intraracial resistance. An unenthusiastic black and Latino electoral base, a small shift in the white vote, and lower turnout among his coalition partners doomed Dinkins's reelection.

Voting along racial lines hardened, with white Democrats supporting Giuliani by a sixty-four to thirty-five margin, whereas in 1989 the difference was at fifty-nine to thirty-nine.[78] Increased turnout on Staten Island, where a secession bill had been placed on the ballot, aided Giuliani. He emerged with a significant lead over Dinkins in Manhattan.[79]

According to election data, Dinkins lost by less than 2 percent of the vote. Though he earned 95 percent of the African American electorate, turnout in that community did not reach the same levels as it had in 1989. Bill Fitch, writing in the *Village Voice*, remarked that "it was in the ghettos of Harlem and central Brooklyn, not simply [in] Staten Island, that Dinkins lost the election."[80] In every borough, he received fewer total votes than in 1989. Much the same was true of Latino voters as well. Support among Jewish voters declined 3 percent, as did his support from both "white liberals" and Democrats in general.

Other factors contributed to Dinkins's defeat. A rising anti-incumbency tide had just begun, which culminated in the 1994 Republican takeover of Congress. White and Jewish populations had begun a more general shift to the right and new immigration patterns made coalitions more difficult to sustain. Jim Sleeper, a former *Daily News* columnist and *New Republic* contributor, argued that rainbow coalitions were doomed to fail as demographics changed and new immigrant groups entered American society. As Sleeper put it, "old style civil rights" politics failed to appeal to new minorities, while others felt betrayed by such movements.[81]

Black commentators viewed Dinkins's defeat in several ways. Some blamed racism, saying, "People feel betrayed . . . people feel that we as black Democrats played by the rules, and the rules were changed."[82] Others believed that Dinkins had "pandered too much to whites," failing to campaign enough in black communities. Some blamed the black community itself, as one campaign worker for Dinkins remarked acidly, "We got what we deserved and I love it."[83] When asked if the lack of mobilization of his base constituency may have contributed to his defeat, the former mayor demurred. Dinkins argued that Staten Island contributed heavily to his defeat, saying, "That's what hurt me more than anything else. People can say Crown Heights, they can say this, they can say the other, I'm saying Staten Island."[84]

Black intellectuals appeared as split over reasons for Dinkins's loss as the larger community. Wilber Tatum, publisher of the *New York Amsterdam News*, denounced the mainstream media for failing to present Dinkins's tenure as mayor and his campaign for reelection honestly.[85] Tatum acknowledged the *Times* endorsement of the incumbent but claimed that "their news and editorials" undermined his hopes of gaining reelection. Others, including white journalists, pointed out similar media failings. *Village Voice* writer Wayne Barrett supported this view; he noted media bias in several areas, arguing that Giuliani's past seemed to be ignored by the city's major papers and media.[86]

African American Pulitzer Prize–winning journalist Les Payne commented that Dinkins had taken his support within the black electorate for granted, placing too much emphasis on winning over white voters.[87] Bob Herbert argued that Dinkins had been elected not because he would eliminate crime or enhance quality of life, but rather because "Mr. Dinkins [would] calm things down . . . if Mr. Dinkins had been perceived as aggressive, he could have forgotten about being elected." According to Herbert, Dinkins suffered from the tranquility that had settled upon the city such that "in a calmer atmosphere voters can look more closely at the conditions in which they are living."[88]

Black intellectuals' opinions regarding Dinkins's failures varied as widely as the electorate itself, but several common themes emerged: Dinkins's lack of black mobilization, especially among the poor; fear of crime; media bias; racial bias; and his own failures of leadership.

CONCLUSION

Ultimately, David Dinkins entered office in difficult times. The city's financial situation, union obligations, debt payments, and shrinking tax base all contributed to limit his options. His promised social programs were slow to develop, leaving many of his minority constituencies frustrated and disillusioned. His probusiness policies produced budget surpluses by 1992, but these were then overshadowed by the Garcia shooting, the September police riots, and the August 1993 release of the Crown Heights report. His accomplishments—more affordable housing, new city contracting laws, balanced budgets, crime legislation, and the Beacon school programs—were often overshadowed.

The former mayor could not outflank a Republican candidate on issues traditionally thought to be GOP strengths, such as crime and economic growth. He was unable to galvanize his base constituencies to offset increased turnout in Staten Island. Incremental losses among Jews, white liberals, and Latinos allowed increased white mobilization to overwhelm his term's "gorgeous mosaic."

Rudy Giuliani took office in 1994. Receiving the lion's share of credit for crime reduction, he had continued many of the provisions that preceded him, a fact that few writers noted. Neighborhood policing, which has been praised for helping to reduce crime in New York, began under Dinkins. The Beacon School Program also garnered support from Giuliani and was later used to his political advantage. Race played a part in Dinkins's defeat, but so too did his failures in the stewardship of the city. Ethnic conflict and his response to it, especially after having been elected as a "healer," undermined his strongest personality trait. Rather than appearing conciliatory, he seemed detached and out of touch. This allowed those few white voters that defected to excuse themselves for voting against him, while dulling black and Latino turnout. It is very possible that Dinkins lost his bid for reelection due in part, to his race. Had he been white, perhaps voters would have been more forgiving of his inconsistencies. Yet, segments of the black and Latino population had not forgiven him for his imperfect four years, reducing turnout in both communities. Blacks and Latinos expected more of Dinkins because of his race, despite the fiscal limitations placed on him by an economy in recession. In contrast, whites expected him to cool racial tensions because of his race, despite the fact that the mayor had little control over outbreaks of spontaneous social rage. In the end, because of race and the differing expectations it brought for each ethnic or racial constituency, David Dinkins was left with little political space in which to operate.

NOTES

1. E. J. Dionne Jr, "The Politics of Race," *New York Times*, April 11, 1989.
2. Ibid.
3. Ibid.
4. Roger Biles, "Mayor David Dinkins and the Politics of Race in New York City," in *African American Mayors: Race, Politics, and the American City*, ed. David Colburn and Jeffery Adler (Chicago: University of Chicago Press, 2001), 138.
5. Tomasky, Micheal, "Identity Politics in New York City," *Nation*, June 21, 1993.
6. Ibid.
7. Though the National Institute on Drug Abuse and other organizations have reported in recent years that the crack problem of the late 1980s and early 1990s was not as statistically significant as the media and government believed, it was perceived that way as evidenced by numerous essays and reports in both left-leaning and conservative news sources. The perception of crime is almost as important as its reality. Thus, even if it was statistically misleading, the media and government emphasized the crack epidemic to such an extent that the public believed it was a problem.
8. Most notably the Queens and Bronx sections of the party.
9. Scott McConnell, "The Making of the Mayor," *Commentary*, February 1990.
10. New York black political leaders Basil Patterson, Charlie Rangel, David Dinkins, and Percy Sutton, all from what is known as the Harlem Pragmatic school, a Democratic machine-based wing of New York black politics.
11. J. Phillip Thompson, *Double Trouble: Black Mayors, Black Communities, and the Call for a Deep Democracy* (New York: Oxford University Press, 2005), 168.
12. Martin Kilson, "Adam Clayton Powell, Jr: The Militant Politician," in *Black Leaders of the Twentieth Century*, ed. John Hope Franklin and August Meier (Chicago: University of Illinois Press, 1982), 267.
13. "J. Raymond Jones: Inside Outside," *New York Daily News*, April 15, 1999.
14. Josh Barbanel, "Dinkins Ties to Clubhouse Under Attack," *New York Times*, October 10, 1989.
15. Ibid.
16. Johnathan P. Hicks, "As Political Lions Go Gray, Harlem Wanes as Center of Power," *New York Times*, February 3, 2003.
17. Biles, "Dinkins and the Politics of Race," 135. John Flateau, who was a dean at Medgar Evers College commented, "They were the beneficiaries of a unique convergence of demographics, personal chemistry and a party political system that gave them a significant

jumping off point . . . but as the black population grew, it dispersed into Brooklyn and Queens. And so did the political power."

18. Jim Sleeper, *The Closest of Strangers: Liberalism and the Politics of Race in New York* (New York: W. W. Norton, 1990), 298.

19. Ibid.

20. Celestine Bohlen, "For Dinkins Styles Range from Calm to Serious," *New York Times*, July 31, 1989.

21. Ibid.

22. Tom Wicker, "Dinkins Out Front," *New York Times*, June 23, 1989.

23. McConnell, "The Making of the Mayor."

24. Biles, "Dinkins and the Politics of Race," 136.

25. McConnell, "The Making of the Mayor."

26. Don Terry, "The New York Primary: For Black Voters, an Evening of Inspiration and Giddy Celebration," *New York Times*, September 13, 1989.

27. Thompson, *Double Trouble*, 190.

28. Biles, "Dinkins and the Politics of Race," 137.

29. David Dinkins, Interview by Ryan Reft, 18 April, Tape Recording, Columbia University, New York, NY.

30. Arian Asher et al., *Changing New York Politics* (New York: Routledge, 1991), 98.

31. Bohlen, "For Dinkins Styles Range from Calm to Serious," *New York Times*, July 31, 1989; as one African American woman commented to the *New York Times*, "Crime is an important issue—crime and drugs. The white media thought in the '60s when we were complaining about police brutality that we didn't want the police. That's not the point. A majority of the black community wants these criminals off the streets and punished."

32. Admittedly, the attempt of Asher et al. to eliminate the Bensonhurst incident along with earlier examples of racial violence—Howard Beach Incident 1986 and the rape of the Central Park jogger 1989—seems at best wishful thinking.

33. Editorial, "A New York Mayor," *Wall Street Journal*, September 14, 1989.

34. Editorial, "Lessons for Republicans," *Wall Street Journal*, November 9, 1989.

35. Mark J. Penn and Douglas E. Schoen, "Don't Minimize Dinkins Victory," *New York Times*, November 11, 1989.

36. Leon Wynter, "Dinkins' Win Tinged with Sadness," *Wall Street Journal*, November 9, 1989. Leon Wynter, that newspaper's minority enterprise reporter at the time, observed hopefully, "Because he is black, Mr. Dinkins can be a bridge, in a city of rivers where the bridges have been falling down."

37. Editorial, *Tri-State Defender*, January 24, 1990.

38. According to Shorris, "No comparable burden is placed on any city in the country."

39. Biles, "Dinkins and the Politics of Race," 139.

40. Michael Tomasky, "Identity Politics in New York City," *Nation*, June 21, 1993.

41. By 1991, federal aid's proportion of the city's budget had declined to 9.3 percent, down from 17.9 percent in 1981.

42. Growth in the city had come to a standstill. Income growth was the lowest it had been since 1982 and employment growth reached the same levels it had in 1980, while finance industry, as a result of the 1987 crash and general economic adjustments, was suffering a 2 percent decline.

43. The city's municipal workforce at that time consisted of 360,000 workers, of whom 250,000 were members of trade unions. New York had one of the highest proportion of city workers per 100,000 than any other city in the United States.

44. The EDC, as it is known, is a quasi-governmental organization that operates as an in-house consultant on planning issues, zoning, environmental review, streets, and other

areas. The organization attempts to create growth rather than simply rewriting zoning laws. Thus, it hopes to expand economic development in five-, ten-, fifteen-, and twenty-year blocks, depending on the specific situation.

45. Harvey Adasko. Interviewed by Ryan Reft 17 April 2006, Tape Recording. Economic Development Corporation, New York, NY.

46. The Morgan Stanley deal secured their presence in Manhattan until 2002 and represented a continuation of Koch's policies. As the *Wall Street Journal* noted, "In the past two years, Prudential Insurance . . . Bear Stearns and four of the city's major commodities exchanges have all made long term commitments to staying in New York in exchange for lucrative tax breaks."

47. Editorial, "New York Mayor to Increase Contracts Given to Minorities," *Wall Street Journal*, February 11, 1992.

48. David Dinkins, Interview by Ryan Reft, 18 April, Tape Recording, Columbia University, New York, NY.

49. Annette Walker, "Construction Industry Agrees to Historic Minority Training Program," *Amsterdam News*, January 2, 1993.

50. J. Phillip Thompson, "The Failure of Liberal Homeless Policy in the Koch and Dinkins Administration," *Political Science Quarterly* 111, no. 4: 655.

51. If these costs totaled $10 million in 1980, by 1992 they exceeded $500 million.

52. Meaning it focused singularly on housing rather than taking a broader perspective.

53. "Time to Fire Ms. Blackburne," *New York Times*, February 22, 1992. A number of financial indiscretions had opened Ms. Blackburne, one of Dinkins's top housing officials, to criticism. Though she had instituted a number of useful reforms in the Housing Authority, including conducting an "internal New York City Housing Authority democracy campaign" and attaining increased federal funding for affordable housing units, she found herself battered by calls for her resignation. For Dinkins's supporters, it became difficult to defend an officeholder who allegedly spent $345,000 "redecorating the authority's executive floor," among other questionable expenditures.

54. Jerry Gray, "Public 'Nuisance' Crackdown Starts with Vice Raid in the Bronx," *New York Times*, June 23, 1991. One example of this new approach emerged in June 1991. The police began enforcing a seven-year-old regulation known as the "Padlock Law," "which allows the authorities to use civil court orders to close sites where there are histories of arrests."

55. David Dinkins, Interview by Ryan Reft, 18 April, Tape Recording, Columbia University, New York, NY.

56. James C. McKinley Jr., "Officers Rally and Dinkins Is Their Target," *New York Times*, September 17, 1992. As one officer lamented, "He never supports us on anything. . . . A cop shoots someone with a gun who's a drug dealer, and he goes and visits the family."

57. "New York Police: Revolt of the Hessians," *Economist*, September 26, 1992.

58. Ibid.

59. Editorial, "New York City Police Department Shamed and Dishonored by a Handful of Bigots," *New York Voice/Harlem U.S.A.*, September 30, 1992.

60. Benjamin F. Chavis Jr., "Stand with NY Mayor Dinkins," *New Pittsburgh Courier*, September 30, 1992.

61. Jane Fritsch, "The Police as Mayor's Political Nightmare," *New York Times*, September 27, 1992.

62. A jury later found the girl to have suffered nothing more than a superficial cut, if that.

63. Some protesters were reported to have made comments such as, "No fortune cookie today."

64. Jim Sleeper, "The End of the Rainbow," *The New Republic*, November 1, 1993. Giuliani commented, "If I were mayor and some Italian-Americans were intimidating a black shopkeeper, I'd come down on them hard and fast."

65. Editorial, "A Long Night in Crown Heights," *New York Times*, August 21, 1991.

66. Elizabeth Kadetsky, "Racial Politics in New York," *Nation*, November 30, 1992.

67. The state report was issued just prior to the primary and general election that summer.

68. Editorial, "He's the Mayor, Not a Magician," *New York Times*, August 23, 1991.

69. Thompson, *Double Trouble*, 255.

70. "He's the Mayor, Not a Magician."

71. David Dinkins, Interview by Ryan Reft, 18 April, Tape Recording, Columbia University, New York, NY.

72. Lester Hinds, "Democrats Endorse Dinkins but Barely," *New York Amsterdam News*, May 29, 1993.

73. "Badillo Seeks Mayor Dinkins' Support as Republicans Woo Him for Giuliani's Ticket," *New York Voice/Harlem U.S.A.*, May 26, 1993.

74. David Gonzalez, "Where Hispanic Voters Sided with Dinkins, Now Defection," *New York Times*, October 14, 1993.

75. Lisa Belkin, "Care for Women is Lacking, Hospital Corporation Admits," *New York Times*, March 13, 1993; Communicare attempted to expand health care into undeserved areas by providing more clinics for patients to visit on a more regular basis, thus avoiding emergency rooms and maintaining better overall health. In its first year of existence the city hoped to increase care visits by 68,000.

76. Neil Barsky, "Back from the Dead," *Wall Street Journal*, July 6, 1992.

77. Ibid.

78. "Tuesday's Tea Leaves," *New York Times*, November 5, 1993.

79. Marvine Howe, "Staten Island Ferry Revives Battle of Boroughs," *New York Times*, April 3, 1994.

80. Bill Fitch, "Road to Rudy: Dinkins Lost Because He Ran an Issue Free Campaign," *Village Voice*, November 16, 1993.

81. Jim Sleeper, "The End of the Rainbow," *New Republic*, November 1, 1993.

82. Felecia R. Lee, "For Blacks, Loss by Dinkins Undermines Hopes of Change," *New York Times*, November 4, 1993.

83. Ibid.

84. David Dinkins, Interview by Ryan Reft, 18 April, Tape Recording, Columbia University, New York, NY.

85. Wilbert A. Tatum, "The Election Wasn't Won: It Was Stolen and Bought," *New York Amsterdam News*, November 13, 1993.

86. Wayne Barrett, "Post Election Memo," *Village Voice*, November 16, 1993.

87. Vernon Jarrett, "Low Black Turnout Hurt Dinkins' Re-Election Bid," *Chicago Sun-Times*, November 9, 1993; Payne summarized Dinkins mayoral career succinctly, "[Dinkins] was to gentle to hurt his enemies and too afraid to reward his friends."

88. Bob Herbert, "The Verdict," *New York Times*, November 3, 1993.

CITY POLITICS AND BLACK PROTEST

THE ECONOMIC TRANSFORMATION OF HARLEM AND BRONZEVILLE

DEREK S. HYRA

MUCH OF THE LITERATURE ON BLACK POLITICS CLAIMS THAT AFRICAN AMERICANS are the most politically uniform group in the United States. According to Pinderhughes (1997, 77), a leading expert on black politics, "The African American population consistently displays the clearest signs of . . . political cohesion; their homogeneous behavior arises out of distinctive historical experiences." If this were true, we might expect similar political behaviors surrounding the economic redevelopment and gentrification of two historic black communities. However, Harlem, in New York City, has a different level of protest politics associated with its revitalization as compared to Bronzeville in Chicago. In Harlem, public dissent and protest is ubiquitous, while oppositional voices in Bronzeville are muted. This difference is rather puzzling, since these communities have very similar racial and socioeconomic characteristics.[1] One major distinction between these two neighborhoods is that they are embedded within cities with drastically different political landscapes. Therefore, I investigate whether the unique citywide political environments in New York City and Chicago influence internal community debates.

Exploring the dynamics related to civic engagement and public dissent within black communities is particularly important since African Americans, compared to

I acknowledge Vincent Carretta, Allison Hyra, and the participants of the Reproduction of Race and Racial Ideologies Workshop at the University of Chicago, whose critical feedback improved this chapter. In addition, I thank the Rockefeller Foundation, the U.S. Department of Housing and Urban Development, the Social Science Research Council's Program in Applied Economics and the Center for the Study of Race, Politics, and Culture for supporting this research.

whites, are more likely to participate in nontraditional political action (Verba and Nie 1972). For instance, African Americans are more likely to affect their community through civic groups than by voting. Although many survey studies investigate individual and community-level determinates of black political action (e.g., Cohen and Dawson 1993; Marschall 2001), few studies explore how conditions beyond the community affect informal political engagement. By comparing the extent of protest politics related to Harlem and Bronzeville's redevelopment, this study explores whether the structure of citywide political environments affect contested politics at the community level.

Harlem and Bronzeville have been American symbols for concentrated poverty and social isolation for the last forty years. These inner-city communities, however, are now experiencing rapid economic development. Harlem, once known for its boarded-up buildings, crack houses, and high mortality rate, now boasts health spas, quaint bed and breakfasts, boutique stores, and posh restaurants. Harlem brownstones, which the city could not give away at one time, today command prices from $1 to $2 million. Moreover, mainstream chain stores such as Marshalls, the Body Shop, and Starbucks have recently opened on the main business strip of 125th Street. Bronzeville, the Harlem of Chicago, has not experienced large-scale commercial development, yet its transformation is very apparent. Real estate values are rising faster than the city's average, and unprecedented amounts of high-rise public housing developments have been demolished and replaced with half-million dollar luxury condominiums and town homes. Major financial institutions that neglected the community for decades are now eager to make loans and are even establishing new branches in the area. As the title of an article in a recent real-estate publication claims, "Bronzeville is Booming."[2]

There has been a substantial amount of positive media attention concerning the economic development in Harlem and Bronzeville. However, there is little community consensus about the redevelopment that is occurring, since it is associated with displacement. Taylor (1944, 149) notes in her study on the reemergence of Harlem, "Improvement efforts in Harlem have stoked the fires of controversy." Generally, homeowners in both communities view this development trend as a blessing and hope this reinvestment returns these areas to their legendary glory days. Others, however, fear that unrestricted development will bring soaring rents and housing prices beyond the reach of many current residents. Smith (2000, 163) describes Harlem's development as a catch-22. He states, "Without private rehabilitation and redevelopment, the neighborhood's housing stock will remain severely dilapidated; with it, a large number of Central Harlem residents will ultimately be displaced and will not benefit from the better and more expensive housing." This same dilemma applies to Bronzeville. One newspaper article states, "Bronzeville is going the way of any number of newly gentrifying city neighborhoods—nice if you've got the money."[3]

The redevelopment of Harlem and Bronzeville provides a unique opportunity to explore the role of black organizations and institutions in the process of transformation. While many revitalizing inner city areas experience an influx of white residents (Smith 2000), these two communities are developing economically with little racial changeover. According to the 1990 and 2000 censuses, Harlem is approximately 80 percent African American, and in the last ten years the white population only increased from 1.5 percent to 2 percent. Bronzeville's racial composition has remained stable, moving from 95 percent to 92 percent African American during the same period. The affluent populations moving into these communities are upper- and middle-income African Americans. Thus, these two communities are perfect localities to study aspects of black civil society.

Dawson (2000) argues that the extreme level of racial segregation in America, as documented by Massey and Denton (1993), justifies the study of black networks and institutions. In this chapter I define black civil society as "institutions and social networks formed by individuals who participate . . . in some type of public-oriented collective action" (Dawson 2000, 3). As stated earlier, much of the past literature on black politics claims that African Americans act in similar ways. While numerous residents in these areas are elated by the economic revitalization, several black-led organizations are attempting to preserve a place for low-income people who comprise 45 percent of the population in these communities.[4] Since these communities are similar on many levels, one would expect equivalent levels of support and opposition from residents and black-led organizations in both neighborhoods. However, the degree of "contested politics" or "black activism" (Jennings 1992) associated with the redevelopment processes is drastically different. Harlem is full of public dissent, while activists in Bronzeville are reluctant to challenge the development process.

This circumstance is plausibly related to the distinct citywide political contexts of New York City and Chicago. New York City and Chicago are cities with different political landscapes. In Chicago the structure approximates a one-party system with strong central control, while New York City's political formation is more decentralized and diverse, a difference that has been repeatedly noted since the 1950s (Fuchs 1992; Greenstone and Peterson 1976; Mollenkopf 1991; Wilson 1960). These unique political milieus at the city level might facilitate specific norms of political engagement (see Clark 1996; Putnam 1993) at the neighborhood level. Hence a comparison of Harlem and Bronzeville can answer a major question: do political differences at the city level translate to alternate circumstances at the community level, and if so, are these distinctions affecting the civic engagement of black-led organizations and institutions?

Ample research suggests that a city's political structure matters for several important outcomes. For instance, district elections, compared to citywide council elections, lead to larger overall voter turnout (Bridges 1997). Additionally, more centralized city political systems facilitate less public dissent throughout the city and smaller budget deficits (Fuchs 1992). Last, strong machine systems, compared to weak party city governments, limit contested politics in low-income neighborhoods (Wilson 1960). Since the structure of a city's political system influences several outcomes, it seems reasonable that the normative and structural differences in city-level politics might also influence levels of activism and resistance within African American communities.

Comparative literature suggests a link between citywide political environments and African American community politics. For instance, Ferman (1996) posits that alternate political climates affect the likelihood of successful progressive movements stemming from minority neighborhoods. She argues that Pittsburgh's political culture, with norms of trust and cooperation, facilitates the incorporation of neighborhood demands, while Chicago's political environment, characterized by suspicion and cynicism, remains rigid, controlling, and resistant to change. Further, Greenstone and Peterson (1976), in their study of the implementation of Great Society programs in several cities, note the importance of a city's political climate on progressive black institutions. They argue that compared to NAACP chapters in other large municipalities, Chicago's is one of the least militant because of the local political climate.

Based on my analysis of data collected through a variety of ethnographic procedures, I argue that the political differences between New York City and Chicago affect the context within which the redevelopment of Harlem and Bronzeville takes place. Political climates at the city levels, in particular distinct structures and norms for political engagement, affect the public debates connected to the redevelopment processes within these two communities. Evidence suggests that New York City's diverse political system facilitates public dissent, while Chicago's one-party, centralized structure inhibits it. My analysis highlights the unique political context of each city as an important explanatory variable to understanding the extent of black-led protest politics and the redevelopment process in these communities.

METHODOLOGY AND APPROACH

The method of this study is an ethnographic, multiple-case design (Yin 2003), commonly known as the comparative approach (King, Leohane, and Verba 1994). Some criticize the ethnographic method by claiming that it lacks scientific rigor; however, by conducting a comparative study, I increase the analytic power of this technique. Furthermore, most studies on black politics use survey research, and, as Dawson (1994, 13) states, "To understand black politics one needs to draw on many methodologies"; thus, this study adds a level of needed depth to black politics research. The strength of this approach is that it allows for tacit knowledge drawn from observing and participating in people's everyday lives. This is one of the first studies on black politics to employ a comparative ethnographic technique. I spent more than three years (1999–2001) studying the redevelopment of Bronzeville and considered comparing this redevelopment pattern with another community. Using the replication logic, I attempted to find a community that matched Bronzeville in many characteristics. Harlem, with its recent economic resurgence and rich African American history, was a viable option.[5] Starting in January 2002, I moved to Harlem and spent two six-month periods, between 2002 and 2003, exploring the redevelopment process there.

PLACE

In this chapter, Harlem means specifically Central Harlem. It is located toward the northern tip of Manhattan and is bounded by Central Park at 110th Street to the south, 155th Street to the north, Fifth Avenue on the east and Morningside and St. Nicholas Parks on the west. It houses many culturally significant black institutions including the Apollo Theatre; Abyssinian Baptist Church, once led by Adam Clayton Powell, Jr.; and the New York Urban League. Harlem is where Marcus Garvey and Malcolm X settled and established their political and social movements. Langston Hughes and Zora Neale Hurston wrote many of their famous literary works in Harlem, and renowned painter Jacob Lawrence lived there as well. Musicians Duke Ellington, Charlie Parker, and John Coltrane performed at venues such as Smalls Paradise, the Cotton Club, and the Lenox Lounge. During the early and mid-twentieth century, these people and many other African American artists, writers, performers, and political leaders developed Harlem's reputation as the "capital of Black America."

Bronzeville is the Harlem of Chicago. It is located on the south side of Chicago and for the purpose of this study is bounded by Twenty-sixth Street to the north, Fifty-first Street to the south, Cottage Grove Avenue to the east, and the Dan Ryan Expressway to the west.[6] During its heyday, Bronzeville inspired the work of literary figures such as Richard Wright and Gwendolyn Brooks, as well as artists such as Archibald J. Motley, Jr. It houses many important black institutions, including the Chicago Urban League, Olivet Baptist Church, and the *Chicago Defender* newspaper, which still sponsors one of the largest annual African American parades in the country. Many important political leaders such as Ida B. Wells, Oscar DePriest, and William Dawson resided in Bronzeville. In addition, during the 1920s, 1930s, and 1940s, numerous singers and musicians, including Ella Fitzgerald, Louis Armstrong, and Earl Hines, performed in neighborhood venues like the Regal Theater, the Palm Tavern, and the Parkway Ballroom.

Bronzeville and Harlem are similar on many levels. These communities have almost identical histories of development throughout the twentieth century (see Clark 1965; Drake and Cayton 1993; Hirsch 1998; Johnson 1991; Lemann 1991; Osofsky 1996; Spear 1967). Both began in the 1890s as white, middle- to upper-income suburbs with exquisite housing stocks, then became culturally significant, mixed-income black communities between 1920 and 1940. This was followed by periods of significant decline, with population loss and extreme levels of concentrated poverty. Starting in the 1990s, these areas began to slowly transition to more mixed-income environments as property values rose with increased commercial and residential investment.

Aside from their histories, these areas have other analogous qualities. First, both are located near the central business districts (CBD) of their respective cities. Proximity to the CBD is important because of indications that distance from the primary area of business is related to patterns of gentrification (Sassen 2000). Second, both of these communities are targets of federal programs, such as the Empowerment Zone Initiative. Last, and most important, the 1990 and 2000 censuses indicate that Bronzeville and Harlem are similar in social and economic demographics, including racial composition, household income, home value, home ownership, and educational level (see the appendix). Moreover, both areas have enormously high concentrations of subsidized housing. These similarities minimize the possibility that claims about differences in the extent of contested politics are attributed to distinct social and economic conditions.

Although it is important to establish their likeness, these two communities have some noteworthy differences. First, Harlem contains more people and is more densely populated than Bronzeville. Second, Harlem's reputation as a symbolic center of black life is stronger than Bronzeville's. Third, different types of displacement are occurring in these communities. In Harlem, low-income residents are more likely to remain since public housing is not being demolished, while in Bronzeville the public housing is being razed, leading to an exodus of many low-income people. In Harlem, displacement is occurring among small businesses and working-class residents who occupy private market housing. These differences could lead to alternative explanations about the levels of contested politics. However, despite these variations, I argue that there are enough similarities between these two communities to warrant a comparative study.

ETHNOGRAPHIC PROCEDURES

Following in the tradition of other ethnographic studies, such as Gans (1982), Pattillo-McCoy (1999), and Whyte (1955), I used a variety of data-collecting techniques, including participant observation, interviews, and archival materials to understand the process of redevelopment. While living in these neighborhoods, I attended hundreds of community meetings hosted by block clubs, public housing tenant associations, coalitions of civic leaders, and social service organizations. I also interviewed approximately thirty-five individuals in each community through scheduled hour-long sessions. I spoke with heads of public-housing tenant groups, social-service organizations, community development corporations, elected officials, staff in city agencies, and business leaders. In addition, I had countless informal interactions with people on the streets and in homes, restaurants, bars, coffee shops, barbershops, Laundromats, and recreational centers. Last, I gathered archival material, including newspaper articles, city documents, meeting minutes, recent academic reports, and census data.

CONCEPT OF PROTEST POLITICS

Protest politics and opposition are public and private acts of informal collective actions taken by organizations and individuals to contest the economic development. My notion of protest moves away from nonspecific and abstract forms of resistance discussed by historian Robin Kelley (1994). His definition of resistance, such as alternative "dress codes," is too broad for the politics of community development. Powerful forces are escalating the real estate markets and only concrete acts of opposition, such as protest at public meetings, are likely to slow the development process. I do agree with Kelley, however, that community organizations are important mechanisms in "black working-class political struggles" (38). In this study, I examine actions taken by organizational leaders and everyday individuals in civic forums attempting to directly impact public-redevelopment decisions.

POLITICAL CONTRASTS

Harlem residents, compared to Bronzeville's, are more vocal and almost unruly at public meetings. In Harlem, people are more willing to denounce the actions of their local politicians and further, the political leaders are more likely to attend public meetings where these exchanges take place. After a local official presents at a community forum, a woman concerned about rising rents stands and shouts, "The elected officials here in Harlem are part of the problem. If I vote for you and you can't help me, you don't get my vote the next time." Shouting in public at political officials occurs on a much less frequent basis in Bronzeville.

Even though Bronzeville and Harlem are similar communities, they are embedded in contrasting political environments. During an interview with a Harlem politician, State Assemblyman Keith Wright notes this difference. When asked to describe the political environment in New York City, he comments that compared to New York City, Chicago is "more politically stable." As we continue to talk, he describes how the stability in Chicago comes from the fact that it is a single-party, Democratic town, while New York

City is more fragmented. He points out that the fragmentation, in part, stems from the prominence of the Republican Party in New York City. He comments that this is illustrated by the recent elections of two Republican mayors, Giuliani and Bloomberg, while he notes that a Republican mayor has not been elected in Chicago since 1931. An excerpt from my field notes suggests that the existence of a rival party in New York City, to a certain extent, impacts the political environment in Harlem.

> I am getting my hair cut in Jackson's Barbershop on 135th. This is the second time I have been there and the barber, Joe, remembers that I live on 137th. As he cuts my hair the other barber in the shop asks if we know if there are term limits for the governor. I say, "I don't think so, but I'm not exactly sure." He replies, "I'll tell you what, Pataki [the Republican governor at the time] is going to win." Joe, who has lived in Harlem for 36 years, responds, "After all the money he's invested in Harlem, I'm going to vote for him." He then stops cutting my hair and says, "I'm a Democrat, but if I like the other candidate I'll vote for him." The other barber in the shop calls out, "Me too." Joe continues to cut my hair and says, "I am what you call a smart voter; I go by the candidate not the party."

Joe's perception that a Republican official is investing in the community suggests one party does not dominate Harlem politics. In addition, the lack of loyalty the barbers express toward the Democratic Party is an example of the diversity of New York City politics.

In contrast, the Democratic Party dominates Chicago politics. During my time in Bronzeville, rarely does a political discussion center on a Republican candidate. In many local elections in Chicago, no Republican candidate runs due to lack of support. People in Bronzeville commonly refer to this one-sided, Democratic government system as "the Party" or "the Machine." Simply put, "In Chicago [the] party and the government [are] indistinguishable" (Ferman 1996, 138).

Fuchs (1992), in *Mayors and Money*, discusses how the diversity in New York City's political system compared to Chicago's monolithic Democratic machine has consequences for fiscal stability. She argues that during the 1970s fiscal crisis, Chicago weathered the predicament because of "the mayor's ability to control," while New York City's deficit spun out of control because of its decentralized and fragmented political system (16). She declares, "Chicago and New York are at the opposite ends of the spectrum," with Chicago dominated by a hierarchical machine "while New York City has more group competition" (251). She contends that this structural difference affects the proliferation of protest politics and requests for funding. In New York City the fragmented system facilitates constituent demands, while the machine dictates the terms of budget negotiations. Although this citywide difference has previously been documented (e.g., Greenstone and Peterson 1976), I show that these differences affect community structures and norms, influencing internal political debates and actions.

STRUCTURAL AND NORMATIVE DIFFERENCES

The cities' different government structures are evident at the community level. In New York City, the five boroughs are divided into fifty-nine community districts, each with its own community board. These boards function as local planning bodies and vote on community development projects in their districts. The community boards in New York City date back to 1947 and officially became part of the city charter in 1961.[7] They originated as a government reform strategy by creating "competing legitimate entities to neighborhood party organization(s)" (Katznelson 1981, 142). The community boards are official components of the political system in New York City, but they have an "advisory" role. For example, the board members vote on development plans but official approval comes from the city council. However, area councilmen attend these board meetings, giving members and residents the opportunity to influence the decisions made by their local politicians. Community Board 10 presides over Central Harlem. Its meetings are open to the general public and are the structural spaces in Harlem where residents and organizational leaders have the opportunity to voice their opinions about redevelopment. Every month the board, consisting of approximately forty politically appointed residents, meets, debates, and votes on community planning proposals in their district. Developers who receive city funds are required to present at these monthly meetings.

Chicago has no structural equivalent to the New York City community boards.[8] No regularly occurring public forums or gatherings exist for political leaders and developers to report their activities to residents. In Bronzeville, public meetings are held by community-based organizations, such as the Mid-South Planning and Development Commission, the Grand Boulevard Federation, and the Gap Community Organization. At these meetings residents are updated on community issues; however, these gatherings are not formally connected to the city's political structure. For instance, developers are not required to attend these meetings, and if they show up, they simply present their plans without serious consideration of resident input. Furthermore, elected officials rarely go to these meetings and when they do the tenor of the exchanges between city officials and residents is much different than in Harlem. During elected officials' visits, they are greeted with cordial, almost reverent exchanges.

New York and Chicago have different expectations and norms for political engagement. In Chicago, city officials, whether from the Chicago Housing Authority, the City Planning Department, or the local aldermen, are confident in the power of the machine and interact with residents in a commanding and almost patronizing manner. One community leader in Bronzeville states, "[Chicago] is the most unusual city in the country. No other city functions like this. I've lived in Cincinnati, in New York City, and in Boston. . . . In these places your representatives actually . . . sit down [with you] and act like they work for you. Here nobody [political leaders] works for you, you work for them, you know, so that's the way it is. Maybe that's only in the black community but that has been my experience here, I work for the alderman, you know, she doesn't work for me." Another community leader in Bronzeville comments, "You know in Chicago . . . the aldermen have a tradition of being sort of autocratic powers in their wards for the most part and they tend to run things according to their own terms and according to their own interests." In Bronzeville, when elected officials speak, people usually praise them or stay silent, while in Harlem residents and organizational leaders often raise their voices and publicly castigate their political leaders. Distinct party strength, community structures, and expectations for citizen engagement within the political systems of these two cities help explain the extent of community-level protest politics.

DEBATES IN BRONZEVILLE

In Bronzeville I attended the meetings of the South Side Partnership, an organizational membership group that gathers to discuss and act on community issues.[9] The partnership is composed of approximately fifteen organizations, including a leading banking institution, several local social-service agencies, a neighborhood block group, a neighborhood planning organization, two local advocacy organizations, two major educational institutions, and several area hospitals. Many organizations are themselves groupings of smaller block clubs and other service organizations in the community, making the membership of the South Side Partnership representative of a diverse set of people in the community. I attended and participated in the bimonthly meetings of this group for a two-year span between 1999 and 2001.

The city's plan for public housing transformation is debated constantly during this period. The plan calls for the demolition of the majority of high-rise public housing buildings in Bronzeville (Chicago Housing Authority 1999). The implementation of this plan will result in the displacement of a significant percent of Bronzeville residents.[10] Many social-service organizations in the partnership express concern about displacement because a large percentage of their clients live in public housing. Other organizations in the partnership, such as the block group association, which is dominated by homeowners, want the public housing removed as quickly as possible. After considerable internal debate, the partnership agrees to attempt to influence the relocation and displacement aspects of the plan. They collectively declare, as stated in their meeting minutes, "We need to make a deliberate effort to ensure the current residents are able to remain in the community and that redevelopment can and should be done without massive displacement." Toward this end, the partnership decides to invite the head of the Chicago Housing Authority (CHA) to discuss how the partnership can help guide the implementation of the CHA plan. Although the CHA director is formally invited, the chief officer for CHA's development division is sent instead.

The interactions during this meeting illustrate how the political climate is Chicago typically differs from New York City. At this gathering, the CHA officer discussed the transformation plan in detail. His presentation emphasized that community groups and other institutions were eligible for both social service money and management contracts for some of the remaining CHA buildings, and it only touched upon the consequences for public housing residents. Even though, at prior meetings, the members discussed and fiercely debated the issue of displacement, none of the social-service agencies questioned the CHA representative about relocation or displacement. After the meeting, a social-service agency director showed me a report that indicated the extent of displacement outlined in the CHA plan. However, he and others chose not to question the CHA representative about the expected level of displacement.

The relationship between Chicago's centralized, political structure and the lack of debate concerning displacement in Bronzeville became evident after I interviewed several of the members of the South Side Partnership.

One organizational leader states,

> In terms of Chicago politics, there is this thing where you have the strong mayor and the weak aldermanic system. So there is the movement afoot to not really challenge

the mayor because it wouldn't be politically astute to really fight [since] . . . the mayor has the resources. Some people will always say, "Well, who's speaking up for CHA residents?" You know, who's taking a lead on these things and you look at these organizations [in Bronzeville] and some of them, us included, are laid back and part of the reason why you're laid back is because you don't want to upset the pot, because your livelihood depends on it. So in a lot of ways people are co-opted through the structure of the way their funding works, through the local government, through the whole CDBG [community development block grant] process.

This comment suggests that the fear of direct reprisals, such as the removal of grants from social service organizations and community development corporations by the reigning political machine, in part, influence the lack of opposition at the South Side Partnership meeting. It is well known in Chicago that the current mayor, Richard M. Daley, fully supports the CHA plan. The plan originated from his office, and, furthermore, he appoints the CHA's director. Members of the South Side Partnership are aware of this relationship and many of the social service agencies receive grants and contracts from the city government. Therefore, some of the social services agencies and housing advocates do not challenge the CHA plan for fear of retaliation from the mayor. Under Daley's father, Richard J. Daley, who reigned as mayor of Chicago from 1955 to 1976, "the slight hint of militancy was enough to bar a group from being funded" (Fuchs 1992, 263), and this norm of retaliation against grassroots opposition remains a reality in Chicago.

Although some claim that Mayor Richard M. Daley's administration is not as heavy-handed as his father's (Clark 2001), others argue that it contains many of the same qualities (Betancur and Gills 2004; Grimshaw 1992; Simpson 2001). Because of the Shakman decree, a law making it illegal to fire public employees for political reasons, patronage positions are less available today; however, Richard M. Daley quickly built a new machine by consolidating power once he was elected. According to Grimshaw (1992, 217), a political scientist who specializes on Chicago politics, Daley's early actions in his administration "effectively disempowered groups that had been empowered by [Harold] Washington," Chicago's first black mayor. Grimshaw concludes, "The few black ward leaders with a genuine commitment to reform are now doing the suffering, ducking for cover, issuing private complaints, and waiting more or less patiently for happier days to arrive" (224).

The strength of the current administration is well documented. A *Chicago Tribune* writer comments, "Since being elected in 1989, the current Mayor Daley has used his considerable political skill to slowly neuter the City Council and re-create a new version of the Democratic machine that is nearly as potent as his father's."[11] Simpson (2001), a former member of Chicago's city council and professor of political science, argues that even though the current mayor does not hold an official position in the party, as his father did, he effectively controls the political scene in the city. Through the use of the carrot (city grants, contracts, and campaign support for aldermen) and the stick (the removal of party and city support), Richard M. Daley has created a new political machine known as "machine politics, reform style" (Grimshaw 1992).

The ability to administer direct sanctions is associated with Chicago's centralized, Democratic-dominated political system. As a current alderman in Bronzeville explains, "Chicago politics is like a feudal system, where Mayor Daley is king and the aldermen are the lords and ladies of their wards." This level of political centralization and control inhibits public debate around issues such as displacement in Bronzeville. One community activist in Chicago insists that public dialogue and debate on displacement and redevelopment in Bronzeville is virtually absent. When speaking about the massive demolition of CHA high-rises in the community, he rhetorically asks, "How can this be happening . . . with so little public discussion, public challenge, [and] public scrutiny?" He continues, "There is no public discourse remotely commensurate with the gravity and scale of what's happening."[12]

Another recent study highlights the lack of sustained dialogue and organizing efforts around public housing in Chicago. Venkatesh (2000) notes a lack of political engagement by longstanding social service organizations in the Robert Taylor Homes, a project in Bronzeville. He asserts, "Only three agencies [of the many that surround the housing project] saw the need to intervene on the behalf of Robert Taylor tenants in politicized matters" (201). One resident, interviewed by Venkatesh, comments, "The [social service organizations] all just say they got to protect themselves . . . against what?" My findings suggest that normative expectations of political consequences are one reason why many of these institutions are not more politically involved.[13] While the political environment in Chicago is hierarchical and residents and organizational leaders in Bronzeville are, at times, intimidated by public officials, residents and politicians are on more equal footing in Harlem.

DEBATES IN HARLEM

The open political environment in New York City allows Harlem's community leaders and residents to publicly attack and question their elected officials and real estate developers. After a developer presented his proposal for a new market-rate housing development at a Community Board 10 meeting, a resident asked, "What is the price for a two-bedroom?" The developer responded, "It will cost between $250,000 and $3000,000." A woman sitting next to me stood up and shouted, "Families for these units ain't coming from Harlem!" She then turned to a city housing department employee and explained that it angered her that developers were receiving city funds to build housing beyond the means of many current Harlem residents.

In Harlem, numerous community meetings, forums, and conferences focus on gentrification. The Harlem Tenants Council, an association that advocates for affordable housing and tenants rights, sponsors several of these gatherings. When local political figures attend, residents and community leaders air their redevelopment concerns. During one session, a local housing activist described to a group of concerned residents how Harlem's economic development threatens its cultural integrity:

> The activist tells the residents that many black landlords are renting to whites and not blacks. One woman in the crowd shouts out, "It's disgusting." The activist follows this by saying, "The elected officials, they know about it." She speaks about how the local politicians engage in symbolic politics by changing the signs of the streets, like Lenox to Malcolm X but that "if Malcolm knew what was happening on 125th and Lenox he'd be turning over in his grave." Lenox Avenue at 125th now has a Starbucks, McDonalds, and an AT&T cell phone store, and there are plans to build a Gap store across the street. She says how some people think the Gap mural on 125th, which is up on President

Clinton's office building, looks nice because it has Danny Glover on it wearing a Gap button-down shirt, but she shouts, "I don't see anything around there looking African." She then says, "We have a managerial class [of African Americans] in Harlem from places like Harvard and Yale," who are orchestrating the redevelopment for "outside wealthy white folks." She continues, "You know what [the director of the Upper Manhattan Empowerment Zone (UMEZ)] does with plans that come from the community. This is what he does," as she vigorously tears up a piece of paper and throws it into a nearby garbage can. She explains that she has been trying to get the attention of the chairman of the board of directors for UMEZ, to have the director removed.[14]

While it is apparent from this excerpt that intraracial class conflict and the interracial divide are perceived as critical factors in the redevelopment process, my central point is to demonstrate that public displays of dissent, especially ones directed at local officials, are far more common in Harlem.

A plausible explanation for why groups in Harlem are more vocal is the diverse structure of New York City politics. New York City, Greenstone and Peterson (1976, 39) note, is "the pluralist's dream." Others describe New York City's political landscape as "an ethnic 'poker game'" in which no single group commands most of the chips, providing "numerous entry points" for contested politics (Abu-Lughod 1999, 417). Community groups in Harlem are able to obtain resources from a variety of places, allowing them more latitude to be vocal on development issues. In fact, many community organizations receive funds controlled by both Democrats and Republicans. With local structures such as the community boards and, more important, a weak party system, no person or group, as in Chicago, controls the political process.

With a more diverse political system and formal local structures for public dialogue, the issues surrounding the redevelopment and displacement in Harlem are heavily debated in public forums. Bill Perkins, Central Harlem's former councilman, is quoted in a *New York Times* article saying, "There's a growing, small entrepreneurial movement that is screaming about unaffordability of commercial spaces. This we hear *loudly* in Harlem" (italics added).[15] Many businesses and residents in Bronzeville face a similar situation; however, public opposition and debate is considerably less apparent.

THE PALM TAVERN VERSUS SMALLS PARADISE

The different structures and "rules of the game" in New York City and Chicago politics are illustrated by exploring the processes by which two historic businesses, the Palm Tavern in Bronzeville and Smalls Paradise in Harlem, are redeveloped. The transformation of these properties indicates how the local political context—that is, the structures and norms for political engagement—facilitate contested dialogue in Harlem, while the political landscape in Bronzeville inhibits it.

The Palm Tavern is a bar and nightclub in Bronzeville where many jazz greats played. It is located on Forty-seventh Street, just a few blocks east of Martin Luther King, Jr., Drive. Drake and Cayton, in *Black Metropolis*, note that Forty-seventh Street in the 1940s was the social center of Bronzeville. Today, Forty-seventh Street still has some viable businesses but, as a whole, is rundown. To stimulate development, the city designated the street a redevelopment area and a tax increment financing district and condemned and seized certain structures along Forty-seventh Street. The Palm Tavern, which was operating at that time, is shut down. Many leaders in Bronzeville claim that the closing of the Tavern occurred without sufficient public input.

In an article on the closing of the Palm Tavern, Harold Lucas, a longtime resident and preservationist who heads the Bronzeville Tourism Council, states,

> I don't know of any community participation [concerning the tavern], and I've lived around the corner [from Forty-seventh and King] for 15 years. What we're talking about is maximum feasibility participation and citizen involvement. . . . Do political agendas supersede the will of the people? In this case, I guess they do. It's absolute demagoguery. . . . The city wants [development] on their terms—that's the problem. . . . They [local officials] should represent the entire community, not just represent your own fiefdom and act like lord over the people and violate the public trust.[16]

Lucas is not the only person concerned by the way the Palm Tavern was closed. In the same article, Ron Carter, the former head of the Forty-seventh Street Merchants Association, states, "Bottom line, there has been no business and community participation. . . . There was no opportunity to take part." He recounts that when he was head of the Forty-seventh Street Merchants Association, city plans to seize the land for redevelopment were being made. However, he claims that city officials were constantly telling him and other Forty-seventh Street merchants that such plans did not exist. During an interview, one community leader commented that trying to find clear and accurate information on city redevelopment plans was like *Mission Impossible*. The city's lack of clear communication with business owners and residents inhibits the ability of citizens to act.

There was very little community dialogue and protest concerning the takeover of this site. The local alderman at the time, Dorothy Tillman, was virtually silent. Alleged handouts or payoffs by the city surrounding this situation had been reported. Some speculated that "the flow of money into the neighborhoods has effectively muzzled former critics such as Ald. Tillman," who had "benefited from major projects" in her ward "partly funded by the city."[17] Furthermore, the owner of the tavern, who rents the property, received $100,000 from the city for the memorabilia in the bar.[18]

The tavern is now boarded up while infrastructure improvements are made in the area. At this point, the city has not announced the future use of the tavern. However, there are plans to redevelop Forty-seventh Street and make it into a blues district for tourists.

Like the Palm Tavern, Smalls Paradise in Harlem showcased many famous jazz musicians and big bands in the 1930s and 1940s. The building where Smalls once operated is located on the southwest corner of 135th Street and Adam Clayton Powell, Jr., Boulevard and has been abandoned and boarded up for several years. When news came that Abyssinian Baptist Church's development corporation planned to redevelop the site with the use of public funds, opinions were mixed. The point of contention was the church's plan to include an International House of Pancakes on the ground floor. In comparison to the tavern case, the redevelopment process of Smalls was more open and transparent.

Activists publicly opposed Abyssinian's plan and took their concerns to Harlem's Community Board 10. At one meeting, Henry Michael Adams, a local historic preservationist, sought the board's support to obtain an emergency designation for Smalls Paradise from the city's landmark commission. If enacted, it might prevent the pancake restaurant from being built on what Adams considered a historic site. During the meeting, Adams told the board and the seventy attending residents, "There is a law called the Historical Housing Preservation Act, which prohibits landmarks from being impaired with federal and state funding, and since we have the Empowerment Zone in our area, and since they have ignored this act. . . . It seems to me very important for this board . . . to identify [and preserve] all of the historically significant, architecturally significant and culturally significant structures in Harlem that make up the African American cultural capital."

The board, by majority vote, approve to support the emergency landmark designation for Smalls. However, the city's landmark commission ignored the community board vote, and Abyssinian continued with its initial plans. At the redevelopment groundbreaking ceremony, Adams and his small group of activists protested the event, shouting repeatedly, "Save Paradise, save Harlem."[19] As *The New Yorker* reported, Reverend Calvin Butts of Abyssinian stated during the ceremony, "Our goal here today is economic revitalization. Now, you hear some people . . . say they want to save Harlem, Save Harlem. Sure. But you know what wise men say. They say, money on the wood makes the game go good. And so I need the money to save Harlem. So I went to the politicians with my hat in my hand . . . [and] these people came through. Throughout the ceremony, Adams continued to shout, "Save Harlem now. Save Harlem from pancakes." Shortly after the event, Butts, speaking to reporters about the protest, said, "The issue is economic. Land marking, preservation—these things cost money. Maybe they add twenty percent to your costs. If you're waiting on the money to do preservation work, that retards your progress. And Mr. Adams, much as I respect his position and appreciate him as an individual, a person—I don't think he's got any money."

The protest at the community board and outside of the groundbreaking ceremony did little to affect the original plans for Smalls, but Adams's voice and others were heard. What is important is that it was a relatively open process in comparison to the situation with the Palm Tavern. Few opponents in New York City complained of covert development plans. Abyssinian's Development Corporation regularly presented at the Community Board 10 meetings, and residents were aware of their plans. The redevelopment of Smalls was an open public process, at least compared to the Palm Tavern situation, where city authority was used to acquire properties and viable establishments, while residents and business leaders were shut out of the planning process.

DISCUSSION

The political contrast between New York City and Chicago is important for understanding the role of black organizations in Harlem and Bronzeville's redevelopment. Chicago's monolithic structure inhibits debate concerning redevelopment, while New York City's decentralized, fragmented, and diverse political system facilitates it. My results coincide with Fuchs (1992, 276), who claims that the structure of the "Democratic machine" in Chicago enables the mayor "to control the demands of neighborhood groups." I have made the case that Harlem and Bronzeville are very similar, and that different levels of political discourse surrounding redevelopment is a function of city-level political circumstances. My study suggests that the features of citywide political structures affect black protest, a finding echoed in the social movement literature (McAdam 1982).

Often research on black civil society involves large-scale survey research of individuals, which sometimes fails to capture key variables that affect black organizations. This study looks at two comparable African American communities with analogous black institutions. It demonstrates that although black attitudes often appear identical in the aggregate, organizational behaviors can differ based on the metropolitan political climate. Katznelson (1981, 200) asserts that when conducting urban community research, "it proves necessary to comprehend how external social forces pattern and inform local events and behavior." I suggest that city-level political structures, "external social forces," pattern behaviors and events related to the process of redevelopment in both Harlem and Bronzeville. Aspects of black civil society act differently based on alternative structures and norms (e.g., expectations for political consequences) in these two communities. These findings are equivalent to certain assertions in James Q. Wilson's seminal study *Negro Politics*. Wilson comments that black "politics cannot be understood apart from the city in which it is found" (23). My findings also illustrate this point: in order to understand the actions of black institutions, the metropolitan context in which they are embedded must be considered.

METHODOLOGICAL CONCERNS AND LIMITATIONS

My overall argument has several concerns and weaknesses. First, one tension running through this project, common to ethnographic field research, is the constant movement between observation and theory, an oscillation between inductive and deductive inquiry. When I arrived in Harlem, I had a broad agenda. I wanted to understand the factors related to its development so that I could compare this circumstance to those in Bronzeville. My initial framework had been influenced by the urban literature represented by such works as Sassen (2000), Wilson (1996), and Logan and Molotch (1987). These studies highlight external community conditions such as economic globalization, the national economy, and federal policies as central to neighborhood development. However, in Harlem I was struck instantly by the differences in local political behaviors and the broader citywide and political landscape, as noted by Fuchs (1992). Thus, my research focus developed from both my observations in the field and factors highlighted by previous research. Therefore, my aim is not to test theories concerning city politics, community politics, and urban development, but to generate findings, questions, and hypotheses that critique past research and contribute to further explorations.

Second, even though I spent sufficient time in both neighborhoods, my data are a small sample of meetings, organizations, and individuals in these communities. To alleviate this limitation, I focused on organizations that are well known in these communities and represent different factions, such as antigrowth and progrowth interests. I would argue that my sample is representative since after presenting various community leaders with a list of the meetings attended and people contacted, I was often told that I have spoken with the main players. However, due to the immense size of these communities, I only interacted with a tiny fraction of the people and organizations important to the economic development process.

Third, I make some sweeping generalizations about the similarities of these communities in order to isolate the political environment as a potentially important variable. Although there are many striking similarities between these two communities, there are several important differences. For example, Harlem's reputation as the "Black Mecca" is stronger than Bronzeville's standing within black America. Harlem's symbolic meaning as the most important black community in the country might make its redevelopment more controversial. It is possible that there exists greater sentiment toward Harlem resulting in a higher level of resistance to the gentrification process (Firey 1945).

Fourth, there are more individuals in Harlem (see the appendix). This demographic difference may lead to higher levels of progressive politics in Harlem simply due to the greater number of people. However, I am confident that if I were to incorporate parts of other African American areas surrounding Bronzeville, my results concerning limited contested politics would remain stable. Fifth, the distinct type of displacement occurring in the two communities might affect the level of protest politics. In Harlem, displacement is occurring more among those residing in the private market, whereas in Bronzeville, the majority of those being removed live in public housing. Private market renters often have more financial resources and thus may have greater levels of political participation. Based on this potential confounding variable, my argument concerning the relationship between the contrasting political contexts and alternative behaviors might be overstated.

Finally, other striking differences at the city level could be related to the level of contested politics. For instance, Manhattan's real-estate market might be tighter than Chicago's. Further, the level of racial segregation in the two cities is different: Chicago is more segregated than New York City (Massey and Denton 1993). While there is some fear that whites will move to Bronzeville, there seems to be greater concern that whites will infiltrate Harlem. This perception in Harlem may be related to the high level of controversy and protest politics surrounding its redevelopment.

FURTHER RESEARCH

The contrasting political climates in New York City and Chicago may affect the intensity of debate concerning redevelopment and displacement in Harlem and Bronzeville. An important question becomes, will the increased debate in Harlem alter public policies geared toward accelerating development? Both communities are part of the federal Empowerment Zone Initiative and are also being affected by newly enacted national public housing reform (i.e., the Quality Housing and Work Responsibility Act of 1998). Moreover, sections of these communities are business improvement or tax increment financing districts, which provide incentives to stimulate economic growth. These federal and local policies might be implemented differently depending on the amount of local resistance. The relationships among the citywide political contexts, internal community debates, and the execution of public policies need to be further explored.

CONCLUSION

A major shift, the bifurcation of the income structure, is occurring within black America. While a large proportion of African Americans are experiencing increased income and wealth, others are seeing their prospects for sustainable living diminish (Dawson 1994). As this is taking place, certain African American inner city areas, such as Harlem and Bronzeville, once mired in poverty, are beginning to experience resurgence, as middle-income blacks are returning to the communities a past generation fled. However, the situation is associated with the displacement of many low-income individuals and small businesses. As a result, certain members of these communities are voicing dissent related to the recent economic changes occurring in these neighborhoods. This chapter demonstrates that in order to understand the function of segments of black civil society in the community transformation process, it is vital to examine how distinct city politics, that is, unique political structures and norms, affect the actions of black-led organizations. Thus, while noting that global and federal forces affect black civil society (Dawson 1999), it is equally important for scholars to acknowledge the influence of metropolitan-level dynamics.

APPENDIX

DEMOGRAPHIC INFORMATION

Table A1. Population by community area

	1980	1990	2000
Bronzeville*	89,441	66,549	54,476
Central Harlem	105,641	99,519	107,109

* Douglas and Grand Boulevard community districts.

Census data.

Table A2. Percentage of population black and white by community area

	Black 1990 (%)	White 1990 (%)	Black 2000 (%)	White 2000 (%)
Bronzeville	95.0	2.5	92.0	4.0
Central Harlem	88.0	1.5	77.0	2.0

Census data.

Table A3. Median household income by community area

	1980	1990	2000
Douglas	$14,377	$10,577	$24,835
Grand Boulevard	$11,640	$8,371	$14,178
Central Harlem	$10,872	$13,252	$19,920

Census data.

Table A4.   Median home value by community area

	1980	1990	2000
Douglas	$25,900	$124,632	$208,499
Grand Boulevard	$23,400	$61,601	$179,849
Central Harlem	$53,873	$199,025	$250,000

Census data.

Table A5.   Percentage of owner-occupied units by community area

	1980 (%)	1990 (%)	2000 (%)
Bronzeville	5.6	5.5	10.0
Harlem	3.5	4.6	7.0

Census data.

Table A6.   Percentage of population with BA or higher by community area

	1980 (%)	1990 (%)	2000 (%)
Bronzeville	8	13	18
Harlem	5	10	15

Census data.

NOTES

1. Owing to high levels of poverty and changing class structures in these communities, some might expect that intraracial class conflict would be related to the level of support or protest. Class antagonism is a line of research and theory I explore elsewhere (Hyra 2008). In this chapter, class discord can be seen as a control variable since both communities are experiencing similar levels of income diversification and intraracial class conflict.
2. Barry Pearce (2001, August), "Back to Bronzeville," *New Homes*.
3. Curtis Lawrence (2001, August 5), "Saving Bronzeville," *Chicago Sun-Times*.
4. I define low income as households that earn under $15,000. These percents come from the author's tabulation of the 2000 census.
5. While conducting research in Bronzeville, I tracked Harlem's redevelopment from a distance. I chose Harlem, in part, because I am familiar with it. I grew up in a northern suburb of New York City and while in high school played for a basketball team based in Harlem.
6. There is some controversy surrounding the present boundaries of Bronzeville. The designated Bronzeville area described in this study consists of the Douglas and Grand Boulevard districts. This area is smaller than the original Bronzeville outlined by Drake and Cayton (1993) in *Black Metropolis*. Most of the community leaders I spoke with viewed this smaller area as today's Bronzeville. However, some still considered sections of adjacent districts, such as Washington Park and Northern Kenwood/Oakland part of the broader Bronzeville community.
7. The authority and form of the community boards have changed several times. Their present structure resembles the 1975 revision of the city charter (Fainstein and Fainstein 1991).
8. A few communities in Chicago are designated as conservation areas and these areas have entities that function similar to the New York City community boards, but these structures

are rare (see Pattillo 2007). There is no conservation area in Bronzeville. Further, the mayor is influential in appointing members to these "community boards."

9. The South Side Partnership was established in 1989. The participating groups came together in order to advocate for educational improvements in the community. Since that time the partnership has broadened its mission to include community development concerns.

10. Cory Oldewiler and Brian Rogal (2000, March), "Public Housing: Reading Between the Lines," *Chicago Reporter.*

11. Andrew Martin (2002, August 11), "Hizzoner's Doormat," *Chicago Tribune.*

12. There are some groups external to Bronzeville that are creating dialogue and putting forth progressive actions concerning displacement, such as the Coalition to Protect Public Housing. Many of these groups, however, are not black-led, nor do they have established relationships with the internal organizational structure in Bronzeville.

13. Based on spending over six months at one of the public housing projects in Bronzeville, I would also argue that political consequences are one of the reasons why onsite organizations, such as the Local Advisory Councils, which are made up of residents, are not more vocal about displacement.

14. Direct excerpt from my field notes.

15. David Dunlap (2002, February 10), "The Changing Look of the New Harlem," *New York Times.*

16. Jeff Huebner (2000, December 1), "Whose Blues Will They Choose?" *Chicago Reader.*

17. Andrew Martin (2002, August 11), "Hizzoner's Doormat," *Chicago Tribune.*

18. Beverly Reed (2001, June 25), "Palm Tavern Owner Surrenders to City's Offer," *Chicago Defender.*

19. Adam Gopnik (2002, April 22–29), "Harlem for Sale," *The New Yorker.*

REFERENCES

Abu-Lughod, Janet L. 1999. *New York, Chicago, Los Angeles: America's global cities.* Minneapolis: University of Minnesota Press.

Betancur, John J., and Douglas C. Gills. 2004. Community development in Chicago: From Harold Washington to Richard M. Daley. *Annals, AAPSS* 394 (1): 92–108.

Bridges, Amy. 1997. Textbook municipal reform. *Urban Affairs Review* 33 (1): 97–119.

Chicago Housing Authority. 1999. *Five-year plan for fiscal years 2000–2004.* Submitted to U.S. Department of Housing and Urban Development Office of Public and Indian Housing. Chicago: CHA.

Clark, Kenneth B. 1965. *Dark ghetto.* New York: Harper & Row.

Clark, Terry N. 1996. Structural realignments in American city politics. *Urban Affairs Review* 31 (3): 367–403.

———. 2001. Chicago's new political order: Trees and real violins. Paper presented at the Semiotics: Culture in Context Workshop, University of Chicago.

Cohen, Cathy J., and Michael C. Dawson. 1993. Neighborhood poverty and African American politics. *American Political Science Review* 87 (2): 286–302.

Dawson, Michael C. 1994. *Behind the mule.* Princeton: Princeton University Press.

———. 1999. Globalization, the racial divide, and a new citizenship. In *Race, identity and citizenship,* ed. Rodolfo D. Torres, Louis F. Miron, and Jonathan M. Inda, 373–85. Malden, MA: Blackwell.

———. 2000. *Blacks and civil society/black civil society project: An agenda for research.* Center for the Study of Race, Politics and Culture, University of Chicago.

Drake, St. Clair, and Horace R. Cayton. 1993. *Black metropolis: A study of negro life in a north-ern city*. Chicago: University of Chicago Press.

Fainstein, Susan, and Norman Fainstein. 1991. The changing character of community politics in New York City: 1968–1988. In *Dual city*, ed. John H. Mollenkopf and Manuel Castells, 315–32. New York: Russell Sage Foundation.

Ferman, Barbara. 1996. *Challenging the growth machine*. Lawrence: University Press of Kansas.

Firey, Walter. 1945. Sentiment and symbolism as ecological variables. *American Sociological Review* 10 (2): 140–48.

Fuchs, Ester R. 1992. *Mayors and money: Fiscal policy in New York and Chicago*. Chicago: University of Chicago Press.

Gans, Herbert J. 1982. *Urban villagers*. New York: Free.

Greenstone, J. David, and Paul E. Peterson. 1976. *Race and authority in urban politics*. Chicago: University of Chicago Press.

Grimshaw, William J. 1992. *Bitter fruit*. Chicago: University of Chicago Press.

Hirsch, Arnold R. 1998. *Making the second ghetto: Race & housing in Chicago, 1940–1960*. Chicago: University of Chicago Press.

Hyra, Derek S. 2008. *The new urban renewal: The economic transformation of Harlem and Bronzeville*. Chicago: University of Chicago Press.

Jennings, James. 1992. *The politics of black empowerment*. Detroit: Wayne State University Press.

Johnson, James W. 1991. *Black Manhattan*. New York: Da Capo.

Katznelson, Ira. 1981. *City trenches*. Chicago: University of Chicago Press.

Kelley, Robin D. 1994. *Race rebels*. New York: Free.

King, Gary, Robert O. Keohane, and Sidney Verba. 1994. *Designing social inquiry*. Princeton: Princeton University Press.

Lemann, Nicholas. 1991. *The promised land*. New York: Knopf.

Logan, John R., and Harvey L. Molotch. 1987. *Urban fortunes: The political economy of place*. Berkeley: University of California Press.

Marschall, Melissa L. 2001. Does the shoe fit? Testing models of participation for African-American and Latino involvement in local politics. *Urban Affairs Review* 37 (2): 227–48.

Massey, Douglas S., and Nancy A. Denton. 1993. *American apartheid*. Cambridge, MA: Harvard University Press.

McAdam, Doug. 1982. *Political process and the development of black insurgency, 1930–1970*. Chicago: University of Chicago Press.

Mollenkopf, John H. 1991. Political inequality. In *Dual city*, ed. John H. Mollenkopf and Manuel Castells, 333–58. New York: Russell Sage Foundation.

Osofsky, Gilbert. 1996. *Harlem: The making of a ghetto*. Chicago: Elephant Paperbacks.

Pattillo, Mary. 2007. *Black on the block: The politics of race and class in the city*. Chicago: University of Chicago Press.

Pattillo-McCoy, Mary. 1999. *Black picket fences*. Chicago: University of Chicago Press.

Pinderhughes, Dianne, M. 1997. Race and ethnicity in the city. In *Handbook of research on urban politics and policy in the United States*, ed. Ronald K. Vogel, 75–91. Westport, CT: Greenwood.

Putnam, Robert D. 1993. *Making democracy work*. Princeton: Princeton University Press.

Sassen, Saskia. 2000. *Cities in a world economy*. Thousand Oaks, CA: Pine Forge.

Simpson, Dick. 2001. *Rogues, rebels, and rubber stamps*. Boulder, CO: Westview.

Smith, Neil. 2000. *The new urban frontier*. New York: Routledge.

Spear, Allan H. 1967. *Black Chicago: The making of a negro ghetto, 1890–1920*. Chicago: University of Chicago Press.

Taylor, Monique M. 1994. Gentrification in Harlem: Community, culture and the urban redevelopment of the black ghetto. *Research in Race and Ethnic Relations* 7: 147–88.

Venkatesh, Sudhir A. 2000. *American project*. Cambridge, MA: Harvard University Press.

Verba, Sidney, and Norman H. Nie. 1972. *Participation in America*. New York: Harper & Row.

Whyte, William F. 1955. *Street corner society*. Chicago: University of Chicago Press.

Wilson, James Q. 1960. *Negro politics*. Glencoe, IL: Free.

Wilson, William J. 1996. *When work disappears: The world of the new urban poor*. New York: Sage.

Yin, Robert K. 2003. *Case study research: Design and methods*. Thousand Oaks, CA: Sage.

TOWARD A PRAGMATIC BLACK POLITICS

FREDRICK HARRIS

THE ELECTION OF SENATOR BARACK OBAMA AS THE FOURTY-FOURTH PRESIDENT OF the United States has changed the contours of African American politics for years if not decades to come. His election, in many ways, symbolizes the maturation of black politics; from the protest tradition through the process of incorporation as players in the political system to the possible beginings of a process of normalization. As a style of politics rooted in protest and the quest for dignity and full citizenship, is black politics turning a corner and entering a new phase that spells the demise of its existence in the American political landscape? Will black politics become like the politics of other ethnic groups, such as the Irish and the Italians, in which individuals from the group benefited from ethnic voting patterns and inter- and intragroup connections as a stepping stone up the political ladder without making direct policy demands on behalf of their kin? Is it possible that black politics will vanish into the vast ocean of mainstream American politics?

Or have blacks become more pragmatic about electoral politics, demanding less in terms of policies that target black communities and seeing themselves more as individuals and Americans than part of a stigmatized racial group whose economic and political fates are bound with "the black community"? These are questions to ponder as African Americans consider the implications of president-elect Obama's successful presidential campaign for the practice and substance of black politics. What is the meaning of a campaign that received strong support from black communities on behalf of a candidate that played down the existence of racial inequality in American society and made no direct promises of targeted public policies that would assist in eradicating those inequalities?

SYMBOLISM AND UNIVERSALISM

Many commentators and analysts asked whether the Obama campaign's approach to wooing black support was more about symbols than substance. Certainly, the 2008 campaign cycle was not the first time that a Democratic Party nominee for president had used symbols rather than policy positions to gain the support of black voters. Indeed, some would argue that the Democratic Party's attempt during the Clinton campaigns of the 1990s to distance itself from issues that were in the mind of white voters associated with blacks—crime, welfare, and affirmative action—was important to the party's success. And many consider President Clinton's three-strikes-you're-out Crime Bill and his signing of the Welfare Reform Bill before the 1996 election as a betrayal to his loyal black constituents. Nevertheless, President Clinton was able to maintain the confidence of black voters by appointing African Americans to visible positions in his administration and through his extraordinary ability to emotionally connect to black audiences.

Critics have also argued that symbolism over substance characterized aspects of Senator Obama's relationship to black voters during the campaign while others argued that Obama was deploying a wink-and-nod approach in gaining support from black voters. There was little difference in the policy positions of the two leading candidates during the Democratic Party primaries, which partly explains why black opinion polls showed that black likely voters were split between Senator Hillary Clinton and Senator Obama before the Iowa Caucus. Indeed, the left-of-center domestic policy positions of former Senator John Edwards were closer to the preferences of black voters than the two leading Democratic candidates.

Many black opinion-makers felt that if Obama advocated policies that would explicitly address issues facing black communities his campaign would have been derailed by his rivals in the primary and general election. Obama's "race-neutral" strategy is a campaign strategy that minority candidates have been using since the 1980s. Fearful that white voters would be turned off by policy positions that steered too closely to black interests, black candidates running before majority or near-majority white constituencies have to adopt campaign strategies that deemphasize their race. These strategies deemphasize or neglect discussions about racism but take up the banner of racial unity and public policies that appeal to all citizens as a way to allay the concerns of white voters. While this can be a winnable strategy for black candidates running in statewide and national campaigns, it often leaves issues that are specific to the concerns of black voters off the public agenda.

Senator Obama noted during the campaign that his positions on health care, the economy, and education appealed to all Americans, not just to African Americans. Echoing themes of the need for personal responsibility among blacks that first emerged in presidential politics during the Reagan era, Senator Obama delivered speeches before majority black audiences about the need for personal responsibility and tolerance but in those very same speeches offered little in the way of policy initiatives that address the needs of marginal black communities. Though black voters enthusiastically supported the Obama campaign, black voters did not hear much about how the candidate would deal with the HIV-AIDS epidemic that still disproportionately affects their communities, the astronomical high rates of black youth unemployment, racial disparities in health care, subprime and predatory lending in black neighborhoods, racism in the criminal justice system, the displacement of low- and middle-income blacks in gentrified neighborhoods, or poverty that plagues a quarter of the black population.

OBAMA AND SHIFTS IN BLACK POLITICAL ATTITUDES

Does Obama's solid support among African Americans signal a shift in black political attitudes from a more liberal to a more moderate or pragmatic perspective that acknowledges the existence of racial inequality and racism in society but sees individual solutions as a cure rather than government intervention? And is a sense of group solidarity, or what political scientist Michael Dawson refers to as "linked fate," diminishing among African Americans? What does a sense of solidarity mean when half of the black population thinks that blacks should get away from thinking of themselves as part of a racial group while the other half thinks that black solidarity is important?

Columbia University's Center on African-American Politics and Society (CAAPS) and the ABC News Polling Unit conducted a national survey of blacks, whites, and Hispanics by telephone from September 11 to 14, 2008, that asked questions about the Obama campaign and feelings about racial group solidarity. The CAAPS/ABC News Black Politics Survey was comprised of a national random sample that includes 1,941 adults. Among the 1,941 respondents, the survey was comprised of an oversampling of African Americans (n = 1032) and Hispanics (n = 315). The survey was conducted in association with *USA Today*. The results from the full survey have a two-point margin of error.

If we look beyond the symbols of racial solidarity and gauge how black Americans feel about what are the best strategies for group success, black Americans are divided. And Obama's success as a candidate, as well as the messages of personal responsibility that Obama delivered before majority black audiences, was well received by African Americans. While some pundits were arguing that talking to black audiences about taking responsibility for their actions were attempts to shore up support from white working-class voters who are more likely to believe that many domestic government programs favor blacks, most black voters did not perceive Obama's speeches that way.

The CAAPS/ABC News survey asked the following: "Obama has made some speeches calling on black Americans to take responsibility for their actions and pull themselves up in society. Do you think he's made those comments more to appeal to blacks, or more to appeal to whites?" A little more than half of blacks—52 percent—believed that those messages were targeted exclusively to the black community while only 12 percent believed the messages were targeted for whites. A quarter of blacks—25 percent—believed that the messages were targeted equally for blacks and for whites. Clearly, a majority of blacks thought that the messages of personal responsibility from Obama were not an attempt to score points with white voters and an additional quarter thought that Obama's message served dual purposes, as a way to communicate to both blacks and whites. This interpretation of Obama's intention in speaking about blacks' personal responsibility is also reflected in the response to a question about whether Obama was addressing issues of special concern to blacks or avoiding discussion black issues.

During the campaign, Obama did not address issues traditionally associated with the policy priorities of black communities. Obama noted early in the campaign that he was concerned about universal policy issues such as health care and education, initiatives that would benefit all Americans rather than policies specifically targeted toward blacks and other minorities. When the survey asked, "Do you think that as a candidate Obama has been mostly addressing issues of special concern to African Americans?" about seven of ten blacks (71 percent) thought that Obama did compared to four in ten Latinos (43 percent) and three in ten whites (32 percent).

As results from the CAAPS/ABC News Black Politics Survey (Figure 4.1) reveal, Latinos and whites were more likely than blacks to think that Obama was avoiding issues of special concern to blacks. Of the 39 percent of whites who thought that Obama was avoiding the discussion of black issues, a majority (58 percent) attributed the avoidance not to whether they thought those issues would be unpopular with white voters but to Obama's aim of trying to transcend race. Only 31 percent of whites thought that Obama was avoiding speaking about black issues because doing so would be unpopular with whites.

Black and white voters in particular looked through different lens when evaluating whether Obama discussed issues of special concern to blacks. It is likely that blacks perceived universal policy issues and the call by Obama for more personal responsibility as speaking directly to the special concerns of African Americans. Whites on the other hand may evaluate Obama's discussions about blacks' personal responsibility in nonpolicy terms and that his emphasis on universal policies as efforts to "reach beyond race." It appears that blacks and whites have been attaching different meanings to Obama's speeches and comments on the need of blacks to take personal responsibility.

But despite blacks feeling that Obama spoke about the special concerns of blacks during the campaign and the campaign's deracialized political strategy, most blacks reported that they have personally experienced racial discrimination and a plurality feels that racial equality in the United States will not be achieved anytime soon. When asked, "Have you personally felt that you were being discriminated against because of your race?" approximately three-quarters of blacks reported that they had while nearly a quarter—23 percent—reported that they have never experienced racial discrimination. Of those that reported experiencing racial discrimination, 21 percent reported that it happened often, 38 percent agreed that discrimination happened occasionally, and 17 percent stated that they rarely experienced racial discrimination. As we will see later when we take a closer look at black attitudes toward strategies for group progress,

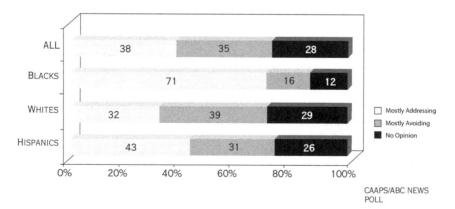

CAAPS/ABC NEWS POLL

Figure 4.1.   Is Obama Addressing Issues of Special Concern to Blacks?

the frequency of perceived discrimination among blacks has a strong influence on determining what course of action is good for the group.

The CAAPS/ABC News Black Politics Survey also asked the following: "Do you think blacks have achieved racial equality, will soon achieve racial equality, will not achieve racial equality in your life time, or will never achieve racial equality?" As shown in Figure 4.2, the results from black respondents indicate that despite the progress that the country has made in wake of the Obama candidacy, African Americans are considerably less likely than whites and Latinos to see racial equality being accomplished in their life times. Only 11 percent of blacks reported that the nation has achieved racial equality compared to 39 percent of whites and 25 percent of Hispanics. A larger percentage of blacks felt optimistic about the prospects of the country achieving racial equality in the immediate future. Forty-one percent of blacks compared to 36 percent of whites and 41 percent of Hispanics think that racial equality in the United States will happen soon. However, a substantial core of the black population is skeptical about the prospects of the country achieving racial equality—44 percent believe that racial equality will not be achieved in their lifetimes or will never be achieved. A smaller proportion of whites (20 percent) and Hispanics (25 percent) are pessimistic about the prospects of the nation achieving racial equality compared to blacks.

TWO BLACK AMERICAS, ONE CANDIDATE

Though Barack Obama received universal support from African Americans, across social class and political ideology, African Americans are divided over what should be the best strategies for improving the status of blacks as a group. These strategies involve protest over mainstream approaches, whether blacks should think of themselves as individuals or as part of a group, should play down their racial identity in order to advance in American society, or see themselves primarily as blacks or as Americans. These questions are part of the subtext of the Obama's use of a deracialized political strategy that includes the candidate's emphasis on Americans getting beyond racial, ethnic, and religious divisions.

When asked the standard survey question measuring a sense of shared fate with other blacks (Do you think what happens generally to black people in this country

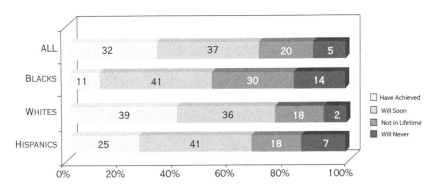

Figure 4.2   Have Blacks Achieved Racial Equality?

will have something to do with what happens in your life?), 64 percent of blacks share a sense of linked fate with other blacks compared to 32 percent who expressed that they do not share that sense. One of the most important factors that distinguish those who feel that they have a shared fate and those who do not is perceived experience with racial discrimination. Blacks who report that they are frequently discriminated against are more likely to express stronger feelings of shared fate with other blacks (74 percent to 23 percent) than blacks that report never having been discriminated against (48 percent to 47 percent).

However, despite the recognition in the general population among a majority of African Americans that blacks share a similar fate in American society, African Americans have divergent views about how to achieve group success. For instance, the CAAPS/ABC News Black Politics Survey asked whether black respondents agreed or disagreed with the following: "Blacks should stop thinking of themselves as a group and think more of themselves as individuals." Those agreeing with the statement would be less supportive of racial group solidarity. An affirmative response would also reflect a perspective that is more in line with a core value in American society—the virtue of individualism—and reflects the viewpoint blacks should become more assimilated into American society. On this question blacks are nearly evenly divided—49 percent think that blacks should stop thinking of themselves as a group, while 48 percent disagree. There are small educational differences in the black population to the response of this question, suggesting that class matters less in how black communities think about the questions of whether they should think of themselves as part of a group or as individuals. However, one factor that does matter is, again, perceived racial discrimination. Only 36 percent of blacks that say they are often discriminated against agree that blacks should think of themselves as individuals; 60 percent of blacks that often experience racism disagree. But for those blacks who reported never experiencing racial discrimination, 66 percent believe that blacks should think of themselves as individuals compared to the 30 percent that disagree with the statement.

Not only does half of the black population express support for blacks thinking more of themselves as individuals, nearly half of the black population feels a greater national loyalty than racial group loyalty. Respondents were asked, "In your own personal identity do you think of yourself as black first, as American first, or what?" Reflecting the divisions in attitudes toward blacks thinking of themselves more as individuals, 45 percent reported thinking of themselves as black first while 46 percent think of themselves American first. About 5 percent of the respondents report thinking of themselves as equally black and American. Like the other indicators measuring attitudes toward group strategies for success, there is virtually little variation in response to this question by social class. Once again, perceptions of racial discrimination are one of the main factors that separate those who exhibit stronger racial group loyalties than national loyalties.

Turning to a question that reflects support for a "deracialized" strategy for black progress, the CAAPS/ABC News poll asked, "Do you think that blacks have to play down their racial identity to get ahead in American society, or do you think blacks can express their racial identity and still get ahead?" Again, as a matter of group strategy for mobility, black Americans are divided. Nearly half—49 percent—think that blacks have to play down their racial identity to get ahead while 46 percent believe that blacks can express their racial identity. Thus, for those blacks who believe that it is important for blacks not emphasize their racial identity to get ahead, the Obama campaign's deracialized political strategy would not have presented any contradictions or concerns to them.

Additionally, blacks are also divided over whether protest is an effective tool for group progress. The CAAPS/ABC News Survey asked black respondents whether they agreed or disagreed with the following statement: "Black people would improve their position if they spent less time protesting and more time working within the system." A slight majority of blacks—51 percent—agreed that blacks would improve their position in society if they spent less time protesting while 43 percent disagreed. Those blacks reporting never experiencing racial discrimination were more likely, by 10 percent, to believe that blacks would progress if they worked more within the system (60 percent).

CONCLUSION

These results indicate that there are fundamental differences within black communities about what are the best strategies for group progress. The Obama candidacy has either heightened these differences or benefited from these shifts in more moderate, pragmatic public opinion in black communities. Given the debates over the past decade about the role of personal responsibility in black America—first initiated during the 1980s by black and white conservatives and more recently by Bill Cosby—it should not come as a surprise that African Americans are divided over whether society is to blame or if blacks as individuals making bad choices are to blame for the social ills facing black communities. It will be interesting to see if the deracialized campaign strategy will be the same approach that president Obama deploys as a governing strategy when it comes to domestic social policies. While the absence of discussions by a presidential Democratic candidate on how to deal with poverty and racial inequality would have raised eyebrows among black political elites in the recent past, the turn in the discourse toward politics of respectability and away from the government's responsibility in assisting the poor has, in a subtle and at times not so subtle ways, helped to elect the nation's first president of African descent. Welcome to the new black politics.

On Black Leadership, Black Politics, and the U.S. Immigration Debate

Mark Sawyer

> We must learn to live together as brothers, or perish together as fools.
>
> —Martin Luther King, Jr.

In the wake of the massive mobilization of immigrants in the United States in the spring of 2006, I have looked in fascination and sometimes concern at the lack of response from black leadership. While for some the response to anti-immigrant legislation has been formally clear, given the potential for racism and human rights abuses, the response from black leadership has been extraordinarily muted. In the context of that vacuum, the media has portrayed the feelings of African Americans as ranging from anti-immigrant to ambivalent. Many African Americans are fearful, some are hateful, and some just do not care. Black leadership has failed to grasp what is at stake in this debate and continues to fail to articulate a clear message on a number of social and economic issues of relevance to the African American community. On moral grounds, African Americans must stand by their tradition of being the guiding light for freedom and human dignity in the United States and around the world and support the legalization of the more than 12 million people in the United States who are struggling for basic rights and desperately trying to obtain what so many Americans take for granted: their citizenship. However, we as a community and leaders of our community must educate ourselves and make sure the media do not allow fear to drive our choices. But how do we fill the vacuum?

The immigration debate engages age-old questions for African Americans. Booker T. Washington, in his famous Atlanta Exposition Address, urged U.S. industrialists not to turn to unknown foreigners who might take the country in unknown and negative directions, but to work closely with the known quantity of African Americans (Washington 1995). However, Washington and current black leadership both have failed to understand the ongoing nexus between conceptions of race, nation, and citizenship and the dynamics of racial exclusion and class issues. These are especially salient in the post–civil rights era. When Washington's counterpart (and sometimes nemesis) W. E. B. Du Bois proposed the concept of double consciousness, it was in profound recognition of the tension between a black identity placed outside of the boundaries of being authentically American (Du Bois 1987). The same has been the case for Latinos and Asians, who are consistently constructed as both racialized and colonial subjects within the United States. Thus, while we recognize that Latinos are not a "race," not even in our nonscientific folk conception of such, we still understand that Latinos—and especially Mexican Americans—have in many cases what is known as racialized ethnicity (Martin-Alcoff 2000; Grosfoguel 2003). That is, they are perceived to be endowed with a set of negative and immutable characteristics that, like African Americans, make them unassimilable and therefore unworthy of full citizenship rights. Why, then, is this not seen as a civil rights issue?

Much of black leadership, academia, and the media have accepted a hegemonic definition of the civil rights movement that focuses primarily on the social dimensions of racial exclusion and thinks of civil rights in entirely domestic terms. This narrative ignores the more inclusionary aspects of racial domination, that is, the process of labor exploitation, cultural appropriation, colonial disruptions, and forced and semiforced migrations that have been the hallmark of the development of Western nations in general and the United States in particular (Sawyer 2006). Thinkers and activists such as W. E. B. Du Bois, Malcolm X, Martin Luther King, Jr., Paul Robeson, A. Philip Randolph, James Baldwin, and Ella Baker saw the process of racial oppression of African Americans in the United States as intimately related to earlier processes of slavery and colonialism and the aggressiveness of U.S. foreign policy in the region (Plummer 1996; Von Eschen 1997; Dudziak 2002; Singh 2005). African Americans were not brought to this country simply to be the objects of racial hatred, genocide, and cultural destruction, but also in order to integrate them into a political economy of race that allowed them to be simultaneously dehumanized and exploited for their labor (Robinson 1991; Du Bois 1995).

There is nothing new about Mexican migration or migration from Central America and the Caribbean, and it all follows a similar pattern. The racist and nativist rants against Mexicans in particular, but also against Dominicans, Asians, and other migrants, demonstrate this integrative process. The employability of Latinos in America's worst jobs demonstrates how the construction of illegality and its maintenance through the racialized rhetoric of the perpetual, and inferior colonial foreign subject, both legally and in practice, marks undocumented migrants (particularly brown, indigenous ones) for labor exploitation and segmented participation in labor markets.

This is not to deny the psychological and at times psychosexual nature of racial animus. However, it is to note that if we make the mistake of thinking of racial oppression as only about creating social distance, we miss the workings of political economies of race that seek to extract labor at an unfair price from racialized domestic and immigrant populations. Thus, the history of U.S.–Mexico relations and efforts such as the Bracero Program, as well as U.S. colonial adventures in Central America and the Caribbean, demonstrate the link between our current immigration debate and the inextricable connection between race, racism, and nation. If we understand

U.S. racism and white supremacy in their international forms in relation to colonial-ism and slavery as well as in racial constructions of national belonging that repeat themselves in places like the United States, Canada, and Europe, we then understand that the struggle for rights for immigrants and against labor and other forms of exploi-tation is not a struggle that is alien or beyond the concern of African Americans. It is only if we hold a domestic and social definition of the civil rights movement that we can turn a deaf ear on the concern for immigrant human rights.

We also must recognize the racialized and frequently racist language that has char-acterized the immigration debate in ways that should give African Americans pause. Samuel Huntington's book *Who Are We?* set off a profound debate on Latinos and immigration (Huntington 2004). Singling out Latinos (and especially Mexican migrants), Huntington suggested that they are unassimilable and pose a threat to the Anglo-Protestant culture that has made America the great country it is. Pundits such as Lou Dobbs and Patrick Buchanan have taken a similar line in attacking Latinos. How-ever, some Latino academics and commentators and their liberal defenders have made a tremendous mistake in response. In order to reply to Huntington, rather than denounce the obvious racism of his attacks, they have taken to emphasizing Latinos' worthiness for citizenship by casting them as "ethnics" in a process of assimilation, similar to Italians and the Irish and in negative contrast with blacks. These authors never challenge either Huntington's implicit construction of a "white" dominant culture in America or his argument that race no longer plays a role in the life-chances of people of color.

Authors such as Richard Alba, David Hayes Bautista, and Gregory Rodriguez also take this line and suggest that Latinos are the quintessential hardworking Americans who are seeking to assimilate into the norms and ideals of the United States They emphasize that—unlike African Americans—Latinos do not seem to be adopting a "culture of pov-erty." The picture is clear. For these pundits, Latino acceptance depends on assimilation, racial distancing from blacks, and not adopting an oppositional racial consciousness similar to blacks. African Americans are rightly upset by these responses. However, these scholars are wrong on both normative and analytical grounds. Clearly, they do not speak for the entire Latino community. There is nothing "new" about Latino immigrants: Mexicans in particular have been a part of the American landscape for a long time and have consistently been racialized as both other and inferior. The virulent reactions to Mexicans and their children by white racist and mainstream organizations speak to their ongoing racialization in American society. Similarly, these debates ignore the existence of Afro-Latinos and black migrants from Africa and the Caribbean.

Thankfully, people on the street are not adopting this stance. Unlike pundits and some academics, the people on the street at the immigrant marches saw what they were struggling against as racism. Their signs expressed antiracist slogans and chal-lenged the exploitation of their labor. They made the connection between the idea that current immigration policy makes them available for labor exploitation, just as Jim Crow and other manifestations of racism continue to make African Americans available for labor exploitation. As African Americans have learned to use their citi-zenship rights to challenge exploitation, employers have shifted to a new source of exploitable labor: undocumented immigrants.

While this might lead one to believe that Latinos are "taking African Ameri-can jobs," the reality is far more complicated. There is no clear economic data that suggests that Latinos have taken African American jobs where there have been cases of employer preferences for Latinos. These employers have tended to use undocumented Latinos' lack of rights in order to guarantee their exploitation. The nexus between race, class, gender, and citizenship status reveals a complex web in which employers "prefer" the most exploitable labor, not individuals whom they see as equals, coethnics, or conationals. Thus, preference for immigrant labor should not be interpreted as a form of assimilation for Latinos. Further, these employers do not see, nor are they creating, a path for upward mobility for Latino laborers. This is why whites in places such as Orange County, California, simultaneously exploit Latino gardeners, nannies, and pool cleaners while developing ordinances to increase deportability, deny educational access for their children, and apply restrictive zoning to maintain their marginality (Lacayo 2007). In this way, Latino barrios are far more similar to South African Bantustans than any of us might care to admit. The sting of de facto apartheid is felt just as sharply.

However, this alone does not overcome concerns from the African American community. One major fallacy that is repeated often is the idea that Latinos have either taken African American jobs or are responsible for African American unemployment. The history of Los Angeles and other places that have received large numbers of immigrants tells a different story. African Americans moved from the South to the North and West in massive numbers, not to work as domestics, gardeners, and busboys, but to work in a growing manufacturing sector that offered middle-class wages and opportunities for upward mobility. Those jobs that helped build the black middle class have gone overseas. They have not been "taken" by Mexican workers. Furthermore, black teachers, postal workers, and bus drivers in the unionized public-service sector have benefited from immigration. Immigrants curbed the slide in urban populations around the country that was causing cutbacks in city budgets and reducing public services and jobs for the black middle class. A recent PPIC study reveals that workers benefit from immigrant labor in both jobs and wages. These direct effects are masked by the countervailing forces mentioned earlier.

What is true is that black and Latino workers share similar difficulties. Blacks and Latinos are dropping out of high school at alarming rates. Far from realizing the immigrant American dream, Latinos are fast becoming an intergenerational group of low-skilled exploitable workers who in subsequent generations face rates of incarceration similar to that of African Americans. To all of our detriment, black and Latino political leadership have not pushed a policy agenda that challenges exploitation, deportability, and mass incarceration for black and brown youth. Further, to the extent that wages for low-skilled workers are declining, the prudent response is to support unionization, human and labor rights, and a higher minimum or living wage. The recent efforts to improve the minimum wage and to support "card check" unionization that allows workers to overcome intimidation tactics by employers who fear workers with rights are steps in the right directions, but how often do African American political elites place these issues at the top of the agenda? These are the issues that also link the concerns of African Americans and Latinos together in ways that move beyond perceptions of group difference, threat, or both. Unfortunately, there has been a significant retreat from these issues on the agendas of national and state politics. As the Latino high school dropout rate approaches and tops 50 percent in many communities, we are not seeing the next great American success story but a group that will likely be left behind as the new economy moves forward. Black leadership must redouble its efforts on central issues like job development, fair wages, prison reform, sentencing reform, crime prevention, universal health care, and quality education. These issues that are rarely on the front of the national political agenda are essential to both African Americans and Latinos. Further, an enforceable "living wage" is also in the interests of African American and immigrant workers of all colors and consistent with values of fairness and ethical assistance. Work should pay in America—and too often for black, brown, white, and yellow workers, legal or undocumented, it does not.

Even if you do not agree with what I have written so far, it is clear that turning 12 million people in the United States into felons will not be good for African Americans. It will redirect scarce resources toward the capture and incarceration of such people. It will make them more vulnerable to employer exploitation and is simply inconsistent with values of human rights embodied by the African American struggle. The racism inherent in such a policy fuels a beast that again will consign African Americans to irrelevance and will cast Latinos into further exploitation. The ordinances being passed by cities and towns to prevent renting to the undocumented and that turn migrants into virtual fugitives invite not only discrimination against immigrants but also discrimination against all Latinos regardless of status. Legalizing racial discrimination anew is a profoundly dangerous road. Furthermore, the policies are not meant, as anthropologist Nicholas de Genova suggests, actually to achieve deportation of Latino immigrants but to produce "deportability." Deportability relegates Latino immigrants (and natives, too) to a fugitive status from which they can be freely exploited, since they cannot exercise normal citizenship rights under fear of deportation. Note that we have been here before with the Fugitive Slave Act, *Plessy v. Ferguson*, and myriad aspects of Jim Crow that—while not mentioning race—were no less directed at a particular racial group and were no less pernicious.

Perhaps our leaders do not understand how far in reverse we may go. In 2007, the Texas state legislature began considering the possibility of challenging the current interpretation of the Fourteenth Amendment such that children born of undocumented immigrants would not be considered citizens. This radical change in the U.S. citizenship regime strikes at a core thread that guarantees those born in the United States the rights and some version of the privileges of citizenship. *Jus solis* rather than *jus sanguine* citizenship rights have been the hallmark of American democracy since the abolition of slavery. This is in jeopardy. We are looking toward a citizenship regime that will create new forms of racially stratified citizenship that will in turn condemn multiple generations of Latinos and other immigrants to marginal status.

Further, the racialized language that casts Latinas as having "anchor babies" in order to stave off deportation and attempt to guarantee their own ability to remain in the United States bears a striking resemblance to the racist rhetoric that characterizes African American women as having children to obtain welfare benefits. This racialized and racist language should be shocking to those concerned about America's racial history.

The prospect of creating new and overtly racial forms of citizenship at the local and/or federal level is a dangerous slippery slope that is not merely about policies but about fundamental principles of fairness and human rights. This shocking attack on a community and the proposals to convert millions of people living in our midst into felons drew the convulsive response that constituted some of the largest protests in

American history. I attended the May 1, 2006, rally in Los Angeles and the march-ers saw their struggle as one for citizenship and empowerment and against racism, as many of their signs read. Others were in solidarity with displaced African Americans from Hurricane Katrina. Immigrants fighting for their rights are not picking a fight with black folks. Do we, as African Americans, think we can go it alone and achieve our political goals in the future? What about the fact that a good two million Latinos are "black," not to mention African and Caribbean immigrants? What have African Americans ever gained from joining with white racists? How will it harm African American interests to have twelve million more voters who will likely support more social spending, unionization, and a range of other policies that are in line with the policy preferences of African Americans and especially the poorest among us?

By supporting this movement and fair, humane, and rational immigration policies; a living wage; unionization; and battling racism wherever it exists, African Americans can make long-term and powerful political allies. Together, we can transform politics in this country rather than play a game of divide and conquer. Like it or not, African Americans are no longer the largest minority in the United States. That is a fact that will remain unchanged. If we do not stand for our principles and we stand with rac-ists, we guarantee our own future irrelevancy and moral decline. The bottom line is that African Americans need to help move the immigration debate and stand on prin-ciple rather than on narrow "interests" or "ethnic competition." That means attacking racism and mobilizing around issues that will help African Americans advance. If we cannot stand with Latinos on this issue, we will all fall.

The perfect example of this lack of vision was in the ultimately successful Proposi-tion 187 campaign in California, which attempted to strip basic rights from immi-grants and garnered a majority of African American votes. It gave momentum to the conservative ballot initiative movement and paved the way for Proposition 209, the anti–affirmative action initiative, now being considered in other states as a result of its wins in California, Washington, and Michigan. There is a domino effect we need to understand. African Americans unwittingly sowed the seeds of our own destruction by not standing with Latinos on this issue.

On the other hand, victories by forces for democracy, rights, and citizenship can have the same momentum. Just as the victory for civil rights by African Americans helped create minimum wage laws, more humane and less racist immigration policies, and other positive reforms in the United States, this movement can have the same effect. Now that Latinos are fighting racism and for citizenship rights, we—as African Americans—have a stake in their winning. If they and we win, our next fights will be for unionization, expanded voting rights, living wages, more funding to public education, and universal health care. These are all issues that immigrants, Latinos, and African Americans share. Further, we will also fight for affirmative action together because Latinos have been and continue to be supportive of these policies.

Currently, the immigrant rights movements are the most vocal element shattering the immoral right-wing orthodoxy in America and fracturing the Republican Party. It is great that Latinos are, in many ways, exposing the hypocrisy of the Republicans and their failed policies by carrying the struggle to the streets. The power structure fears this movement, but if we are righteous, we have nothing to fear. No one imagined that such a mass mobilization of people was possible in this era. "Americans are too apathetic, too comfortable, to try to change the world," they say. But there are those among us who see the injustice of racism and exploitation and through their own lack of basic rights are best positioned to remind us of how tenuous, incomplete, and threatened those rights are. We have all lamented this apathy, but we must be ready to act when we see a movement that challenges injustice.

This is an enormous opportunity for us, both politically and analytically. As academics, we must understand the growth and diffusion of this movement and develop strategies and tactics to understand how so many people can be mobilized so quickly. Further, we must take advantage of the opportunity to educate members of the African American and Latino communities about our shared struggles for meaningful citizenship rights and against either their denial or proffering as second-class citizenship of any kind. It is a living struggle, and we must struggle with our friends who share our values for justice and who also struggle against racism. As Martin Luther King, Jr., once said, "In the end, we will remember not the words of our enemies, but the silence of our friends." Thus, it is both pragmatic and righteous to support legalization now for the twelve million undocumented immigrants in the United States and to support a rational immigration policy that respects human and labor rights above ethnic pride and national purity.

Black leadership must now stand on principle. These principles must guide black leadership even if in some local contexts Latino labor may mean short-term harm to vulnerable black workers. The basic bedrock principles of racial equality and universal rights have been too hard-fought for African Americans to throw them away over a few minimum wage jobs. This is the trade-off that must be discussed in moral terms and in terms that articulate what has been our strongest high ground as African Americans.

THE POLITICAL ORIENTATIONS OF YOUNG AFRICAN AMERICANS

DAVID A. BOSITIS

PROBABLY THE MOST POLITICALLY IMPORTANT GENERATIONAL DIFFERENCES AMONG African Americans are in the area of partisanship and political participation. Younger African Americans are significantly less attached to the Democratic Party than African Americans over fifty years old, and their levels of political involvement are considerably lower than their elders. Furthermore, they hold several beliefs, quite different from those of their parents and grandparents, that account for their diminished political involvement.

There are three main dimensions to these generational changes. First, younger African Americans are more likely to identify themselves as political independents than older African Americans, and younger African Americans are more likely to have a diminished sense of political efficacy. Self-identified "independents" lack attachment to one of the major political parties. They are not "ticket-splitters," voters who cast ballots for both Democratic and Republican candidates. Ticket-splitters generally identify with one of the major parties but frequently cast votes for selected candidates of the other party. Second, in consequence of their diminished partisanship and levels of political efficacy, younger African Americans are less likely to participate politically; this includes voting as well as other political activities, such as contributing money and working for political campaigns. Third, a significant portion of younger African Americans—between one-third and two-thirds—hold several policy views that could be fairly described as more Republican than Democratic. These include views on such issues as school vouchers and retirement policy.

There are some significant subgroup differences among African Americans under thirty-five years old. Younger black women, like all women, tend to be more Democratic than younger black men. Also, younger college-educated African Americans are more likely than those with less education to identify themselves as Democrats. Since younger black women and those with a college degree are more likely to vote than younger black men and those with less education, the ballots cast by younger black voters continue to be predominantly on the Democratic Party line.

Finally, younger black elected officials, while obviously more politically active than younger African Americans generally, share some of the policy issues of their younger peers. This suggests that some of the generational trends visible among younger African Americans will eventually be manifest among the cadres of elected African Americans.

PARTISANSHIP

While young African Americans show little attraction to the Republican Party—with Generation Xers (those twenty-six to thirty-five years old) being the most Republican-leaning cohort—they express much less loyalty to the Democratic Party than do African Americans over fifty years of age (Table 6.1).[1] In Joint Center National Opinion Polls between 1998 and 2002, younger African American age cohorts were substantially less attached to the Democratic Party than were black seniors (80 percent),[2] African Americans between fifty-one and sixty-four years old (77 percent), and black baby boomers (71 percent). Black Generation Xers (63 percent), and African Americans between eighteen and twenty-five years old (55 percent) were together 26 percent less Democratic-identified than were black seniors.

Republican identification among all African Americans remains low, with those over fifty years being the least Republican (about 5 percent). As noted, Generation Xers have tended to be the most Republican-identified cohort over time, averaging 13 percent Republican between 1998 and 2002, with a high-water mark in 1998 (26 percent). In general, African American identification with the GOP tends to be higher during midterm election years, when state-level races dominate, than in presidential years.

One-third of African Americans between eighteen and twenty-five years old, and 24 percent of those between twenty-six and thirty-five years old, are self-identified independents. This contrasts with one in ten seniors, and one in six African Americans between thirty-six and sixty-four who identify themselves as independent. Those in the youngest age cohort are more than three times more likely than those over sixty-five years to identify themselves as political independents.

As is true in the general population, there are partisan gender differences among younger African Americans. Black women between eighteen and thirty-five are more Democratic (70 percent) than are black men (52 percent) of similar age. Black men of that cohort are almost twice as likely to characterize themselves as independent (39 percent) than younger black women (22 percent). Further, younger African Americans with some college or a college degree are more likely to identify with the Democrats (68 percent) than are younger African Americans with a high school education or less (54 percent).

Among younger African Americans, there is a generational trend toward not identifying with the two major parties. That change is being driven by young black men and those without college. Thus, the prototypical black independent is a young black man with no college experience.

Table 6.1. Black partisanship by age cohort, 1998–2002

	Democratic %				Independent %				Republican %				(N)			
	1998	1999	2000	2002	1998	1999	2000	2002	1998	1999	2000	2002	1998	1999	2000	2002
18–25	58	58	51	54	33	30	36	34	9	7	9	9	127	123	76	116
26–35	57	67	70	56	17	26	24	29	6	4	5	15	168	149	148	169
36–50	73	66	79	65	13	26	18	21	14	4	4	12	257	248	234	233
51–64	93	69	77	70	5	20	18	21	3	5	3	5	175	234	173	154
65+	83	80	82	75	8	13	13	16	9	4	1	7	88	140	150	123

Source: Central National Opinion Polls, 1998, 1999, 2000, 2002.

POLITICAL EFFICACY

Younger African Americans differ from older African Americans not only in their partisanship, or rather lack of it, but also in their lower levels of political efficacy. Younger African Americans are less likely to believe that their participation in the political process will have a positive impact on their lives (Table 6.2). In surveys, political efficacy is measured by a series of questions representing reasons for not voting. When 750 African Americans between eighteen and thirty-five were presented with this series of reasons for not voting in 2000,[3] 46 percent they always vote; 62 percent of those with at least a college degree said they always vote; but only 35 percent of those with a high school degree or less said they always vote.

When the younger African Americans who indicated they do not always vote (54 percent of the total) were asked which reasons applied to them, their responses were illustrative of why voter turnout is low among this population—and how they differ in their views from older African Americans.[4]

The first reason the nonregular voters gave for not voting was that "neither candidate was worth supporting"; 41.7 percent of black nonregular voters between eighteen and thirty-five years old said that was a reason they did not always vote. A majority of that cohort (56.1 percent) said they did not always vote because "politicians don't keep their campaign promises." About one-third said they did not vote because "their one vote won't make any difference to the outcome" (31.4 percent) or that "not voting is a way to sow dissatisfaction with the system" (33.8 percent). Finally, almost half (47.5 percent) of these nonregular voters said they did not always vote because "they don't have enough information about the candidates." As noted, education is a key factor in predicting voting behavior, and those with less education are disproportionately among these nonregular voters.

While there was some variation across various subgroups in agreeing to these reasons for not voting, one subgroup consistently stood out—political independents. While 54 percent of Democratic and Republican partisans said they always vote, only 28 percent of independents said they always vote. Further, the extent of agreement

Table 6.2. Reasons for not voting, over 50 black population in 1997 and 18–35 black population in 2000

	1997 50+ years	2000 18–35 years	
Reason for not voting	Total %	Total %	Nonvoters %
Neither candidate is worth supporting	7.8	22.2	41.7
Politicians don't keep their campaign promises	6.5	30.3	56.1
Your one vote won't make any different to the outcome	0	17.0	31.4
Not voting is a way to show dissatisfaction with the system	1.2	18.3	33.8
Don't know enough about the candidates	5.7	25.7	47.5
(N =)	245	750	408

to the aforementioned reasons for not voting was consistently higher among those respondents identifying themselves as independents.

The significance of generational differences among African Americans with respect to partisanship and political partisanship is quite clear. Older (fifty-plus years) African Americans, when asked about these reasons for not voting, generally agreed with none of them. Older African Americans are much more likely to be partisans (Democrats) and to vote. While 20 to 30 percent of eighteen- to thirty-five-year-old African Americans agree with the aforementioned reasons for not voting, zero to 7.8 percent of older African Americans agree with these sentiments.

POLITICAL PARTICIPATION

The changing partisanship across generations in the black population has as yet had little impact on its vote[5] because the levels of voter participation across the age cohorts of the black population vary substantially, with African Americans over fifty years old participating at much higher rates than younger African Americans (Tables 6.3–6.5). Some of this difference represents life-cycle effects (age is one of the most powerful determinants of voter turnout), and young white voters are just as disadvantaged relative to older whites. In addition, candidates and the political parties target seniors more than younger adults for their get out the vote efforts.

The consequences for black power and representation associated with these different (age-based) rates of participation are significant because of the different demographics of the Black and white populations. Young adults (eighteen to twenty-four) make up 16 percent of the black voting-age population; seniors are only 11.8 percent of the black voting-age population. In contrast, young white adults are only 11.4

Table 6.3.   Black voting and registration by ages and gender, November 2000 (census population reports)

	Total	Report registered		Reported voted	
		(N)	(%)	(N)	(%)
Male	10,771	6,416	59.6	5,327	49.5
18–24	1,838	847	46.1	577	31.4
25–44	4,900	2.787	56.9	2,304	47.0
45–64	2,922	1,945	66.5	1,715	58.7
65–74	739	539	73.0	487	65.9
75+	371	299	80.6	244	65.8
Female	13,361	8,932	66.8	7,590	56.8
18–24	2,106	1,048	49.7	758	36.0
25–44	5,916	3,924	66.3	3,337	56.4
45–64	3,662	2,726	74.4	2,425	66.2
65–74	1,014	779	76.8	707	69.7
75+	773	455	79/8	374	54.9

Table 6.4.   Black voting and registration by ages and gender, November 2002 (census population reports)

	Total	Report registered		Reported voted	
		(N)	(%)	(N)	(%)
Male	10,428	5,651	54.2	3,757	36.0
18–24	1.775	614	34.6	299	16.8
25–44	4,425	2,278	51.5	1,394	31.5
45–64	3,175	1,978	62.3	1,470	46.3
65–74	669	491	73.4	377	56.4
75+	384	290	75.5	218	56.8
Female	13,128	8,325	63.4	5,764	43.9
18–24	1,988	894	45.0	441	22.2
25–44	5,550	3,400	61.3	2,297	41.4
45–64	3,863	2,754	71.3	2,086	54.0
65–74	924	690	74.7	536	58.0
75+	803	588	73.2	405	50.5

Table 6.5.   Political activity by age cohort

Political activity	18–25 (%)	26–35 (%)	36–50 (%)	51–64 (%)	65+ (%)
Performed volunteer work for a political organization in the previous year	8	5	19	15	13
Contributed money to a political organization in the previous year	5	7	13	12	25
(N =)	125	176	268	161	84

percent of the white population, and white seniors are 18.7 percent of it. If older adults vote at substantially higher rates than younger adults, this demographic difference (between the black and white populations) represents a substantial structural advantage for whites and a disadvantage for African Americans.

In the 2000 presidential election, African Americans over fifty years old turned out at a rate of 63.4 percent, almost twice the rate for young black adults (33.8 percent), and at a rate 21 percent higher than for African Americans between 25 and 44 years. In the 2002 midterms, African Americans over fifty turned out at a rate (54.9 percent) more than twice as high as young black adults (19.7 percent), and 48 percent higher than for African Americans between twenty-five and forty-four years old.

There are not only generational differences in voting rates, as discussed earlier, but there are also significant gender differences in voting rates. In the 2000 presidential election, eighteen- to twenty-four-year-old black women (36 percent turnout rate) had a 14.6 percent higher turnout rate than their male peers (31.4 percent); black women between the ages of twenty-five and forty-four (56.4 percent) outvoted their male counterparts (47 percent) by 20 percent. In the 2002 midterms, the differences were even greater, with eighteen- to twenty-four-year-old black women (22.2 percent) having a 32.1 percent higher turnout rate than their male peers (16.8 percent); twenty-five- to forty-four-year-old black women (41.4 percent) also outvoted their male counterparts (31.5 percent) by 31.4 percent.

There were also generational differences in other types of political activities, namely doing volunteer work in politics or contributing money to politics (Table 6.5). Older African Americans volunteered for political activities more than the younger cohorts. Seniors—most likely due to their advanced age—volunteered at a lower rate (13 percent) than baby boomers (19 percent) and those fifty-one to sixty-four (15 percent), but still at a higher rate than those in the younger cohorts. Black Generation Xers were again the least engaged (5 percent). In the area of political contributions, consistent patterns by age cohort also emerged, with seniors (25 percent) most likely to contribute, and young adults (5–7 percent) least likely to contribute.

POLICY VIEWS AND PARTISAN DIVERSIFICATION

The movement of young African Americans from identifying with the Democratic Party is likely partially a reflection of a changing policy environment, because on a significant number of important public policy issues, a sizable proportion of them—between one-third and one-half—are sympathetic to Republican Party issue positions. This represents a generational divergence in the black population, since African Americans over the age of fifty are solidly aligned with the Democratic Party in both their voting behavior and their issues' agenda.

Based on the Joint Center's most recent national survey of African Americans,[6] black attitudes on several issues suggest that the Democrats might expect to be less successful in appealing to younger African Americans. First, 25 percent of this population comprises self-described conservatives and 31 percent self-described moderates. On education policy, 66.4 percent support school vouchers for public, private, or parochial schools—a signature Republican issue. On social security, a signature issue of the Democratic Party, 61.2 percent of young African Americans believe they will get back less from social security than what they pay in, and a substantial 79.3 percent favor partial privatization. On the values front, a majority (52.9 percent) of these young African Americans attend church at least once a week. These are not insubstantial issues, and alone or cumulatively they could have the effect of diminishing young African Americans' political, economic, and psychological attachment to the Democratic Party.

As of yet, the compatibility between their views and these Republican issue positions has meant little due to the overly conservative and predominantly white southern branch of the national Republican Party. This keeps young African Americans—when they vote—firmly in the Democratic column. However, it also keeps a large proportion of them from participating in the political process.

POLICY VIEWS AND YOUNG BLACK ELECTED OFFICIALS

The differences in policy views between younger and older African Americans are somewhat mirrored in differences between younger and older African American elected officials.[7] The views of younger ones were similar to those of younger African Americans generally, and they stood in the same relation to the views of older black elected officials as did the views of younger African Americans to older African Americans. First, 33 percent of them are self-described conservatives, and 29 percent self-described moderates. On education policy, a plurality (49 to 44 percent) support school vouchers for public, private, or parochial schools, while more than 70 percent of black elected officials over forty years oppose school vouchers. On social security, 47 percent of young black elected officials lack confidence that social security is going to pay future retirees comparable benefits to those received by senior citizens today.

Younger black elected officials remain closer in views to older ones than is true for younger and older African Americans in the public, since the youngest black elected officials tend to be ten to fifteen years older (on average) than young black adults. However, changes in policy views can already be seen between young and older black elected officials and are likely to be magnified in the future as more young African Americans become elected officials.[8]

CONCLUSION

The increasing political independence of young African Americans is more a cause for political concern than a welcome development because they lack political choices. The reality of the 2004 political environment is that most African Americans, including younger African Americans, do not trust the Republican Party to defend their interests. Thus, African Americans have a choice between supporting the Democratic Party or remaining on the political sidelines and having others determine their political leaders. To older African Americans, this presents no problem because they strongly identify with and support the Democratic Party, and they do not believe in disengagement from the political process. A sizable proportion of younger African Americans, especially young black men and those with limited education—and limited opportunity—do not identify with the Democrats, and hence confront a choice between supporting the candidates of a party to which they feel no psychological, economic, or political bonds, or disengaging from the political process. Their levels of participation suggest a majority of them opt for disengagement.

Neither party has probably even entertained the notion that this group of younger African Americans should be effectively courted and made a part of their core constituencies. In areas like criminal justice, education, and retirement policy, the parties are indifferent to these individuals. Unfortunately, the U.S. political system has laws that effectively enshrine the two major parties in their current status, and that is unlikely to change. Since third-party challenges are largely ineffectual within this legal framework, younger politically disengaged African Americans will be confronted with limited choices until, at minimum, there is a genuine two-party system for African Americans.

NOTES

1. Joint Center National Opinion Polls in 1996 and 1997 found similar results. In a Joint Center national survey of 750 African Americans between eighteen and thirty-five years old conducted in 2000, 62 percent identified themselves as Democrats, 6 percent as Republicans, and 30 percent as independents.
2. The figures cited are the averages over the four surveys.
3. Data are from the Joint Center's 2000 African American youth survey.
4. The 1997 data are from the Joint Center for Political and Economic Studies 1997 National Opinion Poll.
5. In the 2000 U.S. presidential election, black voters gave the Republican nominee 8 percent of their votes, the lowest share since 1964.
6. Data are from the Joint Center 2002 National Opinion Poll.
7. Data are from the Joint Center 1999 National Survey of Black Elected Officials.
8. For further elaboration on this point, see Joint Center for Political and Economic Studies, "Changing of the Guard: Generational Differences Among Black Elected Officials" (2001).

THE CASE FOR A NEO-RAINBOW ELECTORAL STRATEGY

DANNY GLOVER AND BILL FLETCHER, JR.

THE FRUSTRATIONS OF THE 2004 ELECTION RESULTS, AND THE DISAPPOINTMENT WITH the Kerry presidential campaign, led many left-wing and progressive activists to seek new solutions to the quandary of the struggle for power in the United States. It is within this context that a new or revised approach to electoral politics must be considered—in this case, an approach that derives to a great extent from the Rainbow insurgency of the 1980s, including the 1984 and 1988 presidential campaigns of Rev. Jesse L. Jackson, as well as the initial building of the National Rainbow Coalition, a progressive, mass-based organization formed under Jackson's leadership, with the stated purpose of developing an independent presence in the electoral arena. The approach that Jackson offered—building an organization and campaign both inside and outside the Democratic Party—points progressives in the direction we should be advancing. In suggesting this approach, we recognize the failure of the Rainbow Coalition movement of the 1980s to live up to its potential.

LESSONS FROM THE RAINBOW

The Rainbow Coalition movement and Jackson's 1984 and 1988 presidential campaigns were about far more than Jesse Jackson. One may need to be reminded that prior to 1983 there was a degree of growing distrust in Jackson in many quarters, in part because of the perception of him as jumping from issue to issue, raising a flag,

This chapter is a longer version of an article published under a different title in the *Nation*, February 14, 2005. The opinions expressed here are those of the authors and do not necessarily represent the views of any organization with which the authors are affiliated.

and then disappearing to surface on yet another front. Yet, in 1983, the call "Run, Jesse, Run" arose in cities across the United States.

Although to many people on the ground it appeared as if the call came from nowhere, the reality is that Jackson had a well-developed national base. This base was the result of Jackson's work in the Southern Christian Leadership Conference (SCLC), the formation of Operation PUSH (People United to Save Humanity) in the early 1970s, the campaigns in which he involved himself (for example, the Save Black Colleges movement) and his activity in the international arena. Thus, the emergence of Jackson-the-person as a presidential candidate should not have been surprising.

That said, it is critical to note that Jackson's emergence took place within the context of a larger black-led electoral upsurge that witnessed campaigns such as the successful Harold Washington run for mayor of Chicago to the unsuccessful but no less inspiring Mel King campaign for mayor of Boston. These campaigns were both a reaction to the early years of the Reagan-Bush administration and its economic attacks on working people and veiled attacks on people of color, as well as being focused around the notion of black political power in light of the weaknesses of the civil-rights victories from two decades earlier.

Jackson seized the moment to speak nationally on behalf of these movements, but he did something even more important than that. He had the vision to articulate a set of politics that while based within the African American experience, did not represent solely a "black candidacy" or "black politics." In this sense, his effort went way beyond that suggested by groups such as the National Black Independent Political Party, formed in 1980, to open up a new sphere for black political intervention.

Instead, Jackson tapped into a growing anger and frustration arising on the U.S. political scene among groups of historically and newly disenfranchised sectors. He spoke to issues of economic injustice while not abandoning the question of race. As such, he did not fall prey to the classic error of white populists who attempt to build unity by only addressing economic issues. Jackson linked these issues. His appearances before white farmers and workers brought forth a response that hitherto had been unpredictable.

Jackson also tapped into three other key constituencies: the African American political establishment, the African American Church, and the Left (anticapitalist, anti-imperialist forces). Jackson, to put it in its bluntest sense, was not a threat to the political base or organization of established black politicians. By seeking to operate at the national level, and specifically at the level of the presidency, he was not infringing on the sphere of other elected officials. Thus, established politicians could choose to hitch their wagons to Jackson or remain separate, depending on their specific objectives. The role of the black political establishment became problematic, particularly as the politics of election year 1988 unfolded.

The Left, on the other hand, became a key force both within the 1984 campaign, but especially in its aftermath with the construction of the National Rainbow Coalition and the lead-up to and actuality of the 1988 presidential run. Sections of the organized Left, ranging from semi-Maoists through social democrats, as well as countless independent Leftists, involved themselves in the building of the Rainbow Coalition and the respective campaigns. In many cases, key positions in both the Rainbow

Coalition and the campaigns were occupied by individuals who were of the Left (in some cases very openly). Mike Davis ends his book *Prisoners of the American Dream* with a pointed critique of the failure of sections of the Left to understand the importance of the 1984 Jackson campaign. By 1988 there was far more involvement by the Left, as individuals and organizations sensed that there was something deeply significant and different about what was unfolding.

Jackson was additionally able to tap into networks within the African American Church. These networks became major sources for campaign leadership and mobilization across the United States. In the 1984 campaign he was additionally able to tap into the Nation of Islam, which, breaking with tradition, became integrally involved in the campaign in its earlier stages.

What was sensed by sections of the Left, as well as other social forces, was that the Rainbow Coalition and Jackson presidential candidacies suggested a means for progressive forces to involve themselves in real world politics that were connected to a fight for power. No one expected Jackson to receive the Democratic Party nomination, let alone win the presidency, but the power of the movement and the potential for something longer lasting signaled the importance of this initiative.

As obvious as it may seem, it is worth adding that the significance of this movement was also to be found in it emerging explicitly out of the African American people's movement. Thus, this effort was not one with which many of us have become familiar: a liberal or progressive white candidate stepping forward, with people of color being add-ons. The campaign was black-led but was remarkably inclusive of nonblacks. And, as noted earlier, it was not a traditional protest candidacy or a candidacy engaged solely in symbolic politics. The entire Rainbow movement, including the 1984 and 1988 campaigns, had very specific political objectives. These objectives were not always consistent, it should be noted. Within the Rainbow movement and the candidacies existed different agendas; sometimes overlapping, other times clashing. In either case, these were agendas that went far beyond simply shouting against racism and exclusion.

Let us add a final point. The Rainbow movement and candidacies had both the strength *and* the weakness of possessing a charismatic leader. Jackson is an outstanding leader and speaker, and succeeded in capturing the imagination of millions of people. Swift, humorous, well-read, outspoken, and a master at timing, Jackson served as the *maximum* leader for the movement. In doing so, however, he did not consistently practice the approach taken toward leadership by his mentor, Martin Luther King, Jr., who felt comfortable surrounding himself with very intelligent, independent-minded individuals. He did not feel threatened by this. Jackson, on the other hand, seemed insecure when he was not in the limelight. Many of his most loyal and hard-working supporters found themselves excluded from decision making if they somehow seemed to outshine Jackson himself. Loyalty, in the Rainbow movement, came to be based on personal loyalty to Jackson himself, rather than loyalty to the movement and its objectives. Understanding this helps one to understand the factors that influenced the Rainbow Coalition crisis of March 1989. For many people, including significant leaders in the Rainbow movement, silence rather than open disagreement with Jackson was seen as the best course of action in the face of differences of opinion.

DISAPPOINTMENT AND DILEMMA

In a fateful gathering of the executive board of the National Rainbow Coalition in Chicago in March 1989, Jackson sealed the fate of the movement that had emerged from his two presidential campaigns. In a move that shocked and outraged many of his most loyal supporters, he turned the National Rainbow Coalition—the core of his movement—into a personal political operation. All hope of a nationwide, mass democratic and progressive political/electoral formation faded almost immediately. Most local Rainbow Coalitions, with a few notable exceptions, such as Vermont, Alabama (which had already become the Alabama New South Coalition), and New Jersey, devolved into oblivion. Irrespective of Jackson's continued progressive rhetoric, the political strategy that he had originally advanced was abandoned. Many of the most dedicated Rainbow activists turned their backs on him, and in some cases on electoral politics altogether.

In the wake of Jackson's coup against himself, so to speak, and the implosion of Rainbow politics, alternative views and strategies relative to progressive electoral and mass initiatives began to surface. These included the following:

* The former agricultural commissioner from Texas, Jim Hightower, advanced a proposal for a "Democratic-Populist Alliance" to fill the void left by the collapse of the Jackson Rainbow Coalition.
* The late, long-time trade union leader Tony Mazzocchi, onetime secretary-treasurer of the Oil, Chemical and Atomic Workers (OCAW), pressed forward with the notion of the need for a Labor Party. Galvanizing thousands of trade union activists, the Labor Party was formed in the late 1990s.
* Suggesting a unique and provocative approach to electoral politics, Dan Cantor and Joel Rogers advanced a proposal for a fusion approach to politics—later undermined by a Supreme Court decision in 1997—whereby independent parties could achieve a separate voting line while votes for said party could also be used to support parties endorsed by the smaller independent party.
* Former National Rainbow Coalition Executive Director Ron Daniels decided to make a run as an independent for the presidency in 1992, attempting to base himself largely among dissatisfied African American voters.
* The populist Association of Community Organizations for Reform Now (ACORN), during the 1980s and early 1990s, flirted with establishing its own political presence, reminding activists of the history of the Midwest Non-Partisan Leagues of the early twentieth century.
* The Green Party emerged on the local level often successfully running for municipal and county positions on a progressive platform.

While it is the case that these and other efforts, to varying degrees, contributed to advancing discussions concerning independent progressive political action, and some efforts more than others gained degrees of momentum, an honest appraisal would probably conclude that the balance sheet has not been favorable. This is true irrespective of intent, commitment, and vision. Something has seemed to have been missing. The easiest answer, of course, is that there has not been someone of Jackson's stature to lead such a new political movement, but such an analysis is superficial at best. It also misses the fact that we *can* do something now to introduce a new political practice.

THE FAILURE OF POST-RAINBOW ELECTORAL INITIATIVES

Time and space do not permit an exhaustive examination of the failure of each post-Rainbow electoral initiative. The failures had certain things in common but largely failed on their own terms.

Among the problems shared in common, however, the conjuncture—the political moment—has been an important fact. The Jackson campaigns emerged under specific conditions, including the Reagan-Bush era, the demise of the civil rights and Black Power movements, and, as noted earlier and most especially, the black-led electoral upsurge. Such conditions provided a popular energy reserve that cannot be invented out of thin air. While this does not mean that a Jackson-like movement cannot reemerge, it does mean that understanding the moment is always key in politics and that movements cannot simply be replicated, irrespective of the lessons drawn.

The importance of race and the political movements of people of color is an additional issue that is often overlooked. Certainly Ron Daniels's campaign understood race, but it failed to galvanize much of a mass response for other reasons. Most other efforts, however, have failed to appreciate the centrality of race as a central factor in the U.S. political scene. Race is not simply an add-on any more than people of color should be. Race largely defines U.S. capitalism and has since its founding. Thus, attempts to address U.S. politics, issues of economic injustice, and the like, in the absence of understanding race, inevitably fail. Certainly the collapse of the Populist movement at the tail end of the nineteenth century should be an example for all those interested in the future of progressive electoral politics. Yet, despite this historical rhetoric, white liberals, white progressives, and all too many white Leftists fail to grasp this lesson, evidenced in the practice of most union organizing, community organizing, and populist political efforts.

Related to race is the issue of a base among communities of color. The Rainbow movement not only addressed race as a programmatic and thematic point, but having a base among African Americans, this movement gained a certain moral authority to challenge the collective injustice of U.S. society. Other sectors rallied to this movement in large part because it was so rooted. This was not a movement of the margins, but rather a movement of the dispossessed. The difference is decisive.

Most of the post-Rainbow efforts have failed to grasp the importance of a united-front approach to politics. Jackson found a place within his tent for various political forces. As mentioned earlier, the Left, the Black Church, and the black political establishment could be found within the Rainbow movement. This was not, it should be noted, a relationship of comparable power between these three sectors. The black political establishment and the Black Church were always in a stronger position vis-à-vis the Left, but Jackson made overtures to include disparate forces, not allowing the movement to be defined by one specific tendency. His approach, while not as inclusive as Boston's Mel King (the person who actually rehabilitated the term "rainbow coalition" after its disuse for more than a decade), nevertheless included active outreach to and involvement of Asians, Latinos, Native Americans, the women's movement, organized labor, and the environmental movement. The outreach sought leaders from within those movements with which Jackson could ally.

The failures of most post-Rainbow initiatives for the most part shared an additional fact in common. They failed to appreciate and unite with a central strategic conception of Jackson's, a conception that made the Rainbow movement that much more relevant. The Rainbow movement, exercising the legacy of the Non-Partisan Leagues and the Labor Non-Partisan League from the early to mid-twentieth century, was an effort both within the Democratic Party but as well existing independently. It is the latter factor that made the Rainbow so unsettling to the Democratic Party establishment and why they were so anxious to encourage Jackson's personalist tendencies in undermining his own movement (this beginning with the successful effort to discourage Jackson from running as an independent for Senate in South Carolina in 1984). However, the former factor of also being inside the Democratic Party frightened many people on the Left who have had a quite justified skepticism, if not antipathy, to the politics and practice of the Democratic Party officialdom. It is this central strategic conception that must be revived and serve as a basis for the next round of progressive electoral politics.

THE REALITIES OF THE UNDEMOCRATIC U.S. ELECTORAL SYSTEM

The winner-take-all system of U.S. electoral politics has always been an acknowledged obstacle to genuine democracy. Forty-nine percent of the voting electorate can be completely disenfranchised due to the manner of this system's operation. Added on to this are the entire conception of voter registration and the complexities of actually voting, not to mention electoral theft (as we witnessed in November 2000 in Florida, and, indeed, through U.S. electoral history), and the fact that the U.S. system actually discourages voting, accommodating itself to something that is cynically referenced as a "mature democracy."

The entire system of electoral politics in the United States encourages party blocs rather than ideologically defined or constituency based political parties. The Democratic and Republican parties, therefore, serve more as united front vehicles pulling together very diverse constituencies. These party blocs are far from amorphous, but their manner of construction permits the possibility of electoral victories and the ability to overcome the demographic, financial, and other barriers to achieving political power for any one particular group. Such a system, in addition to being undemocratic, is biased in favor of moneyed interests as well as favoring stability. In this sense, the famous nineteenth-century aphorism about the U.S. political system remains true: the two political parties are the equivalent of two wings of the same evil bird of prey. Yet this aphorism does not replace a concrete analysis of the realities of U.S. politics and does not answer questions of strategy.

Major sections of the Left and progressive movements have attempted to avoid the practical realities of the undemocratic nature of the U.S. electoral system. Seeing in the party bloc system the corruption and dumbing-down of politics, many left-of center activists have simply made the call for breaking with the two-party system and forming something else. While this may be the correct longer-term goal, such a call does not speak in any way as to how one gets there. The Labor Party is a case in point.

The late Tony Mazzocchi made an eloquent case for the need for the U.S. working class to have its own political party. Yet, the construction of this party did not emphasize a programmatic vision, but rather the willingness of people to support the *idea* of such a party—that is, if one believed that there should be a Labor Party, then one should sign onto the party process. First, little attention was given to the political character of such a party. Second, the party, being an idea rather than an expression of a political project, failed to acknowledge the central importance of the political movements of people of color. While Mazzocchi himself was a strong and dedicated antiracist, the Labor Party effort, in basing itself within organized labor, failed to factor in the larger political movements that have been essential in shaping and reshaping the United States. Third, Mazzocchi correctly cautioned against premature electoral interventions lest the Labor Party be forever consigned to the political margins. At the same time, the Labor Party had an approach that postponed electoral interventions pending fulfillment of a criteria (actually a good approach) but never quite factored in how to address the inevitable electoral losses that would be suffered if/when Labor Party candidates ran against both Democrats and Republicans (resulting in not only electoral losses to the Labor Party but also losses that would favor the Republicans, period).

At the other end of the spectrum have been symbolic runs for the presidency. This includes both Ron Daniels's 1992 campaign but as well Ralph Nader's 2000 campaign, not to mention the various minor party campaigns that periodically surface. Independent candidacies normally have a rationale associated with them. One common rationale is that they will inspire local activists to run for local office. Another is that an alternative must be heralded in order to lay the basis for some future genuine, mass-based progressive politics. This is actually just another way of saying that all of the existing candidates are bad and that something new needs to be implanted.

Symbolic independent presidential campaigns can bring with them great fanfare, and they often get off to an exciting start. Yet, at the end of the day, they tend to accomplish little unless they are somehow attached to a political movement. The problem is largely to be found in the pragmatic reality of our situation. On election day, the voters must decide whether they are content to register a one-time protest or whether they will hold their nose and vote for someone who *may* happen to change reality in a manner favorable to the voter. Most U.S. voters choose the more pragmatic course—or they simply sit out the election altogether.

Independent protest candidacies for the U.S. presidency generally exist outside of any notion of strategy. Rather than analyze the actual conditions under which a progressive political movement can grow in this country and the necessary building blocks, the independent protest candidacies simply assert the need for a new set of politics, sort of along the lines of running an idea up the flagpole to see who salutes.

In many respects, the Green Party has taken electoral politics most seriously. While they have backed specific independent presidential initiatives, for instance, Ralph Nader in 2000, they have tended to concentrate at the local level where they have realized some impressive victories. Nevertheless, they too have run into a specific quandary: how does one build a political practice that gets beyond school committee, town council, and so forth, and challenges for office in larger cities and counties, not to mention at the state level? The practice advanced by the Green Party is better suited for nonpartisan elections, ironically enough, but here, too, arises the question of what sort of electoral united front they are capable of building beyond a certain scale.

EXPLORING A NEO-RAINBOW APPROACH TO ELECTORAL POLITICS

The failure of most post-Rainbow progressive electoral initiatives has resulted in several tendencies: (1) throwing up one's hands and accepting the terms of operation within the Democratic Party, (2) throwing up one's hands and accepting electoral marginalization through symbolic electoral interventions, (3) throwing up one's hands and abandoning electoral politics in favor of what appear to be more pure social action movement, or (4) just throwing up.

In some respects, what each of the four tendencies has in common is a degree of despair as to the possibilities of a progressive political practice in the electoral arena. Overcoming this despair must be tied directly to constructing such a practice because in the absence of a credible electoral movement, it is unlikely that any sustained movement for substantive, not to mention transformative, politics in the United States will ever see the light of day. Despite the high degree of abstention in the electoral arena, there is a deep belief that the system should work, even if it does not. Standing on the sidelines criticizing the political system without demonstrating the ability to bring into being an alternative is nothing more than a recipe for marginalization. The system must, itself, be challenged both as a step toward fighting for political power as well as a means of actually demonstrating the fault lines in the system itself.

The problem, then, is one of developing a progressive majoritarian bloc within the context of U.S. electoral politics. This is a majoritarian bloc, it should be added, not in some idealistic or utopian sense, but rather a bloc within the context of the existing political system. Taking up this strategic challenge means coming face to face with the problem of the Democratic Party.

As much as many progressives may wish for the replacement of the Democratic Party by a Leftist/progressive party of struggle, this is unlikely for the near future. The establishment of independent political parties in the U.S. context in the recent past has simply failed to ignite widespread populist electoral activity. This does not mean, however, that one should expect that the Democratic Party will itself become the party of the dispossessed in the United States. That is unlikely, given all the factors familiar to progressives.

Instead, activists should look upon the Democratic Party as itself a field of struggle and little else. Such a view flows from a realization of the undemocratic nature of the U.S. electoral system and the dilemmas that creates. In that context, the fight that needs to take place in the electoral arena must take place both within and without the Democratic Party. To carry out such a struggle necessitates organization, vision, and strategy. It also needs the right core to anchor it in reality and build the sort of united front that such an effort or insurgency must represent. These depict the parameters for the development of a neo-Rainbow electoral strategy.

Before we explore the potential elements of such a strategy, it is worth making some preemptive remarks, so to speak. Experienced activists do not need to go through a vitriolic exchange on the nastiness of the Democratic Party or the opportunists that often cling to its label. We know that. As mentioned earlier, the

Democratic Party exists as a party bloc rather than as a genuine political party. It is a front of various forces, many of which are at odds with one another. But it exists and is able to sustain itself largely because of the nature of the U.S. electoral system, which encourages the tendency toward two-party blocs rather than a proliferation of other political formations.

Second, it should be obvious, but it is often not, that discussions about a neo-Rainbow electoral strategy are grounded in a desire to *win*. Many of us on the Left and the progressive side of the aisle are so accustomed to losing and existing under siege, that the prospect of winning is not only beyond our belief system, but is often scary. Winning necessitates political alignments, compromises, and tactics that are often far from pure. Winning certainly carries with it the potentiality of selling out. This is a risk, however, that any social movement must be prepared to accept if it is in the least bit serious about its own integrity and objectives, not to mention the fight for power.

Third, building a strategy around a particular candidacy carries with it profound dangers as well. The collapse of the Rainbow movement through Jackson's personalist decisions and approach were clearly evidence of this. In the more recent period, Congressman Dennis Kucinich's failed bid for the Democratic nomination should have been additional evidence. Kucinich's campaign, particularly in light of his courageous anti–Iraq War stand, could have been a tremendous vehicle for organization and political action. It turned out not to be. Kucinich ran into the same problems as most white populists in shelving race in the name of economic justice. Additionally, he had the wrong core for both a campaign and a movement. While Kucinich could have used his campaign—knowing full well that he would not get the nomination—as sort of a strategy center or springboard for the building of a Leftist/progressive bloc of political forces for the long term, his campaign was nowhere near as inclusive as it needed to be. Driven, as it was by the demands of the campaign and the primaries, there was also little room for the sort of longer-term discussion so badly needed.

Thus, thinking through an alternative electoral strategy really must begin with a severing of the connection or dependency between that alternative and a particular personality. While an alternative electoral strategy will need strong personalities and candidates to champion the causes that must be championed, it cannot rely on or expect stability based upon charismatic figures.

KEY ELEMENTS TO WORK WITH

A neo-Rainbow electoral strategy needs to contain the following elements:

1. An identifiable, accountable organization that operates inside and outside the Democratic Party
2. At its leading core, people of color and a base among African Americans and Latinos (not to the exclusion of others)
3. A united-front approach to growth, encouraging diverse constituencies
4. Proequality populism in its politics, heralding the unity of the struggles for racial, gender, and economic justice as the cornerstones to a larger stand in favor of consistent democracy

5. A program for change in U.S. foreign policy toward what can be called a democratic foreign policy

6. The recognition that while race is the tripwire of U.S. politics, class represents the fault line, therefore rooting itself among working people and their issues

7. The development of a ground-up approach, with ward and precinct organizations, and a targeted effort to build political power in key strategic zones

Let us briefly summarize these components.

1. An accountable organization operating both inside and outside the Democratic Party. Drawing on the history of the Rainbow candidacies and organization, as well as other efforts, such as the Non-Partisan Leagues, an inside/outside approach seems to most correspond to the actual political constraints of the U.S. electoral system. The failure of the Rainbow movement lay not with following this strategy—contrary to criticisms often raised by the ultra-Left—but by the failure to build a democratic organization that was both sufficiently rooted as well as independent of one personality. If there was a mistake in 1989, it was that the activists who had truly been the foundation of the Rainbow movement permitted a situation to exist where Jesse Jackson could carry out the coup against himself with little significant opposition. The tendency, even among committed progressive activists, to defer to Jackson's decision was disastrous. The fact, by way of example, that a prominent black elected official could say, with a straight face, that Jackson had the "right" to *his* own organization, illustrated the political weaknesses of the movement itself.

To be clear, working inside and outside the Democratic Party means establishing an organization—which is not an independent political party, but is an independent organization—that runs candidates within the Democratic primaries, runs in nonpartisan elections, and runs independently, all based on an assessment of the actual situation rather than on a cookie-cutter format. Working inside and outside the Democratic Party does not mean, however, placing a great deal of time and attention on occupying specific positions within the Democratic Party itself. Such decisions need to be made in the context of a longer-term political strategy.

2. An initiative that has a leading core of people of color. As discussed, the Rainbow movement had the advantage of having been based, first and foremost, on the black-led electoral upsurge of the early 1980s. In other words, it was rooted in a movement. In addition, the core was people of color who linked racial justice with broader social and economic justice issues. As such, this effort represented the continuity of the demand for consistent democracy within the United States. It avoided many of the problems of white populism, which seeks an end-run around the question of racial justice. While white populism can and often does attract adherents of color, it does not achieve a political base among communities of color, at least in the current era.

It is not sufficient, however, to have a core that is majority of color. Those in the room in the very founding of such an effort must bring credentials to the table, that is, they must be leaders in their own right, irrespective of their titles and positions. Thus, they must represent a constituency. A neo-Rainbow effort, in other words, cannot be defined alone as the gathering of a group of activists, the majority of who are of color, but must represent an initiative deeply rooted and carry with it popular credibility.

A final point: the changing demographics of the United States, along with a different strategic situation, necessitates that a neo-Rainbow approach does not seek to replicate the "black and . . . " approach of the past. The necessity for a partnership and the recognition of a key alliance, particularly between African Americans and Latinos, must be at the core of renewed progressive politics in the United States.

3. A united front approach. Jackson's willingness and ability to reach out to diverse constituencies marked one of the most significant aspects of the Rainbow movement.

Largely through the activities of the Left, additional constituencies were tapped, constituencies with which Jackson had little history. Asians and Latinos, particularly, became well-organized segments of the campaigns and movement.

An intriguing aspect of the 1980s Rainbow movement was its ability to gather together various political tendencies, including the Left, the Black Church, and segments of the black political establishment, as noted earlier. The growing class divides in the United States and the emergence of more conservative political tendencies within the political establishments of people of color made such an effort more complicated in later years. Many of the assumptions from the civil rights and immediate post–civil rights era could simply not be made. This became evident in black politics when, in the aftermath of the U.S.-inspired coup against Haiti's President Aristide of February 2004, the Congressional Black Caucus as a whole was divided on how to respond.

That said, the project of neo-Rainbow politics cannot afford to be a project exclusively of the Left, but it must represent a coalition of Leftist/progressive forces; otherwise, it will face certain doom.

4. The need for proequality populist politics. This theme has run throughout this chapter, so little needs to be reiterated. An anticorporate, antifinance speculation approach to politics is essential if progressive politics are to reemerge. This can be seen in the works and views of diverse political actors, including Jim Hightower, Michael Moore, and Barbara Ehrenreich. Yet, U.S. history repeatedly demonstrates that this is insufficient to sustain a progressive alternative. Building the linkage between the fights for economic, political, and social justice, and specifically between the fights for racial, gender, and economic justice, will lead to a movement resonating particularly within communities of color rather than limiting ourselves to social criticism.

When one considers once more the Kucinich campaign in 2004, one sees a missed opportunity. As good as his stands were, Kucinich did not represent a breakthrough on the race divide. His message was about those things that we have in common but did not speak to the Grand Canyon of U.S. reality. As such, he did not position himself to be a candidate of people of color, essentially deferring that role to Al Sharpton and Carol Mosley-Braun, to different degrees. The latter two, particularly Sharpton, became the "race" candidates, and Kucinich became the antiwar and economic justice candidate. Neo-Rainbow politics must establish a means of linking these. A similar criticism could be made of Ralph Nader in 2000 and again in 2004, who seemed to avoid race and racial justice issues like the plague.

Proequality populist politics is fundamentally about inclusion and in that sense is not about watering down unity. Jackson began this in the 1980s, for example, in his open, public embrace of gays and lesbians at a point when many, if not most, traditional political leaders kept this sector at arms' length. Twenty-first-century proequality populism must be just as courageous and as inclusive.

5. A democratic foreign policy. One of the strengths of Jackson as an individual, and of his Rainbow candidacies, was his willingness to stake out new ground on foreign policy. Again, breaking from the notion that the Rainbow movement was simply a Black protest movement, the Rainbow movement spoke out on international issues, albeit inconsistently.

In light of the international situation during the Bush years and the aggressive, maniacal U.S. foreign policy matched by the general spinelessness of the official Democratic Party, a neo-Rainbow movement would need to articulate an alternative vision of international affairs and foreign policy. This democratic foreign policy, so to speak, would need to be built on multilateralism, mutual respect among nations, against U.S. interventionism, the search for nonmilitary methods of problem solving, and the support of self-determination of nations. While this is not a Leftist program, it would represent a significant reform in the realm of U.S. foreign policy.

6. Class and the roots of the neo-Rainbow project. The Labor Party attempted to carve out the turf of class as its sphere. In so doing, it handled the question of race ambiguously. A neo-Rainbow project and politics needs to look at working people as more than simply another constituency—which is the standard approach in established electoral politics—but rather look at working people as the fundamental base of the neo-Rainbow politics. This means that the language of the movement, as well as the literal base areas, must be centered on working people. It also means that labor unions should have a central role in building a neo-Rainbow project.

The additional aspect of this is that the neo-Rainbow project itself should have as central to its existence the redistribution of wealth and power in the United States and the restriction on the right of capital to run roughshod over the people of this country and, for that matter, the world.

7. Building with a ground-up approach. The neo-Rainbow project cannot be limited to being a formal coalition that comes together around a specific candidate or set of candidates. First, it must be a national project, although there will need to be targeted, geographic areas in which the project will first seek to take root. As a national project, it must seek to articulate a compelling social vision that helps to break the isolation of Leftist/progressive activists and movements, focusing them on the strategies toward and possibilities of achieving political power. At the same time, this project must be rooted in communities, through ward and precinct organizations; that begins with a process of consolidation of committed activist/leaders (leaders with a small "l") around the mission and vision of the project. To that extent, the project must begin not with the notion of launching a candidacy for president, or for that matter, a candidate for any other office. Rather, the project must come together with a notion of fighting for power and to change the relations of power in the United States.

Building the neo-Rainbow project, then, would be connected with analyzing the power structures in various communities, understanding the real issues of the people, linking with community- and workplace-based organizations, identifying potential candidates for office and the issues around which they should organize their campaigns, and, ultimately, running for office.

THE FIRST STEPS ARE OFTEN THE HARDEST

In the Rainbow movement of the 1980s we saw elements of what a new type of politics could be. It led some of us to believe that a political realignment could be brought into existence by the beginning of the twenty-first century. For a host of reasons, this did not come to pass. Yet we can draw upon that movement for far more than inspiration. We can see in that movement the outlines of a direction that our journey must take us. In that sense, while the direction may look somewhat familiar, it will truly be a direction toward the fabled undiscovered country—a journey into the future.

THE ETHICS OF COLIN POWELL

GRANT FARRED

As for the person answering the question, he too exercises a right that does not go beyond the discussion itself; by the logic of his own discourse, he is tied to what he has said earlier, and by acceptance of dialogue he is tied to the questioning of the other.

—Michel Foucault

Only a radical gesture that appears "impossible" within the existing coordinates will realistically do the job.

—Slavoj Žižek

THE ETHICAL QUESTION, THE ONLY QUESTION THAT CAN BE DEEMED ETHICAL, is one that refuses any proscription. It is the question that does not, in its asking, prescribe any limits. The ethical question, the question dedicated to pursuing the "common good" (to borrow the notion from the Stoics), is the enemy of the perfunctory, of "civil discourse," because it does not belong to that mode of inquiry that already knows its answer, knows itself as an answer—or, worse, the answer—in advance of its asking before it is even asked. The ethical question is the question that will not adhere to the circumscription of the question posed because it recognizes, in declaring itself to be unwilling to "dialogue," the inherent insufficiency of the "original" question. It is the perfunctory question that, because of what it constitutively is, makes necessary, if politics is to be conducted, its own invalidation. The ethical question is the question that must make itself, as it were, a question because no other articulation of the problematic can achieve the "will to truth," to borrow from Foucault's definition of ethics.

The ethical question derives its philosophical standing from its ability to emerge not only as an interrogation—the asking of—but as a political challenge. The ethical question matters because it stages, as if for the first time, a deliberate confrontation

I would like to thank Matthew Abraham and Sajay Samuel for their thoughtful reading of this essay.

with and an outright rejection of the political "common sense" of the day. Because the perfunctory, the question that is, in fact, not a question at all, is the question that must be gainsaid, the ethical question is what must be asked in place of what is civil, innocuous, polite; it is only the ethical question that can be trusted to perform the function of the interrogative.

However, what is most salient about the ethical question is that it cannot, both because of and despite what it is, know itself in advance. The ethical question cannot know who will ask it. The question might very well emerge as the utterance of the subject who might be deemed, in other circumstances, to be or have been, unethical. For this reason there is a disconcerting proximity—and intimacy—between the ethical and not only the unethical but also, significantly, the perfunctory. Both because of contingency and the rote expectations that too often characterize it, the perfunctory might, if its terms are rejected (either inadvertently or directly), function as the staging ground for the ethical. In this delineation, then, the ethical question is marked by undecidability. This means that there is nothing settled about the articulation of the ethical question. It does not promise "safe passage"[1] in advance of its asking. On the contrary, the matter of the ethical question can only be decided—and, often, only for that moment—in and through the act of doing politics. The question becomes ethical by, insistently or unexpectedly, addressing itself to the political.

Because of its constitutive undecidability, the unethical subject—he or she who has lied or cheated or broken the law—is entirely capable of posing the ethical question in response to the perfunctory inquiry. The ethical question, the question that addresses itself to truth, is not the sole prerogative or property of the ethical subject—recognizing, of course, how difficult it is to imagine such a subject but nevertheless not dismissing such a political possibility. The question of the radical renegade state (or extrastate) operative Jack Bauer (of the television series 24, and a pure figment of the American right wing's imagination, some would say), is apropos here: "Where do the rules of engagement end and the crimes begin?"[2]

As a question, the ethical cannot itself know when it will manifest itself—when, that is, it will obtain its ethicality. The ethical has no a priori way of knowing when it will disrupt the terms, too often accepted, too easily adhered to in the cause of "civil dialogue" (as we well know, that moniker always signals the death of the political), and articulate itself as more than simply a formulaic response to what I am naming the "original" or perfunctory "nonquestion"—that is, the question that has no commitment to the interrogative, that "performs" itself only as the impossibility of knowledge or truth.

It is only through the ethical question, in demanding that it be addressed, that it becomes possible to exceed the dominant rhetoric of the civil. This is not to suggest that the ethical question is not girded, beforehand, by a radical political imperative. It is, rather, to acknowledge that the ethical can, in general, not know the moment of its speaking or that it might, in fact, emerge not as a question in or for itself but could come into itself in the process of engaging the "nonquestion." The (ethical) question supersedes the (non)question.

No recent event in American politics makes the case for the contingent quality of the ethical question more dramatically than the *Meet the Press* interview on October 19, 2008. The interview marks the pivotal electoral encounter in which the host,

Tom Brokaw, talked with retired general and former and first African American U.S. Secretary of State Colin Powell. Explaining his decision to break ranks with his party, the Republicans, and vote for Barack Obama for president, Powell responded to Brokaw's question with what can only be termed his ethical challenge. Powell's answer, it has to be said, constitutes itself as an ethical question that extends itself not only to Brokaw's inquiry—the performative question—but well beyond the NBC studios. The challenge addresses itself to the Republican Party, the American polis, and, most importantly, the candidate—the historic African American candidate—Powell was at that moment endorsing:

> I'm also troubled by, not what Senator McCain says, but what members of the party say. And it is permitted to be said such things as: "Well, you know that Mr. Obama is a Muslim." Well, the correct answer is, he is not a Muslim, he's a Christian. He's always been a Christian. But, really, the right answer is, what if he is? Is there something wrong with being a Muslim in this country. The answer's no, that's not America. Is there something wrong with a seven-year-old Muslim-American kid believing that he or she could be president?[3]

Powell's answer, in unequal measures rebuke (to the Republicans), defense of Obama, and what Slavoj Žižek might understand as the "radical gesture" that disrupts the "existing coordinates," demonstrates clearly how the protocols of dialogue are inadequate to the ethical demands of the political encounter.

Before all else, Powell's response is a stinging critique of the Islamophobia that was mobilized by the Republicans and the U.S. right wing to attack Obama—unsuccessfully, as we now know. Playing the Islamophobia card involved everything from the repeated invocation of Obama's Arab middle name (Hussein is frequently used by Christians as well as Muslims in the Middle East and the diaspora, but the attack was intended to arouse suspicion that Obama was a Muslim) to, in the spirit of our post-9/11 times, suggesting that the Democratic candidate would be "soft on terror" and more sympathetic to Islamic extremism. It is the figure of the Muslim that Powell will not, and this is critical, so much rehabilitate—that is, make palatable for the American political; render as "safe" and unthreatening for the viewing public; and distinguish between Islam as a faith of peace and those extremists who have perverted it—as instantiate, uncompromisingly, as a citizen. Powell is definitive: if the native-born or naturalized Muslim is a member of U.S. society, the Muslim is, without apology, an American citizen.

What Powell does, then, is infinitely more important than simply not accede to the terms of the Brokaw interview. Because of how Powell takes up the performative question as a question of ethics (what he takes to be the "good" of America, what is "proper" for America, what can rightly be expected of America) and not merely as the opportunity to state his electoral preference, the key moment in this interview is not, as I have just explained, the refutation of what is deemed to be a political slander—that Barack (Hussein) Obama is not a Muslim but a Christian. The ethical manifests itself in Powell's ability to shift rhetorical gears, his ability to change, rapidly, unexpectedly, from refutation to the positing of the challenge.

The moment of ethical record is encapsulated in the conditional—and a brief conditional, at that—two words: "What if?" That is, as Shakespeare's Prince Hamlet might have it, the question. And it is not only the question that will not operate on the terms of the dominant discourse but also, rather, the question that makes itself, after it has been aired, because it is so self-evident as a truth, as the only question that matters. "What if?" How is that question to be answered, posed as it is by a diasporic black American of Jamaican descent, a venerated military man, who also, of course, presented untruths to the United Nations?

It matters, of course, that Colin Powell was not truthful in his presentation to the UN in making the Bush administration's case for the ill-begotten, ill-conceived invasion of Iraq. Powell was himself unable to rise to the challenge in March 2003, when he appeared before the UN Security Council and made the case to invade Iraq, despite international opposition and the UN Charter's prohibitions against acts of aggression in the absence of a casus belli. The irony, then, is that, as the public face of the United States, Powell more than any Bush administration official paved the way for the "war against Islam" with his presentation. The invasion of Iraq was, to his credit, a war that Obama, in his turn in 2002, so properly and firmly opposed. Finally, however, all that this paradox reveals is the force of Jack Bauer's question—the disconcerting and dangerous proximity of the ethical to the unethical. While Powell is now the source of the ethical question, he possesses an unethical past; similarly, the earlier proponent of ethical opposition, Obama, is now unable to sustain that ethicality.

Hence the status of the Powellian question: "What if?" How is that question to be answered without it being overwhelmed by (the articulator's) disrepute and hypocrisy? In truth, there is no way around this. The question can be addressed only through risking—as Powell might have sensed—that his past would not invalidate or obscure his moment of intervention. As a question, then, the ethical may have a certain veracity, but it is never, in its moment of locution, either politically innocent or pure.

If America understands itself, however problematically, to be "democratic," then the question "what if?" stands as the most profound defense against bigoted or racist or ethnophobic exclusion. The question must be refuted—the Other must, however provisionally, bitterly, or reluctantly, be admitted to the polis, because without the nominal inclusion (the granting of membership), the entire edifice of American democracy will, according to Powell's terms at least, collapse. "What if?" acts to disqualify, linguistically and politically, those who would disenfranchise through their pejorative naming—those who would, through impugning Obama, evoke Islamophobia not only against his candidacy but also, implicitly, against all Muslims, putative or otherwise. Powell's "what if?" is aimed against those who posit, with strategic intent, "Hussein" as the Other, as the political candidate designated untrustworthy, because he is not, as it were, of America by the electorate. "What if?" transforms itself into that most American of rhetorical gestures because, in working to disable the disqualifiers, it insists upon the inclusivity of the nation's founding narrative: the myth of, say, Europeans arriving at Ellis Island and then, retrospectively, inscribing themselves into a historic American subjectivity.

By arguing that Muslims' full belonging to and in America is an inalienable right, Powell's ethical challenge asserts itself as an unarguable truth. The only "right answer" to those who would invoke "what if?"—and all the pernicious intent that goes under its name—as an instrument of exclusion is outright rejection. And, as such, rejection constitutes the only answer tolerable to an ethical American political—that which truly adheres in a common membership in the United States. And, Powell, whatever our reservations of or discomfitures with him might be, clearly subscribes to such a vision of this country.

If we are to follow Žižek in his critique of the Palestine-Israel situation, then we might say that it is precisely in Powell's commitment to the radical that we can imagine an ethical politics. That is, taking up the radical as the only "impossible" way to do politics against the "existing coordinates"; the radical is, in this case, to be found in Powell's adherence to America as a common good for all of its citizenry, regardless of their faith; it is in this radical gesture that the political truth of this country might be located. It is out of Powell's belief in America as fully democratic that we can, at the very least, ask the ethical question.

THE ETHICAL QUESTION

We are still far from having taken the measure of a thought.

—Geoffrey Bennington

What marks the question as ethnical rather than merely an inquiry resides in its ability to determine not what the question should be, as Powell so unequivocally states, but what the question is. It is through the ethical that the question ascends to the status of political axiom—the political truth made self-evident. In its Powellian instantiation, the ethical question is made to do the work of politics. It restores politics to the question and, as I have said, it reneges on the public agreement of discursive nicety because the "ethical subject"—if we might, temporarily, and only ambivalently, of course, grant that status to Powell, our speaker of the question—acts in the spirit that it is only through political confrontation that the political can be addressed.

Central to Powell's case, of course, is his argument for the Muslim, as the target of Islamophobia, as the figure of the immigrant, the (American) "kid" of Powell's imaginary, or the dead soldier at Arlington National Cemetery, whom he also invokes in the Brokaw interview, as commensurable with, intimate to, the American self. (The dead Muslim soldier, as Powell recalls it for Brokaw, provides a poignant event. In a visit to Arlington National Cemetery, he observes a Muslim mother at her son's graveside; a burial site is at once indistinguishable from the other graves but also marked as different by the scimitar and the star that adorn the headstone; so different, for Powell, from the more numerous Christian crosses and the Jewish stars of David. The Muslim mother, for Powell, is demonstrably American in her mourning and yet distinct but it is her grief, and his recognition of the sacrifice she has made for the United States, that makes her, above all else, the mother of a fallen soldier.) In his delineation of the "kid" and the soldier as full citizens, the Muslim becomes for Powell the figure who is no longer—and here I am borrowing Giovanna Borradori's terms—*du lointain*, far away, but instead *du proche*, near.[4] By Powell's political calculus, the Muslim is neither Other nor geographically removed to, of course, the Middle East, that site of unending historic antagonism with which the Muslim is, invariably pejoratively, associated. Rather, the Muslim is, without qualification, American.

The Muslim is one of "us" because, as Powell's frames his Socratic question and answer, there is nothing "wrong with being a Muslim in this country." The Muslim is transformed, because of the ethical question, from the figure that can be kept, by the prejudicial terms of American politics, *du lointain* or marked by irreducible difference to the full subjectivity—to standing *du proche*. The Muslim stands as/with/alongside/ among the always epiphenomenal "us." The Muslim lies as one of the heroic dead— the place of the Muslim is, as it were, at the very heart of where America honors its own, Arlington. Or, most especially, because what could matter more for the Jamai- can-born retired soldier than dying on the field of battle for one's country? *Dulce et decorum est pro patria mori*—"It is glorious and noble to die for your father country," in the words of the Roman poet Horace.

There is, for this reason, more at stake politically than the recognition of death as integral to national belonging. There is more, even, in Powell's ethicality about the Muslim—his terse response to those who inveigh the name "Muslim" as the pejorative and the marker of inveterate disqualification—than his assertion that it is the right of the Muslim to not only be part, in life and death, but to lead. To be president, as either Christian or Muslim, it matters not which—it must not be allowed to matter, it is not, however simplistic such an imagining might be. And yet . . .

Without such thinking—without a lineage that goes back centuries, twisting and turning in the midst of slavery and Reconstruction, Jim Crow, and the civil rights era—there would be (could be, we can definitively say) no such reality as an Obama presidency. The imagining of a different African American condition wends its way through the verse of a Phyllis Wheatley and the fierce advocacy of a Freder- ick Douglass; it is audible in the proud intonations of a W. E. B. Du Bois and the towering prophecy of a Martin Luther King, Jr.; and it takes the form of "terrible beauty" that is the inscape of Toni Morrison's fiction. The black body—already so overdetermined, so violently overinscribed, so xenophobically desired—cannot but now, in the Obama moment, in the person of the diasporic body, traceable to the vast distances and differences that now bind Kenya to Kansas, recall itself as the invocation of the Middle Passage. It is this fleeing, come-home body (half come from Africa body) that has come to stand—to be internationally recognized—as the American nation. The face of the nation; the nation made to face itself, its past. The past that will both now trouble and assuage the American polis because this is the confrontation with self, the confrontation that is also an accounting for the self. Obama represents the spectral reality—black equality and full citizenship—that the nation has always feared as much as it has (or at least some within in it have) hoped for. Obama is historic, like Lincoln freeing the slaves or Kennedy overcoming the bias against Irish Catholics.

Unarguably, the Obama presidency is a historic and momentous the event. January 20, 2009, was the inauguration that singularly exceeded itself by breaking with, break- ing into, the traditions of the past. However, the Obama presidency does not, in and because of Powell's question, represent the threshold of the American political. There is something more, someone, some other figure, some Other who stands as yet beyond: the Muslim. By extending rather than delimiting the historic moment (in making it, literally, the moment to come), by thinking—then, in October 2008, already, before the event of electoral victory or inauguration had even taken place—after Obama, after our conjuncture, that is where the most provocative and searing element of the ethical chal- lenge of Powell's question resides. Again, it is Powell's rhetorical economy that we must heed: "Why not?" the general asks. Why can the Muslim child not grow up, as Obama did, to lead the nation? What can stand in the way of this dream but America itself? It is only through the ethical that it is possible to begin to speak—to imagine—the truth; it is only through the ethical that the common good can overcome prejudice, racism, xenophobia. In short, the ethical stands against American history as it is being, has been, continues to be, in all its delimitation, thought. It is the ethical alone that makes a different future—one in which the Muslim might be president—possible.

This is what, after a female presidential candidate who lost a close Democratic primary (2008), a second female vice-presidential candidate (2008; who also lost), and a Jewish vice-presidential candidate (2000), it means to say, with Bennington, "we are still far from having taken the measure of a thought." What Powell's allusion to the Muslim (as potential national leader) reveals is how little serious thought has been given, even in the wake of an Obama triumph, to reconceptualizing the future of the American polis. The matter extends beyond Obama's triumph over historic racism. That is where, if we are to partake fully in Bennington's reading in *Derridabase*, our thinking—and Powell's, which is what makes his questions so ethically arresting, so demanding of our thought—merely begins. We can be sure that the imagined inauguration of the Muslim or the woman or the Jew will not represent the event of final thought.

The act of "measuring" demands attention because in the figure of president Obama or in the Muslim "kid" who would be president (or, at the very least, aspire to the same office), we are not dealing with the unthought. At the very least, these figures, the African American and the Muslim, precisely because they are so, at once, *du proche* and unthinkable, occupy the status of the irrepressible; these figures are like the restless ghosts of a Toni Morrison novel or the excitable figures who animate Ishmael Reed's fiction. These figures, along with some others (among whom the "illegal immigrant" features prominently), are fully alive at the edge of the nation's consciousness and also, unfalteringly, discernible in the nation's imaging of its (present) self. We understand this presence in the form of the anxious inquiries that marked Obama's campaign: who knows what political shape the next Obama-like figure will take? (Is Obama the harbinger of the Republican Catholic convert governor, Bobby Jindal?) What might her name be? Do we already know her? How can we not, since she is already among us, already one of us?

In the phrasing of the ethical question, we acknowledge not only what has been thought but also what has to be thought. The ethical question reminds us that the urgent conditions of our political has been thought, is already available to us; it has already found so many valences, has been audible in so many bastardized utterances, found its voice in the several anxieties, animosities, and fears that surround the figure of a president Obama or the aspirant Muslim child. However, simply because the ethical question is known does not mean, as Powell understands, that it does not present itself as threat. In truth, its greatest threat may derive from, paradoxically, its ethicality—its presentation of itself as (nothing but) the axiomatic extension of the common good.

The (Other's) claim upon belonging to the "common," then, is precisely the gravest threat to the "common" because it now requires the reconceiving of what has historically been presumed to be a settled matter. (The ethical question challenges the exclusionary politics of the "common" by arguing against its historic circumscription, through its determination to achieve a more democratic logic of belonging.)

It is Powell's insistence on the Muslim as full citizen in life and in death that, contra Foucault, goes beyond the "discussion itself." Powell will not be "tied to what" has been said earlier because that is precisely where the problem, as it were, resides: in the deliberate, publicly sanctioned exclusion of the Other. The willful act of what was said earlier is the first, and thus most susceptible, prohibition on the political. It is to what has been said, either explicitly or implicitly, that Powell addresses himself: it is that ethical conjuncture that Powell is determined not only to revisit but also to open up to questioning—the political force of the question, the right question (and "answer," Powell would assert) in the most propitious moment. Powell is asking the question of the Muslim (the question about the Muslim; in the name of "America"), the one near but also, because of the logic of extension as it applies to the figure of the Muslim, the one who is far away yet never, of course, far away enough. As will be discussed shortly, Powell's ethical question, and it could not be different because of the current ethos of American politics, is framed and haunted by that always present, always resonant figure of the Muslim as Palestinian so that the Islamicization of Obama is, in advance of itself, already audible in several additional (local and international) political registers.

Powell asks the question of the Muslim because, it should be said, the question has never been asked—in the face of national audience deciding a historic election in which race, gender, and ethnicity have, by turns, complicated and superseded each other—quite so ethically before. "Why not?" must become the question, in other words, if the dialogue is to have any political meaning. The question becomes, to invoke Foucault, not only the ethical challenge but the very substance of thought, especially pertinent to our thinking of the American political: "The work of philosophical and historical reflection is put back into the field of the work of thought only on condition that one clearly grasps problematization not as an arrangement of representations but as a work of thought."[5] Reading Foucault and Bennington we have thought as ethics; thought is the ethical. We are at once provoked and enriched by the question. What other way is there to "measure" the work of thought?

BARACK OBAMA: THE PALESTINIAN ISSUE

Have we forgotten the 17,500 dead—almost all civilians, most of them children and women—in Israel's 1982 invasion of Lebanon; the 1,700 Palestinian civilian dead in the Sabra-Chatila massacre; the 1996 Qana massacre of 106 Lebanese civilian refugees, more than half of them children, at a UN base; the massacre of the Marwahin refugees who were ordered from their homes by the Israelis in 2006 then slaughtered by an Israeli helicopter crew; the 1,000 dead of that same 2006 bombardment and Lebanese invasion, almost all of them civilians?

—Robert Fisk

Jamaican-born and raised in the American military, Colin Powell exhibits a profound sense of the political. It is striking, for precisely this reason, that the very man he was endorsing in that interview, the candidate who is now president, should prove himself so profoundly incapable of recognizing the historical force of ethics. Barack Obama's very first public address on the day after clinching the Democratic nomination on June 3, 2008, was to no less an organization than the American Israel Political Action Committee (AIPAC). That day of Obama's AIPAC address, June 4, was, as history would have it, the nineteenth anniversary of the Tiananmen Square crackdown, a notably violent event of our recent past. Speaking, he said from "his heart," Obama proclaimed that he "understood the Zionist idea—that there is always a homeland at the center of our story."[6] Is the "heart" impervious to the violence of history? Is the "heart" of American presidential candidates constitutively unfeeling toward the violence that is routinely visited upon the Arab by the Israeli Defense Force (IDF)? Is the heart of American presidents indifferent to the violence that has been committed against the Arab population of Palestine for more than sixty years now?

More pointedly, how does one speak on Tiananmen Square day and not, for a single moment, acknowledge the tragedy, al Naqba, that went before the establishment of this "homeland?" Why does Obama not take the measure of Israel and ask, as several Israeli and Arab scholars (Rashid Khalidi, Benny Morris, and Ilan Pappé) have, how the "homeland" was acquired? How does one not reflect upon the fate of those who once lived in, and are now denied access to, this self-same space as their homeland? Surely one would have to be entirely "heartless" in order not hear, in evoking "homeland," the cries of those who can no longer live in theirs? What of the pain inscribed in the Palestinian poet Mahmoud Darwish's existential question: "Without exile, who am I?"

If we are to believe Ralph Nader, a putative opponent in the 2008 presidential election, then Obama's strategic decision to address AIPAC rather than any other forum on the very day after securing the nomination marks the culmination of a process of, shall we call it, readjustment by the president-elect. Interviewed on Meet the Press, this time by the late host Tim Russert (who would be replaced by Brokaw), Nader presciently mapped the Obama trajectory in February 2008: "He [Obama] was pro-Palestinian when he was in Illinois before he ran for the state Senate. . . . Now he's supporting the Israeli destruction of the tiny section called Gaza with a million and a half people. He doesn't have any sympathy for a civilian death ratio of 300:1; 300 Palestinians to one Israeli." Bad enough, then, for the residents of Gaza in February 2008.

So much worse in the publicly declared "war on Hamas," dubbed "Operation Cast Lead" by the Israelis, of December 2008 to January 2009. Robert Fisk's arithmetic can only begin to reveal the full brutality of the Israeli onslaught against the Palestinian people: "Twenty Israelis dead in 10 years around Gaza is a grim figure indeed. But 600 Palestinians dead in just over a week, thousands over the years since 1948—when the Israeli massacre at Deir Yassin helped to kick-start the flight of Palestinians from that part of Palestine that was to become Israel—is on a quite different scale. This recalls not a normal Middle East bloodletting but an atrocity on the level of the Balkan wars of the 1990s."[7] Fisk's invocation of the Balkans recalls, as he intends us to, the camps of Srebrenica where in July 1995 some eight thousand Bosnian Muslims men and boys were murdered by Serbian forces under the command of Bosnian Serb Ratko Mladi? As much as any invocation of the camp, of course, cannot but evoke the specter of the Holocaust, the event of the winter of 2008 to 2009 (December 27, 2008–January 18, 2009) may provoke, with some eleven hundred dead and 5,000 injured (by mid-January 2009, as opposed to thirteen Israeli dead), a rethinking of the efficacy of Gaza as the "camp" of our times produced, of course, by those who claim their historic status as those who first endured the fate of the original camp. Might we

then not ask: Is the paradigm of the "camp" adequate as a marker for the Palestinian condition? Is the "camp" concept enough to critique Israeli military violence when the atrocity is committed by those who know the devastation and inhumanity of the camp? How do we think beyond the camp? What is the name for a violence that is unapologetically excessive in its determination to "destroy Hamas" and with it as many of the residents of Gaza as necessary?

What is, as Žižek asks, "committing an act of terror to a state waging war on terror?"[8] Because the Israeli state does not acknowledge the actions of the IDF as "terror," there is only one word to describe the Israeli response to the violence it perpetrates: nothing. The terror it commits against the Palestinians means nothing—insofar as the Israeli state has shown itself immune to critique and relentless in its determination to "destroy Hamas"—because, according to its logic, there is no violence against Gaza that cannot be justified in the name of its "war on terror." Israeli violence against the Palestinians does not fall under the rubric of "terror" because, as Lummis, Bardacke, and Lustig so convincingly argue, what "matters in the definition [of terror] is not what is done, but who did it."[9] Israel can commit the atrocities it does, it can violate the UN Charter, it can make war on civilians on the flimsiest of pretenses, it can provoke a war and then proclaim that it is "defending" itself,[10] and all this not because it has immunized itself against the charges of terrorism. All this can be done by simply naming any form of Palestinian opposition to Israeli colonialism and violence, first the PLO and Fatah and now Hamas, as "terrorists." So, instead of acknowledging that it is committing unthinkable terror, it considers itself as doing "nothing" more than protecting its security (even though a key aspect to terrorism is the "intentional killing of noncombatants"[11]—that is, the overwhelming civilian population of Gaza). In the process, Israel reveals itself to be a truly capable of terror because it is a state that "hasn't yet obliterated the 'founding violence' of its 'illegitimate' origins, repressed them into a timeless past. In this sense, what the state of Israel confronts us with is merely the obliterated past of *every* state power."[12] Israel's refusal to understand itself as committing terrorism means that it has no qualms about, when it thinks fit, instilling pure terror into the people of Gaza.[13] The Gazans are a people who, because of Israel's historic occupation of their land, have no place to hide from the IDF violence, who can have their access to basic resources cut off at any moment, and are, finally, a people who must live without any guarantee of civility;[14] without even the meager right to bare life. "Operation Cast Lead" is nothing but "Operation Cast Dead": cast the Palestinians of Gaza, especially the vulnerable women and children, into death, crushed by the weight of Israel's superior military might.

What, then, is the proper name for those victimized in Gaza? Or, is "Gaza" now the new and only proper name for the post-Agambenian camp? Is Gaza in fact the name of genocide in our time, as Pappé, John Pilger, and others argue? How could it not be? If this is the case, and there is little reason to believe it isn't, then Gaza is truly a frightening name because this tiny strip of land is where the Palestinians live as the dead—either as the already dead or the not-yet dead or the soon-to-be dead. Gaza is the new space, the only proper name, of and for the Israeli politics of death. Gaza is where "genocide," because that is what it would be called without hesitation if the Israelis were on the receiving end of this form of violence, and the Palestinians deserve no less, so we should insist that "Operation Cast Lead" was a war crime, is the order of the day refused by the American political establishment and the mainstream media. Gaza is the language of militarized death applied willfully to the Palestinian living. Gaza is the biopolitically fatal place precariously "lived" in by those whom the Israelis believe should be dead and whom the IDF has killed in extreme numbers in a very short period of time—eleven hundred dead in three weeks. How long before Gaza is able to function again so as to ensure that it will not collapse entirely under the weight of "Operation Cast Lead's" bombardment and a critical lack of supply of basic resources that marked that attack on Palestinian life?

In 2007, when there was a relative state of calm in Gaza, Obama offered a spirited defense of Israeli policy: "When Israel is attacked, we must stand up for Israel's legiti-mate right to defend itself." Not once did he ask how the Palestinians might protect themselves from the terror that is committed against them. Writing almost a year earlier than the Nader interview, in an article titled, mockingly and despondently, too, "How Barack Obama Learned to Love Israel," the *Electronic Intifada's* Ali Abunimah echoed Nader's criticisms and added a couple of his own:

> Obama offered not a single word of criticism of Israel, of its relentless settlement and wall construction, of the closures that make life unlivable for millions of Palestinians.
>
> While constantly emphasizing his concern about the threat Israelis face from Pales-tinians, Obama said nothing about the exponentially more lethal threat Israelis present to Palestinians.
>
> Palestinian-Americans are in the same position as civil libertarians who watched in dismay as Obama voted to reauthorize the USA Patriot Act, or immigrant rights advo-cates who were horrified as he voted in favor of a Republican bill to authorize the con-struction of a 700-mile fence on the border with Mexico.[15]

Many Palestinians, activists and ordinary Palestinian Americans alike (such as Hussein Ibish, a "senior fellow for the American Task Force on Palestine"), express the sentiment that President Obama, unlike any of his predecessors, will be more—in lieu of a more poetic phrase—"evenhanded" in his Middle East approach. The Pales-tinians believe this in part because of who Obama is and in part because of his early (as Nader points out) connections to the Palestinian struggle in Chicago (where his friendship, now lapsed, with Rashid Khalidi, then at the University of Chicago and now a Columbia University professor, was once presumed instructive if not influen-tial in shaping Obama's thoughts on the conflict between Palestinians and Israelis). And in part because Palestinian advocates remember, even as he scrambled rapidly to qualify himself afterward, how once, on a snowy Iowa day during the first Demo-cratic caucus in 2008, Obama showed that he might indeed have a "heart" for the Palestinian people: "Nobody is suffering more than the Palestinian people," he said.[16] Obama's heart, it seems, had uttered an incomplete thought because, in the wake of the furor that followed, he qualified, through extension and reattribution (or, proper attribution, Obama might argue), his view. The Palestinian people were "suffering" neither of their own accord nor because of Israeli violence. Obama laid the blame squarely at the door of the "Hamas-led government's refusal to renounce terrorism and join as a real partner for peace."[17]

Either despite or because of Obama's rhetorical fleet-footedness—his skill in retaining his sympathy for the "suffering Palestinian people" while scapegoating

Hamas, Palestinians, their supporters, and an observer or two—claim, with timeworn restraint, that the American president's public and private positions on Palestine are markedly different. (Given the obvious pandering to the Israeli lobby in the United States, it might be more accurate to describe Obama's qualification as a rhetorical leaden-footedness.) The hope is that President Obama will bring with him to his dealings with the Middle East more of his Chicago past than his AIPAC present.

At best, of course, this is a matter for speculation but, on the evidence of his Tiananmen Square day address, surely there are few reasons for, to use that much Obama-ized word, "hope."

In any event, Obama's response to "Operation Cast Lead" put an end to any potential reason for optimism. By and large, the then president-elect was silent as Israel committed what Ilan Pappé calls, in his critique of Zionism as an ideology, "massive massacres" and the "genocide in Gaza."[18] But silence, as we well know, is not the same as saying nothing. The act of not speaking inscribes within it the power of (presidential) articulation. Silence in this matter is nothing so much as the continuation of the United States' Israeli-centered policy: effectively consenting to Israel's right to "destroy Hamas" and with it, of course, the lives of many Gaza residents. Silence accedes to what Robert Fisk correctly calls the "lie": "that Israelis take such great care to avoid civilian casualties."[19] How much more violence can be tolerated in the name of this lie? When does the lie become so intolerable that the people of Gaza do not, alone, have to bear its costs? Why can we not hear, as John Pilger does in the verse of Yevgeny Yevtushenko, "when the truth is replaced by silence, the silence is a lie?"[20]

The life of the lie, history teaches us, is not infinite, but it is always deeply unjust in its capacity to exact a toll on those who are "silenced." The project, then, must be to terminate the lie that, as Pilger and Fisk both point out, is now sixty-one years old, beginning even before the founding of the state of Israel. The lie, or the truth of Israeli violence, goes back to 1948 (Deir Yassin and Eilaboun, among others) and runs bloodily through 1982 (Sabra-Chatila), 1996 (Qana), and 2006 (Marwahin and the invasion of Lebanon). What are we to make of Obama's silence in the face of the lie? That he knows that (his) silence is a biopolitical power? That he understands the power of death that the Israeli state holds over, daily, the Palestinian people in Gaza but will not act? Surely he cannot believe that his silence will immunize him from history's charge that he willfully and strategically contributed, in his silence, to the very "suffering" he was for a single moment bold enough to champion? Obama's silence in the face of "Operation Cast Lead" renders him, practicing Christian that he is, analogous to that most deadly noninterventionist Biblical figure: Pontius Pilate. How does the president wash his hands of the Gaza dead, killed in the act of him saying nothing as president-elect?

It is because of Obama's silence that, even if there is a disjuncture between the American president's public and private position on the Palestinians, even if we might deem this divided representation worthy of the possibility of thought, there remains the ethical problem. The Palestinians always have to make do with hidden hermeneutics.[21] Denied articulation in the aftermath of Obama's Iowa pronouncement, the Palestinians are left with nothing but the political shred and rhetorical aporia that is hopeful interpretation. For the Palestinians and those who support the justness of their cause, there is little but the proverbial reading between the lines, the Sisyphean determination to insist upon a political possibility other than what is publicly articulated, the search for hope in what is not—what cannot—be said, publicly, at the very least. On the other hand, the Israelis, their American allies, and the American public can demand public accountability.

And so, in order to secure his status as "friend of Israel," Obama offers his assurances to AIPAC that locate him to the right (how far right exactly, we might wonder) of the American political spectrum. "Jerusalem will remain the capital of Israel, and it must remain undivided," Obama proclaimed. Not even George W. Bush was willing to cede all of Jerusalem to Israeli rule; not even Bush was willing to give up the possibility of East Jerusalem as the capital of a future Palestinian state—an always an indeterminable, infinitely postponable future Palestinian state. It bears thinking that Obama is, on this issue, at least, to the right George W. Bush, an American leader who could by no stretch of the imagination be deemed an ally of the Palestinians. Obama denounces Hamas as "terrorists" in the face of radically disproportionate deaths—eleven hundred to thirteen; twenty Israeli dead over ten years before this event to six hundred Palestinian. How is this imbalance thinkable? How does this inequality in the number of dead not demand that it be phrased as an ethical question? Unlike Powell, Obama seems incapable of the succinct ethical question. In this instance, a simple "why?" would, if not suffice, at least open onto the possibility of the ethical questions to follow. More to the point of the event of 2008 to 2009, what of the question that follows directly from Obama's Iowa insight: when will the Palestinian people have suffered too much? Why do the "cocoons of murdered children, wrapped in green, together with boxes containing their dismembered parents and the cries of rage and grief of everyone in that death camp by the sea" not signal that moment?[22]

What is happening in Gaza, we can definitively say, has nothing to do with Hamas, except, of course, in so far as Israel wants to "destroy Hamas." And yet Obama will have nothing to do with democratically elected Hamas. Obama, who is willing to engage Teheran, declares, "There is no room at the negotiating table for terrorists." But, in another failure to pose the ethical question, will not ask, Who is being terrorized? Isn't it the perpetrator of terror who should be reprimanded, who should be brought into line with the terms of the Geneva Convention, who should be named a terrorist? What is to be hoped for when, unlike Powell, Obama will not confront, let alone issue, the ethical challenge by articulating these questions? What if the "rules of (the IDF's) engagement" is already, in its very occurrence, a "crime?"

One is reminded here of that wistful moment in the movie *Clockwise*, when the John Cleese character, the obsessive headmaster Brian Stimpson, offers that memorable line: "I can take the despair, it's the hope I can't stand." For the Palestinians, under an Obama administration, there may be a further, tragic, twist to this formulation; a question that bears asking only because it appears so unfailingly immanent. We might present it as a riddle: for the Palestinian, what is the difference between hope and despair? We could answer, without a hint of nihilism, "nothing." Or, perhaps a proper name will do as well: Barack Obama. That is, "nothing" bestowed with a presidential moniker. Should we not, in our turn, ask, Why is it wrong for the Palestinians to have to stand, for so long, to "stand for despair," to live in such terror?

That, I would suggest, is the ethical challenge we might extract from the thought of Colin Powell. The Republican Colin Powell who, even as he came out in support of the Democratic then-senator from Illinois, remained politically steadfast, militant, even in his ability to understand the imperative of the ethical question. Powell showed himself fully capable of and willing to pose the "right question": the question willing to address itself to a truth, the question without which a truth cannot be achieved, cannot be arrived at. The question that is always, as it were, willing to take the measure of our time. In our turn, it is necessary to take our measure of Obama. This is not to refuse his historicity or to fail to acknowledge the ethicality of his decision, within two days of taking office, to close Guantanamo Bay and to review U.S. detention and interrogation tactics.

Rather, it is to publicly state our expectations of him. It is to recognize that Obama's historicity only means if he does not fulfill the terms of his office. The only way in which he can succeed in his historicity—that is, make something of the presidency that it could not conceive of itself, much as it could not, did not want to, conceive of him as eligible for (or electable to) the office—is to break with the expectations of American politics. He must, most importantly, and with due urgency, produce a mode of thinking that approaches the ethicality of the Powellian question. Obama must learn, quickly (because it is already costly that he has not acquired this "skill"—if we want to think roughly of ethics as instrumental), to find in his address to the question the right answer. The answer, of course, that is agile and restless enough to take on the mode of the ethical question.

Colin Powell, whom we could figure as a conservative capable of the radical reorganization of the existing coordinates, converted a rote inquiry on a Sunday morning (pre-election) news talk show and articulated it as a political challenge. In the act of revealing the ethical force of the question, of making the question—for us—a signature ethical device for our time, Powell made every American political actor (from Obama to McCain), every political constituency (Republican, Democrat, Christian, Muslim, Jewish), near and far (from the United States to the Middle East), ethically equal and ethically accountable, Barack Obama not least of all.

We need to know what (in addition to Guantanamo Bay and water boarding) Obama is willing to ask? What inquiry is he capable of extending into a question? For which vulnerable people can he sustain his sympathy?

If it is impossible to predict where the ethical question will emerge from, then the ethical becomes, in this thinking, the act that is decided upon—produced or contingently produced might be the proper term—only in the doing of politics. The ethical is the act of doing a politics that is committed to the right answer. The ethical question recognizes the truth in itself—"Nobody is suffering more than the Palestinian people," claims that truth for itself, and never countenances violence through silence. Nor does the ethical obliterate, post ipso facto, its own truth through misattribution.

There is, then, at least one thing that the "radically conservative" black Republican can teach the erstwhile outspoken black Democratic president: the art of posing the ethical question.

NOTES

1. John Caputo, *Against Ethics: Contributions to a Poetics of Obligation with Constant Reference to Deconstruction* (Bloomington: Indiana University Press, 1993). I am using Caputo's argument against ethics here, his notion that it provides a "safe passage" to make precisely the opposite case—much as I have regard for what Caputo is suggesting—for the ethical question. There is nothing that is either "safe" or decided, in my argument, about the ethical question.

2. *24*, episode no. 147 (Season 7, Episode 3), "Day 7: 10:00 AM–11:00 AM," first broadcast January 12, 2009 by Fox, directed by Brad Turner and written by Manny Coto and Brannon Braga and episode no. 148 (Season 7, Episode 4), "Day 7: 11:00 AM-12:00 PM," first broadcast January 12, 2009 by Fox, directed by Brad Turner and written by David Fury and Alex Gansa. (These two episodes originally aired together.)

3. Colin Powell, interview by Tom Brokaw, "Oct. 19: Former Secretary of State Gen. Colin Powell (Ret.), Chuck Todd, political roundtable," *Meet the Press*, NBC, 19 October 2008. http://www.msnbc.msn.com/id/27266223/print/1/displaymode/1098.

4. Mustapha Chérif, *Islam & The West: A Conversation with Jacques Derrida* (Chicago: University of Chicago Press, 2008), xvii.

5. Michel Foucault, *Ethics: Subjectivity and Truth*, ed. Paul Rabinow (New York: New, 1997), 119.

6. Barack Obama, Remarks at AIPAC Policy Conference (speech, Washington, DC, 4 June, 2008). http://www.barackobama.com/2008/06/04/remarks_of_senator_barack_obam_74.php

7. Robert Fisk, "Why Do They Hate the West So Much, We Will Ask," *Independent*, January 7, 2009.

8. Slavoj Žižek, *Violence: Six Sideways Reflections* (New York: Picador, 2008), 117.

9. Douglas Lummis, Frank Bardacke, and Jeffrey Lustig, "What Matters Is What's Done to the Victims," *Counterpunch*, March 19, 2003.

10. See, among others, John Pilger, "Holocaust Denied: The Lying Silence of Those Who Know," *Antiwar.com*, January 8, 2009. http://www.antiwar.com/pilger/?articleid=14015. and Bruce Robbins, "It's Past Time for U.S. to Cut Off Israel," *The Providence Journal*, January 15, 2009, http://www.projo.com/opinion/contributors/content/CT_robbins15_01-15-09_SACUBS8_v12.3ed085b.html. Both these authors provide a careful delineation of how Israel engineered the conditions so as to wage "Operation Cast Lead."

11. Ibid.

12. Žižek, *Violence*, 117.

13. Rashid Khalidi makes this very point. Terror is practiced for a very simple ideological purpose: the "Palestinians must be made to understand in the deepest recesses of their consciousness that they are a defeated people" (Khalidi, "What You Don't Know About Gaza," *New York Times*, January 10, 2009).

14. In tracing the history of the concept, Lummis, Bardacke, and Lustig find that "terrorism originally referred to an action of government" that has only been effaced by a "politically motivated campaign to make state terror invisible." What Israel's attack on the people of Gaza does is return terror to its state-determined roots and expose how terror is always legitimated, or delegitimated, by the state—as, Lummis and his colleagues argue, has been the case with the United States' "war on terror" in Iraq and Afghanistan. In his critique of how the Israeli media follows the IDF line, Jonatan Mendel offers, inter alia, the example of how "Israel never *kidnaps*: it *arrests*"; Mendel, "Diary," *London Review of Books*, March 6, 2008.

15. Ali Abunimah, "How Barack Obama Learned to Love Israel," *Electronic Intifada*, March 4, 2007.
16. "Obama's Palestinian Comment Draws Fire," http://www.msnbc.com/id.17631015/print/1/displaymode/1098.
17. Ibid.
18. Ilan Pappé, "Israel's Righteous Fury and Its Victims in Gaza," *Electronic Intifada*, January 2, 2009.
19. Fisk, "Why Do They Hate Us."
20. As quoted in Pilger, "Holocaust Denied."
21. See, for example, Peter Wallsten's piece, "Allies of Palestinians See a Friend in Barack Obama," *Los Angeles Times*, April 10, 2008; then, see, for example, the change in those expectations following his AIPAC speech (June 4, 2008).
22. Pilger, "Holocaust Denied."

THE MEANING OF
BARACK OBAMA

FIRST LADY IN BLACK

MICHELLE OBAMA AND THE CRISIS OF RACE AND GENDER

GERALD HORNE AND MALAIKA HORNE-WELLS

SHE HAS "JANE FONDA'S BIG MOUTH," ACCORDING TO ONE DYSPEPTIC CONSERVATIVE, referring not to Michelle Obama's physiognomy but to her ideas.[1] She "does sound aggrieved," according to another right-winger, which in these circles—if you're not a right-winger yourself—is considered the ultimate offense. Worse, says this same source, she is "to his left politically," referring to her spouse, Barack Obama, and, besides, is a tribune of "militant social democracy," which not so long ago could have led to ostracism, a lengthy prison term, or worse. Those of her ilk in her spouse's circle are said to be tribunes of "crude populism with a quasi-Marxist [approach]," combined with a "strong dose of one-world multiculturalism."[2] Contrarily, says another comrade from the starboard, her now fabled thesis at Princeton exuded "separatism," as evidenced by her critique of the "low number of tenured black faculty at Princeton, the small number of university recognized organizations geared specifically toward blacks and other minorities and [the] undersized nature of the African-American studies program."[3] "She appears to have begun the presidential race in an angry mood," says Byron York, yet another aspirant to the perch once held by the now-departed William F. Buckley, the godfather of modern conservatism. Dumbfounded as he listened to a speech she gave in Charlotte, North Carolina, York remarked acerbically, "It was an hour-long tale of resentment and anger."[4]

Lest one think that this characterization of the first African American First Lady is not the monopoly of the far right of the political spectrum, this image has invaded other circles, as evidenced most dramatically by the notorious July 21, 2008, cover of the *New Yorker*, which portrayed Mrs. Obama in the Oval Office of the White House with a rifle slung across her back, a hairdo reminiscent of Angela Davis circa 1968, giving what has been referred to as a "terrorist fist jab" to her spouse, who is attired in clothing—including a turban—routinely worn by Muslims in East Africa, the region where his father was born.

Even would-be friends of Michelle Obama have evinced a curious interest in the details of her life, with one sympathetic female ally speaking admiringly of her posterior,[5] and another wondering querulously about her hairdo (she is a "no-lye lady!"—no lie?).[6] Journalists have turned inspection of her outfits into a minor cottage industry, with one sniffing that her election-night outfit was "an eyesore": "the sweater seemed to throw off the dress's proportions and obliterate its lines," it was reported breathlessly.[7]

Until mid-September 2008, when the economy showed imminent signs of collapse, it seemed that the hard Right was well on its way to an escalation of its "swift-boating" (remember "lipstick on a pig?"), perfected against Democratic presidential nominee John Kerry in 2004, but this time stepping things up a notch by deploying this subterfuge against a nominee's spouse. Thus, a leading poll released during the summer of 2008 found that only 24 percent of white voters held a favorable view of Michelle Obama, which may be an all-time low for a spouse of a presidential nominee.[8] On the other hand, perhaps the most progressive sector of the U.S. body politic—African American women—differed sharply with this viewpoint: Michelle Obama was the "very image of affirmation," claimed the *Washington Post* after surveying a sample of black women.[9]

What is going on here? How could two groups scrutinize the same person—often in the same settings—and come to such sharply differing conclusions?

To answer this query requires an examination of not only how her spouse shocked the world by winning the White House but also the larger forces that led to this surprising result. For the fact is that despite the exceedingly competent campaign run by Barack Obama, his own positive personal qualities and the enormous sums of money he raised, the objective situation then obtaining, as much as any other factor, propelled him to the highest office in the land. When historians come to examine how a junior senator from Illinois with reputedly a "liberal" record—when this term was still seen as the height of opprobrium—emerged triumphant on the first Tuesday of November 2008, inevitably they will point to his prescient opposition to the war in Iraq, support of which destabilized his fellow Democrats (particularly his chief opponent, Senator Hillary Rodham Clinton), as it vitiated their claims to possessing valuable experience: if experience led you to support a war that resulted in the deaths of thousands of U.S. nationals and tens of thousands of Iraqis, then—voters seemed to say—what was needed was fresh thinking, not years marinating in Washington.[10]

But, perhaps more than this, what benefited the Obama campaign was the mid-September acceleration of what may very well be the most significant economic downturn in the capitalist world since the Great Depression of the 1930s. Simultaneously, this crisis discredited the conservative nostrums that had led directly to the hemorrhaging of jobs and profits alike. Suddenly, the much ballyhooed "Washington Consensus" of privatization, deregulation, "free markets," "keeping government off the backs of the people," and the other bromides popularized by Ronald Reagan began to fade into insignificance as the federal government began nationalizing financial institutions, bailing out big businesses and creating what jokesters in Beijing hilariously referred to as the "construction of socialism with American characteristics."

Of course, this was not socialism—at least not as the radical Left sees it—and the specter of our tax dollars being shoveled into the pockets of Wall Street moguls was hardly funny. Yet, as the man who manages $200 billion worth of China's $2 trillion stash suggests,[11] the United States has reached a fork in the road: borrowing from Asia to finance consumption for goods made in Asia is a model that is reaching the point of exhaustion. More than this, the era of the United States as the "sole remaining superpower" has proven to be remarkably brief. Indeed, just as the baton of global leadership passed from London to Washington in the twentieth century, even the *Wall Street Journal*[12] seems to be fretting about the distinct possibility that U.S. profligacy has paved the way for the rise of China. This is a bitter pill to swallow for a number of reasons: after spending trillions to bring about the "death of communism," the United States now seems poised to endure the specter of the ascendancy of the most populous nation on earth—which happens to be led by the Communist Party.

Perhaps worse, according to some on the hard Right, this would also mean the rise of a "non-European" power to preeminence, a reality long in making that is perceived as incongruent with the theory and praxis of white supremacy, a founding doctrine of this nation.[13] Patrick J. Buchanan, former GOP presidential aspirant and epigone of ossified conservatism, has been remarkably explicit in delineating the racial implications of this new global reality, along with its domestic counterpart, the imminence of the United States itself no longer having a comfortable white majority.[14]

Buchanan, an editorial writer for the fortunately defunct *St. Louis Globe-Democrat*, which poured gasoline on the flames of racist resentment in the 1960s, was picked by Richard Nixon as a top aide: there he was present at the creation as Nixon led a counterrevolution against the Civil Rights Act of 1964 and the Voting Rights Act of 1965, sowing a "white backlash" that led to conservative hegemony for decades to come. Anti-Washington rhetoric resonated in the Deep South particularly, since it was the federal government that had expropriated billions in slave "property" during the Civil War, impoverishing numerous Euro-Americans, while leaving in their midst numerous African Americans.[15] The financial meltdown of 2008 not only paved the way for the erosion—if not outright collapse—of conservative hegemony but also, in a deliciously ironic trick of history, did so in the person of triumphant African Americans: the Obamas.

Unfortunately, conservative hawks have not seen fit to peruse history and note that the epochal historical reversal that the United States is now undergoing on a global scale is nothing new: France little recognized that when it assisted to power anticolonial rebels in North America in the late eighteenth century that it was not only scoring a triumph against John Bull but also creating a nascent superpower. A century ago, London hardly recognized that it was sealing the doom of its empire in Asia when it appointed Tokyo as its watchdog in the region—presumably this was recognized by December 7, 1941. When President Richard M. Nixon traveled to Beijing some thirty-five years ago to broker an anti-Soviet alliance, little did he know that he was in the process of creating one of this nation's most formidable creditors—and a rising military power to boot.

In this context, propelled by a deteriorating economic climate that has undermined traditional conservatism and a global climate that is inconsistent with the historical trajectory of white supremacy, the Obamas have arisen and have become the target of a free-floating anxiety that this crisis has generated, made all the more virulent by the white majority's difficulty in articulation of this crisis, not least since "whiteness" itself has been constructed as "invisible," the norm that need not speak its name, and not least since this majority was deprived of the tools for explicating capitalism itself during the ill-fated cold war.

Thus, in many ways the Obamas—particularly Michelle Obama—are viewed in these circles as the visible evidence of the decline of U.S. imperialism, the crisis of white supremacy, and the rise of a force bent on overturning the conservative consensus of recent decades. That this force may not prove to be unavailing is suggested by the journey of Francis Fukuyama, who after the collapse of the Berlin Wall was hailed and touted for his alleged prescience when he bruited the idea of "the end of history," by which he meant that capitalism had triumphed for all time and socialism, it was thought, had been forced into the mother of all yard sales and bargain-basement liquidations.[16] But today this same highly regarded intellectual is touting "the end of Reaganism"[17]—a surprisingly sane response to the era of Enron, Bernard Madoff, Wall Street bailouts, and corporate greed run amok.

Still, it is Michelle Obama who has been the lightning rod for a good deal of this hostility generated by these epochal shifts, perhaps to a greater degree than her spouse. The American president is both head of government and head of state—Gordon Brown and Queen Elizabeth combined—and it is the latter (and the latter category) that is routinely given a fair amount of deference as the embodiment of the nation and not just its administrator. Mrs. Obama has no such shield. Furthermore, there is a lengthy tradition—perhaps stretching back to Adam and Eve and the apple and Pandora and the box—of the sly woman leading a deluded man down the primrose path of destruction. Thus, when W. E. B. Du Bois joined the Communist Party, it was said to be the handiwork of his much younger spouse, Shirley Graham Du Bois, who was said to have inveigled and enticed the then elderly activist scholar.[18] This hoary tradition dovetails neatly with yet another atmospheric anxiety—that of many men who are challenged and threatened by the challenge to male supremacy and its counterpart: the rise of strong women unwilling to accept ancient stereotypes about female subservience.[19] Michelle Obama, an accomplished attorney and administrator, embodies this rise. That she is also of African ancestry, and therefore a symbol of a perceived "racial" challenge, only heightens, multiplies, and magnifies the antagonism toward her.

In addition, the "First Lady" historically has served as a symbol of womanhood—as defined by patriarchy. The adoring gaze of Pat Nixon and Nancy Reagan as their husbands addressed audiences is the outward manifestation of this trend.[20] Historically, Democratic Party first ladies such as Eleanor Roosevelt and Hillary Rodham Clinton have been the exceptions, which is one reason they both received so much incoming fire. Comes now Michelle Obama, a first lady in black who challenges the patriarchal stereotype—not to mention the racial construction of the femme ideal—in the midst of chaotic worldwide change and a demographic transformation that is changing the face of the nation. Unsurprisingly, she has become a target of deeply rooted—though rarely articulated—anxiety, which makes it all the more perfidious and difficult to extirpate.

Michelle Obama's spouse, on the other hand, has done a remarkable job thus far of deflecting antagonism by his calming persona and his political strategy of bringing diverse forces together, leaving her to absorb the anger and hostility in the ether as the nation and the world lurch toward a new reality. This situation is aided immeasurably by reigning stereotypes of African American women that inevitably influence the public perception of any within this group—not dainty but sizeable, not retiring but confrontational, not subservient but matriarchal. Moreover, her spouse, as is well known, is not a direct descendant of enslaved Africans in North America and therefore does not attract the stigma and hostility routinely directed at the descendants of lost fortunes in the former slave South.

Michelle Obama's great-great-grandfather was born in the mid-nineteenth century and lived as a slave, at least until the Civil War, on a sprawling rice plantation in South Carolina. Jim Robinson toiled on this same plantation as a sharecropper, living in the old slave quarters with his wife and their children; apparently, he could neither read nor write.[21] Having a black majority at various points in its tortured history, the Palmetto State was notorious for the notable viciousness of its slavery, its terrorism and racist bestiality of its political leadership.[22] Rice was the major product of this region, and it has been reported that slave traders in their hunting of the enslaved targeted a specific area of West Africa where this crop was grown.[23] Michelle Obama's ancestors were among these rice growers. In this region, often-outnumbered white elites had even more reason to recognize that their misbegotten wealth was grounded in the basest form of exploitation, thus heightening their fear, anxiety, and cruelty.[24]

Fraser Robinson, Sr., Michelle Obama's great-grandfather, was born in Georgetown, South Carolina, in 1884, at a time when Ku Klux Klan terrorism was ascending. He died in 1936, after a hard life and existence as a one-armed kiln laborer. At some point in the 1930s, many of the Robinson clan pulled up roots and, like so many Negroes of that era, fled—in their case to Chicago, where her father, Fraser Robinson III, was born.[25]

In January 1964 Fraser Robinson III started work for the city's water department, sweeping, mopping, scrubbing, emptying garbage pails, hauling litter, and unloading trucks. Within days after he assumed his post, his spouse, Marian, gave birth to their second-born child, Michelle. (Their first-born, Craig Robinson, played basketball for Princeton University and is now basketball coach at Oregon State University.) Michelle was born into a nation where Jim Crow—apartheid—was still the law of the land, though it was then under ever-stiffer challenge. This was particularly the case in Chicago, as the nation discovered when Martin Luther King, Jr., brought his protest movement there and was compelled to endure a virulent racism that shocked the conscience.[26] The passage of the Civil Rights Act of 1964 and the Voting Rights Act of 1965, while she was still in infancy, seemed to assure that Michelle Robinson would gain a more secure livelihood than her parents or ancestors. But bigotry had a durable shelf life in Chicago, as evidenced when Black Panther Party leader Fred Hampton was murdered by the authorities in his bed on December 4, 1969.

To a greater degree than its counterparts, black Chicago had a lengthy progressive tradition, as evidenced by the presence of the famed novelist Richard Wright, premier Communist intellectuals such as Claude Lightfoot and William Patterson, the celebrated writer Margaret Walker, and many other figures. Black Chicago then was to bequeath to the nation the presidential ambitions of Rev. Jesse Jackson and the trailblazing political leadership of Mayor Harold Washington. Fraser Robinson III became politically active within the Democratic Party, more specifically within the fabled "machine" of Mayor Richard Daley, whom Washington, the African American insurgent, succeeded. It has been suggested that the job Robinson held was a patronage post dependent upon political participation.

Michelle's mother, on the other hand, was the "mom-in-chief," pouring her time and effort into her two children as the father went off to work. Secure employment and a loving family facilitated Michelle's academic excellence at the Whitney Young Magnet School, which—as the name suggests—was no ordinary schoolhouse but a product of both desegregation and educational loftiness to which the teenaged girl had to travel a long distance to attend. This academic preparation proved useful when she arrived at Princeton University in the early 1980s.

Princeton had only begun to admit both women and African Americans in more than minute numbers as a direct response to the tumult of the 1960s. Its most celebrated alumnus, Woodrow Wilson, famously screened the cinematic love letter to the Ku Klux Klan, *The Birth of a Nation*, in the White House during his presidency, which was consistent with his effort to impose strict segregation in Washington, D.C. The architecturally distinct campus was littered with dormitories where the privileged once kept their slaves, and the campus during Michelle's tenure continued to contain clubs that rarely if ever had admitted African Americans of any sort. conservatism, in sum, was alive and well at Princeton during her time there, and one of its central preoccupations was railing against the admission of students like Michelle Robinson.[27]

It was at Princeton that she began to blossom politically, for, like Chicago, Princeton too had a tradition—admittedly not too lengthy—of activism. After all, it had been the birthplace of Paul Robeson, the legendary actor, singer, intellectual, and political activist, and though he had been barred from admittance at the university, he cast a lengthy shadow in his hometown, helping to inspire particularly militant antiapartheid activism that rocked this bucolic campus from the 1960s through her presence there in the 1980s. The Third World Center was one product of this activism, and Michelle spent a considerable amount of time there, once attending a seminar that featured the last surviving member of the renowned "Scottsboro Boys," nine young men whose frame-up in 1930s Alabama on charges of rape had marked a new stage in the evolution of progressive politics.[28]

Princeton undergraduates are required to produce a senior thesis. Most such documents are instantly forgettable, but Michelle Robinson's has been scrutinized like the Dead Sea Scrolls—and some conservative critics have castigated it because of purported evidence of "racial separatism." Her citation of the activist once known as Stokeley Carmichael has been trotted out as evidence of this supposed subversion, but "Princeton-Educated Blacks and the Black Community," read more carefully, is actually instantly recognizable to those familiar with African Americans who have been plucked from the working class and parachuted into elite institutions: inevitably, there is ambivalence, an instantaneous recognition that, perhaps, one is being groomed for a role as a comprador, which generates a struggle to break free from this class prison. The young woman who would become Michelle Obama wonders if she is being educated to be alienated from the community from which she sprang. This sentiment was not unique to her but is reflected in the views of a wide range of black

Princetonians interviewed by Melvin McCray in a remarkable documentary about their time at the university both before and after her admission.

This reluctance to become yet another sated and alienated member of what black Chicagoan and well-known sociologist E. Franklin Frazier referred to somewhat contemptuously as the "black bourgeoisie" was also part of her makeup at Harvard Law School. During her time there, this otherwise staid institution was a hothouse of dissent and brooding radicalism, as evidenced by the prominence of a school of thought referred to as "critical legal studies," which sought to argue that the law, far from being neutral, was actually a key tool of class rule and hegemony.[29] Critical race theory quickly followed, and it, too, established a toehold at Harvard—particularly in the corpus created by Derrick Bell—as it sought to rip away the mask that shrouded the presumed beneficence of elites, which to that point had been giving this group undue credit in explicating gains in civil rights law and human rights generally.[30] Bell, who was the most prominent African American member of the faculty during his time there (he departed prematurely because of the dearth of black women on the faculty, a deficiency that was not corrected until Lani Guinier was hired in 1998), influenced a generation of law students at Harvard and beyond, helping them to reconcile the tension and ambivalence that Michelle Robinson had experienced at Princeton with his thoughtful delineation of what he called "ethical ambition," or the ability, inter alia, to do good and do well.[31]

In short, Harvard Law School was not firmly within the conservative mainstream at this juncture, and it provided fertile conditions for Michelle Robinson to flourish. She volunteered her growing legal skills at Gannett House on campus. Her future spouse was to spend a good deal of time there later, though he was on the top floor of this white-porticoed Greek revival edifice, in the commodious top-floor offices of the illustrious *Harvard Law Review*, which he led. She, on the other hand, worked on a lower floor on behalf of poor and working-class clients with pressing problems of evictions and other nettlesome civil matters.

Decamping from Harvard, she returned to Chicago and, though she still lived at home with her parents, joined a prestigious law firm, then called Sidley & Austin, where she practiced business law. It was there that she met her future spouse, but it was also there that she decided that this kind of profit-making enterprise was not her métier, and she soon departed to work for Public Allies, an organization of organizers and activists; for the planning department of the city of Chicago, once responsible for helping to create this metropolis' unenviable reputation as more segregated than most; and, finally, as an administrator at the medical school of the University of Chicago.

In the meantime, she and the law student she supervised, Barack Obama, had become ever closer. They married, and they had two daughters. But theirs was no bed of roses, as they struggled with paying back student loans that financed their elite educations, and as he established himself as a lecturer at the University of Chicago Law School while practicing law and serving as a state senator. Barack's crushing schedule and regular travel to the capital at Springfield often left Michelle as the sole caretaker of their two young daughters, which sheds light on her White House crusade on behalf of working mothers. As she told one inquiring journalist in words that have resonated with many women, "What I notice about men, all men, is that their order is me, my family. God is in there somewhere, but me is first. And for women, me is fourth, and that's not healthy."[32] At times, this attempt to strike a work-family balance—yet another illustration of the notion that the "personal is political"—left her and her busy spouse "barely on speaking terms."[33] Yet, ironically, this all-too-close peek inside a human relationship helped to solidify the ability of similarly situated women to identify with her and combat the strenuous conservative attempt to portray her as an "elitist"—unlike, presumably, Cindy McCain, she of the $100 million fortune, the five-carat diamond rings, and the fabulous Oscar de la Renta outfits.[34]

Michelle Obama, the first lady in black, represents a departure for this nation—but this departure is difficult to comprehend without consideration of the wrenching changes the nation and the world is now undergoing: a new world is in birth and sharp pangs of pain are inevitable. Even if a sector of the U.S. electorate rails furiously against sane measures dictated by a financial meltdown, it is apparent that the international community—particularly the powerful in Asia that help to keep this stupendously debt-ridden nation afloat—will no longer accept the cowboy capitalism that has inhered in conservatism and that has its roots in a rebellion of rapacious slaveholders. The Obama presidency is a direct outgrowth of these trends, and Michelle Obama, a descendant of enslaved Africans (some of whom helped to construct the White House itself), will no doubt continue to be a target of anxiety. Yet it must be stressed that this anxiety is only secondarily about her: most of all, it is a product of a new balance of power abroad, which has helped to propel a general crisis of race and gender at home.

NOTES

1. *National Review*, August 18, 2008.
2. *American Conservative*, April 21, 2008.
3. *Human Events*, March 3, 2008.
4. *The Hill*, May 8, 2008.
5. *Washington Post*, November 21, 2008.
6. Regina Jere-Malanda, "Black Women's Politically Correct Hair," *New African Woman* 5 (December 2008): 14–18.
7. *New York Times*, November 6, 2008.
8. *The Hill*, August 25, 2008.
9. *Washington Post*, November 21, 2008; for a similar perspective, see the *Cleveland Plain Dealer*, November 9, 2008.
10. See, for example, Joseph E. Stiglitz and Linda J. Bilmes, *The Three Trillion Dollar War* (New York: Norton, 2008).
11. See the fascinating interview with Gao Xiqing in the December 2008 *Atlantic Monthly*.
12. *Wall Street Journal*, December 22, 2008.
13. For more on these intriguing possibilities, see Gerald Horne, *Blows Against the Empire: U.S. Imperialism in Crisis* (New York: International Publishers, 2008); Gerald Horne, *Race War! White Supremacy and the Japanese Attack Against the British Empire* (New York: New York University Press, 2004); Gerald Horne, "Tokyo Bound: African-Americans and Japan Confront White Supremacy," *Souls: A Critical Journal of Black Politics, Culture and Society* 3, no. 3 (Summer 2001): 16–28; Gerald Horne, "The Asiatic Black Man? Japan and the 'Colored Races' Challenge White Supremacy," *Black Renaissance/Renaissance Noire* 4, no. 1 (Spring 2002): 26–38; Gerald Horne, "Race to Insight: The U.S. and the World, White Supremacy and Foreign Affairs," in *Explaining the History of American Foreign*

Relations, ed. Michael J. Hogan and Thomas Paterson (New York: Cambridge University Press, 2004), 323–35.

14. Patrick J. Buchanan, *Death of the West: How Dying Populations and Immigrant Invasions Imperil Our Country and Civilization* (New York: St. Martin's, 2002); Patrick J. Buchanan, *State of Emergency: The Third World Invasion and Conquest of America* (New York: Thomas Dunne, 2006).

15. Dan T. Carter, *From George Wallace to Newt Gingrich: Race in the Conservative Counter-revolution, 1963–1994* (Baton Rouge: Louisiana State University Press, 1996).

16. Francis Fukuyama, *The End of History and the Last Man* (New York: Free Press, 2006).

17. Francis Fukuyama, "A New Era," *The American Interest* 4, no. 3 (January–February 2009): 124–25.

18. See Gerald Horne, *Race Woman: The Lives of Shirley Graham Du Bois* (New York: New York University Press, 2000); *Black and Red: W. E. B. Du Bois and the Afro-American Response to the Cold War* (Albany: State University of New York, 1986).

19. See Dianne M. Pinderhughes, "Intersectionality: Race and Gender in the 2008 Presidential Nomination Campaign," *Black Scholar* 28, no. 1 (Spring 2008): 47–54. See also Theda Skocpol et al., eds., *Inequality and American Democracy: What We Know and What We Need to Learn* (New York: Russell Sage, 2005).

20. See Carl Sferrazza Anthony, *First Ladies: The Sage of the Presidents' Wives and Their Power* (New York: Morrow, 1990); Maurine H. Beasley, *First Ladies and the Press: The Unfinished Partnership of the Media Age* (Evanston, IL: Northwestern University Press, 2005); Betty Boyd Caroli, *First Ladies* (New York: Oxford University Press, 2003); Lewis L. Gould, ed., *American First Ladies: Their Lives and Their Legacy* (New York: Routledge, 2001).

21. *Chicago Tribune*, December 1, 2008.

22. See Peter Wood, *Black Majority: Negroes in Colonial South Carolina from 1670 through the Stono Rebellion* (New York: Norton, 1996); Lou Falkner Williams, *The Great South Carolina Ku Klux Klan Trials, 1871–1872* (Athens: University of Georgia Press, 1996); Stephen Kantrowitz, *Ben Tillman and the Reconstruction of White Supremacy* (Chapel Hill: University of North Carolina Press, 2000).

23. Edda Fields-Black, *Deep Roots: Rice Farmers in West Africa and the African Diaspora* (Bloomington: Indiana University Press, 2008); Judith Ann Carney, *Black Rice: The African Origins of Rice Cultivation in the Americas* (Cambridge, MA: Harvard University Press, 2001).

24. Though it did not receive as much attention, there was yet another connection to slavery represented in the 2008 race for the White House. Senator John McCain descends from a family that owned scores of slaves in Teoc, Mississippi. Just as Michelle Obama's great-great grandfather was a slave, his great-great grandfather was a slave owner. Intriguingly, the African Americans in this town that carry the name McCain were raised to believe that they were "blood relatives" of the "white McCains," stretching back to the antebellum era. *Wall Street Journal*, October 17, 2008.

25. The following is indebted to the work of Liza Mundy, notably *Michelle: A Biography* (New York: Simon & Schuster, 2008).

26. James Ralph, *Northern Protest: Martin Luther King, Jr., Chicago and the Civil Rights Movement* (Cambridge, MA: Harvard University Press, 1993).

27. *New York Times*, November 27, 2005.

28. Mundy, *Michelle*, 71.

29. Duncan Kennedy, *Legal Education and the Reproduction of Hierarchy: A Polemic against the System* (New York: New York University Press, 2004); see also Richard Bauman, *Critical Legal Studies: A Guide to the Literature* (Boulder, CO: Westview, 1996).

30. See Kimberle Crenshaw et al., eds., *Critical Race Theory: The Key Writings That Formed the Movement* (New York: New Press, 1995).

31. See Derrick Bell, *Silent Covenants: Brown v. Board of Education and the Unfulfilled Hopes for Racial Reform* (New York: Oxford University Press, 2004); Derrick Bell, ed., *Race, Racism and American Law* (New York: Aspen, 2004); Derrick Bell, *Ethical Ambition: Living a Life of Meaning and Worth* (New York: Bloomsbury, 2002).
32. Mundy, *Michelle*, 139.
33. David Mendell, *Obama: From Promise to Power* (New York: HarperCollins, 2008), 134.
34. *The Observer*, November 2, 2008.

REFERENCES

Bai, Matt. 2008. Is Obama the end of black politics? *New York Times*, August 10.

Bracey, Christopher Alan. 2008. *Saviors or sellouts: The promise and peril of black conservatism, from Booker T. Washington to Condoleezza Rice*. Boston: Beacon.

Branch, Taylor. 2006. *At Canaan's edge: America in the King years, 1965–1969*. New York: Simon & Schuster.

Frederick, Don. 2008. John McCain endorsed by high-profile (and very rich) Hillary Clinton fundraiser. *Los Angeles Times*, September 17.

Hacker, Andrew. 2008. Obama: The price of being black. *New York Review of Books* 55 (September 25).

Hill, Rickey. 2008. Obama, race, racial domination, and the burden of history. http://www.blackpoliticalanalysis.blogspot.com (accessed August 6).

———. 2008. Yes we can! http://www.Kingpolitics.blogspot.com (accessed November 6).

Hill, Rickey, and P. Lee Tazinski. 2008. The politics of racial domination and the criminalization of young black males: Contextualization and the Jena 6. Paper presented to the National Conference of Black Political Scientists, Chicago.

Jones, Ricky L. 2008. *What is wrong with Obamamania? Black America, black leadership, and the death of political imagination*. Albany: State University of New York Press.

Kennedy, Randall. 2008. *Sellouts: The politics of racial betrayal*. New York: Pantheon Books.

King, Martin Luther, Jr. 1967. *Where do we go from here: Chaos or community*. Boston: Beacon.

Lewis, David Levering. 1993. *W. E. B. Du Bois: Biography of a race, 1868–1919*. New York: Henry Holt.

Lizza, Ryan. 2008. Making it: How Chicago shaped Obama. *New Yorker*, July 21.

Obama, Barack. 2004. Keynote speech to the Democratic National Convention.

———. 2006. *The audacity of hope: Thoughts on reclaiming the American dream*. New York: Vintage Books.

———. 2008a. Philadelphia "A More Perfect Union" speech on race. Philadelphia, PA.

———. 2008b. Speech to the NAACP convention. Cincinnati, OH.

O'Reilly, Kenneth. 1995. *Nixon's piano: Presidents and racial politics from Washington to Clinton*. New York: Free.

Purdum, Todd. 2008. The 2008 Election: Raising Obama. *Vanity Fair*, March.

Steele, Shelby. 2008. *A bound man: Why we are excited about Obama and why he can't win*. New York: Free.

THE RACE PROBLEMATIC, THE NARRATIVE OF MARTIN LUTHER KING, JR., AND THE ELECTION OF BARACK OBAMA

RICKEY HILL

ARGUABLY, RACE HAS BEEN AND REMAINS THE MOST INTRACTABLE PROBLEM IN the United States. Race defines and shapes the dichotomous social and human relations that have historically specified the juxtaposition of the supremacy, right, privilege, and morality of the "white" and the "non-white." In specific terms, race is a marker that describes, informs, and bounds white and non-white people within structures of power and domination. If we accept race as a social construction, then we must also accept it as a category by which all groups in the American society are identified. We must also understand that while whites possess race, they are not *raced*. To be *raced* in the American society is to be identified as non-white. Historically, this especially has been the case for black people.

This chapter attempts to analyze the race problematic as it played out within Barack Obama's quest to become the first black person to run for and win the presidency as the standard bearer of one of the two major political parties in the United States. My effort is to interrogate the race problematic within the paradigm of Martin Luther King, Jr.'s narrative of a *beloved community* and Barack Obama's odyssey of winning the presidency while not propounding his identity as a black man.

What is the race problematic? How did it inform the national discourse on whether white people were prepared to support and elect a black person as president of the United States of America and "leader of the free world," as it were? I want to examine those questions here. Second, during the 2008 presidential election cycle, the legacy of Martin Luther King, Jr., was invoked as a sort of brook of fire through which Obama had to cross in order to convince many people that he was not running as a black candidate, but rather was *transracial* or *postracial* in his campaign to win the presidency. In considering that legacy, I will I argue that the King narrative did inform the discourse on whether, as Obama believes, "white guilt has exhausted itself." The race problematic played out in Obama's presidential victory, but in some surprising ways.

THE RACE PROBLEMATIC

Race and racial specificity are interwoven into the civil society, legal system, mores, norms, cultural and social etiquette, and the body politic of American society. Consequently, the problem is not race per se. Rather the problem is racial domination. Racial domination in America is structured by power relations. White people, in very specific terms, have exercised power over black people and other non-white groups in fundamental ways that have oppressed, exploited, and aggressed against their human and civil rights.

Conceptually, race specifies a system of ideas and values, of advantages and disadvantages. Racism is the ideology that rationalizes racial domination and white supremacy. Moreover, racism gives framework to the superstructural, substructural, and infrastructural processes and institutions that practice racial exclusion, circumscription, and proscription. In broad terms, racism in the United States operationalizes a racial contract of *whiteness*. Whiteness is about privilege and the normality and visibility of white people as the dominant group and class in American society. Historically, whiteness has privileged white people over and against non-white people as the "Other." Moreover, whiteness socially categorizes white people into a dominant power relationship with non-white groups. This conceptualization accounts for the differentiation in the resources, power, authority, and influence among white people writ large.

In highly racialized polities, such as the United States, whiteness occupies the superior position in the racial hierarchy, because white people—as the dominant group and class—reproduce the power, social arrangements, and ideology that frame social reality. Over the history of the United States, citizenship, for example, has been a highly racialized commodity.

During the era of chattel slavery, African people were considered property. They were rationalized as subhuman and had no rights that white people were obligated to respect. To be a citizen, a person had to be white and a property owner. As slaves, black people were not white, were not free, and were not citizens. They were inferior, unfree, and property. Therefore, citizenship was a racialized standing. Article 1, Section 2, of the U.S. Constitution refers to black people as "three fifths of all other Persons." Amendments 13, 14, and 15 codified black people into the social contract in order to place limits on postslavery racial discriminatory practices by the states. From the mid-nineteenth century to well into the early twenty-first century, black people have engaged in political and social protest, social movement, civil litigation, and the struggle to exercise the vote in order to secure and utilize the basic citizenship rights guaranteed by the U.S. Constitution.

Therefore, for black people, the question of citizenship has been tied to questions of race, power, and racialization. In the main, the black struggle for freedom has been a struggle for inclusion into the white body politic. Not only was citizenship closed to black people, but the limits, boundaries, and provinces of citizenship were also proscribed by rules and laws forbidding black people from entering the inner citadels of white civic society. The major dominant group and class institutions, organizations, and social relations—politics, law, economic activity, religion, cultural apparatuses, and residential life—have been structured by the racial order. While *de jure* racial segregation no longer exists, there remain obvious de facto practices of racial constraints in institutional life in America.

After a long, arduous, and protracted struggle against racial segregation and for inclusion, black people do enjoy and exercise some measure of citizenship rights. However, it must be observed that, in the early twenty-first century, such exercise is still constrained by race and racial determinants on the extent and limits of freedom and access.

Today, the race problematic is evident in a litany of empirical indexes validating racial constraints that are not simple social constructions: (1) nationally, one in three black males is in prison, on parole, or on probation; (2) nationally, a higher percentage of black females are in the criminal justice system in disproportion to their numbers when compared to the number of white males; (3) black women have accounted for at least 72 percent of new HIV cases over the last decade; (4) black people do not enjoy transformative assets—inherited wealth required to lift families beyond their own achievements over generations; (5) in the twenty largest metropolitan areas, where 36 percent of all black people live, residential segregation pervades basic dimensions of life; (6) at least 70 percent of all black school-age students are in racially segregated schools; (7) in the lowest quintile, the net worth (the difference between what one owns and what one owes) for the typical white household is $17,066, while black households have a net worth of $2,400; among the highest-earning households, white median net worth is $133,607, while the net worth for black households is $43,806; and (8) more glaringly, net financial assets (liquid assets, that is, assets that are immediately available) are even more revealing along racial lines; at the middle quintile, typical net financial assets for white households are $6,800, while for black households they are $800. Among the highest-earning households, they are $40,465 for whites and $7,448 for black people. These indexes are illustrative of the disparities we find among other non-white groups when compared to whites. While class is an active variable in explaining these disparities, the race problematic is a significant determinant.

While race continues to be regarded as a dilemma in American institutional life, few observers wish to confront racial domination as it is manifested in everyday life. Whether race is rejected as a biologistic concept or accepted as a social construction, the very practices of the race problematic give conceptualization and operationalization to race as an orienting concept in dichotomizing and managing people along distinct lines of color differences. Moreover, in the context of the United States, race seems to operate as an immutable category, characterized by color lines between white people and non-white people that have been defined, circumscribed, and enforced institutionally.

Once a group or an individual has been raced, then it is difficult to become "der-aced." When cultural and social ideologues think and speak in terms of race, then they usually do not have white people in mind. They usually have reference to black people or other people of color. The historical annals are replete with cases of black people who have been so raced that they prefer being identified with the dominant white group or any other group that may approximate some of the attributes of the dominant white group. The phenomena of passing and racial self-hatred readily come to mind (Kennedy 2008; Bracey 2008).

As social practice, race ascribes a particular racial etiquette that codifies and conceptualizes how people are to act along racial lines. This racial etiquette in turn gives rise to a racial ideology that fixes people into differences that are rationalized by social practices and law. Such was the history of slavery and *de jure* racial segregation in the United States. The social practices are quite evident today in the ways in which black people are being criminalized, overrepresented at the lower end of the income and occupation hierarchies, and underrepresented in positions of economic and political power, while institutionalized racism remains a powerful determinant of black life chances (Hill and Lee 2008).

The race problematic remains an active variable in the thinking and practices that define and shape human and social relations in twenty-first-century America. Race is always just beneath the surface in public discourse. Racism and racial domination continue to operate in subtle and glaring ways to make clear that there is a dominant white group and class that maintain and benefit from the racial order.

The narrative on the race problematic has not changed much over the last forty years. When Martin Luther King, Jr., was assassinated in 1968, the civil rights movement had not achieved his beloved community. While measurable, marginal change in the racial status of black people has occurred, the life chances of black people are continually retarded by the racial order.

KING'S NARRATIVE

Martin Luther King, Jr., has been invoked during this presidential election cycle for obvious reasons. The least of them is Obama's status as the first black person to become the presidential candidate for one of the two major parties. Perhaps more critical is the fact that Obama, it was argued, represented a transracial or postracial politics in which race was not the central thesis of his bid for the White House. While it was the case that Obama set out determined not to run as a black candidate, he had to confront the conundrum of having black stalwarts in the Democratic Party, and some black neoconservatives consider him "not black enough." The black Democratic stalwarts were supporting Hillary Rodham Clinton because of the claim that black people owed something to the Clintons, especially since Bill Clinton had been the figurative "first black president." As a self-identified black man, born of an African father from Kenya and a white mother from Kansas, and primarily raised by his white grandparents in Hawaii, Obama did not want to be perceived by the white electorate as black.

While not making the claim himself, Obama may have been vicariously and intuitively assuming the personification of King's beloved community. Not only did Obama not represent the traditional biography of passage to national black leadership, but his cultural and social narrative was also constructed with appropriated language that did not altogether jibe with the race-specific experiences of mass black communities. From his beginnings as a community organizer, Obama had constructed his political résumé and portfolio within an urban terrain that required him to coalesce with individuals and groups across ethnic, racial, class, and cultural lines. His Chicago experience led him to cultivate relationships with whites, Jews, Gentiles, Middle Easterners, Latinos, conservatives, liberals, South Side black politicos, black residents of the city, and the white movers and shakers on Chicago's lakeshore. To become at once a member of Jeremiah Wright's Trinity United Church of Christ and be mentored by one Abner Mikva, a former Illinois congressman and federal judge, did not represent a contradiction for Obama (Purdum 2008; Lizza 2008). Rather, it demonstrated his capacity to reach across racial and ethnic lines to see that his political viability was inextricably linked to a broad, complex human mosaic. Arguably, this strategy was quite Kingian in its intent.

Martin Luther King, Jr., believed in and propagated the idea of America becoming a beloved community in which black people and white people, as "brothers and sisters," had to reconcile their racial differences and come together as "children of God" in order to establish America as the "Kingdom of God." Though King reluctantly became the president of the Montgomery Improvement Association, the leading black political organization in Montgomery, Alabama, in 1955, he came to understand, in short order, that the success of the civil rights movement also required the organization and mobilization of the surrounding white community. King believed that white people were morally mutable. He believed they could change to the point of recognizing black people as "children of God." Thus, King set out to shame white people into changing the racial order and the dominant culture.

King was the consummate liberal Christian who believed that the American dream of freedom, justice, equality, and democracy could be realized and enjoyed by black people. In King's thinking, racial segregation prevented white people from seeing the American dream as having transformative powers for both black people and whites. Moreover, King believed that the American racial order could be transformed by appealing to the moral conscience of whites.

The America that King saw in the mid-twentieth century was being awakened by a post–World War II international mobilization to end settler colonial rule in Africa, Asia, the Caribbean, and Latin America; a domestic politics in the United States organized against cultural and social intolerance; and the consolidation of the decades-long civil rights struggle to end racial segregation and the draconian nadir that had kept black people mired in an inferior state. King came to interpret the black freedom struggle in America as "part of an overall movement in the world in which oppressed people are revolting against imperialism and colonialism"(King 1967a, 59). King's conceptualization of what he saw was constructed in universal terms. He saw racial segregation in America and colonialism in the Third World as the denial of human dignity and worth.

As a liberal Christian, King wanted America to live up to its professed virtues as a liberal democracy by fully granting and protecting black citizenship rights and providing black people with access to freedom, justice, and equality. He knew these things could happen only in a rapidly growing materialistic society, such as America, if America ended its racial order, reckoned with its racism, promoted social equality, and instituted racial integration.

King came to believe that black people represented the moral conscience of America. Through the black freedom struggle, King believed that he could appeal to the rationality of white people. While this was not a new motif—W. E. B. Du Bois, of particular note, began his scholarly and intellectual career believing that white people were rational enough that one could appeal to their moral rationality in making the case to end racial domination—King believed his appeal was to get white people to do "God's will" (Lewis 1993). Obviously, King knew and understood that a race problem existed in America, but he believed that the "essential goodness" of white people would lead them to accept black people as full citizens into the body politic.

As the moral conscience of America, King called on black people to commit to the protracted struggle against racial domination. From the church pulpit and through his public speeches, King urged black people to practice their human dignity and worth by not resorting to retaliatory action against white people for their racial violence. Consequently, King preached and practiced nonviolent direct action.

King's narrative was the establishment of a beloved community in which black and white peoples could live together in integrated racial unity. If, as King believed, the racial order could be overturned, then black people could achieve access to freedom, justice, and equality. However, the march of human events that led King into the broader struggles for economic justice, against the Vietnam War, and in solidarity with Third World peoples also led him to become disillusioned with America's capacity to throw off the racial order.

A close examination of King's thinking from 1965 to his assassination in 1968 will reveal that King was rethinking his earlier beliefs about the moral rationality of white people. During his last three years of life, King had seen the bloody beating on the Edmund Pettus Bridge in Selma, Alabama; the killing of black people in the Watts district of Los Angeles, California; the four little girls killed in the bombing of Birmingham's Sixteenth Street Baptist Church; and black garbage workers in Memphis violently denied their human dignity and worth (Branch 2006).

King loved America deeply. He articulated a vision of hope and possibility in a country of extreme racial oppression, exploitation, and domination. Nevertheless, King believed that people in the United States had to move toward "fundamental structural changes in their values, economic and political structures, and leadership." He believed that the race problematic could be solved if white people in America were to "yield to the mandates of justice" (King 1967).

King did not live long enough to realize his dream of the beloved community. Over the last forty years, much cosmetic change has taken place in the social status of black people. There are more than nine thousand elected black officials in the United States. Approximately 60 percent are located in the American South. The black members of the U.S. House of Representatives comprise a critical voting bloc, and the one black member of the Senate, Barack Obama, has been elected president of the United States. Since 1965, black persons have been elected mayors of most of America's major cities. Black individuals have served in high posts in U.S. presidential administrations, including two black secretaries of state. Some black persons have made notable strives in the corporate sector, including chief operating officers at AOL-Time Warner and Merrill Lynch. Three black persons from the entertainment industry have become billionaires—Oprah Winfrey, Robert Johnson, and Shirley Johnson. While we can conjecture that King would probably be proud of these and other notable individual achievements, he would, perhaps, note they have not lessened the levels of poverty and dispossession that continue to structure black everyday life inside the United States.

In the final analysis, it was inevitable that Obama would be compared to King. But we cannot place the burden of history on King, a man who spoke so eloquently to the black predicament in mid-twentieth-century America, to take up the cause of freedom, justice, and equality in the twenty-first century. King left a legacy on which others can build. The unfinished work of transforming America rests with these times and with individuals who want to continue the struggle for King's dream of the beloved community. Obama is faced with the dilemma of knowing that the dream has not been realized and the possibility that America has not matured enough to put aside the racial order. How did the race problematic play out in Obama's quest to win the presidency?

THE RACE PROBLEMATIC AND THE PRESIDENTIAL CANDIDACY OF BARACK OBAMA

The race problematic has been at play in presidential election cycles long before the use of the phrase "race card" gained currency in the public lexicon. In the Black Belt of the American South, racial demagoguery was employed by white politicians desiring to "outnigger" their opponents by trying to convince white voters that by voting for them rather than their opponents they could be assured that black people would be kept in their place and that nothing would be done to relax the racial order. In explicit terms, the use of the race problematic in presidential campaigns has been characterized as the "southern strategy" (O'Reilly 1995).

In 1964, Senator Barry Goldwater of Arizona, the Republican presidential candidate, employed the southern strategy by making "law and order" the major thrust of his campaign because he believed black people, by employing political protest, were responsible for the "violence in the street." Goldwater was opposed to and voted against all the major civil rights legislation of the era. (It is of particular note here that Hillary Clinton was then a "Goldwater Girl.") Goldwater's southern strategy so concerned Lyndon Johnson, the 1964 Democratic presidential candidate, that Johnson asked the major civil rights leaders to halt all demonstrations until after the November elections. Roy Wilkins of the National Association for the Advancement of Colored People (NAACP), Martin Luther King of the Southern Christian Leadership Conference (SCLC), Whitney Young of the National Urban League (NUL), and A. Philip Randolph, the noted labor organizer, agreed to do so because they thought such demonstrations might seal Goldwater's victory. Only John Lewis of the Student Nonviolent Coordinating Committee (SNCC) and James Farmer of the Congress of Racial Equality (CORE) refused to do so.

Goldwater lost the 1964 election, in large measure, because Johnson received the majority of the white vote. This, however, was not the end of the southern strategy.

Richard Nixon employed the southern strategy in 1968 by declaring that liberalism, as represented by Hubert H. Humphrey, the Democratic candidate, was a "doctrine sympathetic to the excessive demands of blacks." While Nixon has been more pronouncedly identified with the southern strategy, many presidents before Nixon and since have used it (O'Reilly 1995). Ronald Reagan did in his infamous 1980 speech in Philadelphia, Mississippi, in which he called for states' rights. Once elected, among other racially charged decisions, Reagan decentralized community development programs. For a generation, community development programs had been central to infrastructural and civil society developments in black communities.

George H. W. Bush gave crime a black face by using the infamous Willie Horton ads against Michael Dukakis, the Democratic candidate, to frighten white people into believing that black men were going to rape and murder their women. Bush also employed the Nixon mantra against liberalism in order to consolidate the ranks of white conservatives.

Bill Clinton was more clever and perhaps more sinister than any other presidential candidate in his use of the southern strategy. In 1992, while enjoying the glowing support of the black political elite, Clinton was at once the arbiter of black folks' interests and their paternalistic benefactor. Clinton had crafted for himself a portfolio that made him look quite anomalous as a white boy growing up in racist Arkansas, who could make the generic claim that "some of my best friends are black." Clinton claimed to have regarded segregation as a sin. And, as well, he claimed to have admired Martin Luther King, Jr.

However, during his 1992 presidential run, Clinton was determined to prove to white voters that, unlike Michael Dukakis, he was a strong prosecutorial governor. During the New Hampshire primary, Clinton returned to Arkansas to preside over the execution of one Ricky Ray Rector, a brain-damaged black man. To prove, unlike Walter Mondale, he would not kowtow to Jesse Jackson, Clinton used the occasion of Jackson's Rainbow Coalition conference to blast Sister Souljah for suggesting that "if black people kill black people every day, why not have a week and kill white people." Jackson submitted that "the attempt to align me with her is an attempt to malign me with her." James Carville, Clinton's campaign manager, later admitted that "the campaign wanted to bait a prominent African American." Jesse Jackson was certainly among the most prominent African Americans of the time. Clinton went on to win two terms as president. Not only did he manage to sustain the support of the black political elite, including Jackson's, but he also enjoyed the figurative status as "the first black president."

George W. Bush played the southern strategy in both of his presidential campaigns. Bush exploited the denigration of the liberal label to convince white conservatives to vote for him. Bush's appeal was to the same racist tropes that had been used since the Goldwater and Nixon days. He also made a convincing case that he represented ordinary people because he was not endowed—despite the fact that he came from privilege, was a Yale and Harvard graduate, and the scion of the George H. W. Bush—with great intellect. In the final analysis, Bush's notion of "compassionate conservatism" became a cloak to continue retrograde policies against the interest of people of color. Bush's compassionate conservatism was on full display in his regime's ineffectual response—or lack of response—to the Hurricane Katrina tragedy in New Orleans in 2005, in which hundreds of black people died.

The southern strategy was employed by Senator Hillary Clinton, Bill's Clinton's wife, in her long-fought but failed bid to wrestle the Democratic nomination away from Obama. By all estimations, Clinton's campaign was revitalized when she made a blatant appeal to white working people during the Pennsylvania primary by convincing them that Obama was an elitist. By appealing to the base racial instincts of rural white, conservative voters, Clinton validated the longstanding sociological understanding that the very political organization of the white working class was a racial project.

John McCain, the Republican presidential nominee in the 2008 contest, appropriated the themes used by Hillary Clinton. McCain employed the fallacy that Obama did not have the experience to be president. In addition, McCain attempted to make the case that a vote for Obama would be risky. During the September 26, 2008, debate, McCain repeatedly stated that Obama "just doesn't understand." The implication, of course, was that, as a black man, Obama does not have the capacity to grasp the nuances of U.S. foreign policy. This came from a man who chose as his vice presidential running mate a person, in Alaskan Governor Sarah Palin, who believed she had derived her "foreign policy experience" from Alaska's proximity to Russia. (According to McCain insiders, Palin thought Africa was a country, and not a continent. Palin, they said, also could not identify Africa on the map.)

The Obama presidential candidacy was confronted with a long, engrained history in which the race problematic has been played. During this history, a critical mass of white voters have been convinced that it would not be in their interest to elect persons to the presidency perceived to be to the left of the so-called American mainstream. The two Democrats—Jimmy Carter and Bill Clinton—to win the presidency over the last twenty-eight years were conservative. Consequently, race and moral ideology have dominated presidential politics that have tended to advantage moderate to conservative candidates across party lines.

We must recall that, with the election of Ronald Reagan in 1980, conservatives fostered the idea that race no longer characterized the dominant human and social relations between black people and whites. The black middle class had aggregated to a measurable level. Civil rights gains had eclipsed any residual racial problems. Martin Luther King, Jr., had been appropriated as a proper icon for conservative consumption. Race came to be discussed in metaphoric language: "the race card," "driving while black," "angry white men," "affirmative action babies," "quota queens," and the like.

Barack Obama entered national politics at a time when it was perceived that the period of overt racist public statements and actions had passed from the scene and any residual cases of such were anomalies. Some white journalists even wondered aloud, "Is Obama the end of black politics?" (Bai 2008). This is the view that Obama accepted as a given. In his speech to the 2004 Democratic National Convention, Obama observed, "There is not a black America and white America and Latino America and Asian America—there's the United States of America" (Obama 2004). Two years later, in his book *The Audacity of Hope: Thoughts on Reclaiming the American Dream*, Obama rationalized the point:

> In a sense I have no choice but to believe in this vision of America. As the child of a black man and a white woman, someone who was born in the racial melting pot of Hawaii, with a sister who's half Indonesian but who's usually mistaken for Mexican or Puerto Rican, and a brother-in-law and niece of Chinese descent, with some

blood relatives who resemble Margaret Thatcher and others who could pass for Bernie Mac, so that family get-togethers over Christmas take on the appearance of a UN General Assembly meeting, I've never had the option of restricting my loyalties on the basis of race, or measuring my worth on the basis of tribe.

Obama believes that this rationale buttresses his view that "whatever preconceived notions white Americans may continue to hold, the overwhelming majority of them these days are able—if given the time—to look beyond race in making their judgments of people" (Obama 2006).

Obama also believes that racial domination has receded enough that "white guilt has largely exhausted itself in America" (Obama 2006). His optimistic and perhaps uncritical hope is that "even the most fair-minded of whites tend to push back against suggestions of racial victimization and race-based claims based on the history of racial discrimination in this country" (Obama 2006). But is Obama's view hopeful or merely naive? Is he playing to the perverse politics that argues that America has arrived at a transracial or postracial era?

What we saw in the 2008 presidential election cycle indicated that the race problematic was played within the same old framework of the racial order, only with different conceptual usages. For example, with Hillary Clinton and John McCain, one did not have to convince whites to vote against Obama because he is black. All one needed to do was to make the case that he was inexperienced. One need not have argued that Obama did not understand the circumstances of the white working class because he was black. All one needed to do was to convince the white working class that Obama was an elitist, too aloof, and too professorial. No matter how the framing or spinning was done, subliminally, it would come out in racial terms. If Obama was perceived as inexperienced and elitist, then the message was that he was an inexperienced and elitist black man. And, as McCain attempted to do, if the racial framing was not palpable, then the argument would be to make Obama a "socialist" and a "redistributionist," and to charge him with "palling around with terrorists."

Unmistakably, out on the political hustings, Obama self-identified himself as a black man. Therefore, he is not naive about how black males are stereotyped and phenotyped in American culture. He must know, intuitively at least, that he is and will be burdened with all those negative characterizations and invectives that color the place of black males in American society: "Black males are violent, angry, shiftless, and prone to sexual obsessions for white women" and the like. Moreover, despite his racial hybridity and a biography that is unframed by a history of racial subordination, the narrative from which he spoke was not untouched by the experiences of black people writ large. The nature of America's racial order did not and will not permit Obama to forget or obscure that he is black. Some whites may not sense that Obama carries a racial grievance, as it were, but they are not comfortable that Obama's very being reminds them that he is black. And, while many whites might view Obama as an exemplar of American success, this does not necessarily translate into their desire to have him regarded as "the leader of the free world." Given the entire history of black subordination in this part of the world, that would be a bit absurd.

Though Obama has not presented himself as a deracialist, he does believe that "an emphasis on universal, as opposed to race-specific, programs isn't just good policy, it's also good politics" (Obama 2006). He believes that past public policies shaped in universal terms have worked to bring black people into the American mainstream and will work in the future. Obama observes,

> When I look at what past generations of minorities have had to overcome, I am optimistic about the ability of this next generation to continue their advance into the economic mainstream. For most of our recent history, the rungs on the opportunity ladder may have been slippery for blacks; the admittance of Latinos into firehouses and corporate suites may have been grudging. But despite all that, the combination of economic growth, government investment in broad-based programs to encourage upward mobility, and a modest commitment to enforce the simple principle of nondiscrimination was sufficient to pull the large majority of blacks and Latinos into the socioeconomic mainstream within a generation. (Obama 2006)

Obama was undeterred from this optimism. His candidacy was built on the belief that he is just the right person and the right voice to use the presidency to complete the work of moving black people, Latinos, and other oppressed minorities into the American socioeconomic mainstream.

Obama was consistent in guarding against any detraction from his broader mission. In response to the national media's fury over what was interpreted to be racially incendiary speeches by his pastor, Reverend Jeremiah Wright, Obama resigned from Trinity United Church of Christ and delivered a nationally televised speech in Philadelphia, Pennsylvania, on March 18, 2008. Obama attempted to lay bare his concerns about Reverend Wright within the context of how the United States had handled the problem of race. Obama was sensitive to the implications that, since Reverend Wright was his pastor, he must have agreed with his statements. In some way, while the speech could be considered a "compromise," Obama did place in some critical relief that the problem of race must be understood in historical terms and that people in the society brought different perspectives to what they experienced. Obama declared that Jeremiah Wright "expressed a profoundly distorted view of this country—a view that sees white racism as endemic, and that elevates what is wrong with America above all that we know is right with America" (Obama 2006).

Obama wants to be identified with the view that he will not employ race to formulate and implement public policy. In his July, 14, 2008, speech to the national convention of the NAACP, Obama said, "If I have the privilege of serving as your next president, I will stand up for you the same way that earlier generations of Americans stood up for me—by fighting to ensure that every single one of us has the chance to make it if we try" (Obama 2008b). In a Kingian sense, Obama made clear that to stand up for such a principle "means removing the barriers of prejudice and misunderstanding that still exist in America. It means fighting to eliminate discrimination from every corner of our country. It means changing hearts, and changing minds, and making sure that every American is treated equally under the law" (Obama 2008b).

Most observers will agree that Obama has said and done everything reasonable to convince doubtful whites they should not be worried about how he would perform as the nation's first black president. His selection of Senator Joe Biden of Delaware should have made that message unequivocally clear. Senator Biden has been in the U.S. Senate for thirty years. He is a moderate Catholic who has represented the values of the white working class in his native state of Pennsylvania and his adopted state of Delaware. Biden also has longstanding foreign policy credentials from his leadership on the Senate foreign affairs committee.

Yet, during the rather intense Democratic primaries and caucuses, Hillary Clinton ventured that Obama was not prepared to take the proverbial 3:00 a.m. telephone call announcing some national emergency, and Kentucky Republican Congressman Geoff Davis questioned Obama's lack of preparedness to handle nuclear policy, saying, "That boy's finger does not need to be on the button." After Clinton conceded that she had lost her bid for the nomination, one of her ardent supporters, Lady Lynn Forester de Rothschild, declared, ironically, that she would not support Obama because he was elitist. In 2000, Forester de Rothschild married Sir Evelyn Rothschild of the famed British banking family, the CEO of the worldwide holding company EL Rothschild. Forester de Rothschild then threw her support to John McCain (Frederick 2008).

The cover of the *New Yorker* magazine of July 21, 2008, featured Barack and Michelle Obama celebrating with a fist bump in the Oval Office in front of a portrait of Osama bin Laden and an American flag burning in the fireplace. Michelle Obama is portrayed as a militant radical with a bushy Afro hairstyle and an AK47 hanging from her back. Barack Obama is portrayed in full Muslim garb. In response to public reaction, the *New Yorker*'s editor declared that the cover was "a satirical lampoon of the caricature Senator Obama's right wing critics have tried to create." However, the cover pointed to the fact that even in white high culture, the race problematic plays out in blatant offensive ways. In September 2008, Georgia Republican Congressman Lynn Westmoreland described the Obamas as "uppity" because they did not display the characteristic subservience that some whites still expect black people to exhibit.

Even as Obama attempted to overcome the blatant messaging to his race and his fitness to be president, he still had to contend with the perception that he was Muslim. Although Obama stated in many venues that he is a Christian, he was unable to shake the perception that he is Muslim. The September 18, 2008, a Pew Center for Research survey found that 19 percent of McCain supporters said that Obama was a Muslim. Among white voters, 17 percent of those who have not completed college said Obama was a Muslim. Among white college graduates, 7 percent said Obama was a Muslim (Pew Center for Research 2008). If Obama had lost his bid for the presidency, it would probably have been, in some measure, because his failure to prevent the perception that he is a Muslim "de-Americanized" him.

Obama overcame the "Bradley effect," a phenomenon named for Tom Bradley, the first black mayor of Los Angeles, California, who ran for governor of California in 1982. In the gubernatorial race, every poll indicated that Bradley would win. He did not. It was determined that many white voters who were polled lied and said they would vote for Bradley. On the day of the election, the white support for Bradley, as indicated in the polling, did not materialize. During the last two months of the 2008 presidential campaign, it was widely speculated that *the* Bradley effect would be at play. According to the Pew Center for Research survey, "less educated white voters are nearly as likely as white college graduates to say that many will not support Obama because he is black—42 percent vs. 47 percent." Nearly 20 percent of whites polled also believed that Obama was a Muslim.

Obama received 43 percent of the white vote on November 4, 2008. Comparatively, Obama received the second-highest percentage of the white vote for Democratic candidates in the last ten presidential election cycles. Jimmy Carter received 47 percent of white vote in 1976, and Bill Clinton received 43 percent of the white vote in 1996. The black vote was a record 13 percent of the national electorate. Obama received 95 percent of the black vote, higher than any Democratic candidate in the last ten election cycles. The 67 percent of the Latino/Hispanic vote that went to Obama was the third-highest in the last ten presidential election cycles. At 62 percent, the Asian vote for Obama was the highest in the last ten presidential election cycles. Equally important, the effort to paint Obama a Muslim faded in the 78 percent of the Jewish vote that Obama garnered.

Obama also beat McCain in critical cohorts across the national electorate. Obama carried 56 percent of women's vote and 49 percent of men's vote. McCain received 48 percent of men's vote. Obama beat or drew even with McCain in every age cohort except that sixty or older. Obama's highest percentage of the vote in the age category came from voters ages eighteen to twenty-nine. Among this cohort, Obama received 66 percent of the vote. In the education category, Obama beat McCain in every cohort. Most notably, Obama received 63 percent of the vote from persons who are not high school graduates. Among voters in big cities, Obama received 70 percent of the vote. From voters in small cities, Obama received 59 percent of the vote. He received 50 percent of the suburban vote, which has gone to Republican candidates in eight of the last ten election cycles. In the family income category, Obama beat McCain among voters earning under $15,000 and among voters earning $15,000 to $29,999, $30,000 to $49,999, $75,000 to $99,999, and $200,000 and more. McCain beat Obama by 1 percentage point among the $50,000 to $74,999 cohort. Obama and McCain evenly split the vote among the $100,000 to $200,000 cohort. In the geography category, Obama won majorities in the Midwest, Northeast, and West. McCain won the South.

Along with winning the overwhelming vote of black voters, Latino/Hispanic voters, voters under the age of thirty, and a pivotal share of the white vote, Obama made inroads among critical swing voters, including suburbanites, independents, and Catholics. He also won the upper southern states of North Carolina and Virginia and the southern exceptional state of Florida.

Obama was right all along: people wanted and needed change. Going into the election, nearly nine in every ten persons thought the country was on the wrong track. Obama received 89 percent of that vote. Especially telling, among white voters earning less than $50,000 a year, Obama received 52 percent of their vote. And in Ohio, the home state of the McCain caricature Joe the Plumber, six in ten voters called the economy the most important issue. Obama received a majority of their vote, and he won Ohio. Similar results occurred in Indiana, Michigan, and Pennsylvania, where, as in Ohio, white working-class voters were expected to reveal their true racial sentiments on Election Day and vote against Obama.

Through it all, Obama succeeded in not allowing his Democratic and Republican opponents to bait him into morphing into the archetypal angry black man. Obama knew that if he was to win enough white votes to defeat John McCain, then he had to be careful in his utterances and his messaging. In many ways, Obama won the presidency because he remained the racially ambiguous candidate. Like the image of Martin Luther King, Jr., Obama had to be enough of a blank slate to become an acceptable political icon for the comfort of whites. Obama's victory was transformative. It crossed the objective boundaries of race, class, creed, and national identity.

CONCLUSION

Hillary Clinton said that she appealed to race because the polling data implied that it was salient (Hacker 2008). During the Democratic primaries in Pennsylvania, Ohio, and West Virginia, polls showed that 15 to 20 percent of white voters said that race was indeed a factor in their vote (ibid.). Yet Barack Obama overcame the appeal to the saliency of race. He enjoyed an historic turnout among black voters, 43 percent of the white vote, and 67 percent of the Latino/Hispanic vote. Obama overcame the Bradley effect, and on November 4, 2008, he was elected the forty-fourth president of the United States.

Barack Obama is the first black person to accomplish this achievement in the history of the American polity. By any measure, given the long, draconian racial ordeal suffered by African people inside the United States, his victory is momentous for all the obvious reasons. His is a victory for all the storied virtues that have defined and shaped the American idea. In our lifetime, a black person was able to overcome the fallacy of inferiority and the dreadful racial stereotypes and phenotypes to speak a new and different truth to the American body politic. Some will argue that Obama's victory will mean an end to black grievance. Others will argue that a revolution has occurred and the color line has ended. And still others will declare that Martin Luther King's narrative has been manifested and that his dream is now a reality.

As we rejoice in Obama's transformative victory, vigilance must be the watchword. The racial order is still in place, Obama has not transcended race, and we have not achieved postraciality. Equally so, we must recognize that democracy is a contested ideological commodity, requiring a fierce urgency to imagine an America that is only possible within the lived experiences of everyday people. We must remember the past in order to understand that Barack Obama has arrived at this historic epoch through the crucibles of colonialism, the middle passage, slavery, racial segregation, and millions of ravaged black bodies and souls.

REFERENCES

Bai, Matt. 2008. Is Obama the end of black politics? *New York Times Magazine*, August 10.
Bracey, Christopher Alan. 2008. *Saviors or sellouts: The promise and peril of black conservatism, from Booker T. Washington to Condoleezza Rice.* Boston: Beacon.
Branch, Taylor. 2006. *At Canaan's Edge: America in the King years, 1965–1969.* New York: Simon & Schuster.
Frederick, Don. 2008. John McCain endorsed by high-profile (and very rich) Hillary Clinton fundraiser. *Los Angeles Times*, September 17.
Hacker, Andrew. 2008. Obama: The price of being black. *New York Review of Books* 55 (September 25).

Hill, Rickey and Tazinski P. Lee. The politics of racial domination and the criminalization of young black males: Contextualization and the Jena 6. Paper presented to the National Conference of Black Political Scientists, Chicago, Illinois, March 19–22, 2008.

Kennedy, Randall. 2008. *Sellouts: The politics of racial betrayal.* New York: Pantheon Books.

King, Martin Luther, Jr. 1967. *Where do we go from here: Chaos or community.* Boston: Beacon.

Lewis, David Levering. 1993. *W. E. B. Du Bois: Biography of A Race, 1868–1919.* New York: Henry Holt.

Lizza, Ryan. 2008. Making it: How Chicago shaped Obama. *New Yorker,* July 21.

Obama, Barack. Keynote speech to the Democratic National Convention. Boston, MA, July 27, 2004.

———. 2006. *The audacity of hope: Thoughts on reclaiming the American dream.* New York: Vintage Books.

———. 2008a. A more perfect union. Philadelphia, Pennsylvania, March 18, 2008.

———. 2008b. Speech to the NAACP Convention, Cincinnati, Ohio.

O'Reilly, Kenneth. 1995. *Nixon's piano: Presidents and racial politics from Washington to Clinton.* New York: Free Press.

Purdum, Todd. 2008. The 2008 election: Raising Obama. *Vanity Fair,* March.

The Pew Research Center. 2008. *Presidential Race Remains Even. Washington, DC. September 18.*

FROM *IDOL* TO OBAMA

WHAT TV ELECTIONS TEACH US ABOUT RACE, YOUTH, AND VOTING

SHERRILYN IFILL

CONTRARY TO POPULAR OPINION, AMERICANS LOVE TO VOTE. IN 2004, AT least thirty-two million Americans voted for twelve consecutive weeks. Many voted over and over again and with passion and intensity. Most of the voters were young. The election was marked by racial politics and single-shot voting. The election was for the American idol, and over the course of six years, millions of viewers participated week after week in a series of electoral contests as hard-fought, emotional, and divisive as any between the nation's major political parties.

The year 2004 was a banner year for *American Idol*. Launched in 2002, the show was modeled after a British program. Featuring amateur singers from all over the country and three "professional" judges who eliminate singers each week, the show hits its peak in its final twelve weeks, when viewers are permitted to vote by phone for their favorite singers. Those singers who receive the lowest vote tally go home.[1] In the show's third season, the lineup of "final twelve" singers contained what were arguably the best singers to ever participate in the competition. One competitor, Jennifer Hudson, a beautiful big girl with a powerhouse voice, went on to win an Academy Award two years later for playing Effie White in the film *Dreamgirls*. Her rendition of the signature song "And I Am Telling You" may be the single most powerful musical performance in motion picture history. Hudson was voted off the *Idol* program in the seventh week of the final twelve episodes.

Another dynamic singer in the 2004 season of *Idol* was LaToya London. Beautiful and petite, with a near flawless voice, London's farewell rendition of Barbra Streisand's classic "Don't Rain on My Parade" when she was voted off the show three weeks after Hudson left a stunned audience with the uneasy sense that a mistake had been made.

I am grateful for the research assistance of law student Michelle McLeod.

In fact, by the time London was voted off the show, racism had emerged as an ugly but unmistakable factor in the voting. Hudson, London, and Fantasia Barrino, another powerhouse black singer, were consistently voted as the bottom two or three contestants in successive weeks. Elton John, who'd made an appearance as a guest singer and coach for the competitors in an earlier week had been deeply impressed by Hudson, London, and Barrino (who were now being referred to as "The Three Divas" by the press). John attributed the low placement of the three strongest singers in the competition to racism. John argued that "these three girls would have the talent to be members of The Royal Academy or Juillard . . . [t]he fact that they are constantly in the bottom three . . . I find it incredibly racist."[2] Jennifer Hudson did not call the voting racist outright, but she argued that the voting was not based on "talent." She reasoned, "if it was, all three of us wouldn't have been in the bottom three. Maybe one, [but] not all three."[3] London was more coy, stating, "I don't like to blame racism."[4] As the show seemed to increasingly get out of hand, host Ryan Seacrest appealed to the voting audience at home: "You cannot let talent like this slip through the cracks."[5] Black recording artist Missy Elliot promised that even if Fantasia Barrino lost the competition, she would offer the young singer a recording contract. Similar public statements of intent were directed at LaToya London.

Meanwhile, Jasmine Trias, a sixteen-year-old Asian American native Hawaiian with a thin, shaky voice but a sweet demeanor and winning smile, was proving amazingly resilient. She was one of the final three contestants. Critics charged that native Hawaiians were using the Pacific Time difference to pull off a surge of late-night voting for Trias. Her singing voice was embarrassingly threadbare, but Trias seemed blissfully unaware of that fact and of the increasingly uncomfortable racial dynamics taking hold of the competition. When Trias received more votes than Barrino in the week of London's departure, the young Hawaiian's excited smile faltered into confusion when the live audience began to boo after the results were announced. Perhaps more racially savvy than Trias, Dianne DeGarmo—a white teenager from Georgia with an increasingly strong presence and voice—appeared shaken and horrified when Seacrest announced that Trias had beat Barrino in the vote tally. Ultimately, Barrino won the contest after singing a near-perfect and emotional version of the song "Summertime" from Porgy and Bess, beating Diana DeGarmo by 1.3 million votes.[6]

All in all, by the final six weeks, the *Idol* contest had become as exciting and complex as any contemporary American election. Voters were showing tremendous sophistication and dedication to their "candidates." Racial politics were discussed at the watercooler and on the editorial pages of the nation's papers.[7] Using a form of single-shot voting, some voters withheld votes from some of their favorite candidates in order to multiple vote—sometimes up to fifty times—for a candidate they also preferred but who the voter reasoned lacked sufficient support within the larger electorate of viewers. Turnout was regarded as the key to keeping your candidate alive. Like long lines at the polling booth, receiving a "busy" signal when calling in votes caused some viewers to give up; therefore, viewers were exhorted to be persistent and to keep calling back until their votes were recorded. Indeed, millions of votes were cast each week. During the final week of the contest, sixty-five million votes were recorded—at that time, the highest in *Idol* history.[8] Since then, voting has only increased on the show. The finale for the seventh season of *Idol* in 2007 garnered 97.5 million votes.[9] Even assuming multiple voting, the number is staggering and represents an electorate of tens of millions of viewers. The show remains the most single most watched regularly scheduled program in African American households and in the top ten for general audiences as well.[10]

THE 2004 PRESIDENTIAL ELECTION

Ironically, at the same time that *Idol* was making its ascent in the Nielson ratings and attracting the participation of millions, voting experts were decrying the lack of participation of Americans in voting, and many were lamenting the use of voting machinery and techniques that seemed to inhibit rather than encourage voting. With the debacle presidential election of 2000 fresh in voters' minds, a new sense of suspicion had developed about voting. Issues that black and Latino voting activists have complained about for years—voter list purges, voter suppression and intimidation tactics, changes in polling places, long lines, faulty election equipment—had made it onto the front pages of major newspapers and into the larger public's consciousness.

The year 2004 presented an opportunity to right some of the wrongs of 2000. Principal among these for many was the (s)election of George W. Bush as president after a contested election. The Supreme Court's decision to stop the recount and, in essence, permit Bush to become president before all the votes in Florida were recounted,[11] compounded by President Bush's near-unilateral insistence on starting a war with Iraq, had provided a sense that the stakes in the 2004 election were high. Senator John Kerry (D-MA) accepted the nomination from the Democratic Party just as the number of U.S. soldiers killed in Iraq reached the 1,000 mark. Reports put Iraqi civilian deaths between 300,000 and half a million.

A good portion of the focus for this election among Democrats and liberal groups was on the youth vote. Efforts were made by scores of grassroots organizations to interest young people in voting. Hip-hop entrepreneur Sean "P. Diddy" Combs launched a campaign dramatically exhorting members of the hip-hop generation to "Vote or Die." Complete with T-shirts, concerts, and MTV promotion, "Rock the Vote," "Vote or Die," and other similar efforts sought to "politicize" millions of young people.[12] The unspoken but implicit expectation was that this potential voting cohort would vote to oust then President Bush.

Other grassroots organizations focused on states that outlawed voting by ex-offenders and made efforts to change or challenge state constitutions that contained these disenfranchising provisions. Still, others sought to monitor and curb repeats of the voter list purges that had resulted in hundreds of wrongfully disenfranchised voters in Florida in 2000. And then, of course, the traditional "get out the vote" efforts of the two major political parties and major civil rights organizations used standard canvassing and registration techniques to increase the voter rolls. In the end, 64 percent of the electorate, or 126 million people, voted in the 2004 general election.[13] This level of participation did not break voting records, although it was the highest level of electoral participation since 1992. Fifteen million more voters turned out and voted in 2004 than in 2000.[14] The voting rate increased 11 percent for voters between the ages of eighteen and twenty-four from 2000 to 2004.[15]

But the hoped-for outcome of the election was not to be. George W. Bush squeaked by and won the election (although voting irregularities in Ohio, where the Republican

Secretary of State Kenneth Blackwell insisted on certifying Bush as the winner, made even this Bush win suspect to some), and many regarded the success of "get out the vote" efforts as having won the battle but not the war.

REALITY TV AND REAL-WORLD VOTING

Ironicallly, the two voting paradigms unfolding in 2004—*American Idol* and the presidential election—seemed to operate in separate universes. Although *Idol* was experiencing overwhelming voter turnout and enthusiastic participation, no apparent efforts were made by the purveyors and shapers of the political contests to capture and duplicate the success of *Idol*'s voting scheme. And yet the lessons and techniques of *Idol* voting were clearly worth studying. As previously stated, *Idol* showed that many Americans—especially young voters—are quite interested in voting. But this interest in voting flourishes under certain conditions. First, young people are attracted to telegenic, entertaining, *young* candidates. This should not be discounted. More than 16 percent of eligible voters age eighteen to twenty-four who did not vote said that they either "weren't interested" or "didn't like the candidates."[16] *Idol* also provided the opportunity for voters to vote in a way that was convenient (wherever they had access to a phone), using technology with which young people are most comfortable (telephone calls and text messages). This also should be closely examined. Twenty-three percent of eighteen to twenty-four year olds who did not vote in 2004 and nearly 28 percent of voters twenty-five to forty-four years old reported that they did not vote because they were "too busy" or had "conflicting schedules" with polls hours.[17] As one nineteen-year-old young man with two jobs and a pregnant girlfriend explained to a reporter, "I should have voted, but I got a lot to do."[18]

Finally, *Idol* permitted voters to vote passionately and as expressively as possible (multiple voting for preferred candidates). In other words, voters were not only willing to vote for their favorite candidates but were also invested in voting multiple times—even when doing so would cost them something. Although *Idol* phone calls are toll-free, voting either by phone call or text message for *Idol* candidates from a cell phone uses all-important cell phone minutes—a currency often scrupulously guarded by young cell phone users.[19]

Idol also reveals the dark side of modern voting. Electronically disseminated information about candidates has resulted in problems for 3 Idol candidates since the show's inception. Two of the three candidates were people of color. The first, Frenchie Davis, was a African American plus-sized powerhouse singer, who—it was revealed— had appeared in racy photos and appeared on an adults-only Web site.[20] In 2007, racy cell phone photos of Antonella Barbra threatened to railroad her participation in the contest.[21] In 2008, internet rumors that contestant David Hernandez had worked as a stripper at a gay nightclub were later substantiated.[22] Among the three, only the black woman *Idol* contestant, Frenchie Davis, was actually removed from the show by the producers for her photo "scandal." Barbra and Hernandez were voted off the show by viewers—each within two weeks of the revelations involving their conduct. The failure of the producers of the show to remove Barbera for her nude photos 3 seasons after Frenchie Davis was dismissed from the program for largely the same issue—especially when it was revealed that Smith had fully disclosed her work for the adult Web site when she auditioned for the show—resulted in charges of a racial double-standard. Talk show host Rosie O'Donnell called the decision to keep Barbra on the program "racist," in light of the show's earlier summary dismissal of Davis.[23] Of course, the "racial double standard" is a feature of almost every election involving black and white candidates. The racial double standard featured prominently in the 2008 presidential election, particularly as it related to the difficulties candidate Obama faced for his association with his pastor, the Rev. Jeremiah Wright. Youtube, the Web site devoted to amateur videos, played a central role in the controversy. Video clips of Rev. Wright's inflammatory sermons in which, in the tradition of the black church he called America to account for its history of racism and militarism, were used to challenge and question Obama's patriotism and judgment. Yet white Republican candidate Sen. John McCain was given virtually a pass on his association with John Hagee, pastor of a megachurch in Texas, who famously made statements insulting the Catholic church. The controversy over Rev. Wright and the broadcast of Youtube loops of particularly inflammatory sections of Wright's sermons, nearly sank the Obama campaign. By contrast, relatively few voters were even aware of some of the most hateful statements of Mr. Hagee. As one columnist explained, "Mr. Hagee's videos have never had the same circulation on television as Mr. Wright's. A sonorous white preacher spouting venom just doesn't have the telegenic zing of a theatrical black man."[24]

The rise of Idol mischief Web sites like Votefortheworst.com may also be instructive. The Votefortheworst.com Web site came to prominence during the 2008 season of *Idol*. That year, a South Asian-American singer, Sanjaya Malakar, threatened to hijack the competition with a bizarre mixture of poor singing, over-the-top hairdos, and a seemingly unshakeable belief in his own Idol-worthiness.[25] Despite his lack of singing ability and the often painful assessment of his talent by the show's judges, Malakar managed to eke out enough votes week after week to remain on the show. It was revealed that Dave Della Terza, an Idol watcher and critic had created a Web site designed to challenge the very premise of the show. Della Terza noted that in the initial auditions many "good [singers] are turned away and many bad singers or over the top personalities are kept around."[26] As such, Della Terza noted that Idol "is not about singing at all . . . The show starts out every year encouraging us to point and laugh at all of the bad singers who audition." To expose the hypocrisy of the show as a talent competition, Della Terza's site encourages visitors to "rally behind one choice so that we can help make a difference and pool all of our votes toward one common goal," not to win the competition, but "to get a controversial contestant as far as possible."[27] The Web site received a huge boost when radio shock jock Howard Stern took up the cause, encouraging his listeners to use the site to "corrupt" the Idol program.[28]

Votefortheworst.com functions, in essence, as an organized protest vote. Like writing-in a fictional candidate, or organizing votes for a patently unqualified candidate in order to protest the perceived illegitimacy of the electoral process itself, votefortheworst. com is yet another expressive avenue for voters. The embrace of Sanjaya Malakar, and the celebration of his mediocrity by many voters, was a way of speaking out against a show that promised democracy, but that "rigged the system" by conducting auditions in a way that weeded out some of the best talent in favor of contestants likely to bring drama (and thus ratings) to the program. One can easily imagine translating such a challenge into a protest vote against candidates selected by either of the two major political parties—candidates selected not because of their qualifications to do the job, but selected because they are telegenic, sexy or otherwise appeal to voters' baser interests. In fact, the 2003 gubernatorial election in California, after the recall vote that ended the term of Gov. Gray Davis featured 135 candidates—a virtual free-for-all that expressed populist anger at the leadership provided by the two major political parties.[29] Republican actor Arnold Schwarzenegger ultimately won the election with over 4 million votes (over the sitting Lieutenant Governor Cruz Bustamente), in a race that included an adult film actress (who garnered over 11,000 votes), a comedian (over 5,000 votes), and a self-described "custom denture manufacturer" (over 2,000 votes).[30]

But votefortheworst.com also exemplifies how organized technological responses to elections can potentially be used for mischief of a good deal more pernicious variety, than merely seeking to expose the hypocrisy of a popular entertainment program. Groups seeking to suppress or otherwise undermine voter participation can use technology to achieve those ends. Such efforts are most likely to be directed at minority groups.

Post civil-rights era efforts to intimidate minority voters or suppress minority voter turnout have been documented for decades. The allegation (on the sworn testimony of two witnesses) that he was involved in such intimidation at the polls in Arizona in the 1960s, nearly derailed Justice Rehnquist's elevation to Chief Justice at his confirmation hearings in 1986.[31] Efforts to scare off black voters through a North Carolina Republican Party "ballot security" program was one of the features of the contentious, racially charged 1990 contest between the late Senator Jesse Helms and the challenger, African American Charlotte mayor Harvey Gantt. [32] The program was ended after the Justice Department under the elder President Bush stepped in. Actions designed to intimidate minority voters were also reported in the 2004 presidential election.[33] Even the firing of U.S. Attorney David Iglesias by Attorney General Alberto Gonzales in 2007 was largely in response to Iglesias' failure to press ahead with Republican efforts to bring voter fraud cases in New Mexico, where although there was little evidence to support it, Republicans insisted that illegal immigrants and ex-felons were being registered to vote. [34]

In past years "robo calls" to minority voters reportedly warned (erroneously) that you cannot vote if you are behind in your child support payment or if you have unpaid traffic tickets. Other calls targeted at minority communities included false claims that the polling place for Election Day had been moved. These calls are nearly impossible to trace—many likely come from out of state.

Technology may make these voter suppression efforts even more efficient. Intimidating or false voter suppression materials can be disseminated to millions of voters by e-mail. Such e-mails, forwarded by millions of readers, can reach exponential numbers of voters in a few days. Even efforts to *support* black voting rights can result in the mass dissemination of false or misleading information, as evidenced by the near-viral circulation of an e-mail in 2005 and 2006 warning that blacks would lose their voting rights in 2006. The e-mail certainly was directed at garnering grassroots reauthorization of Section 5 of the Voting Rights Act of 1965, which was slated to come before Congress in 2006. But the wording of the e-mail and its mass dissemination encouraged many blacks to believe that their right to vote was not guaranteed by the 15th amendment to the Constitution, but was instead subject to statutory reauthorization.

It is true, of course, that many African Americans were unable to effectively exercise their constitutional right to vote until the passage of the Voting Rights of 1965. But the misinformation circulated by the e-mail warning that for blacks the right to vote would "run out" in 2006 inhibited efforts to educate and mobilize black voters about the specific provisions of Section 5 of the Voting Rights Act that were up for congressional reauthorization. Ultimately, voting rights activists were able to successfully mobilize black and Latino voters to ensure that Congress would reauthorize Section 5 of the Act, appropriately named the Fannie Lou Hamer, Rosa Parks, Coretta Scott King, Voting Rights Reauthorization Act of 2006. But mass e-mails containing misinformation, even when they seek to mobilize minority voters can inhibit targeted and efficient organizing to address real challenges to the exercise of the franchise.

An even more disturbing use of technology for the explicit purpose of voter suppression emerged in 2008. For the first time, it was reported on the day of the 2008 Presidential general election, that black voters received text messages on their cell phones steering them away from the polls. The Maryland ACLU received phone calls on election Tuesday from black voters who received text messages that read, "due to long lines today, all Obama voters are asked to vote on Wednesday." [35] Efforts undertaken to trace the erroneous texts proved unsuccessful. But the use of cell phone or internet technology to suppress minority voting should be expected in future elections.

In sum, although the Idol votefortheworst.com movement represented a legitimate protest against the perceived dishonesty of the *Idol* competition, it also represents the use of technology (in this case the internet) to subvert the legitimacy of the voting process. This is a very real threat to political voting in the U.S., and is one most likely to be directed at minority voters.

THE OBAMA CAMPAIGN AND THE FUTURE OF VOTING RIGHTS ACTIVISM

Barack Obama's sophisticated, youth-oriented, Internet-heavy campaign walked directly into this pop-culture voting environment. His campaign had many of the features that *Idol* voters would have recognized: a young, telegenic, talented candidate and multiple opportunities for engagement over the Internet. The ability of supporters to donate $5 or $10 functioned as the equivalent of multiple phone calls for *Idol* candidates. Obama freed the campaign donations from the traditional form of onetime large gift giving—something out of reach for young people and also for many African Americans. Instead, the ability to give $10 or $20 to the Obama campaign multiple times online permitted voters to "invest" in Obama at a level that was doable for them and also enabled voters to build their commitment to Obama's candidacy over months.

Obama's campaign also harnessed some of the convenience that *Idol*-trained voters had come to expect and that so many young and minority voters have identified as key to their participation. Absentee voting and the opportunity to "early vote" in states like North Carolina increased the convenience of voting for millions. Not surprisingly, candidate Obama emphasized over and over again to his supporters that early voting would be key to his victory and urged voters in the weeks before the election to engage in early voting if possible.

Barack Obama's campaign for the presidency successfully tapped into the electoral environment created by shows like *Idol*. My point, of course, is not to attribute Obama's win to a reality show. His campaign will one day be recognized as one of the most sophisticated, smart, well-organized, substantive campaigns in the history of U.S. elections. The perfect storm of George W. Bush as a failed president, the collapse of the economy, and the weakness of the John McCain–Sarah Palin Republican ticket created an environment in which Obama's overwhelming talents, intelligence, and magnetic power could be *seen* by an electorate that might otherwise have been blinded by race. The full story of President Obama's electoral success is beyond the scope of this chapter.

Instead, I seek to point out to voting rights advocates that, rather than ignore (or worse, roll our eyes dismissively at idea of) popular culture as a training ground for civic participation, we should open our minds to the possibility that popular culture can not only serve as a means for understanding youth culture but can also provide innovative and important ideas about how to improve and invigorate our ideas about voting rights, in particular, and civil rights, in general.

Most voting rights activists are middle-aged. Our ideas about voting—even what we regard as our most radical ideas—are remarkably traditional. We were victorious in pushing for legislation that requires voter registration opportunities in motor vehicle bureaus and social service organizations.[36] But we have not begun to think about "the mall" as a site for civic development, despite the fact that it has become the equivalent of "the public square" for millions of young people. Social networking Web sites like Facebook and MySpace are transforming communication and the idea of "community" for young people. Yet voting activists have not begun to think through how registration and voting must be transformed to acknowledge these developments.

Many of us resisted efforts to push "early voting" or even massive absentee voting, not only out of a fear of compromised ballots, but also out of a form of "old-fashionedness"—a nostalgic commitment to preserving a certain kind of physical "community" of neighbors at the ballot box on Election Day. We fight to prevent polling place changes in the weeks before Election Day without really confronting the anachronism of the geographically static polling place itself. So many elections are for statewide offices or, in the case of the president, for national office. The geographical residence of the voter within the state is largely irrelevant in these elections. And yet we have not seen real efforts to disconnect elections for president and senators from local election contests so that elections for national office could more effectively or perhaps entirely use electronic or mail voting. This would not only benefit young people. In both 2004 and 2006, "too busy" or "conflicting schedule" was the single most reported reason of twenty-five- to forty-four-year-olds *and* age forty-five- to sixty-four-year-olds who did not vote.[37] The percentages of those offering this rationale for not voting was highest among Latino registrants. Thus the inconvenience of traditional polling place voting is a key issue affecting voter turnout.

The idea that *American Idol* has anything to do with *real* voting will likely be dismissed by many voting rights lawyers and activists. And yet, season after season, this program offers a window into electoral politics, race, ageism, voting behavior, and civic participation. The Obama campaign' s use of the Internet and flexible donation opportunities only touched the tip of the iceberg in its successful, if inadvertent, incorporation of some of the lessons of television voting. Ignoring pop culture's contribution to how voting is learned and experienced on the ground is a mistake. To regard the voting that takes place on TV shows as beneath serious civil rights discourse only impoverishes our thinking and activism.

Without question, there is still a great deal of work to be done in the traditional realm of voting rights activism. Pushing back the litigation challenge to the reauthorization Section 5 of the Voting Rights Act,[38] working to repeal state laws that disenfranchise ex-offenders and addressing voter intimidation and suppression efforts remain critical areas of focus. But we must seek to do more than hold the line or inch forward. We must keep a keen eye out for new, innovative, and nontraditional means of increasing the opportunity for voting.

CONCLUSION

Barack Obama's 2008 campaign for the presidency is, without question, the result of brilliant organizing, strategic thinking, and substantive commitment to ideals. It is also a campaign that was birthed in the midst of *American Idol* and its other televised voting progeny (*So You Think You Can Dance, Dancing with the Stars*, etc.). These television voting programs have introduced and cemented voting as a pop-culture exercise for millions of mostly young Americans. Obama's campaign was able to take advantage of an electorate that had grown increasingly sophisticated and engaged in voting as a form of expression. His campaign, perhaps unwittingly, spoke directly to the needs of young voters. Much of the campaign replicated for young voters the personal connection with the candidate, the electoral conveniences, and interactivity that voters had come to expect from *Idol*. The challenge for us going forward is to draw on all sources that may deepen and broaden the scope of our efforts to fully enfranchise those who live at the margins.

NOTES

1. For a full description of the show's format, see http://www.americanidol.com.
2. Associated Press, "Elton John Says 'American Idol' Vote Is 'Incredibly Racist,'" *USA Today*, April 28, 2004, http://www.usatoday.com/life/people/2004-04-28-elton-john-idol_x.htm.
3. Catherine Donaldson-Evans, "Elton John: 'American Idol' Is Racist," Fox News, April 28, 2004, http://www.foxnews.com/story/0,2933,118432,00.html.
4. James Poniewozik, "The Making of an Idol," *Time Magazine*, May 16, 2004, http://www.time.com/time/magazine/article/0,9171,638335,00.html.
5. Ibid.
6. *American Idol* (season 3), available at http://en.wikipedia.org/wiki/American_Idol_(season_3).
7. Kate Aurthur, "Television; An Excess of Democracy," *New York Times*, May 23, 2004, http://query.nytimes.com/gst/fullpage.html?res=9D06E3D9123FF930A15756C0A9629C8B63.
8. Ibid.
9. "'Idol' Viewers Set a Voting Record," TV Decoder, *New York Times*, May 21, 2008, http://mediadecoder.blogs.nytimes.com/2008/05/21/idol-viewers-set-a-voting-record/.
10. Nielsen Media Research, "Nielsen Issues Most Popular List for African American Audiences for 2006," press release, January 24, 2007, http://www.nielsenmedia.com/nc/portal/site/Public/menuitem.55dc65b4a7d5adff3f65936147a062a0/?allRmCB=on&newSearch=yes&vgnextoid=628813ad7b550110VgnVCM100000ac0a260aRCRD&searchBox=la.
11. See *Bush v. Gore*, 531 U.S. 98 (2000).

12. Jose Antonio Vargas, "Vote or Die?: Well, They Did Vote," *Washington Post*, November 9, 2004, p. C1, available online at http://www.washingtonpost.com/wp-dyn/articles/A35290-2004Nov8.html.
13. Kelly Holder, "Voting and Registration in the Election of November 2004," U.S. Census Bureau, Current Population Reports P20-556 (2006), available at http://www.census.gov/prod/2006pubs/p20-556.pdf.
14. Ibid.
15. Ibid.
16. Ibid., table F.
17. Ibid.
18. Vargas, "Vote or Die," xii.
19. Interestingly, some standard features of political electoral contests—like learning the winner on the night of the election—proved to be dispensable. In *Idol* elections, voting is conducted on Tuesday evenings, and the results are announced on a Wednesday night program.
20. Futura Condensed, "Antonella Barba Will Not Be Disqualified from American Idol for Racy Photos." Associated Content, March 1, 2007, http://www.associatedcontent.com/article/164340/antonella_barba_will_not_be_disqualified.html?cat=2
21. Gael Fashingbauer Cooper, "'Idol' Making Up Rules As It Goes Along," MSNBC, March 6, 2007, http://testpattern.msnbc.msn.com/archive/2007/03/06/81894.aspx
22. Associated Press, "Source: 'American Idol' Stripper David Hernandez Won't Be Disqualified," Fox News, March 4, 2008, http://www.foxnews.com/story/0,2933,334740,00.html.
23. Access Hollywood, "'Idol' Producer Slams Rosie Over Frenchie Rant," MSNBC, March 8, 2007, http://www.msnbc.msn.com/id/17523736/.
24. Frank Rich, "The All-White Elephant in the Room," *New York Times*, May 4, 2008, http://www.nytimes.com/2008/05/04/opinion/04rich.html.
25. Chris Ayres, "Why worst crooner's voice may topple American Idol," Times Online, http://www.timesonline.co.uk/tol/news/world/us_and_americas/article1582430.ece.
26. See, http://www.votefortheworst.com/about_us.
27. *Id.*
28. Edward Wyatt, "Howard Stern Tries to Kill 'American Idol' With Kindness for a Weak Link," *New York Times*, March 1, 2007, http://query.nytimes.com/gst/fullpage.html?res=9801E7DA1130F932A05750C0A9619C8B63.
29. See Rick Lyman, "The California Recall: The Candidates; California Voters Wonder: Is Anyone Not Running?," *New York Times*, August 16, 2003, http://query.nytimes.com/gst/fullpage.html?res=9902E0DC1530F935A2575BC0A9659C8B63.
30. California Secretary of State, Elections Division, Statement of Vote, Vote Summaries (2003), available at http://www.sos.ca.gov/elections/sov2003_special/sum.pdf.
31. See Hearings on Nomination of Justice William Rehnquist to be Chief Justice of the United States, July 29-31, August 1 (1986), available online at http://www.gpoaccess.gov/congress/senate/judiciary/sh99-1067/browse.html
32. Associated Press, "THE 1990 CAMPAIGN; Democrats Accuse G.O.P. of Voter Intimidation in Two States," *New York Times*, November, 2, 1990, http://query.nytimes.com/gst/fullpage.html?res=9C0CEFD61739F931A35752C1A966958260.
33. Joe Conason, "Supreme Injustice," Salon.com, October 29, 2004, http://dir.salon.com/story/opinion/conason/2004/10/29/injustice/print.html
34. Amy Goodman, "Former US Attorney David Iglesias on 'In Justice: Inside the Scandal that Rocked the Bush Administration'" DemocracyNow.org, June 4, 2008, http://www.democracynow.org/2008/6/4/former_us_attorney_david_iglesias_on.

35. E-Mail Report from Deborah Jeon, Legal Director, ACLU of Maryland, November 4, 2008, on file with the author.

36. The National Voter Registration Act (NVRA), 42. U.S.C. 1973gg, known as the "Motor Voter Law," designates as "voter registration agencies" all state social service agencies that provide public assistance. The law was enacted in 1993.

37. Thom File, "Voting and Registration in the Election of November 2006," U.S. Census Bureau, Current Population Reports P20-557 (2008), table 6, available at http://www .census.gov/prod/2008pubs/p20-557.pdf; and Holder, "Voting and Registration in the Election of November 2004."

38. In June 2009 the Supreme Court narrowly upheld Congress's 2006 reauthorization of Section 5 of the Voting Rights Act in *North Austin Municipal District v. Holder.*

PART III

THE 2008 PRESIDENTIAL CAMPAIGN AND BEYOND

CHAPTER 12

RACE, POSTBLACK POLITICS, AND THE DEMOCRATIC PRESIDENTIAL CANDIDACY OF BARACK OBAMA

CARLY FRASER

ON FEBRUARY 10, 2007, SENATOR BARACK OBAMA STOOD BEFORE SUPPORTERS ON the steps of the Illinois State House and announced his candidacy for the presidency of the United States. During the course of a stirring speech, he never acknowledged the historic nature of his candidacy as an African American.[1] As one reporter noted, "Not once did the words 'black' or 'African American' pass Mr. Obama's lips."[2] Yet, as the events of his candidacy unfolded, race proved to be a recurring issue, repeatedly acknowledged by the media, his opponents, his surrogates, and eventually by the candidate himself.

This chapter will trace the role of race in the candidacy of Senator Barack Obama during the Democratic primary season of 2007–2008. I will inspect the role that Obama's background and racial identity has played in his run for office as well as his place in the phenomenon of "postblack" politics. Polling numbers, media coverage of race-related issues in the campaigns, speeches given by Obama and his opponents, and academic articles and op-ed pieces on Obama's role as a black politician all provide evidence on how race played a central role in the Democratic primary.

Barack Obama's parents, Ann Dunham and Barack Obama, Sr., fell in love and married in a civil ceremony while studying at the University of Hawaii in the early 1960s. Dunham, a white woman who was raised in Kansas, and Obama, Sr., who was born and raised in Kenya, came from vastly different backgrounds and married at a time in America when interracial marriages were rare. U.S. census data shows that in ıly 0.4 percent of all marriages were between men and women of different ., compared to 2.2 percent today.[3] Shortly after the marriage, on August 4, 1961, ırack Obama, Jr., was born.

When Obama was still a young child, his father left Hawaii and his family to pursue a scholarship at Harvard. In his memoir, *Dreams from My Father*, Obama describes his struggle with identity, growing up biracial while raised by a single, white mother. Dunham made attempts to instill in her son a sense of pride in his African American heritage by reading to him about heroic acts by African Americans in the struggle for civil rights. The stories his mother told made him feel that "every black man was Thurgood Marshall or Sidney Poitier; every black woman Fannie Lou Hamer or Lena Horne. To be black was to be the beneficiary of a great inheritance, a special destiny, glorious burdens that only we were strong enough to bear."[4]

Because Obama spent several years of his childhood in Indonesia, the home of his mother's second husband, and the rest in Hawaii, he was somewhat sheltered from the experiences of being black in mainstream America. Yet, as he grew older, he would grow more conscious of his differences. Growing up biracial at a time when few others shared this experience often caused anger, loneliness, and confusion for the young Obama.

Obama describes his first real reckoning with his racial identity as occurring when he came across a magazine article that told the story of a black man who had tried to alter his skin color: "When I got home that night from the embassy library, I went into the bathroom and stood in front of the mirror with all of my senses and limbs seemingly intact, looking as I had always looked, and wondered if something was wrong with me." Although he states that "this anxiety would pass," he goes on to say that his "vision had been permanently altered": "I began to notice that Cosby never got the girl on *I Spy*, that the black man on *Mission Impossible* spent all his time underground. I noticed that there was nobody like me in the Sears, Roebuck Christmas catalog that Toots and Gramps sent us, and that Santa was a white man."[5]

As he approached adulthood, Obama describes a continuing struggle with his racial identity. He frequently discussed racism with African American and biracial friends he met as a high school student on scholarship at Punahou, a prestigious Hawaiian prep school, and later as a college student at Occidental College in Los Angeles and Columbia University in New York, schools he chose in part because of their proximity to black neighborhoods. He sought out writings by Langston Hughes, Malcolm X, and other African American figures. *Dreams from My Father* describes Obama's young adulthood as a time of deep reckoning with his identity, amplified by the death of his father in Kenya in 1983.[6]

Obama entered Harvard Law School in the late 1980s, where he would become the first African American editor of the *Harvard Law Review*. This experience would give Obama the opportunity to write *Dreams from My Father*. It is not clear whether or not Obama had political aspirations as a law student, but his choice of topic is an interesting one for a politician of the postblack model. Obama's autobiography centers on his search for racial identity, clearly defining himself has an African American who, at times, felt anger and confusion about the state of race relations in America. Yet, Obama writes in a way that emphasizes the complexities of his background and his desire to embrace all of them. This message of reconciliation is one that appeals to a wide variety of readers.

It is impossible to understand the role of race in Barack Obama's candidacy without examining the idea of "postblack" or "postracial" politics and the evolution of African American politics. At the end of the civil rights movement of the 1960s, African American activists began a steady move into the arena of electoral politics. The leaders who came forward at this time defined their politics through their racial experiences, often referred to as a "race-based" political model.

A generation later saw the emergence of the postblack model of African American politics. In *Beyond Black and White*, Manning Marable defines postblack politics as "the rise of African American political candidates who have relatively few connections with organic black social and political formations and institutions, and consciously minimize their identity as 'minority' or 'black.'"[7] In its avoidance of racial issues, this model stands in stark contrast to the race-based model of politics. Marable cites the fact that white Americans have been reluctant to vote for an African American candidate as a factor in pushing black politicians in this direction.[8] By downplaying race and racial conflict in favor of a nonthreatening rhetoric of unity, white voters would be made more likely to vote for a black candidate. Since the publication of *Beyond Black and White* in 1995, public opinion has changed somewhat, showing that whites today are more open-minded than in the past about the race of a candidate. In 1997, a Gallup poll found that 94 percent of Americans would vote for an African American candidate.[9] Yet, it is still clear that many white voters are still reluctant to vote for a black candidate who does not fit into the postblack model.

African American candidates in recent years have adopted the postblack model to political success. The roots of the postracial model can be seen in the campaign and politics of Harold Washington, Chicago's first black mayor. Elected in 1983, Washington was a charismatic leader who was able to build a coalition of African American, Hispanic, Asian American, Jewish, low-income, and liberal white voters to usurp the power of the Cook County Democratic Party machine, led by boss Eddie Vrdolyak. Washington passed away from a heart attack while in office, and unfortunately, the Cook County machine returned to power shortly thereafter.[10] Yet, before his death, Washington promoted a message of progressive reform and racial unity, as a young Barack Obama working as a community organizer on Chicago's South Side took note. Bearing witness to Washington's administration and use of postblack rhetoric undoubtedly had an effect on the aspiring young politician.

More recently, younger black politicians have adopted the postblack or postracial model, Cory Booker, the thirty-eight-year-old mayor of Newark, New Jersey, and Deval Patrick, who won the 2006 Massachusetts gubernatorial campaign by an overwhelming margin, have, like Obama, been classified as being a "part of an emerging generation of politicians who came up after the major battles of the civil rights movement and say they have outgrown its approach."[11]

Early on, Obama saw the positive reaction he received from whites when he presented himself as nonthreatening. In *Dreams from My Father* he describes the tactic he learned to use as a teenager: "People were satisfied so long as you were courteous and smiled and made no sudden moves. They were more than satisfied; they were relieved—such a pleasant surprise to find a well-mannered young black man who didn't seem angry all the time."[12] This early realization may have molded the kind of politician Obama would become. The idea of racial reconciliation over racial anger has been key to his political career. The black-white breach in public opinion when it comes to matters of race is a key factor in this choice of message, for Obama and other postblack politicians. Polling has consistently shown that white Americans are more likely to think that the United States is largely beyond racial inequality and discrimination than black Americans and are therefore less perceptive to rhetoric on race-based inequality.[13] Although Obama has described how the words of Malcolm X resonated with him as a young man, for him to emulate Malcolm's anger would distance himself from many mainstream white voters—because this breach exists.[14] As Ama Mazama stated in a guest editorial in the *Journal of Black Studies*, "Obama's appeal among white Americans, it seems, rests on his perceived ability to transcend race—that is, not to be a Black candidate but simply an American one."[15]

In 2004, Obama positioned himself as a postracial candidate on the national stage during his speech at the Democratic National Convention, where he famously ended his remarks with the words, "There's not a liberal America and a conservative America—there's the United States of America. There's not a black America and a white America and a Latino America and Asian America—there's the United States of America."[16] Yet, Obama has been careful not to imply that his message of unity means that America has overcome racial division, as he wrote in his 2006 book, *The Audacity of Hope*:

> When I hear commentators interpreting my speech to mean that we have arrived at a "postracial politics" or that we already live in a colorblind society, I have to offer a word of caution. To say that we are one people is not to suggest that race no longer matters—that the fight for equality has been won, or that the problems that minorities face in this country and largely self-inflicted. We know the statistics: On almost every single socioeconomic indicator, from infant mortality to life expectancy to employment to home ownership, black and Latino Americans in particular continue to lag far behind their white counterparts. In corporate boardrooms across America, minorities are grossly underrepresented; in the United States Senate, there are only three Latinos and two Asian members . . . and as I write today I am the chamber's sole African American. To suggest that our racial attitudes play no part in these disparities is to turn a blind eye to both our history and our experience—and to relieve ourselves of the responsibility to make things right.

These words of caution are important because they make it clear that Obama has a profound commitment to the African American community, despite the fact that racial issues are not central to his political message.

Obama's non-race-based rhetoric gained him early support among liberal whites; however, black Americans were less willing to immediately support his candidacy when he announced that he would be running for president. African American political leaders initially hesitated in endorsing Obama, due in part to the generational division in political philosophy between the race-based politics grounded in the civil rights movement and Obama's role as a postracial candidate. Reverend Al Sharpton, for example, was skeptical of Obama's ability to understand the needs of black voters. Shortly after Obama's announcement, Sharpton stated, "Just because you are our color doesn't make you our kind. . . . It's not about his genealogy, it's about his policies. . . . What is it that you're going to represent?"[17] Scholar Cornel West also called on Obama to speak out more forcefully on issues of race.[18] Former presidential candidate Jesse Jackson criticized Obama publicly for not calling more attention to the Jena 6, a group of young black men arrested on attempted murder charges in Jena, Louisiana, for the beating of a white student after three nooses were hung from a tree on their school's grounds in 2006. Obama had released a statement stating that he felt the charges were inappropriate, but he did not have any extended response to the arrests. One South Carolina newspaper reported that Jackson accused Obama of "acting like he's white" regarding the incident. Jackson later said he did not recall making the statement.[19]

Mainstream African American voters were also reluctant to support the candidate. One question raised frequently was whether or not Obama was "black enough" to win the support of African American voters. Obama's white mother, Hawaiian and Indonesian upbringing, and Ivy League education made many African Americans skeptical about his ability to represent their needs. Obama has stated he was "rooted in the black community, but not defined by it."[20] In November of 2007, only 50 percent of black Americans felt that Obama "shared their values," while only 41 percent of blacks with a high school education or less saw Obama "as a part of the black community."[21] Many questioned if Obama could truly understand the needs of black Americans, given that his father had been a voluntary immigrant to the United States rather than a descendant of the involuntary migration of the transatlantic slave trade.

The popularity of former President Bill Clinton among many African Americans posed another challenge for Obama in gaining the support of black voters. Often referred to as America's "first black president" (a name bestowed on him by African American Nobel and Pulitzer Prize–winning writer Toni Morrison), Bill Clinton enjoyed high approval ratings among black Americans due to the appointment of several African Americans to government positions, his support of affirmative action, and his launch of a race initiative during the second term of his presidency to create a national dialogue.

However, the actual positive impact of President Clinton's policies on black Americans is debatable. Scholars like Monty Pillawsky have accused Clinton's gestures toward African Americans as purely symbolic and have criticized his attempts at centrist triangulation, which resulted in a crime bill and welfare reform that did more to hurt than to help black Americans, particularly those most in need. Nevertheless, when Hillary Rodham Clinton, the former first lady and senator from New York, entered the Democratic race, it was evident that much of her husband's popularity among African Americans also applied to her. Early polling showed that African American voters favored Clinton 60 percent to Obama's 20 percent.[22]

While Obama's background may have been difficult for many black voters to identify with, his wife Michelle's more conventional background made her a key voice in speaking to African American communities. Born Michelle Robinson, the candidate's wife was raised on the predominantly African American South Side of Chicago by working-class parents. As an undergraduate she attended Princeton, a predominantly white Ivy League school, where her white freshman year roommate's parents were so "horrified" at the idea of having a black roommate they tried to have their daughter's room reassigned. Michelle went on to major in sociology with a minor in African American studies.[23] In her senior thesis, "Princeton-Educated Blacks and the Black Community," Michelle wrote of the challenges facing black American college students: "I have found that at Princeton, no matter how liberal and open-minded some of my white professors and classmates try to be toward me, I sometimes feel like a visitor on campus; as if I really don't belong. Regardless of the circumstances under which I interact with whites at Princeton, it often seems as if, to them, I will always be black first and a student second."[24]

Her choice of thesis topic shows that issues of race were very much a part of Michelle Robinson's consciousness. Her experiences as the wife of a politician have been no different. When Obama had to minimize race to fit into the postracial model, it was Michelle who spoke to black audiences about how her husband would be the best candidate to represent their needs. Campaigning in Atlanta in January 2008, Michelle Obama spoke to a crowd of African Americans, addressing the issue of race head-on: "I know that the life I'm living is still out of reach for too many women. Too many little black girls. I don't have to tell you this. We know the disparities that exist across this country, in our schools, in our hospitals, at our jobs and on our streets. . . . If my husband were here, he'd tell you that inequality isn't a burden we have to accept, but a challenge to overcome."[25] Michelle Obama's straightforward, no-nonsense approach to campaigning for her husband was crucial in gaining support for her husband's candidacy in primary states with large black electorates.[26]

Soon after the announcement of his candidacy, Barack Obama would be in a position to address black voters on March 4, 2007, the forty-second anniversary of the Selma Voting Rights March. The media presented this event as a "battle" or "showdown" for the African American vote, since Obama would be making a speech to commemorate the event at Selma's Brown Chapel AME Church and Hillary Clinton would be giving a speech at the nearby First Baptist Church, with husband Bill at her side.[27]

Obama used this opportunity to relate his experience to that of the African Americans in his audience:

A lot of people been asking, well, you know, your father was from Africa, your mother, she's a white woman from Kansas. I'm not sure that you have the same experience. And I tried to explain, you don't understand. You see, my Grandfather was a cook to the British in Kenya. Grew up in a small village and all his life, that's all he was—a cook and a house boy. And that's what they called him, even when he was 60 years old. They called him a house boy. They wouldn't call him by his last name. Sound familiar?[28]

The words of the candidate's speech and the ease with which he addressed his audience helped to diminish some of the speculation over Obama's "blackness." The image of an African American presidential candidate speaking on the historic site and his call to black voters to take action presented Obama as a politician who had an investment in the black community. Although his opponent's parallel speech was well received, there was some speculation over whether Clinton's words pandered to the African American audience, as she at times affected a southern accent and described going to hear Martin Luther King, Jr., as a teenager, although in her autobiography she described her support for Goldwater's run for president in 1964, a candidate who opposed the 1964 Civil Rights Act.[29] The combination of these factors contributed to Obama's rise in the polls among African American voters. The momentum had begun before the Selma appearance, with polls showing Obama over Clinton 44 to

33 percent among African American voters in the week before. The results from the upcoming primary states would show African American support for Obama grow even further.[30]

The election season's first caucus was held on January 3, 2008, in Iowa. With a predominantly white population (93 percent), Iowa would be a test of how Obama's message of change and postblack rhetoric had played with white voters. Entrance polling demographics showed that Obama won 33 percent of the white vote in Iowa, over Clinton's 27 percent and North Carolina Senator John Edwards's 24 percent. Polling also showed that most black voters in Iowa were willing to support Obama over the other candidates. Seventy-two percent of African American caucus-goers supported Obama, while Clinton only received 16 percent and Edwards 8 percent.[31] Iowa was a significant turning point for the candidate, for it showed that he had the ability to attract white voters in Middle America in large numbers over two well-known and popular white candidates.

Between the Iowa and New Hampshire primaries, comments made by Hillary Clinton would serve to further damage her popularity among African American voters. Obama's charismatic rhetorical style, youth, and message of unity had drawn comparisons to Dr. King, as well as to President Kennedy. Clinton, faced with her opponent's momentum, responded to the comparisons in a January 7 Fox News interview, saying, "Dr. King's dream began to be realized when President Johnson passed the Civil Rights Act. . . . It took a president to get it done."[32] Although it was unstated, the implication appeared to be that Clinton was to Johnson as Obama was to King; as she used it to reinforce her charge that Obama was merely a speechmaker while she was an action taker. There was much debate over whether or not Clinton's comments diminished the legacy of Dr. King. The media focused heavily on Clinton's comments, and Obama called it "an unfortunate remark" that he believed offended many people. Historical evidence does show that President Johnson was instrumental in passing the 1964 Civil Rights Act.[33] Yet, as John Nichols pointed out in an online article in *The Nation*, "her comment came across as precisely the sort of crude and self-serving interpretation of history that Americans expect from the lesser of our leaders. And that it was. By so casually referencing the complex role that civil rights agitation played in forging racial progress, she invited the firestorm that has come."[34] As more African American voters began to support Obama, Clinton's comments regarding President Johnson and Dr. King resonated negatively with those black voters (and voters of other races as well) who were still undecided, increasing Obama's rise in the polls.

Comments made by Bill Clinton on the morning of the New Hampshire primary were also criticized as being racially charged. Visually upset over the fact that many television pundits were predicting that Obama would shortly become the Democratic nominee and that Hillary Clinton's presidential run, after a third-place finish in Iowa, was coming to an end, Clinton railed against what he classified as Obama's negative tactics and the consistency of his position against the war during an appearance in New Hampshire. He went on to state, "Give me a break. This whole thing is the biggest fairytale I've ever seen."[35] Coming immediately after Hillary Clinton's comments on Dr. King and President Johnson, the issue of race was ignited once again as commentators asked whether Clinton's comments implied that Obama's historic candidacy was a "fairytale." Clinton denied that interpretation of his words, stating that he was only referring to Obama's stance on Iraq, but this statement once again raised questions about the Clintons' relationship to the black community.[36]

Heading into the New Hampshire primary on January 8, 2008, following his success in Iowa, Obama was favored to win in most polls. The Rasmussen poll showed Obama leading Clinton 37 percent to 30 percent.[37] Like Iowa, New Hampshire was another state where the majority of voters were whites (the U.S. Census Bureau statistics show that 95.8 percent of the population of the state is white, while African Americans make up only 1.1 percent).[38] In the media, Obama was predicted to not only win the state primary but also the entire Democratic nomination. Yet, once the votes were counted in New Hampshire, Clinton won the state with 39.1 percent of the vote over Obama's 36.5 percent and Edwards's 16.9 percent.[39]

One explanation for the discrepancy between the polling and the actual result is what is known as the Bradley effect. In 1982, Tom Bradley ran for governor of California. If he won, he would become the first African American governor of the state, and polls showed that he was favored to do so by overwhelming margins. Bradley's white opponent, George Deukmejian, trailed him by double digits. Yet, on Election Day, Bradley lost. Similar trends presented themselves in the 1989 mayoral race between David Dinkins and Rudy Giuliani (Dinkins would win, but by far less of a margin than polls predicted), the Virginia gubernatorial race between Douglas Marshall and Douglas Coleman that same year, and the North Carolina senatorial race between Harvey Gantt and Jesse Helms. A look at polling returns in these cases showed that those voters who identified themselves as "undecided" voted overwhelmingly for the white candidate, suggesting that these voters were unwilling to tell pollsters that they supported the white candidate for fear of appearing racist, or they felt that both candidates were equally capable, but in the privacy of the voting booth could not bring themselves to vote for the black candidate.[40]

The recent elections of Cory Booker in Newark and Deval Patrick in Massachusetts seemed to suggest that the Bradley effect has diminished in recent years, owing to an increasingly progressive white electorate. However, the results of the 2008 New Hampshire primary call into question if the effect was at play in the state. It is possible that undecided white voters, once they entered the voting booth, were influenced by underlying prejudices that prevented them from voting for Obama—a factor that would have been less of an issue in the more public caucus process in Iowa, where fellow community members may question their racial open-mindedness. Alternatively, it may have been the fact that women voted in unexpected numbers, motivated by the prospect of losing their chance to elect the nation's first female president.[41] There was also speculation that the negative reporting on Clinton by the media, a moment of emotion she showed while campaigning in the state, and the sexism exhibited by men at a Clinton appearance shouting "iron my shirt" also played a role in increasing sympathetic female turnout for Clinton at the polls. This combination of factors should be taken into account when analyzing the disparity between the New Hampshire polling and election returns.

New Hampshire proved that the road to the nomination would be neither short nor easy for Obama, yet he had a chance to make a strong showing in the upcoming South Carolina primary. That election, on January 26, 2008, would be the first time in the primary season that a state with a substantial African American population would go to the polls. Demographically, the primary voters were 55 percent black and 43 percent white.[42] With both Obama and his wife Michelle campaigning heavily in the state, Obama won the primary with 55.5 percent of the vote, over Clinton by almost 30 percentage points. An overwhelming 78 percent of black voters chose Obama over Clinton and Edwards.[43] Four days after the South Carolina primary, Edwards suspended his campaign.[44]

Once it was clear that Obama had the support of the majority of black voters over Clinton, his opponents shifted their rhetoric from portraying him as "not black enough" to portraying him as "too black."[45] This process began with comments made by Bill Clinton. After Obama's sweeping win in the state, Clinton spoke to reporters after a rally, saying, "Jesse Jackson won South Carolina in '84 and '88. Jackson ran a good campaign. And Obama ran a good campaign here."[46] The comments were largely criticized, since they appeared to minimize Obama's win as a consequence of the high percentage of African Americans in the state. Further, connecting Obama with Jackson presented him as a race-based candidate rather than a postracial candidate. While Jesse Jackson stated publicly that he had no problem with the comparison, Obama spoke out against the statement, calling it a "certain brand of politics" where "anything is fair game."[47] Whether Clinton's comments should be considered racist for diminishing the importance of states with large black populations, the message of divisiveness was clear, and it would become more prominent as the race continued.

The Super Tuesday primaries on February 5, 2008, would present a different kind of racial challenge for Obama. Several states voting that day, among them California, New Mexico, New York, and New Jersey, had high Latino populations, raising questions over whether Obama would have trouble courting Hispanic votes due to the popularly held view on the existence of a black-brown divide in American politics. The actual existence of this divide has been debated. Political scientist Fernando Guerra has argued against this view, saying, "It's one of those unqualified stereotypes about Latinos that people embrace even though there's not a bit of data to support it. . . . In Los Angeles, all three black members of Congress represent heavily Latino districts and couldn't survive without significant Latino support."[48] Yet, other scholars have argued otherwise. Author Earl Hutchinson has argued that "tensions between blacks and Latinos and negative perceptions that have marred relations between these groups for so long unfortunately still resonate," predicting shortly before Super Tuesday that "there will still be reluctance among many Latinos to vote for an African American candidate."[49]

Although results from Super Tuesday showed that Clinton did win much of the Hispanic vote, the results were more nuanced than most media reports would indicate. Obama showed strong support among Hispanic voters in Connecticut and New Mexico.[50] These complexities make sense, as the term "Hispanic," instituted by the U.S. Census Bureau in the 1970s, encompasses a wide range of Americans with Spanish surnames who do not necessarily share similar values, nationalities, or experiences. However, the fact that many Latino voters supported Clinton helped her to remain in the race. Super Tuesday ended with Obama in the lead in the delegate count, yet Clinton was close enough to continue to be a contender in the race.[51]

With a nominee still unselected after the Super Tuesday primaries, the MSNBC televised debate moderated by journalist Tim Russert on February 26, 2008 was highly anticipated as the two remaining candidates both tried to position themselves as the presumptive nominee. Halfway into the debate, Obama was asked to account for the fact that Louis Farrakhan, the controversial leader of the Nation of Islam, had recently endorsed him in his bid for the presidency. Russert first asked Obama if he accepted to support of Farrakhan, to which Obama responded, "I have been very clear in my denunciation of Minister Farrakhan's anti-Semitic comments. I think they are unacceptable and reprehensible. I did not solicit this support. He expressed pride in an African American who seems to be bringing the country together. I obviously can't censor him, but it is not support that I sought."

After this response, Russert pressed further, asking Obama if he rejected Farrakhan's support. When Obama again failed to use the word "reject," Russert again brought up Farrakhan's record of anti-Semitism. Clinton then interjected to suggest that Obama should "reject" rather than simply "denounce." Obama handled the situation by turning it into a question of semantics, stating that he did not see any real difference between the words "reject" and "denounce," "but if the word 'reject' Senator Clinton feels is stronger than the word 'denounce,' then I'm happy to concede the point, and I would reject and denounce."[52]

The idea that black political figures must publicly denounce black controversial figures like Farrakhan has been prominent for several years and has no equivalent in white electoral politics. Journalist Marjorie Valbrun provided a possible answer to why the "Farrakhan Litmus Test" has become so prominent: "Maybe it's because some white people will always need black leaders to denounce controversial (read: threatening) figures in order to feel comfortable with the very notion of black leadership. . . . Maybe black people have a hard time denouncing—at the command of whites—other black people, especially those who despite their worst characteristics, have also done some good for the larger black community."[53] The double standard in calling for Obama to denounce Farrakhan was made clear on February 27, when Republican candidate John McCain received the endorsement of evangelist John Hagee, who had made public statements claiming that Hurricane Katrina was God's punishment for sin in New Orleans (specifically homosexuality), that the Quran has a clear "mandate" to kill Christians, and that women should "submit" to the lead of their husbands.[54] Yet, on his Sunday morning political program, *Meet the Press*, Russert, who had pressed Obama on the Farrakhan issue at the debate just days before, ignored a reference made about the Hagee endorsement. McCain would eventually reject Hagee's endorsement during the general election.

In early March, race would again be injected into the media dialogue on the Democratic race with comments made by former Democratic vice presidential candidate and Clinton supporter Geraldine Ferraro. In a newspaper interview with a small California newspaper, Ferraro stated, "If Obama was a white man, he would not be in this position. And if he was a woman [of any color] he would not be in this position. He happens to be very lucky to be who he is. And the country is caught up in the concept." The implication that Obama was only enjoying electoral success because he is black struck many as ridiculous and shocking, particularly coming from such a prominent leader of the Democratic Party. Ferraro stepped down from her role as an advisor to the Clinton campaign, and Clinton publicly stated that she "did not agree" with Ferraro. Yet Ferraro continued to defend her comments, insisting on their validity. *Chicago Sun-Times* columnist Mary Mitchell responded by writing that "if being black is the magic ingredient for a successful 'historic' campaign, then Shirley Chisholm, Jesse Jackson, Al Sharpton, Carol Moseley Braun and Dick Gregory" would have been much more successful in their presidential runs.[55]

The historic occurrence of having a woman and an African American as viable candidates for the American presidency sparked considerable dialogue concerning both gender and race in politics. With election returns showing Clinton with much of the female vote and Obama with much of the African American vote, it often appeared that the two historically disenfranchised groups were pitted against one another. In a campaign where there are few policy differences between the candidates, identity became for many voters a major factor in choosing which candidate to support. There was also debate over whether female or black candidates faced more prejudices in running for office. Psychological studies have shown that gender stereotyping is more common than racial stereotyping, yet racial stereotypes are more commonly associated with negative opinions. As one article on the topic notes, "Male chauvinists don't dislike women, they just have particular ideas about their capabilities and how they should behave—but with race, stereotypes tend to go hand-in-hand with prejudice."[56] As this historic Democratic primary unfolded, racist and sexist stereotypes and prejudices were apparent. It was impossible for anyone to judge whether it is "more difficult" to be a black politician or a female politician, as both face challenges, have been historically disenfranchised, and still today women and African Americans (as well as Latinos, Asians, non-Christians, and other groups) are drastically underrepresented in political life.

Besides race and gender, prejudices revolving around religious identity would also play a prominent role in the Democratic primary. Obama's identity as a man of African heritage with an African Muslim name would cause suspicion among many voters. Although all non-white, non-male, and non-Protestant political figures have faced significant hurdles in running for office, in post-9/11 America, Muslim Americans may face the greatest challenge. While recent polls have shown that over 90 percent of American voters could vote for a black candidate and 88 percent for a woman candidate, a 2006 poll showed that only 34 percent of Americans would vote for a Muslim candidate.[57]

Although speculation about Obama's connection to Islam made many voters wary, it would be a news cycle concerning his relationship with his Christian pastor that would prove to be most problematic for him. Since the announcement of his candidacy, Obama's opponents and conservative news networks had been trying to stir the issue of his relationship with his outspoken pastor, Jeremiah Wright, and to portray his church, Chicago's predominately black Trinity United Church of Christ, as dangerously radical. Then, in early March 2008, video clips of Wright surfaced, drawing immediate and overwhelming attention from the media. The clips showed Wright making statements implying that the United States was to blame for 9/11 because of its foreign policy and that the U.S. government was involved in spreading the AIDS virus. Perhaps the most replayed clip from the Wright sermons was one in which the pastor proclaimed that instead of singing "God Bless America," black Americans should sing "God Damn America."

The media and the public immediately questioned why Obama would have such a close relationship with a man who had these views and why he would be a member of his church for so many years. Obama had first started attending Trinity while working as a community organizer in Chicago, where he found the connection to an African American community he had sought growing up. Reverend Wright officiated the Obamas' wedding and baptized their two children, Sasha and Malia. Obama also used the title of one of Reverend Wright's speeches as the title of his second book, *The Audacity of Hope*. Trinity was, and still is, one of Chicago's most prominent churches, boasting a congregation of "Chicago's influential thinkers and leaders," including, at one time, Oprah Winfrey. In an article on Trinity and Obama's membership, the *Chicago Tribune* wrote that "for someone thinking of running for mayor, governor, senator or any statewide office, being part of Trinity would likely be an asset."[58]

Yet, once he entered the national stage, Obama foresaw Wright's potential as a political liability, particularly in an election where appealing to white, working-class voters was crucial to winning the nomination and the general election. Wright, having come of age during the civil rights era, preached messages that were more race-based than postracial. Although Wright had retired as pastor of Trinity, conservative blogs and programs questioned the Obamas' relationship with his pastor early on. In response, Obama asked Wright to step down from his role of giving the invocation at the announcement of his candidacy, a move that was criticized by Reverend Al Sharpton.[59]

Yet, Obama's initial attempts to distance himself from Wright proved insufficient to avoid controversy. The clips of Wright's sermons were played nearly constantly on cable news and became a subject of national discussion. The March release of the clips would pose a significant test for Obama as a postblack political figure. While Obama had sought to present himself as a uniting leader, avoiding discussion of racial divisions, the Wright controversy brought race to the forefront. In the days following the release of the clips, Obama denounced Wright's words, but the media and the American public continued to question Obama's relationship with Wright. This response showed that it was not enough for Obama as a postblack politician to avoid showing anger over issues of racial inequality; he also could not have relationships with African Americans who were publicly angry about the state of race relations in America. The clips also highlighted the black-white breach in public opinion. A poll taken by the Pew Research Center showed that 58 percent of white Americans were personally offended by Wright's sermons, compared with 29 percent of black Americans.[60]

The media firestorm and reaction from the American public made it clear that Obama would need to make a statement regarding his relationship with Reverend Wright. Obama chose to do this through a speech given on March 18, 2008, in Philadelphia, titled "A More Perfect Union," a speech that would address the state of race relations in America. In this speech, Obama faced the challenge of talking about race in a way that would speak to white and black voters of varying backgrounds and attitudes.

He began the speech by recognizing the importance of the American Constitution as well as its "original sin"—slavery. He described his patriotism and desire to build unity despite this fundamental flaw, citing the way his campaign had built a coalition of voters from all racial backgrounds. In addressing Reverend Wright, Obama made clear that he disagreed with his words, particularly their divisive message, but that he would not disown a man who has "been like family" to him. He went on to recognize the good works Wright had done for his community and to say that he could "no more disown him than I can disown the black community. I can no more disown him than I can my white grandmother—a woman who helped raise me, a woman who sacrificed again and again for me, a woman who loves me as much as she loves anything in this world, but a woman who once confessed her fear of black men who passed by her on the street, and who on more than one occasion has uttered racial or ethnic stereotypes that made me cringe."

These phrases made it clear that many in the black community, particularly those like Wright who experienced a time before the civil rights movement, are angry about the state of race relations in America. They also made clear that stereotypes and prejudices still exist and cannot be ignored. While addressing this reality, the ultimate message of Obama's speech was one of hope that the union described in the Constitution could be strengthened.[61] While to many academics and liberals the issues Obama raised were not groundbreaking, the speech was remarkable in its ability to speak to those white voters who may not have given serious thought to racial inequalities before while maintaining his postracial message of unity.

The reaction to Obama's handling of the situation was largely positive. A poll by the Pew Research Center shows that 51 percent of voters familiar with the Wright controversy rated his handling of the situation as "excellent" or "good." Sixty-six percent of Democrats, 48 percent of white voters, and 75 percent of black voters also gave his response a positive rating. Even one-third of Republicans felt that he handled the situation well.[62] Yet, there was media speculation whether Obama had done enough to distance himself from Wright.

Up until the speech, the Clinton campaign had remained largely quiet concerning the Wright controversy (presumably because it was doing enough to challenge Obama's reputation among white voters without their comment), Clinton did tell the Pittsburgh *Tribune Review* that "he would not have been my pastor . . . you don't choose your family, but you choose what church you want to attend." The Obama campaign accused Clinton of making these statements in order to draw attention away from a controversy she herself was negotiating, concerning overstatement of the danger she faced during a trip to Bosnia as first lady.[63] Regardless of her motivations in making this statement, the continuation of the Wright controversy could only benefit the Clinton campaign, particularly when experts were judging her changes of winning the nomination at 10 percent. In order to gain enough delegates to win the nomination, she would need the Obama campaign to experience a significant setback, which the Wright story had the potential to be.[64]

The true test of whether Obama successfully weathered the Wright controversy would be his performance in the Pennsylvania state primary on April 22, 2008, a state with a large white, working-class electorate. As polls predicted, Clinton won the state over Obama 56.6 to 45.4 percent, with 60 percent of the white vote but only 8 percent of the black vote.[65] Although Obama had made gains in the state (early 2008 polling, before the Wright controversy broke, showed Clinton over Obama by 20 percentage points), the win justified the continuation of the Clinton campaign.[66]

As the Obama campaign looked ahead to the upcoming primaries in Indiana and North Carolina and tried to put the Reverend Wright media cycle behind them, the controversy would resurface as Wright made public statements to the media at the end of April. In an interview on PBS, Wright stated that Obama said "what he [had] to say as a politician," insinuating that the candidate did not truly disagree with the opinions expressed in the clips.[67] The next day, in a press conference at the National Press Club, Wright made comments about Louis Farrakhan, 9/11, and the sins of the American government that echoed the divisiveness Obama had rejected from the earlier clips of Wright's sermons.[68]

Obama reacted by publicly severing ties with Wright in a press conference on April 29, 2008.[69] Again, there was speculation over the effectiveness of Obama's handling of the situation. Would Reverend Wright's most recent comments lead voters to believe that Obama shared his pastor's views? Would the complete severing of the relationship reassure voters? Would voters who believed that he shared his pastor's views not have ultimately voted for him anyway? It may be that those who believed that Obama shared his pastor's views would not have noted for him ultimately anyway. A *New York Times*/CBS poll, taken immediately after Obama's most recent press conference on Wright, showed that Obama's connection to Wright had not affected their opinion of him for most voters, but that they thought that the Wright controversy would affect Obama in the general election.[70]

As in Pennsylvania, the May 6 primaries in Indiana and North Carolina were a litmus test for how well Obama weathered the more recent comments of Reverend Wright—and whether the delayed rejection of his pastor was seen as sufficient to a skeptical electorate. Obama was largely expected to win in North Carolina, because of the state's large African American population (33 percent). Indiana, with its largely white and working-class population, was in question. As the results came in Tuesday night, Obama proved that he had been able to weather Wright's incendiary comments. Election results showed that Obama won North Carolina with 56 percent of the vote and Indiana brought essentially a split decision, with Clinton winning by a margin of 1 percent.[71]

The next contests in West Virginia and Kentucky would pose a bigger challenge for Obama. Demographically, both states favored Clinton, with their largely white, working-class populations. On May 13, Clinton won West Virginia with 67 percent of the vote, and on May 20, she won Kentucky with 65 percent.[72] Following her landslide victories in West Virginia and Kentucky, Clinton sought the support of superdelegates by making the case that she was more electable than Obama in important states against John McCain. Racially, this proved to be a problematic argument. Exit pollsters in West Virginia and Kentucky asked voters whether race was an important factor in deciding their vote. Twenty-two percent of voters in West Virginia said that race was an important factor, and 8 percent said that it was the "single most important factor." Twenty-one percent of voters in Kentucky cited race as an important factor, with 7 percent citing it as the "single most important factor."[73] In both states, voters who answered in the affirmative voted overwhelmingly for Clinton. These comparatively high percentages were more alarming when one considers the trend evidenced in the Bradley effect in which white voters who hold prejudices are often reluctant to express them, meaning that the actual percentage of voters who felt that race was an important factor might be higher.

Several newspaper opinion writers and television pundits questioned why Clinton would not denounce the prejudices of her supporters, which would undoubtedly be an ethical but politically complicated action. Clinton instead chose to emphasize her high regard for these voters. In an interview with *USA Today*, Clinton stated that

"Senator Obama's support among working, hard-working Americans, white Americans, is weakening again, and how whites in both states who had not completed college were supporting me."[74] Many commentators felt that these comments, while praising those voters who admitted to racial prejudices, also seemed to suggest that Obama would be unable to win in the general election because white Americans were not ready to elect an African American president. Suggesting this struck many as shocking, particularly coming from a democratic candidate.

As the Democratic primary season came close to an end and Senator Obama maintained a consistent but close lead over Senator Clinton, it became clear that decisions made prior to the primary season regarding Michigan and Florida would need to be addressed again, particularly as the two states would be important in the general election. Because the two states held their primaries before February 5, 2008, the date set by the Democratic National Committee (DNC), Michigan and Florida had been stripped of their delegates. The primaries were still held, although the candidates signed a pledge not to campaign, and Obama, along with John Edwards, Bill Richardson, and Joe Biden, took his name off the ballot in Michigan. Under these circumstances, Clinton won in both states.[75] Voters in Florida and Michigan, who were not responsible for moving the dates, could not be completely disenfranchised, particularly in such a close and historic primary race. Neither could the votes be fully counted in the primaries as they were held. Clinton had a vast advantage in both states because none of the candidates campaigned there (and she was far better known as a former first lady) and in Michigan because voters did not have the option of voting for any of the other main contenders.

On May 31, 2008, the DNC Rules and Bylaws Committee met to make a decision on how to seat the Michigan and Florida delegations. Representatives from both states and both campaigns presented their proposals. Clinton surrogates who spoke at the meeting called for the full seating of the delegations based on the primaries that had taken place, borrowing from civil rights era rhetoric to make their case. In the days leading up to the Rules and Bylaws meeting, Senator Clinton traveled to Florida to make her case for counting the votes in Florida and Michigan as they were placed, in a speech in which she evoked the struggles of "the men and women who knew their Constitutional right to vote meant little when poll taxes and literacy tests, violence and intimidation made it impossible to exercise their right, so they marched and protested, faced dogs and tear gas, knelt down on that bridge in Selma to pray and were beaten within an inch of their lives."

Certainly, taking away the votes of two states would be a significant breach of civil rights. The problem with Clinton's use of civil rights rhetoric to support her view of seating all the delegates is that this action would be equally in opposition to civil rights and would effectively be using unconstitutional elections to, in the eyes of many Americans, "take" the nomination from the first African American nominee to a major political party. Furthermore, Clinton had supported the repeal of voting rights in these states at the outset of the primary season, when she signed the pledge to not campaign in Florida or Michigan. Therefore, the use of this rhetoric caused anger among some commentators, as Ben Smith wrote on Politico.com: "It's not just that she's convinced herself it's okay to try to steal the nomination, she has also appropriated the most sacred legacies of liberalism for her effort to do so."[76]

Following a long and impassioned televised meeting on May 31, 2008, the DNC's Rules and Bylaws Committee, a group containing supporters of both candidates, decided to assign each delegate in Florida and Michigan half a vote.[77]

With Michigan and Florida resolved and a seemingly insurmountable lead, Obama was now widely seen as the presumptive nominee of the Democratic Party. On June 3, 2008, the day of the South Dakota and Montana primaries, a steady stream of superdelegates publicly endorsed the Illinois senator throughout the day. By the early evening, Obama had reached 2,118 delegates, the number needed to secure the Democratic nomination.[78] In announcing this achievement, media outlets paid great attention to the historic fact that Americans had selected the first African American to be the nominee of any major political party.

Yet, in his speech that night to a large crowd of supporters in St. Paul, Minnesota, Obama did not make reference to the historic fact that he was the first African American to be selected as the nominee of any major political party, reflective of his February 10, 2007, candidacy announcement. He again emphasized the postblack message, dedicating the speech to his white grandmother and highlighting the diversity of his coalition, saying, "There are young people, and African-Americans, and Hispanic-Americans, and women of all ages who have voted in numbers that have broken records and inspired a nation."[79]

Senator Obama was not alone in failing to mention the historic significance of the moment. The night he received the amount of delegates needed to secure the nomination, Senator Clinton also gave a much-anticipated speech. Although the Associated Press had reported that Clinton would be conceding, Clinton declared before supporters in Manhattan that she "would not be making any decisions" that night. Yet, to many who were moved by the fact that the country had elected its first African American nominee, it was not that Senator Clinton chose not to concede that they found disturbing, but that she refused to acknowledge that her opponent had achieved this historic goal. When asked by a reporter about the fact that Obama supporters may have been angered by the speech, Clinton campaign chairman Terry McAuliffe exclaimed, "Tonight was Hillary's night!"[80]

Following Clinton's speech on June 3, the Democratic leadership, including many of her own supporters, called for her to suspend her campaign, since Obama had reached the number of delegates needed for the nomination and there was an eagerness to unite a party that had become deeply divided between the two candidates.

The speech ending her campaign was held on Saturday, June 7, 2008, at the National Building Museum in Washington, D.C. Given the long and passionate campaign, Clinton knew that it was important to express her unequivocal support for Senator Obama to urge her numerous supporters, many of whom told pollsters that they would vote for McCain over Obama in the general election.

With the nomination finally secured, Obama's victory brought increased optimism to a large number of African Americans, many of whom doubted they would see a black nominee in their lifetimes. Given that most of the voters who elected Obama as the nominee of the Democratic Party were white, African Americans interviewed for a *New York Times* article expressed feelings of hope, particularly for the opportunities this would provide for their children. As one women stated, "When she's out in, God knows where, some small town in rural America, they'll think, 'Oh, I know someone like you. Our president is like you. . . . That just opens minds for people, to have someone to relate to. And that makes me feel better, as a mom."[81] Pop culture reflected this sentiment, as shown in the lyrics of a song released by rapper Nas in the week Senator Obama received the nomination.

Despite his positive message, Nas also puts forward questions and fears about an Obama presidency, most notably the threat of assassination and whether or not Obama will be committed to the issues facing African American communities.[82] These questions would highlight the struggle that lay ahead as Senator Obama campaigned for the general election.

As the nominee of the Democratic Party, Senator Obama certainly faced more challenges because of his race in the general election against John McCain. McCain did not actively discourage his campaign and his surrogates from engaging in race-baiting tactics, although his family had been the victim of racial attacks targeted at his Bangladeshi daughter (who was adopted as an infant) in the 2000 Republican primaries.[83] The Republican Party also extended efforts to use race to its advantage, as was evident in smears made against Michelle Obama, painting her as an angry black radical. Republican groups tried to connect Barack Obama to controversial black leaders such as Farrakhan and revived the words of Reverend Wright in an attempt to inspire fear in white voters, even though in the final days of the Democratic primary, Obama formally withdrew his family's membership at Trinity following the remarks of a guest speaker at the church who claimed that Senator Clinton felt entitled to the nomination because she was white.

In the end, of course, Barack Obama overcame the many obstacles put in his path, and on November 4, 2008, he won the presidency of the United States by a large margin of both the popular and the electoral vote. Using the postracial model and a message of change, he became the first African American president, just as he had become the first African American candidate with a real chance of being elected president. Although he sought to avoid focusing on issues of race, the realities of being a black presidential candidate—and then president—in a country with deep-seeded divisions and a troubled racial history has made the topic central for the last two years; race will remain a central focus of inquiry and discussion. In that regard, Barack Obama opened a much-needed racial dialogue in this country, one that he will have the opportunity to continue as president.

NOTES

1. "Full Text of Senator Barack Obama's Announcement for President," February 19, 2007, http://www.barackobama.com (accessed May 30, 2008).
2. T. Baldwin, "Obama Seeks 'Stay Fresh' Formula as He Tries to Widen Appeal," *Times* (London), February 12, 2007.
3. "Race of Wife by Race of Husband: 1960, 1970, 1980, 1991, 1992," U.S. Bureau of the Census, June 10, 1998, http://www.census.gov/population/socdemo/race/interractab1.txt (accessed June 12, 2009).
4. Barack Obama, *Dreams from My Father* (New York: Crown, 1995), 51.
5. Ibid.
6. Ibid., 52.
7. Manning Marable, *Beyond Black and White* (New York: Verso, 1996), 203.

8. Ibid.
9. Nicholas Kristof, "Obama and the Bigots," *New York Times*, March 8, 2008.
10. Manning Marable, *Black Leadership* (New York: Columbia University Press, 1998), 127.
11. Damien Wade, "Cory Anthony Booker: On a Path that Could Have No Limits," *New York Times*, May 10, 2006; Frank Phillips, "It's Patrick in a Romp: Bay State Win Makes History," *Boston Globe*, November 8, 2006.
12. Obama, *Dreams from My Father*, 94–95.
13. Claire Jean Kim, "Managing the Racial Breech: Clinton, Black-White Polarization, and the Race Initiative," *Political Science Quarterly* 117, no. 1 (Spring 2002): 55–79.
14. Obama, *Dreams from My Father*.
15. Ama Mazama, "The Barack Obama Phenomenon," *Journal of Black Studies* 38, no. 1 (2007): 3.
16. Barack Obama, "Keynote Address at the 2004 Democratic National Convention," July 27, 2004, http://www.barackobama.com (accessed May 10, 2008).
17. Manning Marable, "Racializing Obama," *Along the Color Line*, April 2008.
18. Ginger Thompson, "Seeking Unity, Obama Feels Pull of Racial Divide," *New York Times*, February 12, 2008.
19. Alexander Mooney, "Jesse Jackson: Obama Needs to Bring More Attention to Jena 6," CNNPolitics.com, September 19, 2007, http://www.cnn.com/2007/POLITICS/09/19/jackson.jena6.
20. "Candidate Obama's Sense of Urgency," *60 Minutes*, February 11, 2007.
21. Juan Williams, "Obama's Color Line," *New York Times*, November 30, 2007.
22. Ibid.
23. Brian Feagans, "Georgian Recalls Rooming with Michelle Obama," *Atlanta Journal Constitution*, April 13, 2008.
24. Michelle LaVaughn Robinson, "Princeton-Educated Blacks and the Black Community" (BA thesis, Princeton University, 1985).
25. Allison Samuels, "Daring to Touch the Third Rail," *Newsweek*, January 28, 2008.
26. Lauren Collins, "The Other Obama," *New Yorker*, March 10, 2008.
27. Anne E. Kornblut, "At Site of '65 March, an '08 Collision," *Washington Post*, March 2, 2007.
28. "Full Text of Barack Obama's speech at the Selma Voting Rights March Commemoration," http://www.barackobama.com, March 2007.
29. Patrick Healy and Jeff Zeleny, "Obama and Clinton Mark Civil Rights Struggle," *New York Times*, March 4, 2007; Dick Morris, "Obama's Selma Bounce," RealClearPolitics.com, March 8, 2007, http://www.realclearpolitics.com/articles/2007/03/obamas_selma_bounce.html.
30. Dan Balz and Jon Cohen, "Blacks Shift to Obama, Poll Finds," *Washington Post*, February 28, 2007.
31. "Profile of the Iowa Caucus Goers," *New York Times*, http://politics.nytimes.com/election-guide/2008/results/vote-polls/IA.html (accessed June 20 2008).
32. Sarah Wheaton, "Clinton's Civil Rights Lesson," *New York Times*, January 7, 2008.
33. Mary Jo Murphy, "Phone Call into History," *New York Times*, January 27, 2008.
34. John Nichols, "MLK, LBJ, Clinton, and the Politics of Memory," *The Nation*, January 14, 2008, http://www.thenation.com.
35. Kate Phillips, "The Clinton Camp Unbound," *New York Times*, January 8, 2008.
36. Carl Hulse and Patrick Healy, "Bill Clinton Tries to Tamp Down 'Fairy-Tale' Remark About Obama," *New York Times*, January 11, 2008.

37. "Election 2008: New Hampshire Democratic Primary: Final New Hampshire Poll: Obama 37% Clinton 30%," *Rasmussen Reports*, January 8, 2007, http://www.rasmussenreports .com/public_content/politics/election_20082/2008_presidential_election/new_hampshire/ election_2008_new_hampshire_democratic_primary.

38. "State and Country Quick Facts: New Hampshire," U.S. Bureau of the Census, http:// quickfacts.census.gov/qfd/states/33000.html.

39. "New Hampshire Primary Results," *New York Times*, http://politics.nytimes.com/ election-guide/2008/results/states/NH.html.

40. Eugene Robinson, "Echoes of Tom Bradley," *Washington Post*, January 11, 2008.

41. Ibid.

42. "Profile of the South Carolina Primary Voters," *New York Times*, http://politics.nytimes .com/election-guide/2008/results/vote-polls/SC.html (accessed June 20 2008).

43. "South Carolina Primary Results," *New York Times*, http://politics.nytimes.com/election -guide/2008/results/demmap (accessed June 20 2008).

44. "John Edwards in New Orleans," *New York Times*, January 30, 2008.

45. Marable, "Racializing Obama."

46. Anne E. Kornblut, "For Bill Clinton, Echoes of Jackson in Obama Win," *Washington Post*, January 26, 2008.

47. Katharine Q. Seelye, "Jackson: Not Upset by Clinton Remarks," *New York Times*, January 28, 2008.

48. Gregory Rodriguez, "The Black-Brown Divide," *Time*, January 26, 2008.

49. Jaime Reno, "Black-Brown Divide," *Newsweek*, January 26, 2008.

50. Nancy Cook, "Race, Ideology Shaped Super Tuesday Vote," NPR.org, February 6, 2008, http://www.npr.org/templates/story/story.php?storyId=18738766.

51. "Super Tuesday Results," Salon.com, htpp://www.salon.com/news/feature/2008/02/05/ election_results.

52. "Feb. 26 Democratic Debate Transcript," MSNBC Online, http://www.msnbc.msn.com/ id/23354734/.

53. Marjorie Valbrun, "To Denounce and Reject," TheRoot.com, February 27, 2008, http:// www.theroot.com/views/denounce-and-reject.

54. Katie Halper, "Top Ten Outrageous Quotes from McCain's Spiritual Advisors," Open-Left.com, May 1, 2008, http://www.openleft.com/showDiary.do?diaryId=5517.

55. Mary Mitchell, "Ferraro Fails to Grasp Why She's So Wrong," *Chicago Sun-Times*, March 13, 2008.

56. Drake Bennett, "Black Man vs. White Woman," *Boston Globe*, February 17, 2008.

57. Kristof, "Obama and the Bigots."

58. Christi Parsons and Manya A. Brachear, "What Led Obama to Wright's Church?" *Chicago Tribune*, May 3, 2008.

59. Jodi Kantor, "Disinvitation by Obama Is Criticized," *New York Times*, March 6, 2007.

60. "Obama Weathers the Wright Storm, Clinton Faces Credibility Problem," Pew Research Center, March 27, 2008, http://people-press.org/report/407/.

61. "Remarks of Senator Barack Obama: 'A More Perfect Union,'" http://www.barackobama .com, March 18, 2008 (accessed Match 19, 2008).

62. "How Has Obama Handled Controversy?" Pew Research Center, March 27, 2008, http:// pewresearch.org/pubs/823/reverend-wright-press-coverage.

63. Patrick Healy, "Clinton: Wright Would Not Have Been My Pastor," *New York Times*, March 25, 2008.

64. David Brooks, "The Long Defeat," *New York Times*, March 25, 2008.

65. "Profile of the Pennsylvania Primary Voters," *New York Times*, http://politics.nytimes .com/election-guide/2008/results/vote-polls/PA.html.

66. "2008 Pennsylvania Democratic Presidential Primary," Pollster.com, January 2008, http:// www.pollster.com/08-PA-Dem-Pres-Primary.php.

67. Julie Bosman, "Wright Says His Words Were Twisted," *New York Times*, April 24, 2008.

68. Kate Phillips, "Wright Defends Church and Blasts Media," *New York Times*, April 28, 2008.

69. Jeff Zeleny, "Obama Says He's Outraged by Ex-Pastor's Comments," *New York Times*, April 29, 2008.

70. Adam Nagourney and Marjorie Connelly, "Poll Shows Most Voters Unaffected by Wright," *New York Times*, May 5, 2008.

71. "Democratic Contests," *New York Times*, http://politics.nytimes.com/election-guide/2008/ results/demmap.

72. Ibid.

73. "Politics / 2008 Primary Results / Exit Polls / West Virginia Democrats," http://www .msnbc.msn.com/id/21226014/, and "Kentucky Democrats," http://www.msnbc.msn.com/ id/21225982/.

74. Suzanne Smalley, "The Raison d'Etre du Jour: Clinton's Latest Line: Obama Can't Win 'White Americans,'" *Newsweek Online*, May 9, 2008.

75. Ben Smith, "Off the Ballot in Michigan," www.Politico.com, October 9, 2007, http:// www.politico.com/blogs/bensmith/1007/Off_the_balllot_in_Michigan.html. ; Jeff Zeleny, "Clinton, Obama, and Edwards Join Pledge to Avoid Defiant States," *New York Times*, September 2, 2007.

76. Jonathan Chait, "Clinton's Shocking Florida Gambit," *New Republic Online*, May 21, 2008.

77. Michael Falcone, "D.N.C. Cuts Fla., Mich. Votes in Half," *New York Times*, May 31, 2008.

78. Jeff Zeleny, "Obama Claims Nomination; First Black Candidate to Lead a Major Part Ticket," *New York Times*, June 4, 2008.

79. "Barack Obama's Remarks in St. Paul," *New York Times*, June 3, 2008.

80. Michael Crowley, "In the Clinton Bunker," *The New Republic*, June 4, 2008.

81. Marcus Mabry, "Many Blacks Find Joy in Unexpected Breakthrough," *New York Times*, June 5, 2008.

82. Nas, "Black President," http://www.lyricsdomain.com/14/nas/black_president.html.

83. Richard H. Davis, "The Anatomy of a Smear Campaign," *Boston Globe*, March 21, 2004; Jennifer Steinhaur, "Mrs. McCain, Demure in 2000, Is Speaking Up in a Steely Tone," *New York Times*, June 19, 2007.

SOVEREIGN KINSHIP AND THE PRESIDENT-ELECT

JOY JAMES

This election had many firsts and many stories that will be told for generations. But one that's on my mind tonight's about a woman who cast her ballot in Atlanta. She's a lot like the millions of others who stood in line to make their voice heard in this election except for one thing: Ann Nixon Cooper is 106 years old.

She was born just a generation past slavery; a time when . . . someone like her couldn't vote for two reasons—because she was a woman and because of the color of her skin. . . .

In this election, she touched her finger to a screen, and cast her vote, because after 106 years in America, through the best of times and the darkest of hours, she knows how America can change.

—Barack Obama, November 4, 2008

A CENTENARIAN BLACK WOMAN AS REPRESENTATIVE OF AMERICA'S NEW MULTIRACIAL consciousness is a powerfully poignant depiction of democracy born in a former slave state. Barack Obama's narrative in his "This Is Your Victory" speech displays popular sovereignty emerging from the biography of a subordinated citizen-in-waiting (albeit an elite one given that Mrs. Cooper came from a privileged black family). Political elites and politicians, however, wield a sovereign kinship that does not easily share power with the populace.

There is evolving multiracial and gender-inclusive popular sovereignty, as represented by Ann Nixon Cooper; and there is emergent multiracial sovereign kinship, as represented by the president-elect. The story woven around Ann Nixon Cooper filtered one hundred years of U.S. American history, culminating in the election of its first black president. Its symbolism sweeps past distinct differences between voters and the political class they install in a representative (rather than a direct) democracy. This symbolism deflects attention from the contradictions of inequalities and dominance in a democratic nation.

Sovereignty is the ability to determine political destinies, one's own and those of others. Popular sovereignty is the myth and matter of modern democracy. In a representative democracy dominated by a two-party system, wealth and remoteness infuse the national political class. The sovereignty of the poor, the colored, the female, the queer,[1] the ideologically independent—as non-elites and non-"mainstream"—is rooted in their agency and autonomy, their ability to lead politicians rather than follow them. Although their more talented and ambitious members may join the ruling elites, historically disenfranchised outsiders to the political realm have had no inherent kinship with the dominant political class. Possessing no sovereign powers stemming from an autonomous political base, they control no governmental, police, military, or economic institutions; through such structures, traditional sovereign kinship exercises its aspirations and will.

Politically marginalized groups might fare less well in a direct democracy; but in such a system, recognizing themselves as the true agents for change, they may more often seek sovereignty to resist both repression and the political class that represents them. Historically excluded from voting, blacks organized economic boycotts to end lynching and segregation. Their contributions to democracy worked beyond electoral politics from which they were often barred. The end result is that U.S. representative democracy has become more "participatory," as defined by a more diverse electorate and its desire to elect representatives who reflect that diversity. Out-groups remain hopeful that elected officials will function as their advocates rather than pursue conventional power shaped by a two-party system and sovereign elites.

Yet, in 2000, the U.S. Supreme Court demonstrated its sovereign kinship against the majority vote. The political class designed the Electoral College to override the popular vote. However, by installing George W. Bush as president, the Supreme Court intervened in the Florida recount to determine the electoral vote. The failure of the defeated party to contest this suggests that these battles for high office are intrasovereign affairs. Even if the "improbable journey" of the president-elect seems at odds with that interpretation, one should note how singular and symbolic representation of blackness remains within federal government. Among its three branches, only the Supreme Court and executive branch have surpassed the Senate in racial segregation.

Polymorphous politicians seek to represent all things good to all people voting. Their purpose is to consolidate and exercise power. As "centrists" synthesizing two powerfully entrenched parties, they can ignore critical third parties while skillfully transferring agency to a kinship of political insiders. Electoral politics is a marvelous route by which sovereign kin pose as "outsiders." On the campaign trail, they become "regular" folks—intimates with Joe six-packs and plumbers, churchgoers, hockey moms, beer guzzlers, and misguided bowlers. The difference between grassroots activism and Astroturf organizing is that the primary role of activists is to determine policy—not to elect politicians. Activists seek sovereignty, not representatives of it. The mobilization of the "grass roots" or "Astroturf"—Internet-based communication that simulates or stands in for a mass movement—permits voters to relinquish or transfer agency to elected officials. A less controlled democracy ensues from mass participation that is not reduced to mass rallies, technological social networking, national days of service, or mobilizations to buttress state policies. The seductive appeal of U.S. democracy lies in its ability to make the electoral changing of the guard synonymous with political power in the mind of the citizen. The power of seduction depends on the desire to surrender; in the absence of that, it is just political rape.

Voters can select from among the political class to replace sovereign kin. The tyranny of the majority—portrayed by a homogenized mainstream that provided the "darkest hours" for Ann Nixon Cooper's kin—has often been directed or manipulated by its representative political class. With social and ethnic minorities within its ranks, the multicultural majority in making history on November 4, 2008, appears to have vanquished racial tyranny. America can and does change.[2] Its dependence on political elites and restrictive right to rule may not. Rather than enable independent political parties and populist self-rule, sovereign kin promote a more diverse or multiracial political class.

As a member of this political class, the president-elect becomes progenitor and founding father of a millennial multiracial democracy. That impressive feat is not necessarily synonymous with "power to the people." Of the varied independent or outsider spaces to be corralled under one flag, the president-elect represents the one that, more than class, gender, sexuality, or political ideology, became the defining mark for the failure and promise of American democracy—race. The phenomenon of the 2008 election may not be the electoral victory understood as a triumph over racism, but the sovereign kinship and the sovereign whiteness that permitted this achievement. Lacking poverty, queerness, femaleness, and ideological independence, Barack Obama's form of blackness became an asset, an embraceable opportunity traceable through improbable political bloodlines.[3]

A GENEALOGY OF THE POLITICAL CLASS: A FORTY-FIVE-YEAR MARCH ON AND TO WASHINGTON

Barack Obama debated Hillary Clinton at the flagship university. But he did not campaign in the home place of the men who contributed most significantly to his becoming America's first black president-elect. (Refusing to credit them, he instead invoked Kennedy and Reagan.) Perhaps in 2008 Obama knew he could lose a red state not quite ready for purple, yet sweep the Electoral College. Texas had not gone for a Democratic presidential candidate since Lyndon Baines Johnson's election in 1964.[4] The conservative state prides itself on having been the residence of three presidents: Johnson (1963–68), George H. W. Bush (1988–92), and George W. Bush (2000–2008). The first president led the nation deeper into an unpopular war with genocidal results: 58,226 Americans died while contributing to the deaths of more than two million Vietnamese. The United States escalated the war in Vietnam based on Johnson's deception about a fabricated August 4, 1964, attack on U.S. naval destroyers in the Gulf of Tonkin. President Johnson built up John F. Kennedy's war and, in turn, was surpassed in mass casualties by President Richard Nixon and Secretary of State Henry Kissinger, who expanded the war with secret bombings of Cambodia. Although Johnson's interventionism squandered American wealth and lives, that did not stop two other Texans from emulating him.

Unlike his foreign policy violations of the human rights and national sovereignty of nations resisting colonizers, Johnson's domestic policies promoted democracy and economic opportunities for the formerly enslaved. His presidential alter ego propelled the 1960s civil rights agenda and antipoverty programs. He witnessed the assassinations of John Kennedy, Robert Kennedy, and Martin Luther King, Jr.: two sovereigns and one agitator who disturbed his equilibrium. Nonetheless, while King built the moral pillars, Johnson installed the legal foundation—as he strong-armed the 1964 Civil Rights Act and the 1965 Voting Rights Act through Congress—for a foreseeable Obama victory. Liberal sovereigns and progressive activists created new expressions of democratic rule, incorporating fictive kin to create a future multiracial political elite. This elite though would emerge at the expense of a broad-based pacifist insurgency against repression.

Reverend King would stand beside President Johnson as he signed key legislation that transformed the political and electoral landscape. He had also stood behind this sovereign leader as he deflected television cameras from Student Nonviolent Coordinating Committee (SNCC) activist Fannie Lou Hamer at the 1964 Democratic National Convention (DNC). As a member of the multiracial Mississippi Freedom Party (MFDP) delegation, attempting to unseat Mississippi's official white supremacist delegates, Hamer's impassioned demand, "Is this America?" seared the airwaves, leaving little room for centrists and accommodating political operatives such as the president's media spokesman, a young Bill Moyers; his vice presidential running mate, the seasoned Hubert Humphrey; and the venerated Christian leader. The three would work to force Hamer and the MFDP delegation into a compromise, with full recognition that the alternative progressives demanding a full franchise lacked the sovereign power to win a presidential election but possessed enough transformative power to destabilize a major party at the polls.

Johnson was so consumed by a devastating and unpopular war that he declined to run for a second term. He would not be the last Texan to leave the Oval Office disgraced in wartime by low approval ratings. Johnson had sold Fannie Mae and Freddie Mac to private interests in order to pay for the war in Vietnam. Bush-the-son would theoretically buy the mortgage lenders back in a $750 billion bailout, ballooning the national debt, after squandering a trillion-dollar surplus inherited from President Bill Clinton. Invading a country his father had stormed a decade earlier to vanquish a foreign enemy that the elder Bush as director of the Central Intelligence Agency had helped to install, Bush-the-son pronounced "mission accomplished" in 2003. That defeated country held no weapons of mass destruction and no ties to al-Qaeda, Osama bin Laden, or the September 11, 2001, attacks on the United States. The invasion of Iraq would help make the United States an internationally recognized human rights violator and debtor nation, as war costs spiraled to more than a $1 billion a month. It would also give in 2007 a novice public servant but shrewd politician a major peace platform by which to differentiate himself from his fellow senators and presidential rivals. Senators Hillary Clinton and John McCain had voted for what would become an unpopular war leading to mass death and genocide.

Between the 1960s retirement and political murders of national leaders and the 2009 retreat by Bush-the-son to Dallas—a city that gained notoriety when Kennedy was shot in his motorcade—Bush-the-father defeated a Democratic rival by running one of the most racist campaigns in the post–civil rights movement era. George H. W. Bush allowed Republican National Committee chair Lee Atwater to make good on his 1988 campaign promise to position convicted black rapist Willie Horton as the running mate of presidential candidate Massachusetts Governor Michael Dukakis. Although Bush deployed the "southern strategy"—where whites vote against their economic interests based on their social fears and antiblack animus, he was routed in 1996 by a husband whose wife's future presidential campaign would be supported by xenophobes and racists among "hard-working whites" and "Hillary Democrats."

Racism's psychosexual politics was increasingly becoming an inside joke for sovereign whiteness. The most incendiary racial baggage tied to the candidate who would be president were (a) President Johnson's former medical attendant, a black marine and Vietnam veteran turned pastor who castigated U.S. racism and imperialism; and (b) false allegations of the politician being both the national and international bête noire. With the economic downturn, the public became disinterested in racial and political outcasts, including an affluent white radical who used mass casualties in Vietnam to justify Weather Underground domestic bombings against government targets. The southern strategy had become an unpredictable regional phenomenon. An electorate going bankrupt can distinguish between Willie Horton and Jeremiah Wright and find both increasingly irrelevant to their pressing economic crises. The violent criminality attributed to the domestic bête noire, now extended to the Muslims,[5] and the political incivility of the preacher were less pressing concerns for mainstream America. Neither the Clinton nor McCain campaigns could foist a faux running mate onto a black candidate who had already established kinship ties with DNC leadership.

DNC CONVENTIONS AND THE FAMILIAL PARTY

After he won the Iowa caucus, America began to take Barack Obama seriously as he continued to campaign against an unpopular war that led the nation toward moral and economic bankruptcy. When he won the North Carolina primary, despite the Clinton surge, it became evident that the notion of race-based sovereignty and familial ties were forever splintered by the autobiography of the candidate: white mother, black African father, devoted maternal white grandmother, loyal Ivy League-educated, Southside Chicago girl-turned-political wife. Read by millions, Barack Obama's *The Audacity of Hope* and *Dreams from My Father: A Story of Race and Inheritance* made consistent claims, echoed insistently on the campaign trail: "nowhere but in America" and "my life is an American story." In gratitude to the nation, the candidate increasingly dismissed charges of antiblack racism against its racial majority and its institutions. Thus, he revealed himself as self-made, aligned with traditional political power rather than sovereign blackness (the existence of the latter is generally doubted). Mixed-race black, unwed mother, abandoned by father—pariah became parvenu through sovereign kinship. Winning more primaries and the delegate count, Obama traveled to Denver to accept the nomination at a skillfully organized DNC.

In Denver, DNC sovereign kin staged a party that surpassed all previous conventions. Before cameras, the Democrats posed as a functional and disciplined family, generations beyond the 1968 Chicago riots and 1972 hawk-and-dove infighting over the war that contributed to their defeat and the election, twice, of Richard Nixon. In 2008, unity and goodwill were such that no discernible fractures shaped by ideology, gender, race, or sexuality (class seemed to have disappeared) showed. On the convention platform, the future first lady, Michelle Obama, who had earlier stated her uncertainty about voting for the former first lady as nominee given the attacks against her partner, thanked Clinton for the eighteen million cracks in the glass ceiling. One-third of those eighteen million voters were male and perhaps not all were pro—women's rights; some were against gay and lesbian rights; a small number publicly indicated that they could never vote for "a black." That all became irrelevant as Michelle Obama's speech displayed a humility and gratitude—as well as a pride in being American—absent from Hillary Clinton's cautious concession. Having sovereign whiteness, Clinton did not need to demonstrate patriotism or belonging when she emphatically stated that she would vote for Obama while releasing her delegates to vote their conscience. The following evening, with extemporaneous remarks fired by the rousing ovation for the former president, Bill Clinton's eloquence overshadowed her reticence to instruct everyone to vote for the president-elect.

A predecessor of Ann Cooper Nixon appeared in Hillary Clinton's concession. Calling out Harriet Tubman as an expression of populist belonging, Senator Clinton, though, did not mention Tubman's specific history in radical politics. Illiterate in antiracist history, most Americans could perceive Tubman as a symbol yet remain unfamiliar with her improbably journey. Just as with Ann Nixon Cooper, there was the burden of slavery (although with closer proximity to violent trauma). While Cooper survived discrimination and hardships long enough to vote for the first black president, Tubman stole and liberated herself. Electing sovereign kin and opposing sovereign powers are both political acts. Yet only the latter is an expression of defiance against injustice through independence from institutional power. Tubman's national political life began as an outlaw freeing slaves, what her detractors and the law defined as looting property.[6] A conductor on the "underground railroad" and supporter of the insurrectionist John Brown (with his sons, the white abolitionist was executed at Harper's Ferry for violent opposition to slavery), Tubman saw her reputation augmented as a distinguished militarist and spy who fought with the Union Army with 200,000 other African Americans to defeat the Confederacy.

Thus Clinton could name her, a black woman who also organized in the suffrage movement, but not cite Tubman's political lineage, as would be done for the white suffragette Susan B. Anthony. To present her with specificity, as more than a symbol, would enable the rebel to appear as a sovereign, in control of her own life and those lives entrusted in her care—even as they wandered, hunted in the wilderness. At the 2008 DNC convention, Tubman would be the first but not last black (female) political figure stripped of agency in opposition to a repressive American democracy.

The democratic presidential nominee chose the forty-fifth anniversary of King's "I Have a Dream" speech and March on Washington as the backdrop to showcase the new multicultural Democratic Party. The final night of the Democratic convention was held on August 28, the anniversary of the 1963 march and the great, hopeful sermon of Reverend King, whose oratory had helped Johnson in his presidential bid. Perhaps seeking inspiration and electoral uplift without the weight of antiracist activism, Obama invoked "the preacher" in his 2008 acceptance speech. Rendering King nameless, he embraced him as an abstraction. The label "the preacher" is conveniently worn by white evangelical conservatives and black liberationist pastors alike. With black liberationists as one-dimensional illustrations, with no acknowledgment of their opposition to state violence, King joined Tubman as symbolic representation of a multiracial democracy embodied in the Democratic Party. Denver's football stadium hosted a political pageant that appropriated political activists who had enabled that historic moment to unfold in time.

During the 2008 democratic primaries, Martin Luther King, Jr., had become a touchstone; he was portrayed as a key relation for Obama and Clinton. April of that year marked the fortieth anniversary of his assassination in Memphis, Tennessee, where he had gone to support striking sanitation workers. The presidential inauguration would take place the day after the national holiday commemorating King's birth. During the primary debates, Obama insisted that activism abolished American apartheid. Clinton maintained that the government, through the Johnson administration, was the enabler of King's legacy and the demise of segregation. When asked which of the two Democratic candidates King would have endorsed, Obama replied, "Neither." Yet, that did not prevent the candidates from appending "the preacher" to their campaigns.

Whereas King failed to lead a dominant political class to which he did not belong, Obama forty years later successfully morphed into it as fictive kin. King's diminishing popularity stemmed from his resistance to the Vietnam War, which he described as imperialist, and his critiques of racism and capitalism. His prophetic voice became an anathema to those pursuing imperial powers, and the *New York Times* castigated King for his opposition.[7] Obama's growing popularity and endorsements stemmed from his advocacy of a unified state and the restoration of its imperial might (to be used only for good). Both men understood and acquiesced to America's selective notion of elite leadership and sovereign kinship. Only King would later repudiate the sovereign elite in favor of another form of kinship. That kinship was partly forged in antiblack repression and terror and partly forged in a spirit or spirituality for liberation.

It is unclear if the president-elect, in choosing the anniversary of the March on Washington for his acceptance speech, was aware that the march, largely organized by labor activists such as A. Phillip Randolph, took place on the anniversary of the 1955 lynching of Emmett Till, a black teen from Chicago visiting Mississippi who allegedly whistled at a white woman on a dare. A fourteen-year-old boy from Obama's adoptive hometown, Till's torture, murder, and open-casket funeral would galvanize the civil rights movement that produced Martin Luther King, Jr., as an international human rights icon.[8] From the floor of the Denver stadium, only Jesse Jackson, Sr., also a Chicago adoptee, publicly recalled the Till tragedy in his August 28 interview with *PBS News Hour* correspondent and anchor Gwen Ifill.[9] Few may have heard or remember Jackson's reflections[10] as they uncovered Emmett from anonymity and Americans from amnesia.

While Emmett's lynching was given limited recognition at the DNC, the "four little black girls," immortalized as a nameless collective, received none. In 1963, bombings followed the historic march. The one placed in Birmingham's Sixteenth Street Baptist church killed children activists. Lacking sovereign kinship, these black girls' names, like Emmett's, would not be spoken from a stage in which the contemporaneously slain, sovereigns such as President John F. Kennedy and Senator Robert Kennedy would be honored. Yet, Denise McNair (11), Addie Mae Collins (14), Carole Robertson (14), and Cynthia Wesley (14), and the other teens who would die in the Birmingham riots following the bombing, contributed dearly to this multiracial democracy. Few Americans would have any idea of the price paid so that two little black girls could join their parents on the Denver platform to present themselves to an approving American electorate.

CONCLUSION: HAGAR'S KIN AND BLACK SOVEREIGN RELATIONS

[In the Hebrew Testament, as the African owned by Abraham and the barren Sarah] Hagar's predicament involved slavery, poverty, ethnicity, sexual and economic exploitation, surrogacy, rape, domestic violence, homelessness, motherhood, single-parenting and radical encounters with God. . . . Paul [in Galatians 4:21–5:1] relegated her and her progeny to a position outside of and antagonistic to the great promise Paul says Christ brought. . . . Hagar and her descendents represent the outsider position par excellence.

—Delores Williams, *Sisters in the Wilderness*

At the 1964 Democratic convention, dispossessed activists risked their lives to dispute the claims and qualifications of political elites. Former sharecropper, forcibly sterilized, Fannie Lou Hamer was crippled by a savage beating when jailed for trying to vote. She was fired from her job, and kicked out of her home because of her organizing for a greater democracy. Without radical activists such as Hamer, there would be no franchise for Ann Nixon Cooper and millions of others, and no black president-elect. Positioned by the political class, along with SNCC, as divisive and antagonistic to the promise of an American democracy manifested through Democratic Party victories, Hamer would not be validated by any president. Ideological arborists severed Tubman, King, and Hamer from the political tree, only to selectively graft branches for politicians seeking symbols to stir a populace.

In 1964, President Johnson was so unsettled by a crippled but not yet beaten black woman exercising political power through antiracist and black sovereign relations that he called a press conference to draw away cameras, hoping that Hamer would not touch the screens of American households. At the 1964 Democratic Convention, Hamer demanded that America oust, not forgive, an unrepentant white supremacy and its official delegation. Her ability to galvanize America—not reassure it of its moral standing—by exposing violent repression through personal and collective narratives threatened the power of politicians. Forty-four years after Hamer disturbed America, Ann Nixon Cooper, in a mesmerizing presidential victory speech, comforted us.

Repudiating in part the compromise that left the MFDP unable to unseat white racism, in 1972, Democratic presidential nominee Senator George McGovern and other party reformers ensured that the DNC would never repeat 1964 or mirror the Republican Party. (Current demographics and diminishing numbers have led some to mock the GOP as "the part of [old] white men.") However, disciplining intraparty independence before his stunning defeat to Richard Nixon, McGovern with other liberals worked to destabilize Brooklyn Congresswoman Shirley Chisholm and her supporters. The Chisholm campaign sought political power without loyalty to sovereign elites. Again, the independent leadership and free politics of another black woman "maverick" proved problematic to party regulars.

In order to defeat Hubert Humphrey, his real rival, McGovern needed Chisholm's delegates, whom she refused to release. Although they had initially supported Chisholm's candidacy as empowering all women, white feminists insisted that the black woman defer to the white male standard bearer. (In 2008, white feminists would not insist that the white woman candidate relinquish her delegates to the black male standard bearer.) As the first black woman elected to Congress and one of its most progressive members, Chisholm recognized she would be outside of sovereign kinship. Yet, when fellow black Congressman Ron Dellums defected from her camp to endorse McGovern at the convention and urge that her delegates do likewise, the betrayal stunned Chisholm. She had assumed that Dellums shared her desire for independent black sovereignty. Documentary footage shows the congresswoman in tears saying, "tell Ron to come home" and that she is not angry.

Years later, Chisholm's bid for redistributive economic and political power would be rendered into a symbolic tale serving simultaneously multiculturalism and white supremacy. In Chisholm's 2005 *New York Times* obituary, Gloria Steinem selectively quoted the congresswoman to write that Chisholm had run for president to prove that any girl could attain the highest elected office. In fact, Chisholm had stated, decades earlier, that she ran so that any *black or Puerto Rican* girl would have presidential aspirations. Perhaps Chisholm would not have endorsed either Clinton or Obama. No matter. Few seemed to remember her candidacy during the 2008 Democratic primaries, in which pundits heralded the "first black" and the "first woman" as presidential contenders in the Democratic Party who inspired American voters, failing to note the first black woman to run for president on a major ticket. Unlike Clinton and Obama, Chisholm was an outspoken supporter of feminism. Ulike Clinton and the president-elect, she lacked ties to the Democratic machine and sovereign whiteness. Although offering limitless opportunities for political agency and moral and social transformation, there is little political wealth and personal gain in belonging to outcast struggles. Hence, belief in the value of black sovereign relations is difficult to sustain.

Still, certain facts remain. Activism and creativity, not elected or appointed officials, establish the conditions for political cultures that expanded democracy and civil and human rights. Historically, compromises with sovereign whiteness and sovereign kinship have denied impoverished children and families a viable future.[11] For centuries, popular and political cultures recycled antiblack stereotypes to create an apartheid-based democracy. Today, public and private agencies continue to disproportionately discipline and disenfranchise black life. Black women are selectively monitored for drug use in prenatal and delivery care; black families receive minimal public assistance in housing, health care, food subsidies, and counseling; black children are disproportionately held in foster homes and detention centers under the most substandard conditions. Yet, mainstream democracy, like mainstream Christianity, asks much from subordinated social sectors, providing few guarantees of restorative justice.

December 2008 news featured poverty and genocide: the 40 percent rise in murder rates by and of young black males in the United States; hundreds of Palestinian civilian deaths as Israel bombed Gaza (with weapons financed by the United States) as a way to "signify" to Hamas. Simultaneous news focused on the millions planning to converge on Washington, D.C., for the historic January 2009 inauguration, and the hundreds of parties and balls to follow. The spectacle of American democracy's unique beauty and might overshadows mundane and traumatic suffering. Any popular sovereignty that emerges to keep faith with our highest aspirations for sustainable life will have to create its own compelling expressions of transformative agency.

Having created the conditions for a centrist-liberal black president-elect, progressive activists will have to determine how best to influence a multiracial democracy. Popular sovereignty may yet offer a popular narrative of a great, independent democracy, one in which even the most dispossessed see themselves as directly participating in citizenship and social justice. Such possibilities rest in the wisdom of slave-turned-liberator Frederick Douglass: power concedes nothing without demand and struggle.

NOTES

1. American progress remains framed by the compassion or cruelty of Judeo-Christianity as symbolic template. With California's electoral votes, Barack Obama surpassed John McCain just as California voters passed Proposition 8, which banned gay and lesbian marriage. The same white voters who touched their screens for a black president—one who simultaneously opposed both the proposition and nontraditional marriage—later used racial epithets to denounce blacks who alongside the majority of Californian voters supported the ban. Voters did not use racist language at public rallies against the president-elect when he selected evangelical pastor Rick Warren, a key opponent to gay, lesbian, and transgendered rights and women's reproductive choices, to give the invocation at the inauguration; but they did use such language against non-elite blacks.

    Days after the announcement of Warren's selection, Pope Benedict XVI pronounced from the Vatican that gender theory and gay marriage were threats to "human ecology." Placing progressive initiatives on par with the demise of the oxygen-rich rainforest, the pope asserted that feminism and unchecked homosexuality would end human reproduction, bringing death to the species. Professing a loving forgiveness, ecclesiastics fear and condemn female and queer sovereignty. A sophisticated political class secure in its patrimony, America's elite kin absorb female, queer, and colored sovereignty by assimilating members of out-groups into their ranks.

2. A black presence in the sovereign American body is not new. Public knowledge of Lynne Cheney's family tree, which includes the president-elect's family, led to campaign quips about Obama declining to hunt with her husband Vice President Dick Cheney. Madeleine Albright's adoptive parent was Bush Secretary of State Condoleeza Rice's professor and mentor in Eastern European Studies at the University of Denver. The former Clinton secretary of state has publicly joked about her admonition to Rice in the 1980s upon learning that she was a Republican: "Condi, how could you? We have the same father!" As the political class increasingly recognizes blacks as kinsmen and kinswomen, the independent black sovereign increasingly appears antiquated.

3. On the campaign trail, paternity manifests in religion (God the Father), and dead or ancestral presidents (political sires). Unsurprisingly the American archetype for both remains symbolized by white male authority. Invoking both can help to establish one's belonging to a ruling elite. Emulating Abraham Lincoln, Barack Obama announced his presidential candidacy in Springfield, Illinois, missing a televised state of the black union forum sponsored by Travis Smiley. African American pastors and theologians and academics including Michael Eric Dyson, Cornel West, and James Cone discussed Obama's candidacy and absence. Smiley read Obama's note of regret citing scheduling conflicts, yet panelists and some audience members seemed dissatisfied.

    To view the incident (discussed repeatedly in the black media) as perhaps more than political immaturity, we might consider the value of texts. The copy of the Bible that had not been used since Lincoln's 1861 swearing-in, Americans were told in December 2008, would be used for the president-elect at his January 2009 inauguration. In 1864, African

Americans gave Lincoln a Bible following his signing of the Emancipation Proclamation. Despite Lincoln's uncertainty about whether emancipated or free blacks should remain in the United States or be "repatriated," and despite the fact that the 1864 Bible was cherished by those who most intimately understood the heavy burdens of fighting for freedom, Obama chose the1861 Bible. For only Lincoln's book possessed the gravitas worth holding. (After Lincoln's assassination, the U.S. Senate would alter and then ratify the Thirteenth Amendment to legalize slavery for those duly convicted of a crime, setting a template for disproportionate incarceration of blacks and new forms of labor exploitation.)

4. The connections between the black president-elect and a southern president were noted during the campaign. In an October e-mail encouraging Texas democrats to vote and provide assistance to the Travis County Democratic Party, Luci Baines Johnson wrote, "Dear Fellow Democrat: 2008 marks the centennial celebration of my father's birthday. If Lyndon Johnson were still with us today, I know that he would be proud to cast his vote this year for Barack Obama for President, Rick Noriega for U.S. Senate, Lloyd Doggett for Congress, and every Democrat all the way down the ballot. Among his many accomplishments in office, President Johnson fought alongside Rev. Martin Luther King and other civil rights leaders of the 1960s to pass landmark legislation that helped extend the American dream to everyone in our country. At the time, it was a historic struggle against the status quo. Today, Senator Barack Obama gives us all hope that America is once again ready to turn the page on the status quo and tackle the challenges of the 21st century. In 2008 we are closer than ever to achieving my father's vision—and ours—of a better tomorrow for our children and for our nation. But none of this can happen without you" (e-mail, author's papers).

5. Former Bush Secretary of State Colin Powell's late endorsement of Barack Obama included a condemnation of the Republican Party for inaccurately portraying the candidate as Muslim, and for GOP insults to Muslim Americans. Powell stated that any Muslim American boy should be able to grow up dreaming of becoming president of the United States. (For a transcript, see "Powell Endorses Obama for President: Republican ex-Secretary of State Calls Democrat 'Transformational Figure,'" http://www.msnbc.msn.com/id/27265369 [accessed December 16, 2008]). Both Clinton Democrats and Sarah Palin Republicans challenged Obama's Christian authenticity. In response, the candidate distanced himself from Muslim Americans and Palestinian human rights. The point of asserting that Barack Hussein Obama was not Muslim was to reassure the sovereign whiteness as electorate that any Muslin American boy could *not* grow up to be president of the United States.

6. The complicated relationship of blacks to property bears serious scrutiny. The historical legacy of criminalizing blackness and equating it as having a strong threat to property endures to this day. For example, in 2005, following the breaking of substandard New Orleans levees in the aftermath of Hurricane Katrina, President Bush and Louisiana Governor Kathleen Blanco issued "shoot-to-kill" edicts for mostly impoverished black survivors; the government mandated "zero tolerance" even for those, in the words of 2008 presidential contender John McCain, who were trying to "get bottled water to babies."

7. Martin Luther King, Jr., "Why I Am Opposed to the War in Vietnam," speech given at New York's Riverside Church on April 30, 1967. The Pacifica Radio/UC Berkeley Social Activism Sound Recording Project offers a full transcript of the sermon at http://www.lib .berkeley.edu/MRC/pacificaviet/riversidetranscript.html.

8. Mamie Till-Mobley insisted on an open coffin in a public funeral for her son's decomposing body. White Mississippi officials had packed the casket with lye to accelerate its deterioration as it traveled back to Chicago. The mother demanded that the funeral home defy Southern officials' orders for a closed-casket funeral. The tens of thousands of mourners that passed before it and the millions more that saw the image in the black press (such as

Jet magazine) sparked the southern civil rights movement. Months later in Montgomery, Alabama, when Rosa Parks, Joanne Robinson, and E. D. Nixon asked a twenty-six-year-old preacher with a PhD in theology from Boston University to be spokesman for a bus boycott that they were organizing, Martin Luther King, Jr., agreed.

9. Jesse Jackson, Sr., wrote the foreword to Mamie Till-Mobley's memoir, coauthored by Christopher Benson, *Death of Innocence: The Story of the Hate Crime That Changed America* (New York: Random House, 2003).

10. This had its own sad irony, given that weeks earlier, not realizing that his microphone for a televised interview was still on, Jackson remarked, in cruder language, that he wanted to castrate Obama for dismissive treatment of the concerns of non-elite blacks.

11. During the 2008 campaign, to the consternation of Democratic Party loyalists and the confusion of many progressives, Barack Obama repeatedly cited Ronald Reagan—whose administration exploited racist stereotypes for political gains—as a presidential role model. The original southern strategy was crafted by Lee Atwater for Reagan, whose campaign used Philadelphia, Mississippi, the site of murdered civil rights activists Michael Schwerner, Andrew Goodman, and James Chaney, as a rallying cry for the restoration of white rights. There are legacies. On the September 28, 2005, broadcast of *Bill Bennett's Morning in America*, William Bennett, Reagan's secretary of education, responding to a caller, observed, "If you wanted to reduce crime, you could—if that were your sole purpose, you could abort every black baby in this country, and your crime rate would go down. That would be an impossible, ridiculous, and morally reprehensible thing to do, but your crime rate would go down."

Bennett's moral disclaimer following his final solution to criminality weakly serves as political cover against charges of racism. Nations have historically embarked on the "impossible, ridiculous, and morally reprehensible" in the name of "law and order" and ethnic cleansing; that is the illogic of genocide. Logically, the crime rate would go down if you abort all babies—including white sovereign ones. Yet, Bennett does not advocate multiracial abortions. Antiabortion Christian leaders failed to mount a campaign to force Bennett to apologize to the (black) unborn and their families. Bennett criminalizes not antisocial behavior but black kinship: families reductively understood as mothers warehousing and fathers abandoning children allegedly destined to plague a nation. Perhaps if Bennett had spoken of the first families much-loved young children in this fashion, the outcry would be greater. If so, then class and social standing shield the "new black" from the most excessive forms of rhetorical and physical violence, and shape their political views with increasing distance from non-elites.

CHAPTER 14

YOU MAY NOT GET
THERE WITH ME

OBAMA AND THE BLACK
POLITICAL ESTABLISHMENT

KAREEM CRAYTON

ONE OF THE EARLIEST CONTROVERSIES INVOLVING THE NOW HISTORIC PRESIDENTIAL run of Barack Obama was largely an unavoidable one. The issue beyond his control, to paraphrase his later comment, was mostly woven into his DNA. Amid enthusiasm about the potential of electing an African American candidate as president, columnist Debra Dickerson posed a rather provocative question about Obama's appeal. While Obama possessed many appealing qualities, she suggested, the candidate was not "black" in the sense that many of his supporters claimed. Even while Obama "invokes slavery and Jim Crow," she wrote, "he does so as one who stands outside, one who emotes but still merely informs."[1]

The point was not without some foundation. Biologically speaking, Obama was not part of an African American family in the traditional sense. The central theme of his speech at the 2004 Democratic convention was that only in a place like America could his Kenyan father have met and married his white Midwestern mother.[2] While increasing numbers of Americans are from racially mixed families, Dickerson also noted a more substantive issue about Obama's biography—his apparent lack of experience living in a black community.[3] In his first memoir, Obama traces his childhood search for identity, which ended as an adult in Chicago. His native Hawaii, while racially complex, did not have a significant African American population. More typical Democratic candidates like Bill Clinton, the putative "first black president," grew up in the South, where issues of race dominate the political and social landscape.[4]

These factors actually helped to make Obama an attractive candidate for many non-black voters. For his white liberal supporters in particular, Obama had an uncommon personal and professional profile that embodied their vision of the illusory color-blind society. Obama's personal story also seemed to transcend the typical social lines of race and class. While he could not credibly invoke connections or formative experiences within the black community, neither was Obama burdened by them. And for some liberal voters, Hawaii helped to immunize Obama from the most scarring chapters of America's history on race.

What makes the Obama political ascendancy remarkable is not the fact that he won the presidency but *how* he did it. This candidate began with a core of support among white liberals, which is rare for almost any black politician. Just as surprising, Obama's challenge was consolidating support in the black community, which did not immediately warm to the candidate. In the epic fight for Democratic nomination, Obama faced a climb from obscurity to attract black voters. Even after his spectacular public debut in the 2004 convention, Obama remained a relatively unknown figure to blacks outside of Illinois. Further, his main rival for the party's nomination in 2008 (Hillary Clinton, the initial front-runner) was one of the best-known and most admired names in politics—especially among blacks.[5]

Obama succeeded against these odds using an unconventional strategy for black candidates. Having begun with solid support among white liberal voters, Obama worked to shift black opinions into his favor. He did so, I argue, utilizing surrogates within the existing black political establishment. At times, this strategy involved seeking out credible black public figures for their support and guidance. At certain points, though, Obama marginalized or circumvented these individuals altogether to maintain his cross-racial appeal. In the end, this dynamic political strategy allowed Obama to assume the mantle of a candidate who not only had the capacity to transcend race but who also could legitimately claim part of the black political experience.

In this chapter, I illustrate this political strategy using Obama's relationships with three public figures in the black political establishment. Since he could not appeal to black voters based on his personal history or on his professional record alone, these surrogates leveraged their credibility among blacks to introduce Obama to the community. These individuals vouched for his capability and commitment to the policy concerns of African Americans in a manner that he could not himself. Further, they provided Obama with skills that made him a candidate who later could compete for black votes in his own right. While not perfect in design and execution, the strategy was effective in branding the candidate as a person who could bridge voters in the black community with white liberal constituencies in the Democratic Party.

THE RELIGIOUS MENTOR: JEREMIAH WRIGHT

If any single person deserves credit for the initial rise of Barack Obama as a force in the city of Chicago and for his entry into the world of black politics, the Reverend Jeremiah Wright certainly does. Wright, then the pastor of Trinity United Church of Christ, served as Obama's cultural interlocutor with the South Side's black community. While this relationship was fraught with complexities, Jeremiah Wright offered the mentorship and guidance of a "second father" at an early point in Obama's development as a public figure.[6]

The relationship with Wright provided Obama with three specific political assets. First, the Wright connection helped Obama obtain acceptance in a black community with a notoriously insular social network. Second, Wright aided Obama in developing a religious and cultural identity that could resonate with black communities. The religious elements of Obama's political philosophy and rhetoric largely reflect what he learned as a result of Wright's influence. And finally, Obama's membership in the Trinity church congregation proved a tangible base of support as the candidate readied himself to run for political office.

Most scholarship on black politics acknowledges that the black church plays a role that is quite difficult to overestimate in terms of importance.[7] This institution has been the heart of black political and social life since the founding of the republic.[8] Black Americans have depended on churches both for inspiration, economic support, and political organization from the antebellum period through the twentieth-century civil rights movement. And no other single institution has been more responsible for the development of the nation's most prolific black public figures—from Frederick Douglass to Martin Luther King. Throughout this period, the church has been the major site for the formation and evolution of a distinct black political ideology. Then, as now, the church remains the lone point of contact in black life that has remained largely protected from regulation by the larger society.

In many of these ways, Trinity United Church of Christ has been the institutional anchor for blacks living on the South Side of Chicago. Since its founding in the 1960s, the church has ministered to the city's most vulnerable and depressed neighborhoods. Its congregation welcomes an increasingly uncommon cross-section of the black community, with some members enrolled in public assistance programs and others from the most affluent ranks of the city's professional class. Trinity's mission also includes a directive to cater to the poor, the elderly, and the unemployed. And its professed ideology of being "unashamedly black and unapologetically Christian" captures the dual traditions of racial pride and social activism that run strong throughout the black church community.

When he became pastor at Trinity in the 1970s, Wright arrived with a background that was well suited to lead this religious community. Wright was born in Philadelphia, and he had graduated from traditionally black colleges in Virginia and Washington, D.C. But Wright's credentials also showed his capacity to excel in non-black professional settings as well. For example, Wright interrupted his undergraduate studies to enlist in the U.S. Marine Corps, where he worked as an aide to Lyndon Johnson. His graduate studies included work in Divinity Schools at the University of Chicago and Union Theological Seminary—a school known for a philosophy emphasizing the linkages between religion and social activism. Wright presented himself as a clerical scholar who combined strong roots in the black community with the skills to engage with institutions outside of the community.

During Wright's tenure, Trinity dramatically grew in size from less than a hundred to more than six thousand members. Many members live in neighborhoods that had witnessed economic blight during the 1970s and 1980s, and Wright's message responded to their concerns about economic and cultural decline. As is true for other urban-based ministries, Wright's sermons characterized the problems associated with poverty, drug abuse, and unemployment as both social ills and spiritual challenges. His preaching stressed the need for social activism as a tool for change, and it invoked themes of black consciousness and self-reliance as rallying points. Only by rejecting the social by-products of racism and economic exploitation could people realize their full potential. This religious philosophy influenced the church's community services like childcare, community banking, and affordable housing.

Trinity's burgeoning social network and its charismatic leader played a huge role in Obama's coming of age in Chicago. When Obama arrived in the city as a community organizer, he did not immediately succeed in reaching out to neighborhood groups in the South Side. The longtime residents of the South Side were either skeptical or entirely indifferent to his initial efforts—not a surprising response to someone who was, in many ways, an outsider.[9] Obama had no immediate personal ties to Chicago, he had been educated in schools on the East Coast, and he had no real familiarity with the places and people he sought to serve.

It was in this regard that Wright's intervention on Obama's behalf proved crucial. Wright spoke alongside Obama in a series of meetings introducing him to neighborhood leaders. Reminding residents of his own credibility in helping to advance their group goals, Wright assured audiences that while the young man "needed some help," he could assist in improving their neighborhoods. Since Trinity's reputation was well regarded far beyond the church's membership, community leaders were willing to give Obama a chance to show his worth. But Wright's initial gesture of deploying his influence on Obama's behalf was essential. Wright convinced residents that they could trust Obama, and that effort helped to transform a mere well-intentioned outsider into a committed and capable activist who could assist in improving life on the South Side.

More crucial than the pastor's willingness to lend a professional reference, though, was Wright's influence in shaping Obama's religious identity. Obama acknowledged that church life (Christian or otherwise) had not been an important part of his childhood experience. His lack of affiliation with any church (let alone a black one) was, in fact, one reason that the early effort to reach out to South Side groups had faltered. With his "church home" at Trinity, though, Obama could draw on the church's successes to bolster his own ideas for establishing new community programs.

Accepting Christianity enhanced Obama's abilities as a communicator as well. Intrigued by Wright's sermons that drew on liberation theology, Obama engaged in several conversations with the minister about the role of churches in promoting social change. The relationship directed Obama's thinking about social policy to appreciate both its material and moral aspects. These exchanges also gave Obama access to a powerful interpretation of the gospel, including a vocabulary that could apply to current political and social arguments. Before Wright, Obama's public policy views did not include a decidedly religious tone. The ease with which he now weaves biblical imagery and talk of values into his speeches is entirely a product of his spiritual awakening and study at Trinity. This particular marriage of the scholarly and the spiritual was not uncommon to black churches, but Wright's influence opened the door for Obama to this unfamiliar terrain.

Finally, the political salience of Obama's connection to Wright and Trinity deserves consideration. While a more secular advantage than the aforementioned benefits, membership in Trinity provided a well-developed and valuable political network in Chicago. The congregation was an ideal political base for any candidate to launch a political campaign to represent the South Side, and politicians courted votes there during election seasons. Trinity's size and visibility made it a crucial starting point for attracting votes, soliciting donations, and recruiting organizers. Just as Wright's seal of approval held sway with the neighborhood groups Obama approached as a private citizen, his political endorsement was an even more influential to gain attention and respect among blacks as a candidate who could be an effective public servant in elected office.

In light of Wright's close relationship with Obama, the campaign's decision to repudiate the minister was probably the most daunting issue of the election. Sensing objections to some of Wright's more controversial statements, campaign aides quietly removed Wright from the public launch of the presidential campaign in Springfield. Later, Obama delivered his Philadelphia speech in answer to the uproar over circulation of Wright's more incendiary comments from the pulpit. Taped excerpts from past sermons revealed sharp, sometimes even vulgar, criticisms of the government for its alleged involvement in promoting the drug culture, the spread of AIDS, and for maintaining a racially biased criminal justice system.

In the face of calls to denounce Wright entirely, Obama recognized the risk of alienating voters in the very community he had cultivated at the start of his campaign. Wright was a well-regarded figure in black churches and could not be easily dismissed without exacting a credibility damaging rebuke from Wright or other ministers. At the same time, staying silent about the most volatile comments would undercut the candidate's racially inclusive message to non-white voters. A statement had to place Obama's long relationship with Wright in context and provide a measured but clear expression of disapproval for the pastor's comments. Accordingly, Obama very carefully attempted to separate his own views from Wright's remarks yet also to signal his continued embrace of Trinity and its pastor. After appealing largely to his biography, the candidate summarized his critique of Wright's comments: "The profound mistake of Reverend Wright's sermons is not that he spoke about racism in our society. It's that he spoke as if our society was static; as if no progress has been made; as if this country—a country that has made it possible for one of his own members to run for the highest office in the land and build a coalition of white and black; Latino and Asian, rich and poor, young and old—is still irrevocably bound to a tragic past."[10]

Obama characterized Wright's views about self-reliance and racial pride as, at best, obsolete—at worst, un-American in nature. Obama framed his own ideology as rooted in patriotism and optimism; he dismissed Wright's viewpoint as ossified and provincial. Yet the righteous anger demanding social change is what undergirds the most impassioned sermons within the liberation theology tradition. This perspective is consistent with what brought Wright to Trinity as its pastor and Obama as a member. Obama's analysis suggests that the candidate only discovered his interpretation of Wright's ideology (at least as he described it) during his presidential campaign. Even some of the most ardent Democrats found that this claim of surprise strained credulity.

This speech also addresses America's ongoing debates on the matter of race. Obama compared the anger many Blacks feel about slavery and segregation to the pressure and resentment of whites who oppose race-conscious programs like affirmative action. The press applauded this rhetorical turn for its empathy for each group's plight in these polarizing disputes. While he may have vividly described the terms of this debate, Obama never placed himself within this discourse. He skillfully presented each side in the manner of a concerned, yet not actively involved, observer. While a politically successful effort to defuse a volatile situation, the Philadelphia speech failed to provide a serious account of Obama's own views about these trying and vexing racial issues.

THE LEGISLATIVE OPERATIVE: EMIL JONES, JR.

Reverend Wright was a tremendous emissary for Obama as he engaged with the neighborhoods on the South Side, but it was State Senator Emil Jones who enhanced Obama's résumé as an accomplished legislator. Obama's relatively brief time in the Illinois Senate was notable thanks mostly to help from his political patron—a renowned operator in state government. Jones, the first black legislator to preside over the Illinois Senate, positioned Obama to mount a successful statewide campaign. Given the barriers that normally prevent rank-and-file legislators from becoming standouts, Obama's alliance with Jones made him a favorite candidate for U.S. senator.

An often overlooked part of Obama's résumé is that his first elected position was representing a majority-black constituency. Many political scientists find that this starting point prevents candidates from winning higher office, since the ideological bent of a majority-black (or non-white) constituency differs sharply from a larger statewide electorate.[11] Legislators in these districts sometimes develop records considered "too liberal" to run statewide for governor or senator. This structural factor is common in explanations for the paucity of successful black statewide candidates.[12]

A second factor is an institutional norm that affects all young politicians. Seniority provides the key to exercising legislative power, which means new members must earn their way into the leadership.[13] Even a member of the majority party normally must wait in line before chairing a committee or sponsoring an important bill on the floor of the chamber. Only after a period of close observation and apprenticeship to the more senior members can a legislator assume the responsibilities of institutional leadership.

Within this rigid promotion system, Jones himself developed a mastery of the legislative process and earned a place in the leadership. After serving for a decade in the House of Representatives, Jones won a seat in the Illinois Senate. He advanced in the ranks there with a strategy common for many black legislators—working within the caucus structure to secure projects for his district. His colleagues selected him to become the Senate's Minority Leader in 1993—when Democrats held only twenty-seven seats. He asserted control of the legislative and campaign business of the caucus and quickly moved to improve the party's standing. When Jones retired in 2009, the Senate Democrats had grown to a thirty-seven-member veto-proof majority. Much of that success is due to Jones's heralded ability to recruit, fund-raise, and allocate these resources among the members of his caucus.

Due to seniority norms, Obama's swift emergence as a star in Springfield was remarkable. For one thing, the Illinois Senate was his first experience holding public office. Compared to the other Democratic members of the Senate—including every other black member—Obama was a political novice. Further, his positions on substantive policies were at that time still unknown and untested; others had already demonstrated their loyalty. And at least a few of his fellow senators were rankled because Obama had won by unseating a well-regarded black incumbent. Still, certain elements of his profile were appealing to Jones. Obama's membership in Trinity and affiliation with Wright provided some indication of Obama's political orientation. Jones was not unfamiliar with Obama, since his own senate district bordered many of the South Side communities that Obama represented.[14]

So how specifically did Jones's mentorship enhance Obama's standing as a legislator? First, Jones showered favor on Obama by designating him as spokesperson on high-profile legislation. For example, Obama was the point person for bills on ethics reform in state government, an especially salient issue in light of several major scandals.[15] Obama was also a floor manager for a bill to reform criminal law enforcement standards for interrogation and detention, which many civil rights groups championed.

These assignments would have been rewards for deputies with years of service to their party. A backbencher normally could expect to play a supporting role in the process. Obama had no special expertise with substantive policies like crime or ethics reform beyond teaching a few law school courses. Nor did he enjoy preexisting ties with many of the colleagues whose support required a lobbying effort. However, Obama did have the backing of a senate caucus leader who desired a new front man for the party's legislative agenda.

Jones also provided cover for Obama on controversial votes. Obama remained insulated from the more contentious social policy debates like abortion that might have led to trouble later in his career. Jones rarely exercised his power as caucus leader to demand that Obama vote the party line on these issues. Among the most biting criticisms of Obama as a presidential contender was that he ducked votes on bills to restrict abortion. By voting "present" or missing some roll calls altogether, Obama avoided attacks that he was too solidly in the liberal or conservative camps. Put another way, Jones's protection preserved Obama's reputation in the Illinois Senate as a centrist who could build helpful alliances with his Republican colleagues. Further, the candidate remained free from the more unseemly compromises that legislators sometimes must make in service to the party.

Finally, Jones provided a crucial advantage in the redistricting process. This assistance not only secured Obama's senate seat, but it also ideally positioned him to pursue a run for the U.S. Senate. When legislative districts are redrawn to equalize their populations, members often find that their personal interest in reelection diverges from the leader's concern—protecting the margins for the party statewide. A party leader may transfer enough voters out of an incumbent's district to leave that incumbent vulnerable; however, that same move might be necessary to help the party's chances of securing or gaining seats elsewhere.

These tradeoffs largely helped Obama in the 2000 process, thanks to Jones. Although he was a very junior senator, Obama was permitted to redesign his district with little interference from the party leadership. Looking ahead to a U.S. Senate campaign, Obama desired exposure to the voters living beyond the South Side neighborhoods in his existing district. The change would mean a larger number of professional and non-black voters that could cement his bona fides as a serious state-wide candidate who could obtain the money and deliver the message to win.

With the consent of Jones, Obama redrew his district so that its borders largely ran north to south, rather than east to west. The consequences were quite significant. In the 1990s, Senate District 13 was slightly more than 70 percent black and was solidly anchored near his home base, Trinity. After the refashioning, District 13 traded some of this South Side territory for parts of Chicago's more affluent Gold Coast farther north. Though still a majority, the black population was markedly smaller in Obama's redesigned plan. Obama also removed from his district areas where potential primary challengers for his existing seat lived. Overall, the district's racially heterogeneous voter coalition served as a template for his U.S. Senate campaign in 2004; it allowed Obama to signal that he was a viable politician both inside and outside of the black community. All of the disruption that these changes caused in adjoining districts would have been impossible without the approval of Jones.

An ever-present risk of being a political operator is the propensity to develop strange (and politically damaging) associations. Jones's tremendous influence in state politics brought him close to several moneyed interests that offered their assistance in funding campaigns. Particularly in districts as economically impoverished as some on the South Side, the external sources of support were vital. However, at least one of Jones's prized financial donors posed political and legal problems for Obama as a presidential candidate. Antoin Rezko, the now-convicted real estate baron, played an important role assisting Obama in purchasing a home. The questionable timing of the transaction drew attention when Rezko was arrested on charges of corruption and fraud. Rezko had been a major supporter of the entire Democratic Party ticket in Illinois, but Jones had cultivated him as a principal recruiter of financial support for political candidates including Obama.

As the media investigation into Rezko's web of influence became more acute, Obama's connection with his political mentor became more difficult to defend. Jones had made Obama a credible candidate for U.S. senator, but his continued involvement was a liability with the growing cloud of suspicion. The Rezko matter hastened Jones's retirement from politics, but Obama surprisingly stayed above the fray. His legislative portfolio was dependent on Jones and his style of deal making. And the scandal involved many key allies in Obama's rise to prominence in state politics. Yet Obama bore none of the costs for the choices that helped make his rapid climb possible. Jones was not charged by prosecutors, but he emerged with a tarnished public image due to his political associations with those who were convicted. Meanwhile, Obama turned the focus of his policy expertise on the issues he advocated as a legislator rather than the political patron and ally who made them possible. Severing the public ties with Jones was a relatively simple enterprise in light of the legal and political issues that they created.

THE PARTY POWER BROKER: JESSE JACKSON

The third figure essential to Obama's emergence as a candidate was the Reverend Jesse Jackson. This relationship was perhaps the most vital, if also the most volatile, for Obama's campaign. Unlike the other individuals, Jackson was not heavily invested in Obama's career success. Jackson lived in Chicago, but his network of political supporters was national.[16] Jackson's help was therefore crucial to Obama's effort to secure the nomination. At the same time, Jackson's earlier political campaigns had branded him a divisive personality, at least in some quarters.[17]

As a public figure, Jackson combined strengths of Wright and Jones. Like Wright, Jackson was an ordained minister with civil rights credentials. Jackson was a protégé of Reverend Martin Luther King, Jr., and he became a major leader in his own right during the post–civil rights era.[18] At the same time, Jackson developed a reputation as a power broker within the Democratic Party's national organization. Politicians who desired a strong relationship with the black community viewed Jackson an invaluable ally. Like Emil Jones, Jackson enjoyed tremendous political influence; in Jackson's case, his network led to two path-breaking campaigns for U.S. president. And as with Jones and Wright, Jackson's appeal within the black community was viewed by the larger public as a liability.

Jackson did not have a close tie to Obama like Wright and Jones, but his children were in Obama's ambit. Jackson's son, a U.S. congressman, had signed on early as a statewide cochair of the Obama campaign in Illinois. Jackson's daughter was a longtime personal friend of Obama's wife, Michelle. While he was not as personally connected to Obama as Wright or Jones, Jackson was a major part of Obama's success as a national candidate who could appeal to the black community. Interestingly, Jackson made his contributions long before Obama even entered politics. Specifically, Jackson was responsible for promoting institutional changes in the Democratic Party as a result of his own political campaigns.

Symbolically, Jackson's campaigns put to rest the question of whether a black candidate could seriously contend for the nation's highest office. Shirley Chisholm's advances in 1972 notwithstanding, Jackson developed the first truly national campaign to challenge the Democratic front-runners in both the 1984 and 1988 primaries. He helped transform the civil rights movement from one oriented toward protest into one aimed at governance. The campaign won or placed second in more than ten state primaries during both years and, along the way, raised millions of dollars in support of this cause. Because he outlasted several of his white opponents in the race, Jackson became a pivotal player at the party convention.

More concretely, Jackson pioneered the strategy that Obama's campaign perfected years later. Jackson's innovation was registering new voters in states that had not previously witnessed a close primary contest. His mobilization of new voters not only targeted heavily black counties in the rural South, but it also reached into economically depressed portions of the Midwest and Appalachia. Especially in the South's Black Belt region, Jackson's civil rights background made him wildly popular with black voters. In 1984, more than 869,000 new black voters registered. The achievement translated into real influence with white Southern Democrats, who relied on these voters to help defeat strong Republican opponents.

The most significant contribution was the set of reforms within the Democratic Party's delegate selection system. Jackson prompted changes that would work to Obama's tremendous benefit years later. After the party lost the White House in 1984, the Democrats resolved to tie the nomination more closely to electoral performance.

At Jackson's urging, leaders agreed to award convention delegates proportionally, based on the popular vote in each state's primary. As a result, Jackson's 1988 electoral performance yielded a larger share of delegates than in his first effort. Having won the overall popular vote on Super Tuesday, Jackson moved from holding about 6 percent of pledged delegates to 24 percent. He vaulted to the second place delegate total at the 1988 convention. By contrast, Jackson's close to 20 percent share of the primary vote in 1984 only produced about half that percentage of pledged delegates.

The reform proved even more significant because of the growing number of majority-black legislative districts during this same period. Enforcement of the 1965 Voting Rights Act led to the creation of majority-black constituencies in jurisdictions with records of racial discrimination.[19] In states where the award of delegates was allocated according to the Democratic vote in state legislative districts, the Black Belt region made all the difference for the Jackson campaign. Even when he placed second statewide, Jackson won delegates by winning big in black majority counties that anchored legislative districts. Although he did not secure the nomination, Jackson performed well enough in these areas to gain a larger number of delegates and therefore increased influence in the convention platform.

There is no more central explanation for Obama's nomination than the party rule change that Jackson had championed. In 2008, Obama used Jackson's strategy to prevent Hillary Clinton from building an insurmountable delegate lead with her sizable wins in large states like California. As reflected in Table 14.1, the rule reform allowed Obama to collect delegates by targeting majority-black constituencies in these states, leaving the candidates on equal footing after Super Tuesday. Obama therefore could embark on his February surge—setting up the eventual end of the primary contest.

Jackson also aided Obama during the nomination fight due to his *inaction* at two important moments. The more significant was Jackson's early endorsement to Obama's candidacy. Without Jackson's blessing (or, put differently, his decision not to endorse Hillary Clinton), Obama might have fallen victim to the same internal class divisions within the black community that hobbled Chisholm's bid for the

Table 14.1.   Data collected from 2008 primary exit polls

State	Obama	Clinton	Obama delegate gain	Black share of Democratic electorate
Mississippi	61	37	+5	50%
Louisiana	57	36	+12	48%
Delaware	53	42	+3	28%
Georgia	66	31	+33	52%
North Carolina	56	42	+17	33%
Alabama	56	42	+2	51%
Virginia	64	35	+25	30%
South Carolina	55	27	+13	55%
Maryland	61	36	+14	37%

Sources: http://www.cnn.com/Election /2008/primaries/results; http://politics.nytimes.com/election-guide/2008/results/votes/index.html; http://www.msnbc.msn.com/id/21660890.

nomination. Jackson's approval helped Obama reach into the South in ways that no other single person could.

At the same time, Jackson's silence about the Democratic Party's decision to disqualify results in the Florida and Michigan primaries was also crucial to Obama's success. Both states held primaries in which most voters chose Hillary Clinton; however, the elections were in doubt because they were scheduled at a time that violated the party's rules. Had the party recognized either of these outcomes, Obama's path to the nomination would have been more arduous. Clinton's margin of victory could have yielded enough delegates to surpass him in the nomination fight. Many of her allies argued that ignoring these elections disenfranchised of large numbers of black and Latino voters. Had Jackson publicly adopted this view, the ultimate compromise that favored Obama might never have materialized. Amid the debate about the status of these elections, Jackson remained on the sidelines, allowing both sides to settle their dispute with party officials.[20]

This is not to say that Jackson remained entirely silent throughout the process. Jackson received a public scolding from his son for his off-color remarks about Obama. Jackson objected to statements that he viewed as "talking down to black people" to score political points.[21] Jackson found Obama's statements minimized structural explanations for social problems in favor of conservative value arguments that urged blacks to engage in self-help. For example, improving the education system was surely a priority for government, but blacks also needed to "pull their kids away from the TV," Obama explained in the speech. Jackson noted his strong displeasure with those statements, threatening to "cut his nuts out" to bring him back in line. However, Jackson's was chided by his son in print, who urged his father to "keep hope alive and shut up" during the remainder of the campaign.[22]

CONCLUSION

On the eve of his assassination, the Reverend Martin Luther King, Jr., announced to an audience a vision of the Promised Land. Drawing on themes in the book of Exodus, the prophetic speech conveyed in moving terms King's idea that black Americans would reach the goal of equal rights. But just as Moses could not enter Canaan with the people he led, King cautioned listeners, "I might not get there with you. But we, as a people, . . . will get to the promised land."[23] Forty years later, the possibilities and perils for black politics remain just as true in light of the Obama candidacy. Perhaps with a touch of irony, Obama evoked King's biblical imagery in his speech commemorating the Selma to Montgomery March in 2007.[24] Obama announced that he and other young black politicians were part of the Joshua Generation—those who had received the inheritance of the movement. Few likely recognized that the message Obama might have been sending was not all positive. King had embraced the role of Moses in the Memphis speech, but one could read Obama's invocation of the Joshua Generation as notice to the black political establishment (many of them, in King's generation) who could not cross the river Jordan with him.

No one can seriously doubt that the Obama campaign inherited a legacy from the civil rights movement. Although he was not a direct descendant of that legacy, Obama positioned himself to benefit from it. With the aid of each of the figures described above, he successfully marshaled the language, the skills, and the strategy from the black political establishment in mounting his bid for the nomination. Absent any one of the efforts to legitimate Obama, this candidacy would surely have faltered early. But one must approach this quite laudable moment of achievement with caution. Joshua's entry into Canaan, Obama rightly noted, came at a cost to Moses. To the extent that the black political establishment was the Moses Generation, the years to come may not be entirely filled with celebration. In the days after the nomination fight, very little evidence of Obama's promised change was apparent in his decision making. Wright, Jones, and Jackson all found themselves outside of the inner circle of Obama's policy-making team after the convention. The shift is an especially sobering one for a campaign that was once so reliant on gaining the support of black voters. Perhaps Obama has taken the advice and guidance from these black figures to heart and developed his own sense of a racial mission based on the lessons that the established generation of politicians have taught. On the other hand, it is also possible that his appeal to racial concerns may prove more instrumental than substantive. One therefore must recognize that electing a black candidate for the nation's highest office may certainly be part of the formula for black political power, but it cannot substitute for the enactment of substantive policies that respond to the long overdue calls for racial justice. On this score, the Obama political story largely remains a work in progress.

NOTES

Thanks to Vincent Brown, for the idea for title. Also, I appreciate helpful comments from Mary Dudziak and Meta Jones.

1. Debra J. Dickerson, "Colorblind," *Salon.com*, January 22, 2007, http://www.salon.com/opinion/feature/2007/01/22/obama/.
2. Senator Barack Obama, 2004 Democratic Convention Address (July 27, 2004). Reprinted in Barack Obama, *Dreams From My Father: A Story of Race and Inheritance* (New York: Three Rivers, 2004).
3. Nicholas Jones and Amy Symens Smith, "The Two or More Races Population: 2000," in *2000 Census* (Washington, D.C.: Government Printing Office, 2001). In 2000, 2.4 percent of all Americans described their racial background using more than one of the recognized categories.
4. Toni Morrison, "Comment," Talk of the Town, *New Yorker*, October 5, 1998, http://www.newyorker.com/archive/1998/10/05/1998_10_05_031_TNY_LIBRY_00001650.
5. Jeffrey M. Jones, "Clinton Most Positively Rated Candidate Among Blacks, Hispanics," *Gallup News Service*, June 29, 2007.
6. James Carney and Amy Sullivan, "The Origins of Obama's Pastor Problem," *Time Magazine*, March 20, 2008.
7. Michael Dawson, *Behind the Mule* (Princeton, NJ: Princeton University Press, 1995); Fredrick C. Harris, *Something Within: Religion in African-American Political Activism* (New York: Oxford University Press, 2001). *See also* C. Eric Lincoln and Lawrence H. Mamiya, *The Black Church in the African-American Experience* (Durham, NC: Duke University Press, 1990).
8. William E. Montgomery, *Under Their Own Vine and Fig Tree: The African-American Church in the South, 1865–1900* (Baton Rouge, LA: Louisiana State University Press, 1993).

9. Kenneth T. Walsh, "Obama's Years in Chicago Politics Shaped His Presidential Candidacy," *U.S. News and World Report*, April 11, 2008.

10. Senator Barack Obama, Speech on Race, *New York Times*, March 18, 2008.

11. See, for example, Keith Reeves, *Voting Hopes or Fears* (New York: Oxford University Press, 1997); James M. Glaser, *The Hand of the Past in Contemporary Southern Politics* (New Haven: Yale University Press, 2005); Matthew Streb, *The New Electoral Politics of Race* (Tuscaloosa, AL: University of Alabama Press, 2002).

12. See, for example, Earl Black and Merle Black, *The Rise of Southern Republicans*" (Cambridge, MA: Belknap Press of Harvard University, 2002); David Lublin, *The Paradox of Representation* (Princeton, NJ: Princeton University Press, 1997), 112–13.

13. Robert Peabody, "Leadership in the U.S. House of Representatives," *American Political Science Review* 61 (1967): 675–93.

14. Abdon M. Pallasch, "Jones Took 'Pushy Organizer' Under His Wing," *Chicago Sun Times*, August 24, 2008.

15. Claire Suddath, "A Brief History of Illinois Corruption," *Time Magazine*, December 11, 2008.

16. William Crotty, "Jesse Jackson's Campaign: Constituency Attitudes and Political Outcomes," in *Jesse Jackson's 1984 Presidential Campaign: Challenge and Change in American Politics*, ed. Lucius J. Barker and Ronald W. Walters (Illinois: University of Illinois Press, 1989).

17. Joyce Purnick and Michael Oreskes, "Jesse Jackson Aims for the Mainstream," *New York Times*, November 29, 1987.

18. Mfana Donald Tryman, "Jesse Jackson's Campaigns for the Presidency: A Comparison of the 1984 and 1988 Democratic Primaries," in *Blacks and the American Political System*, ed. Huey Perry and Wayne Parent (Gainesville, FL: University of Florida Press, 1995).

19. See 42 U.S.C. § 1973(b).

20. Cf. Grace Raugh, "Lawsuit Eyed by Sharpton Over Florida," *New York Sun*, March 10, 2008.

21. Jackson was caught on an active microphone whispering to another panelist that he wanted to "cut [Obama's] nuts off" for "talking down to black people." Allison Samuels, "At Arm's Length," *Newsweek*, July 12, 2008.

22. "Jesse Jr. to Jesse Sr.: You're wrong on Obama, Dad," *Chicago Sun Times*, December 3, 2007.

23. Reverend Martin Luther King, Jr., "I've Been to the Mountaintop," April 3, 1968. Transcript available at http://mlk-kpp01.stanford.edu/kingweb/publications/speeches/I%27ve_been_to_the_mountaintop.pdf.

24. Senator Barack Obama, Speech at Selma Voting Rights March Commemoration, March 4, 2007.

BARACK OBAMA AND THE BLACK ELECTORATE IN GEORGIA

IDENTIFYING THE DISENFRANCHISED

KEESHA M. MIDDLEMASS

THE YEAR 2008 WAS DIFFERENT FROM EARLIER ELECTION YEARS. VOTER PARTICIPATION and turnout increased across the country. In 2000, about thirty-one million voters cast ballots in the presidential nominating contest. In 2008, nationwide, that number was easily surpassed: about fifty-five million primary voters went to the polls to cast a ballot. It was the first contested presidential nominating fight in eight years, since both the Republican and Democratic parties did not have an incumbent president running for office, and there was a lot of choice. On the Republican side, there were eleven official candidates, and on the Democratic side, there were nine. All the Republicans were white men, but on the Democratic side, there was a former first lady, Hillary Rodham Clinton, a viable female presidential candidate, and a freshman U.S. senator from Illinois, Barack Obama, the first black presidential candidate with a real chance of victory.

The primary season on the Democratic side was not determined until June, while the Republican contest was decided in early March. The length of the Democratic presidential primary and caucus season meant that voters in states with contests after Super Tuesday, February 5, 2008, had real reason to go to the polls and cast a ballot. Obama and Clinton went back and forth, for weeks, with Obama winning several caucuses and primaries in a row in February simply to be matched by Clinton winning several primaries in a row in March and April. In the end, on June 4, 2008, Senator Barack Obama emerged with enough delegates to secure the Democratic nomination for the presidency of the United States. His prize: A general election campaign against a former prisoner of war, U.S. Senator John McCain.

A single statement cannot adequately describe the 2008 presidential primary and general election, but one underlying theme in many of the state-by-state contests in the South was black turnout. Could Obama win over blacks who had voted for Clinton in southern primaries? Moreover, once he secured the nomination, could Obama challenge McCain in traditionally Republican states that had a large percentage of black voters?

Part of the challenge of get-out-the-vote efforts in the black community is the degree to which felon disenfranchisement laws capture a sizeable percentage of the total potential black electorate. Past elections and scholars have shown that felon disenfranchisement laws matter (Uggen and Manza 2002). For instance, after the fiasco of the 2000 presidential election recount and aftermath, it became quickly obvious that a considerable portion of the otherwise eligible voting population in the state of Florida was not able to vote because of Florida's use of a felony conviction to disenfranchise its citizens. Did disenfranchising laws matter in 2008 in Georgia? This chapter explores felon disenfranchisement laws as a historical marker in Georgia and discusses how the use of such laws impacts voter eligibility today in order to explore the question, Who was disenfranchised and unable to vote for the first black president?

THE GENERAL ELECTION

John McCain clinched the Republican nomination on Tuesday, March 5, 2008, a full three months before Barack Obama wrapped up the Democratic nomination. Even though Obama, who won eleven straight victories in February, did not wrap up the Democratic nomination until June, the Democratic nomination battle, as well as the Republican Party's nominee, McCain, brought a lot of media attention to three critical issues: race, gender, and age. If Clinton had won, she would have made history, becoming the first woman nominated by a major political party to run for the highest office in the land. Another historical marker was the fact that John McCain, if elected president, would have been the oldest man, at seventy-two, to assume the presidency. Last, but significant, was the preoccupation with race and the element that race and "the Bradley effect" would have on the presidential election when voters actually entered the voting booth. The issue of race permeated most, if not all, of the conversations regarding Barack Obama being the first African American candidate for president of one of the major parties. The significance of all three issues—race, gender, and age—played a role in the Democratic nomination battle and voters' choice at the polls. Yet, when the primary contests were complete and Obama and McCain represented their respective political parties in the general election, gender did not become less significant; rather, the nomination of two men—one a freshman U.S. Senator from Illinois just three years removed from the Illinois state legislature and the first black nominee of a major U.S. political party, and the other an elderly former prisoner of war—pivoted on those issues of race and age. Race did not disappear from the political stage, but as the financial meltdown in September 2008 captured the attention of the world and the presidential debates brought the contrasting styles of the two candidates into focus, race became less significant. Obama, of course, raised a huge amount of money that month. Moreover, Obama was calm and steady,

displaying intellectual strength and understanding of the crisis, and he began to garner the support of large swaths of the electorate leading up to the general election.

Obama stretched the political playing field beyond traditional "red" and "blue" states
and used his formidable fund-raising powers to challenge McCain in traditional Republican states, including, for a short time, Georgia, a staunch Republican state with a
Republican governor, two Republican U.S. senators, and Republican control of the
congressional delegation and both state houses. The long Democratic primary battle
allowed Obama to hone his sophisticated get-out-the vote operation, which was augmented by months of organizing before the primary election season, giving Obama the
ability to play offense in many states during the closing days of the 2008 general election
campaign. Media reports indicate that Obama raised $621,984,626 during the 2008
cycle. The month of September 2008 was the largest fund-raising month, ever, as the
Obama-Biden ticket raised more than $150 million. The ability to raise so much money
allowed Obama to do three things: (1) outspend John McCain and the Republican
Party by a ratio of 3:2 on television,[1] which allowed Obama to run negative as well as
positive ads at the same time; (2) run ads in reliably Republican states that George W.
Bush had won in 2004, forcing the McCain campaign and the GOP to spend money
to defend its turf; and (3) conduct vast field operations in every state, making some
traditionally noncompetitive ones, such as North Carolina and Virginia, competitive.

The money advantage allowed for micro-targeted ads as well as a national ad
campaign for the first time ever in a presidential contest. In Georgia, Obama raised
more money than McCain, partly due to his decision to forgo public financing. The
demographics of Georgia's voting population had an effect, too. A poll conducted by
InsiderAdvantage demonstrates that Georgia was competitive for three reasons: the
high percentage of black voters; an unusually high percentage of voters under the age
of thirty; and a high percentage of voters who identified as independents, who largely
supported Obama. Yet, for all of the fund-raising advantage and ability to craft his
message and garner the support of Democrats, Republicans, and independents alike,
Obama did not win Georgia. All the same, it cost the GOP a substantial amount of
money to defend it, and it is less "red" and less Republican for his efforts.

Obama pulled out of Georgia during the waning days of the general election.
According to the *Washington Post*, the following states were visited by one or both
candidates during the closing days of the campaign and ended up being important
in determining Obama's electoral victory on November 4: Ohio, Florida, Virginia,
North Carolina, Pennsylvania, Indiana, New Mexico, and Nevada.[2] In the end, the
only "blue state" McCain and the GOP contested was Pennsylvania, which McCain
lost. Obama won all the states listed, winning a total of 364 electoral votes, while
McCain won the remaining 174.

Even though the entire southern region has gone through a transformation since
the time of one-party dominance, scarce Republicans, and practically nonexistent
black voters, the role of race continues to be a political issue. Georgia has a large black
population, as well as a large poor population. In the past, the combination of felon
disenfranchisement laws and strict voter-eligibility requirements contributed to low
voter turnout, but the year 2008 was different. The level of enthusiasm in the Democratic Party, and in the black community in particular, was high, which was evidenced
by the number of voters who cast ballots in the primary election, contributed to the

Obama campaign, and turned out to vote in November in Georgia. The total number of potential voters was high, but because of felon disenfranchisement laws in Georgia, a certain block of voters could not cast a ballot for the first black president.

RACIAL THREAT IN THE SOUTH

A major strand of the voting rights literature has explored how race explained state differences in terms of political development and policy enactment. Racial threat emerged as the dominant approach to interpret and explain southern politics (Key 1949). Racial percentage measures are not sufficient alone to explain why voting rights policies of the nineteenth century continue to exclude a substantial percentage of potential black voters; group composition and racial position still matter, but even as the number of blacks elected to the Georgia state legislature increased and reached sufficient numbers to constitute a significant minority voting block within the Democratic Party (Wielhouwer and Middlemass 2002), some black voters are disadvantaged.

Race plays a prominent role in shaping social and community interactions, as well as political power and access to government resources, including the formation of public policies (Lieberman 2005). Established before and maintained during slavery, the politics of race in the United States is often about the relationship between blacks and whites and the preservation of a color line that divides the two groups. The line that separates blacks from whites has diminished in terms of the legal sanctions and racialized public policies that followed slavery, but the simple attainment of legal equality for blacks did not equate to equal standing in the political, social, and economic spheres of society.

Key declared that "the politics of the South revolves around the position of the Negro" (1949, 5). This was true until the 1960s. Before the civil rights movement, southern states often adopted laws for the sole purpose of widespread disenfranchisement of the black population. Tactics that include poll taxes, literacy tests, and felon disenfranchisement laws were adapted to individual states' political and racial culture, which ensured the disenfranchisement of a large percentage of the electorate, both black and white, and primarily poor, until the middle of the twentieth century (Keyssar 2000).

The metaphorical color line represents several generations of public policies and social traditions that dictate group position. It is not a firm demarcation, and neither does it adequately represent a single sharp line; rather, the color line, which once "stood fundamentally for [the] denigration of Negroes as inferior and a rejection of them as alien" (Blumer 1965, 323), still extends into many aspects of society, as public policies continue to separate certain groups from the political community, most notably at the ballot box.

Race relations have dominated much of America's legal and political history, and the color line in general has had a profound impact on public policies in the United States (Lieberman 2005; Dye 1971). Slavery is sanctioned as an official public policy in the U.S. Constitution, and even though the words *slave* and *slavery* are not in the document, the peculiar institution's fingerprint is woven throughout. For example, Article I, Section 2, determines the number of representatives in Congress and direct taxes. Figures were determined by counting "free persons" as whole numbers and "all other persons, but excluding Indians" as three-fifths of all other persons for the purpose of apportioning congressional seats in the U.S. House of Representatives and determining the amount of taxes each state owed to the new national government. Although there is no direct reference to whom the "other persons" refer to, there is no mistake that they are slaves.

Additionally, slave-holding states were able to gain invaluable protection via Article IV, Sections 2 and 3. Section 2 explicitly discusses individuals fleeing justice, requiring that if found in another state, they were to be returned to their original jurisdiction, while Section 3 mandates that "no person held to service or labour in one state . . . escaping into another . . . be discharged from such service or labour." The intent of Sections 2 and 3 of Article IV was to ensure that if escaped slaves crossed state lines and were recaptured, they were to be returned to their owners.

Census figures from 1790 demonstrate why slave states were adamant about protecting the institution of slavery via the U.S. Constitution. According to population figures, approximately 20 percent of the overall population in the thirteen southern states in 1790 was of African descent, though not all were slaves. Georgia had 29,264 slaves; Maryland had 103,036 slaves; North Carolina had a recorded 100,783 slaves; South Carolina had 107,094 slaves; and Virginia, with the most, had 292,627 slaves. These figures indicate that approximately 35 percent of Georgia's total population of 82,548 was enslaved, as was 32 percent of Maryland's population (319,728). In North Carolina, 26 percent of its population of 395,005 was enslaved, as was 43 percent of South Carolina's population of 249,073. Virginia, with the largest slave population, had more than 39 percent of its population of 747,550 held in bondage (Historical Census Browser 2004).

The 1790 census was important for many reasons: it demonstrated the number of people who lived in the newly formed nation and also where the largest number of blacks lived. Whites, regardless of their class or status, felt threatened by large black populations and passed restrictive laws to ensure the maintenance of a strict color line between slave and master (Key 1949). Racial-threat theory, however, did not develop as a theoretical model of study until the middle of the twentieth century, traceable to two seminal works: V. O. Key's *Southern Politics* (1949) and Hubert M. Blalock's *Toward a Theory of Minority-Group Relations* (1967).

Key and Blalock spend an inordinate amount of time and energy on the minority percentage in the population and emphasize how areas in the South with large black populations affected whites' responses to real or imagined threats to their social, economical, and political interests. Key (1949) explains state variation, and the political differences and development across southern states and localities by examining the percentage of blacks in the populace. White southerners in the Black Belt embraced strong racist beliefs to implement harsh practices in order to maintain the black-white social order and the political, economical, and life patterns established by and for the benefit of whites. A small white population controlled the larger black population across the South, which was possible because whites controlled the socioeconomic and political systems.

In *Toward a Theory of Minority-Group Relations*, Blalock focuses on social control and the black percentage in the community to explain state policies. Like Key, Blalock examines the relational positions of blacks and whites, but he does so to explain variations in white attitudes and behaviors toward blacks. Blalock asserts that different types of threats, real and imagined, produce varied forms of social control from those in power of the state apparatus. Based on racial attitudes, whites were concerned with social relationships, status and class, and in particular political power; therefore, the relative positions that both groups occupied were more important than the actual percentage of blacks. As the black population, viewed as threatening, increased in numbers, so too did the state response to the potential threat posed by that same population. Blalock argues that the size of the black population explained social control mechanisms used by southern jurisdictions. In the context of Georgia, racial threat and social control may not explain the continued implementation of restrictive voting rights laws in the twenty-first century, but taking into consideration the relative position of whites and blacks helps to explain their continued existence. The electorate in the South was largely restricted to upper-class white men until the mid-1960s.

The passage of the Voting Rights Act in 1965, a major step in securing equal voting rights for blacks, provided the necessary means to combat different kinds of discrimination in the electoral process. The Voting Rights Act granted the federal government unparalleled powers to protect the voting rights of blacks (Scher and Button 1984), essentially enforcing the Fifteenth Amendment almost one hundred years after its passage (Teasley 1987). The passage of the Voting Rights Act, coupled with the passage of other federal legislation and U.S. Supreme Court decisions declaring that "all citizens were entitled to full participation in the political system, and to 'an equally effective voice' in the process" (Ryden 1996, 36),[3] expanded the electorate to include others beyond white men. Yet, in the twenty-first century, one notable state-level restriction implemented in the nineteenth century continues to restrict individuals from casting a ballot: felon disenfranchisement laws, which place an added burden on otherwise eligible voters.

FELON DISENFRANCHISEMENT LAWS

Felon disenfranchisement laws are a patchwork of state laws that systematically restrict a former felon's right to participate in the democratic process. These laws are triggered when an individual is convicted of a crime that the state categorizes as a felony. Voting is an integral part of any democratic society, and in most democratic societies electoral laws are implemented by a set of social and public institutions separate and apart from the criminal justice system; however, electoral laws are inextricably linked to the criminal justice system in forty-eight of the fifty states.

This connection between crime and the loss of civil rights has a long history in the United States (Keyssar 2000). Historically, southern states were more likely than northern states to use an array of techniques designed to disenfranchise potential voters, the most notable of which is the use of felon disenfranchisement laws following the Civil War. Like most southern states, Georgia incorporated felon restrictions into its constitution, though such laws date back to medieval times. In medieval Europe, the loss of one's civil rights followed after an individual was found guilty of committing infamous crimes or crimes of "moral turpitude" (Ewald 2002).[4] Similar disenfranchising practices were adopted in England, where criminals were stripped of their rights to transfer property and access the courts. English colonists argued that those who committed infamous crimes should be restricted from the polity based on the rationale that if one failed to adhere to customary behaviors, then disenfranchisement was a proper punishment, in addition to fines or jail time. The moral argument justified the use of felon disenfranchisement laws, and felons were easy targets (Keyssar 2000). This belief system was brought to the United States. Coupled with racial segregation, felon disenfranchisement laws found their way into state constitutions and state statutes across the South. The randomness by which the list of offenses was crafted, however, demonstrates that felon disenfranchisement laws are a social construct designed for the long-term exclusion of offenders by race.

The use of felon disenfranchisement laws was a way to ban newly freed slaves from participating in the democratic process. Many southern states believed that criminal disenfranchisement was the most effective legal method to exclude blacks from the polity (Shapiro 1993). More than two dozen states disenfranchised black men for committing crimes in the post–Civil War period and into the early part of the twentieth century. Many southern states had detailed measures incorporated into law that included lesser offenses that labeled a large number of black men as felons, thereby automatically disenfranchising them (Keyssar 2000). These lesser crimes included theft, vagrancy, wife-beating, adultery, larceny, bribery, burglary, arson, obtaining money or goods under false pretenses, perjury, forgery, embezzlement, and bigamy (Shapiro 1993). In doing so, state legislatures enumerated a list of crimes that white policy makers believed black men were more likely to commit but did not list crimes such as murder or assault, since they felt that black and white men committed these crimes at equal rates (Shapiro 1993). State laws vary greatly in defining which crimes constitute a felony, inasmuch as states have the statutory power to determine which crimes are sufficiently serious enough to be punishable by death or by one year or more of incarceration in a state penitentiary, one dividing line between felony and misdemeanor.[5] While these laws developed randomly, the denial of voting rights was practically automatic by the early part of the twentieth century. By 1920, all but a handful of states had some mechanism barring suffrage from men who were convicted of a felony. The Supreme Court ruled that administratively state legislatures had the power to determine who could and could not vote.[6]

Originally, the removal of suffrage and other civil rights from criminals had a public dimension articulated in law and pronounced at the time of sentencing (Ewald 2002); however, the loss of one's voting rights is now no longer a part of the official public conviction record. The loss of voting rights is an administrative consequence of a felony conviction that is disclosed to the felon after release from confinement, if it is disclosed by the state at all, and there is no constitutional protection against it (Keyssar 2000). Demleitner (2002) argues that the American policy of disenfranchising felons appears to have the one and only goal of permanent punishment of blacks, turning former offenders into permanently dishonored members of society who are never forgiven their sins (Demleitner 2000). Harvey (1994) argues that disenfranchisement laws cannot be justified. If an individual completes his or her sentence, then society is responsible for proving guilt of a second crime beyond a reasonable doubt, and it does not have the right to punish the former criminal in advance of prospective future criminal behavior. Yet, many states wrote felon disenfranchisement laws into their constitutions following Reconstruction, and those same laws echo today in the number of individuals who are ineligible to vote.

GEORGIA'S CONSTITUTIONAL HISTORY, WHITE SUPREMACY, AND FELON DISENFRANCHISEMENT LAWS

The history over the struggle of blacks to gain the right to vote in Georgia is well documented (McDonald 2003; Keyssar 2000; Perman 2001; Kousser 1974). At the founding of the state, Georgia's white leadership, in an effort to maintain white supremacy, used race, poll taxes, literacy tests, and the grandfather clause to deny blacks the right to vote and hold elected office (Kousser 1974). The legal sanctions imposed upon blacks were formally written into law in an effort to keep blacks in their "place" (Perman 2001; Constitutional Rights Foundation 2008).

Georgia's first state constitution, in 1777, states, "All male white inhabitants, of the age of twenty-one years, and possessed in his own right of ten pounds value, and liable to pay tax in this State, or being of any mechanic trade, and shall have been resident six months in this State, shall have a right to vote at all elections for representatives, or any other officers, herein agreed to be chosen by the people at large; and every person having a right to vote at any election shall vote by ballot personally." From its founding, Georgia focused on allowing only white men over the age of twenty-one and with certain financial means and residency to vote.

A dozen years later, similar language found its way into Georgia's 1789 constitution, except for two criteria. The 1789 constitution dropped the requirement that voters had to have a net worth of at least ten pounds and the requirement of whiteness, replacing it with citizen, which slaves were not. The state, however, maintained the requirement of having to pay taxes in order to be eligible to vote. Article IV, Section 1, states, "The electors of the members of both branches of the General Assembly shall be citizens and inhabitants of this State, and shall have attained to the age of twenty-one years, and have paid tax for the year preceding the election, and shall have resided six months within the county."

Less than a decade passed before Georgia amended its constitution. The 1798 constitution maintained much of the previous language regarding the right to vote. Georgia restricted the franchise to only males of at least twenty-one years of age, and to "citizens and inhabitants," which was an obvious affront to blacks who were bonded in slavery.

Article IV, Section 1, reads, "The electors of members of the general assembly shall be citizens and inhabitants of this State, and shall have attained the age of twenty-one years, and have paid all taxes which may have been required of them, and which they may have had an opportunity of paying, agreeably to law, for the year preceding the election, and shall have resided six months within the county." Georgia passed a new constitution in 1861, on the eve of the Civil War, to reinsert explicitly racial language by designating only white men eligible to vote and added the word "free" to the other eligibility criteria of age, residency, and taxes. Article V, Section 1, states, "The electors of members of the General Assembly shall be free white male citizens of this State; and shall have attained the age of twenty-one years; and have paid all taxes which may have been required of them, and which they have had an opportunity of paying, agreeably to law, for the year preceding the election; and shall have resided six months within the district or county."

Immediately following the Civil War, all of the Confederate states, including Georgia, had to rewrite their constitutions to be readmitted into the Union. During the early aftermath of the Civil War, with Union troops and Freedmen's Bureau officials governing the former Confederate states, Confederate states held state constitutional conventions. The first were held during the summer and fall of 1865, and only white men were allowed to vote and participate in creating the new state governments (Kousser 1974; Constitutional Rights Foundation 2008). During the state conventions, none of the participants considered extending the right to vote to former slaves (Perman 2001; Kousser 1974). The atmosphere at the time is best summed up through the words of South Carolina's provisional governor, who declared that the new constitution created "a white man's government" (Kousser 1974; Constitutional Rights Foundation 2008).

Georgia's 1865 constitution reflected this sentiment, making explicit that only free white male citizens could vote, and that if you were not eligible to vote, you could not hold elected office in the state, which was a blatant attempt to keep former slaves from voting and running for office during Reconstruction. In order to maintain the color line, the white power structure created public policies to ensure that freedmen were not incorporated into the polity. Article V, Section 1, of the 1865 constitution states,

> The electors of members of the General Assembly shall be free white male citizens of this State, and shall have attained the age of twenty-one years, and have paid all taxes which may have been required of them, and which they have had an opportunity of paying agreeably to law, for the year preceding the election, shall be citizens of the United States, and shall have resided six months either in the district or county, and two years within this State, and no person not qualified to vote for members of the General Assembly shall hold any office in this State.

Following the demise of Reconstruction, and beginning in 1890, southern states rewrote their state constitutions in an effort to address "the Negro problem" once and for all (Kousser 1974). Mississippi's constitutional convention in 1890, which was called specifically to disenfranchise blacks, garners a lot of attention, but it was not the first to merge the criminal justice system with the political system. In an attempt to regain control of the black population and allow the state to maintain social, economic, and political control of former slaves, the criminal justice system was used to create a set of crimes thought more likely to be committed by blacks. Purposely expanding the list of offenses committed more frequently by blacks, Mississippi was able to disenfranchise most criminals (Kousser 1984).[7] Mississippi may have been the first to enunciate specific crimes, but it was not the first to use a felony conviction to prevent blacks from gaining political power.

Georgia inserted the word felony and subsequent ramifications of such into its 1868 constitution. Georgia declared that if convicted of a felony, an individual is not eligible to be an elector unless pardoned. In Article II, titled "Franchise and Elections," Section 2, Georgia states, "Every male person born in the United States and every male person who has been naturalized . . . twenty-one years old or upward, who shall have resided in this State six months next preceding the election . . . and shall have paid all taxes . . . for the year next preceding the election . . . shall be deemed an elector, and shall have all the rights of an elector." The section immediately following states, "No person convicted of felony or larceny before any court of this State, or of or in the United States, shall be eligible to any office or appointment of honor or trust within this State, unless he shall have been pardoned." Southern legislatures created such laws with the specific intent to maintain the subservient positioning of blacks and white supremacy.

The ideology underlying slavery did not disappear following the Civil War and Reconstruction; rather, notions of a racial hierarchy, supported by religious and scientific notions about race and physical difference, claimed that social structures based on racial inequity were justified because of innate deviance, lack of cranial ability, and the theory of original sin. The logic held that slaves benefited from taming; blacks without the presence of a racially ordered structure such as slavery were liable to act out innate savage characteristics and therefore become a threat to the safety of whites, particularly the safety of white women. However, the criminalization of blackness was not simply the institutionalization of the view that blacks carried an essential criminal disposition (Muhammad 2009); rather, state constitutions and legislation were used to execute strategic methods to maintain social control over the newly freed black populace and control the labor economy (Wacquant 2000, 2002). Another goal was to ensure that the entire black population could not vote, thereby controlling the political apparatus of each state (Kousser 1974; Perman 2001; Oshinsky 1996). In Georgia, if the county unit system, which gave considerably more power to rural, and whiter, counties, was not sufficient to maintain the white political structure, tests were implemented to discourage potential black voters from voting. When that was not enough, violent means were not excluded (Parker 1990).

Felon disenfranchisement laws were deemed constitutional in the 1974 U.S. Supreme Court decision *Richardson v. Ramirez*.[8] This decision reinforced a state's right to exclude felons from the electorate via Section 2 of the Fourteenth Amendment. Such an interpretation of Section 2 by the U.S. Supreme Court indicates that if a state chooses to disenfranchise individuals with a felony conviction, it would not necessarily be penalized in a reduction of representation in the U.S. House of Representatives.

Georgia's most recent constitution, passed in 1983 but amended several times, declares in Article II, "Voting and Elections," Section 1, paragraph 3, "No person who has been convicted of a felony involving moral turpitude may register, remain registered, or vote except upon completion of the sentence." Although Georgia's constitution does not define moral turpitude, the word *felony* ensures that individuals who are out of prison but on parole or probation are ineligible to vote until completion of their entire sentence. The constitution may have expunged explicitly racial language, but it does continue to use a felony conviction to determine who is eligible to vote.

GENERAL ELECTION: TURNOUT IN GEORGIA

Although John McCain and his running mate, Sarah Palin, won the state of Georgia, it was only by 5.21 percent (52.16 percent to 46.95 percent). Sheinin (2008) argues that Georgia politics has changed in big and small ways and that the outcome of the 2008 election may appear typical, but atypical results lurk just below the surface.[9] For example, with the exception of Georgia-born Jimmy Carter in 1976 and 1980, Barack Obama outperformed every Democratic candidate here since John F. Kennedy. He did not simply challenge the Republican candidate, John McCain, but he also left an infrastructure that the Democratic Party will be able to use in future elections. Democrats also gained two seats in the Georgia General Assembly in unlikely territory, Marietta and Lawrenceville, two key suburban cities outside of Atlanta's inner-suburban and more liberal voting blocks. Georgia, according to election results and voting patterns, is now a two-party competitive state, and recent polls suggest that this will be true for years to come. A 2008 poll indicates that Democrats outnumber Republicans 38 percent to 35 percent, while the remaining 28 percent identify as independents or supporters of another party. A key factor about Georgia's electorate is that the Democratic Party continues to have a strong African American voting base.

In 2004, black voters made up approximately 25 percent of the electorate, and 88 percent supported the Democratic nominee John Kerry. In 2008, black voters comprised nearly 30 percent of all ballots cast in Georgia, and Obama drew 98 percent of their support. Black voters did not just participate at a higher rate in Georgia in comparison to the 2004 presidential election, but they also increasingly chose Obama over McCain. Would Obama have won the state of Georgia if 98 percent of those individuals with a felony conviction had voted and cast a ballot for him? Could Obama have won Georgia's fifteen Electoral College votes if individuals with a felony conviction were eligible to vote did so and cast a ballot for Obama and his running mate, Joseph Biden? In other words, did the McCain-Palin ticket win Georgia because of felon disenfranchisement laws and a suppressed black electorate in a competitive two-party state?

King and Mauer (2004) demonstrate the effect that felon disenfranchisement laws have on the black community in Atlanta, where a sizeable portion of the state's total black population lives. As the criminal justice system in the state has expanded, so too have the number of individuals with a felony conviction. Often, these individuals hail from the same concentrated communities and neighborhoods, which exacerbates the problem because the entire community has diminished voting power. King and Mauer found that one in every eight black men in Georgia was disenfranchised by felony conviction. In Atlanta, the rate was one in seven.

Owing to felon disenfranchisement policies, black men register to vote at a disproportionately lower rate than non-black men. King and Mauer argue that the disparity between registration rates of black and non-black men is a direct function of felon disenfranchisement laws. In Atlanta, they demonstrate that more than two-thirds (69 percent) of the gap between black and non-black men is accounted for by the sole practice of using felon disenfranchisement laws. Moreover, in eleven neighborhoods in Atlanta, more than 10 percent of black males are disenfranchised. In Atlanta, in 2003, 5 percent of the voting age population was disenfranchised. King and Mauer are not the only scholars who have shown the disparate and negative impact of felon disenfranchisement on electoral outcomes that are connected to particular state policies (Manza and Uggen 2005; Uggen and Manza 2002; Travis 2005).

Could felon disenfranchisement laws be the difference in Obama's not winning Georgia, especially since he was able to make major strides in two other southern states with similar demographic characteristics, Virginia and North Carolina? Both Virginia and North Carolina elected Democratic candidates to the U.S. Senate in 2008, and North Carolina elected a Democratic governor. Moreover, Obama won the two states easily. Georgia, however, reelected Saxby Chambliss, a Republican senator, in a special election in December. The special election was required because neither he nor his opponent, Democratic candidate Jim Martin, was able to garner a majority of the vote on November 4. According to the *Atlanta Journal-Constitution*, turnout for the special election appeared to be just over half of what it was for the general election, and Republicans framed the race as "the last stand" against a democratically controlled U.S. Senate.

CONCLUSION

Felon disenfranchisement laws hark back to the days of Jim Crow, when black voters were purposely segregated out of the electorate. In the historical context of race relations, blacks were viewed as potential threats, and the use of felon disenfranchisement laws and their widespread application in the South following emancipation reflects this reality. Felon disenfranchisement laws prevent a particular population from voting, thereby allowing those in power to stay in power.

Who is in and who is out of the electorate is not a new debate; rather, since the founding of this country, an enormous amount of political energy demarcating the polity into voters and nonvoters has been expended. Supreme Court decisions, legislative acts, and constitutional amendments have expanded the electorate to include almost every citizen over the age of eighteen, regardless of race or gender. At the same time, the intensity in which state laws have been designed to restrict access to the ballot by excluding certain populations deemed "other" has been fervent.

Disenfranchisement laws are one clear example of how both the electoral system and the judicial system are burdened with a history of racial injustice and how the two systems work in tandem to create a stratified society (Demos 2003). Wacquant claims that the disproportionate representation of blacks in the criminal justice system is linked to other institutionalized systems of black oppression in American history, most notably four "peculiar institutions" that have "operated to define, confine and control [blacks in] the United States" (2000, 378). He identifies the system of chattel slavery from the colonial era through to the end of the Civil War as the first peculiar institution, which was followed by the Black Codes and Jim Crow. The era of Jim Crow was marked by the passage of legislation that specifically barred blacks from participating in the greater society. Under oppressive racial restrictions, many fled the South for northern cities, where the ghetto segmented and segregated large numbers of blacks from the comparatively prosperous white community. When the ghetto no longer could control the black community, Wacquant argues, the prison-industrial complex effectively reproduced the color line and social stratification similar to that of slavery, creating a system of racial oppression (2000, 2002).

The racial distinctions and development of felon disenfranchisement laws alongside criminal laws more than a hundred years ago continue to have a pronounced effect on the black community and its voting strength. Although the phrase "civil death" is not habitually used anymore, the same outcome persists. A felony conviction removes an individual from the polity, and this experience is acute in the black community. In 2008, the year that was different, felon disenfranchisement laws may have prevented Barack Obama from winning Georgia and banned a large swath of black voters from casting a ballot for the first black president.

NOTES

1. University of Wisconsin Advertising Project, http://wiscadproject.wisc.edu/ (accessed November 15, 2008).
2. Shailagh Murray, Juliet Eilperin, and Robert Barnes, "A Positively Negative Home Stretch: McCain, Obama Break Tradition by Staying on the Attack," *Washington Post*, November 3, 2008.
3. The "one man, one vote" decisions evolved through such cases as *Baker v. Carr*, 369 U.S. 186 (1962); *Gray v. Sanders*, 372 U.S. 368 (1963); *Wesberry v. Sanders*, 376 U.S. 1 (1964); and *Reynolds v. Sims*, 377 U.S. 533 (1964), which together determined that one person's vote in an election was worth as much as another's.
4. In 1958, the U.S. Supreme Court held that an "infamous crime" was one that resulted in imprisonment for one year or more (*Green v. U.S.*, 356 U.S. 165). This definition now essentially equates to the definition of a felony; hence, today an infamous crime is translated into a felony. Originally, infamous crimes were labeled as such based on the nature of the crime, such as treason, murder, or high crimes and misdemeanors, and not on the type or kind of punishment inflicted. Now, however, infamous crimes are determined by the nature of the punishment and not by the character of the crime.
5. Individuals convicted of a misdemeanor are punished by confinement to county or local jail and may be fined.
6. *Davis v. Beason* (133 U.S. 333 [1890]) upholds disenfranchisement laws, stating that these laws were within the discretion of the state legislature to make and the state is able to disenfranchise those found guilty of criminal activity. *Murphy v. Ramsey* (114 U.S. 15 [1885]) upholds disenfranchisement laws and a state's right to use them to regulate the franchise and that political rights are a privilege, which can be regulated by the state. *Oregon v. Mitchell* (400 U.S. 112, 139 [1970]) overturns *Murphy* and argues that the franchise is no longer considered a privileged right. *Richardson v. Ramirez* (418 U.S. 24 [1974]) firmly reinforces a state's right to exclude felons from the polity via section 2 of the Fourteenth Amendment. Interpretation of section 2 by the Supreme Court indicates that if a state chooses to disenfranchise felons, it would not necessarily be penalized in a reduction of representation in the U.S. House of Representatives (see Developments, 2002).
7. The disenfranchising crimes included such acts as fornication, assault with intent to ravish, miscegenation, incest, and petty larceny (Kousser 1984, 35). See also *Ratliff v. Beale* (74 Miss. 247, 265–66 [1896]) for a list of offenses that the Mississippi Supreme Court deemed blacks were more likely to commit than whites and *Williams v. Mississippi* (170 U.S. 213 [1898]) for the U.S. Supreme Court's response.
8. 418 U.S. 24 (1974).
9. Aaron Gould Sheinin, "Georgia a Political Plum: Red State Gives Way to Purple," *Atlanta Journal-Constitution*, November 9, 2008.

REFERENCES

Blalock, Hubert M. 1967. *Toward a theory of minority-group relations*. New York: Wiley.
Blumer, Herbert. 1965. The future of the color line. In *The south in continuity and change*, ed. John C. McKinney and Edgar T. Thompson, 322–36. Durham, NC: Duke University Press.
Constitutional Rights Foundation. 2008. The Southern "black codes" of 1865–66." http://www.crf-usa.org/brown50th/brown_v_board.htm (accessed April 1, 2008).

Demleitner, Nora V. 2000. Continuing payment on one's debt to society: The German model of felon disenfranchisement as an alternative. *Minnesota Law Review* 84:4:753–804.

———. 2002. "Collateral damage": No re-entry for drug offenders. *Villanova Law Review47*:2:1027–1102.

Demos: A Network for Ideas & Actions. 2003. *Democracy denied: The racial history and impact of disenfranchisement laws in the United States.* New York: Demos.

Developments. 2002. "Developments in the Law: The Law of Prisons" *Harvard Law Review* 115:7:1838–1963.

Dye, Thomas R. 1971. *The politics of equality.* New York: Bobbs-Merrill.

Ewald, Alec C. 2002. "Civil Death": The ideological paradox of criminal disenfranchisement law in the United States. *Wisconsin Law Review* 2002:1:10451137.

Harvey, Alice E. 1994. Ex-felon disenfranchisement and its influence on the black vote: The need for a second look. *University of Pennsylvania Law Review* 142:3:1145–89.

Historical Census Browser. 2004. University of Virginia Geospatial and Statistical Data Center. http://fisher.lib.virginia.edu/collections/stats/histcensus/index.html (accessed September 24, 2008).

Key, V. O., Jr. 1949. *Southern politics in state and nation.* New York: Knopf.

Keyssar, Alexander. 2000. *The right to vote: The contested history of democracy in the United States.* New York: Basic Books.

King, Ryan S., and Marc Mauer. 2004. *The vanishing black electorate: Felony disenfranchisement in Atlanta, Georgia.* Washington, D.C.: The Sentencing Project.

Kousser, Morgan. 1974. *The shaping of southern politics: Suffrage restriction and the establishment of the one-party South, 1880–1910.* New Haven: Yale University Press.

———. 1984. The undermining of the first reconstruction: Lessons for the second. In *Minority vote dilution*, ed. Chandler Davidson, 37–39. Washington, D.C.: Howard University Press.

Lieberman, Robert C. 2005. *Shaping race policy: The United States in comparative perspective.* Princeton: Princeton University Press.

Manza, Jeff, and Christopher Uggen. 2005. *Locked out: Felon disenfranchisement and American democracy.* New York: Oxford University Press.

McDonald, Laughlin. 2003. *A voting rights odyssey: Black enfranchisement in Georgia.* New York: Cambridge University Press.

Muhammad, Khalil Gibran. 2009. *The condemnation of blackness: Race, crime, and the making of modern urban America.* Cambridge, MA: Harvard University Press.

Oshinsky, David M. 1996. *Worse than slavery: Parchman Farm and the ordeal of Jim Crow justice.* New York: Free Press.

Parker, Frank P. 1990. *Black votes count: Political empowerment in Mississippi after 1965.* Chapel Hill: University of North Carolina Press.

Perman, Michael. 2001. *Struggle for mastery: Disenfranchisement in the South, 1888–1908.* Chapel Hill: University of North Carolina Press.

Ryden, David K. 1996. *Representation in crisis: The Constitution, interest groups and political parties.* Albany: State University of New York Press.

Scher, Richard, and James Button. 1984. Voting rights act: Implementation and impact. In *Implementation of civil rights policy*, ed. Charles S. Bullock III and Charles M. Lamb, 20–54. Monterey, CA: Brooks/Cole.

Shapiro, Andrew L. 1993. Challenging criminal disenfranchisement under the Voting Rights Act: A new strategy. *Yale Law Journal* 103:537–66.

Teasley, C. E., III. 1987. Minority vote dilution: The impact of election system and past discrimination on minority representation. *State and Local Government Review* 19: 95–100.

Travis, Jeremy. 2005. *But they all come back: Facing the challenges of prisoner reentry.* Washington, D.C.: Urban Institute.

Uggen, Christopher, and Jeff Manza. 2002. Democratic contraction? Political consequences of felon disenfranchisement in the United States. *American Sociological Review* 67: 777–803.

Wacquant, Loic. 2000. The new peculiar institution: On the prison as surrogate ghetto. *Theoretical Criminology* 4 (3): 377–89.

———. 2002. From slavery to mass incarceration: Rethinking the race question in the U.S. *New Left Review* 13 (January–February): 41–60.

Wielhouwer, Peter W., and Keesha M. Middlemass. 2002. Party voting and race in the Georgia General Assembly. Paper presented at the Citadel Symposium on Southern Politics, Charleston, SC.

BARACK OBAMA'S CANDIDACY AND THE COLLATERAL CONSEQUENCES OF THE "POLITICS OF FEAR"

GREGORY S. PARKS AND JEFFREY J. RACHLINSKI

Why would they try to make people hate us?

—Michelle Obama

BARACK OBAMA'S SUCCESSFUL RUN FOR THE PRESIDENCY OF THE UNITED STATES begs the question of what role race now plays in America. Some commentators and pundits contend that the election shows that American society has moved beyond race. Others argue that it proves nothing and that racism remains as much an entrenched part of American society as ever. In light of the 2008 election, however, others have begun to articulate a more nuanced analysis of race in America—that being the presence of racial bias is mostly subtle and unconscious.[1] In this chapter, we address the role that the ugliest aspect of the 2008 presidential election plays in this debate—the threats to and attempts on President Obama's life.

These threats play a surprising role in this debate about the meaning of the 2008 election. Those who claim that Obama's victory means that we live in a postracial society could attribute these threats to the work of a distant fringe or note simply that all serious presidential candidates face death threats. And those who claim the 2008 election proves nothing can point to these threats as modern instantiations of the use of lynching and threats of lynching to combat the ambition among blacks under Jim Crow. They can claim that a populace that would make such vile threats against Barack Obama is no different than the one that spawned the successful assassination of Medgar Evars and Martin Luther King, Jr. Threatening and killing "uppity" black leaders is an age-old American story. We argue, however, that the threats today are different and have a somewhat different source.

We contend that the subtle ways that racism plays out in modern America has a surprising connection with the threats against Barack Obama The connection between unconscious racism and these threats is straightforward. The vast extent of unconscious bias in America made candidate Obama vulnerable to a negative emotional appeal by his political opponents and made for fertile ground for news stories portraying him as a potentially dangerous outsider. In the 2008 presidential campaign, the media's coverage of Reverend Jeremiah Wright and, to a lesser extent, of Minister Louis Farrakhan likely primed some white voters' anxieties about Barack Obama being "too black." In addition, political candidates prime voters with information that is designed to be emotionally evocative and win votes. In the 2008 presidential contest, both the Clinton and McCain-Palin campaigns used religion as well as national and cultural identity to prime whites' fears and win votes. The attacks were designed to encourage white voters to reject Barack Obama as a plausible president, and the news stories were simply designed to attract readers and viewers. But the unintended consequence of this effort was to create an environment in which threats can flourish. Individuals inclined to violence are also exposed to the negative imagery, and they likely surround themselves with others who also accept and embrace the negative imagery that paints Barack Obama as a threat to their cultural identity.

We contend that the threats against Barack Obama cannot be dismissed as the same kinds of threats that other Presidential candidates commonly face. His race and "otherness" underlie them, and unlike the threats directed against other national political leaders, they do not arise exclusively from the ranks of the seriously mentally ill. But neither do they have the same source as a southern lynching or even of the assassination of past black leaders. Successful blacks in the early twentieth century truly were a threat to the white hierarchy under Jim Crow, and so too were many black leaders. Barack Obama is a pathbreaking politician, but he is not a threat to the status white Americans enjoy. Violence directed against him has a different, contemporary origin and nature.

THE THREATS AGAINST CANDIDATE OBAMA

All serious presidential candidates face threats. And since the assassination of Robert F. Kennedy in 1968, many national candidates receive Secret Service protection. One can thus argue that the threats against Barack Obama are just part of the territory, but clearly, things were and are different from other campaigns.

For one thing, the issue of Barack Obama's possible assassination originated with his candidacy. The Secret Service placed him under its protection earlier than any other presidential candidate—in May 2007, some eighteen months before the 2008 national election. The Department of Homeland Security authorized his protection after consulting with a bipartisan congressional advisory committee. The security detail was not prompted by direct threats but by general concerns about the safety of then-Senator Obama as a prominent black candidate. These concerns arose, in part, from the racist chatter found on white supremacist Web sites early in Obama's candidacy.[2]

Senator Obama did not initiate the request for Secret Service protection, but his colleague Illinois Senator Dick Durbin did. Senator Durbin openly acknowledged that his request "had a lot to do with race."[3] At the outset of Obama's presidential campaign, many supporters, including his wife, expressed fears that he would be placed in harm's way.[4] Some black supporters went so far as to state their fear that he would be assassinated and that not to vote for him was a way to protect him.[5] These concerns became so pervasive and widely discussed that even candidate Obama acknowledged them.[6] No candidate in recent memory (except perhaps Jesse Jackson) faced the issues of threats on his life to the extent that candidate Obama did.

During the campaign, several arrests underscored the nature and extent of the threats that candidate Obama faced. In early August 2008, the Secret Service arrested Raymond Hunter Geisel in Miami for threatening to assassinate Obama. In Geisel's hotel room and car, agents found a 9 mm handgun, knives, ammunition (including armor-piercing types), body armor, a machete, and military-style fatigues. Geisel had allegedly referred to Obama with a racial epithet during a bail-bondsman training class and said, "If he gets elected, I'll assassinate him myself."[7] In late August, the Secret Service, FBI, and other law enforcement agencies investigated a possible assassination plot against Obama by white supremacists. They arrested Nathan Johnson, Tharin Gartell, and Shawn Robert Adolf, recovering two rifles. The men told the arresting officers that they planned to shoot Obama from a distance using rifles at Invesco Field in Denver during Obama's Democratic National Convention speech.[8] In September, law-enforcement agents arrested Omhari L. Sengstacke, who was in possession of a gun and a bulletproof vest, near Obama's Chicago home.[9] In October, federal officers undermined an alleged plot against Obama by white supremacists Daniel Cowart and Paul Sclesselman. The two men had planned to go on a killing spree, targeting a predominantly black school and beheading fourteen blacks. They intended for their rampage to conclude by assassinating Obama.[10]

The threats did not end with the election. Obama's victory produced a spate of racial animosity against him. In Maine, the day after the election, citizens rallied against a backdrop of black figures hung by nooses from trees. In a Maine convenience store, an Associated Press reporter noted a sign inviting customers to join a betting pool on when Obama would be assassinated. The sign read, "Let's hope we have a winner." In Mastic, New York, a woman reported that someone spray-painted a message threatening to kill Obama on her son's car. In Staten Island, New York, two white men allegedly beat a black teenager with a bat on the night of the election while they yelled, "Obama." In Hardwick, New Jersey, someone burned crosses in the yards of Obama supporters. In Forest Hills, Pennsylvania, a black man found a note with a racial slur on it underneath his windshield that said, "Now that you voted for Obama, just watch out for your house." In Apolacon, Pennsylvania, someone burned a cross on the lawn of a biracial couple. At North Carolina State University, "Kill that nigger" and "Shoot Obama" were spray-painted in the university's free expression tunnel. At Appalachian State University, a T-shirt was reportedly seen around campus that read "Obama '08, Biden '09."[11]

The threats were, unfortunately, a nationwide phenomenon. In Midland, Michigan, a man was observed walking around wearing a Ku Klux Klan robe, carrying a handgun, and waving the American flag. He later admitted to the police that the display was in response to Obama's win. In a Milwaukee, Wisconsin, police station, police found a poster of Obama with a bullet going toward his head. At the University of Texas in Austin, Buck Burnette lost his place on the football team for posting on his Facebook page, "All the hunters gather up, we have a nigger in the White House." In Vay, Idaho, a sign on a tree offered a "free public hanging" of Obama. Parents in Rexburg, Idaho, complained to school officials after second- and third-graders chanted "Assassinate Obama!" on a school bus. In Orange County, California, two men pleaded not guilty to hate crime and attempted robbery charges after they allegedly beat a black man while shouting racial and anti-Obama epithets. A popular white-supremacist Web site got more than two thousand new members the day after the election, compared with ninety-one new members on Election Day.[12] Federal agents arrested Mark M. Miyashiro in December 2008 for threatening to attack and kill Obama during Obama's scheduled vacation there. The Secret Service confiscated a Russian SKS rifle, a collapsible bayonet, and several boxes of ammunition from him.[13] Obama's critics complain that raising the specter of violence against him is only an attempt to raise his "mythic stature."[14] But the reality is that he faces grave threats.

The notion that the threats against Barack Obama are just the ordinary ones that presidents and candidates face is not right. Unlike the threats against many national leaders, few of the threats against Barack Obama were the product of delusional mental illnesses. National figures are commonly the targets of such threats. The 1981 attack on President Reagan by John Hinckley was the result of his delusional belief that the attack would win the affections of actress Jodie Foster. Similarly, a member of the Manson family launched the 1975 knife attack on President Ford. Among Senator Obama's multiple would-be assailants, only Miyashiro had any history of mental illness. The vague threats and planned assaults all have the same obvious racial overtones.

But are these threats of the same nature as threats of lynching in the Jim Crow South and the assassination of black civil rights leaders? On this point, the case is less clear-cut. The imagery of lynching is, after all, a part of some of the threats against him. But the motivation behind the virulent threats against Obama and those directed against ordinary citizens in the South were part of a cohesive effort to maintain a social order. Black men risked lynching through efforts to raise their social status or by raising the prospect of interracial sexual interaction. Many threats against him, and ultimately the assassination of Martin Luther King, for example, arose precisely because he threatened the social order of the South.

But 2008 is a different time and place. Barack Obama's success does not clearly threaten an established social order in any part of contemporary America. It is a historic moment, to be sure, but not even the most devoted white supremacist believes that racial disparities in America will vanish as a black man takes the oath of office of the presidency. America's other CEOs will still mostly be white, as will most members of Congress, governors, mayors, and so on. More black men will still be in prison than college; the unemployment rate among black Americans will still be higher than among whites, and the infant mortality rate of black children will still be higher than that of white children.

Both the current threats against Barack Obama and lynching share an important property. Each represents extremist reactions, but each arises from the society that facilitates them. Lynchings were overt acts of racism that required the conscious, intentional support of the communities in which they occurred. To maintain a successful campaign of fear, lynch mobs had to have the tacit support of the community and especially the local police. They were the product of explicit, conscious racism. Although those who threaten Barack Obama are also consciously racists, they draw support from the implicit "racism" that now represents the more dominant form of racial bias in America.

Thus, although those who threaten Barack Obama might themselves have motives that are similar to the lynch mobs of old, the climate that inspires them is different. They lack the tacit support of law enforcement—indeed, they are now the targets of law enforcement. Their efforts are not part of an organized campaign by the white community to keep black Americans "in their place." But those who have threatened Barack Obama must still feel that they have support somewhere in modern society. We contend that the campaign themes that were designed to target unconscious racism unintentionally provide this support.

UNCONSCIOUS RACIAL BIAS

People's reports of their cognitive processes are often inconsistent with those actual processes.[15] Often, influences on judgment operate outside of people's awareness.[16] This observation, combined with contemporary brain research, has led psychologists to argue that people rely on two, distinct cognitive systems of judgment. One is rapid, intuitive, and unconscious; the other is slow, deductive, and deliberative.[17] The intuitive system often dictates choice, with the deductive system lagging behind, struggling to produce reasons for a choice that comports with the accessible parts of memory. Accordingly, an intuitive, gut reaction against a candidate can dictate choice. The rational account only follows later, and it might not provide a fully accurate account of the decision.

Voting is not based solely on the deductive, deliberative system of reasoning; intuition and emotion play significant roles in voter choice.[18] Emotional responses to candidates accurately predict voter preferences.[19] Most political advertisements are meant to either inspire voter enthusiasm, thereby motivating their political engagement and loyalty, or to induce fear, thereby stimulating vigilance against the risks some candidates supposedly pose.[20] Political advertisements that provoke anxiety stimulate attention toward the campaign and discourage reliance on habitual cues for voting.[21] Accordingly, politicians prime (that is, use subtle, if not subliminal) exposed and attentive voters to base their voting decision on issues and images emphasized during the campaign.[22] As with most decisions, both passion and reason influence voting. Thus candidates have an incentive to use arguments that evoke emotions such as fear, anxiety, and anger. Such emotional appeals allow politicians to galvanize their base and attract uncommitted voters' support. Moreover, the use of emotionally evocative appeals is consistent with the media's desire for excitement and drama in their reporting.[23] It is no surprise that such appeals influence voting patterns, inasmuch as people's implicit attitudes affect how they vote.[24] And their implicit attitudes about candidates' demographic makeup influence their voting patterns.[25]

Research on "implicit bias" indicates that race biases can influence unconscious, emotional processes, wholly apart from the conscious, rational ones.[26] Psychologists term these unconscious, emotional influences "implicit biases"—attitudes or thoughts that people hold but might not explicitly endorse.[27] These attitudes might conflict with expressly held values or beliefs. Many people who embrace the egalitarian norm that race should not affect their judgment of a political candidate unwittingly harbor negative associations with blacks.[28]

Research on implicit bias suggests that over 70 percent of whites—and more than 60 percent of Asian Americans and Latino-Americans—harbor antiblack or prowhite biases.[29] The proper interpretation of implicit race bias research has been a matter of some debate,[30] but most scholars conclude that what is implicated are invidious biases.[31] There is a striking divergence between explicit attitudes toward race and measures of implicit bias.[32] Although explicit and implicit measures of bias are related, even people who openly embrace egalitarian norms often harbor very negative associations concerning blacks.[33] Within this area of research, even participants who are told that they are being tested for undesirable racist attitudes, despite their explicit self-report of egalitarian attitudes, find it difficult to control their biased responses.[34]

Implicit racial bias is not a mere abstraction. It is linked to the deepest recesses of the mind—particularly the amygdala. The amygdala is an almond-sized subcortical brain structure, involved in emotional learning, perceiving novel or threatening stimuli,[35] and conditioning fear.[36] Neurological research shows that whites react to black faces with amygdala activation, even when shown black faces *subliminally*.[37] This activation does not occur in whites processing white faces. Furthermore, the degree of amygdala activation after exposure to black faces correlates with Implicit Association Test ("IAT") scores.[38] In short, whites who show a high degree of implicit bias react to black faces, whether they know it or not, with some measure of fear and anxiety.

Unconscious biases also seem to affect cognitive processes. People implicitly associate white faces with harmless objects and black faces with weapons.[39] Individuals subliminally primed with the word "white" find it easier to recognize positive words such as "smart" than when they are primed with the word "black."[40] Other studies show even more marked effects when researchers use black and white faces as priming materials.[41] Similarly, whites subliminally primed with black male faces react to a staged computer mishap with much greater hostility than those primed with white male faces.[42] Other work shows that subliminally priming people with words commonly associated with blacks could lead individuals to interpret ambiguous behavior as more aggressive.[43]

Not only do whites, and others, harbor an implicit preference for white over black, but they also harbor an implicit preference for individuals who are phenotypically more white than black.[44] For example, black criminal defendants who present with more Afrocentric, as opposed to Eurocentric, facial features are more likely to be sentenced to death.[45] Analogously, this may also be the case with regard to ideology. Blacks who downplay their race and attempt to assimilate with the larger white society may implicitly be deemed less threatening by whites than blacks seen as more radical, if not angry and militant.[46]

OBAMA AS THE "BLACK" CANDIDATE

Recent interviews with insiders from the Obama campaign have reported that the campaign managers, and candidate Obama, rarely discussed his race. Reports from these insiders have to be taken with a grain of salt, of course; in the modern era, a president's campaign for reelection begins even before he is sworn into the office. But the reports suggest that the campaign believed that the media was paying far more attention to Barack Obama's race than to the campaign itself. Indeed, Omaba's chief strategist, David Axelrod, indicated that the only times that the campaign managers discussed the issue of race was in response to the media's endless discussion of it. While the campaign was obviously aware of the issue of race, his managers report that they consistently thought of Obama as a candidate who happened to be black, not as a black candidate.[47]

Although Barack Obama generally received favorable press coverage, the media focused on his race. In particular, the media focused frequently on Barack Obama's relationship with controversial black leaders. For example, Minister Louis Farrakhan, during the Nation of Islam's Savior's Day gathering in 2008, praised Obama.[48] Tim Russert, during an MSNBC debate between Obama and Hillary Clinton, questioned Obama about this alleged endorsement—prompting an exchange between Obama and Clinton, which resulted in Obama having to "reject and denounce" Minister Farrakhan's support.[49] Moreover, the media was fixated on Obama's relationship with Reverend Jeremiah Wright, playing the most incendiary excerpts of his sermons in an almost endless loop. In doing so, the media may have suggested that Obama endorsed the most radical views of these men, particularly Reverend Wright, since Obama was a long-standing member of his church and he had been Obama's spiritual mentor. Thus the media may have painted Obama as "too black" for some Americans and consequently raised the likelihood that people would plot against his life.

The role of the media in implicitly shaping Obama's image to voters cannot be understated. Implicit antiblack biases are malleable.[50] Thus, exposing whites to negative black representations increases their implicit antiblack biases.[51] And after exposure to negative representations of blacks via news broadcasts, those already predisposed to harbor stereotypes about blacks vis-à-vis those who are not are more likely to support harsher treatment of blacks in certain contexts.[52] Not all those exposed to aggression-related or inducing cues act aggressively; priming with aggressive-related cues increases aggressive cues only among those low in agreeableness.[53] Those who are center-right on the political spectrum tend to be lower in agreeableness than those who are center-left.[54] Not surprisingly, political conservatism is associated with implicit antiblack bias[55] and is disambiguated from mere conservative ideology.[56] This should be no surprise, given that "one major criterion continually reappears in distinguishing left from right: attitudes toward equality. The left favors greater equality, while the right inevitably sees society as hierarchical."[57] Thus, 73.6 percent of conservatives harbor implicit antiblack biases.[58] Moreover, whites who harbor stronger implicit antiblack biases are more likely to engage in acts of racial aggression against blacks.[59]

One cannot blame the news media for this focus on race in the 2008 campaign. Historic events sell papers and attract viewers to television news programs, and Barack Obama's election was historic. But the endless discussion of the historic aspects of the election often supplanted discussion of the issues, making Barack Obama seem like "the black candidate" for president rather than the candidate who happened to be black. Like all campaigns, the efforts on behalf of Obama were designed to ensure that voters generate many positive associations with the candidate. But these efforts, particularly in the primaries, when fewer people had been exposed to Barack Obama, had to swim upstream against the media's focus on his race.

IMPLICIT IDENTITY: OBAMA IS "NOT ONE OF US"

In addition to the likely priming effects of some of the media coverage during the presidential race, both the Clinton and McCain-Palin campaigns also primed voters. The Clinton campaign allegedly e-mailed images of Obama dressed in what was perceived by many to be traditional Muslim garb.[60] Clinton, when asked, pointedly whether she believed he was Christian, failed to clear up any misperception among the public.[61] She not only walked a fine line with regard to addressing whether Obama was a Muslim,[62] but, during the primaries, she also committed a gaffe when she expressly referred to Robert F. Kennedy's assassination to explain why she had not yet dropped out of the presidential campaign.[63]

More significant, however, the McCain-Palin campaign and its surrogates aggressively primed voters regarding Obama's religion, cultural identity, and Americanness. McCain surrogates used Obama's middle name, Hussein, to fuel anxieties and bias.[64] Other McCain-Palin campaign surrogates and supporters drove this issue further by raising concerns about Obama's potential religious and cultural background. For example, Bill Cunningham, a conservative radio show host and supporter of McCain, revved up a crowd prior to Senator McCain's appearance. While doing so, Cunningham repeatedly referred to McCain's opponent as "Barack Hussein Obama."[65] To his credit, Senator McCain tried to walk back some of these attitudes, as was evident when a woman stood up at one of his rallies and indicated that she could not vote for Obama because he was an Arab.[66] At the same time, however, Governor Palin continued to stoke the flames when she described Obama as a man who "launched his political career in the living room of a domestic terrorist," adding that "he's not a man who sees America the way you and I see America."[67] Palin repeatedly accused Obama of "palling around with terrorists," which some viewed as playing on xenophobic, anti-Muslim sentiments. This was all in the shadow of 9/11, which Palin would have known would incite fear and anxiety among voters.[68] As such, her words both gave credence to "the poisonous Obama-is-a-Muslim e-mail blasts" and moved "the brand of terrorism from [the] Vietnam-era variety to the radical Islamic threats of today."[69] It is no surprise that when McCain or Palin mentioned Obama at their rallies, cries of "Treason!" "Terrorist!" and "Kill him!" rose from the crowds gathered.[70] Even the evangelist and conservative political commentator Frank Schaeffer was moved to remark, "If your campaign does not stop equating Sen. Barack Obama with terrorism, questioning his patriotism and portraying Mr. Obama as 'not one of us,' I accuse you of deliberately feeding the most unhinged elements of our society the red meat of hate, and therefore of potentially instigating violence." He went on to describe McCain-Palin rallies as lynch mobs and noted that they were "playing with fire . . . unleashing the monster of American hatred and prejudice [and] . . . doing this in a country with a history of assassinations."[71]

Throughout his campaign, Obama was dogged by false allegations that he did not pledge allegiance to the American flag. Such critiques stemmed from his failure to place his hand over his heart during the singing of the national anthem at an Iowa fair.[72] In addition, critics latched on to the fact that Obama had stopped wearing an American flag pin on his lapel, despite his contention that he believed some politicians used the flag pin as a hollow substitute for patriotic deeds.[73] Because of such actions, critics—often white voters—labeled Obama as unpatriotic.[74]

Such priming correlates with implicit attitudes about religion as well as national and cultural identity. At the implicit level, whites more easily pair American symbols with white faces rather than with black faces.[75] This is so even where the faces are that of black and white U.S. Olympic athletes, both representatives of this country in the international games.[76] White and Asian Americans associated whites with the concept "American" to a greater extent than blacks.[77] Furthermore, when primed with images of the American flag, whites' and Asians' attitudes toward blacks become more negative.[78] Moreover, when they are primed with images of the American flag, their attitudes toward Democrats were not altered but their attitude toward blacks, generally, and Senator Obama, specifically, becomes more negative.[79] People even more easily associated Senator Clinton and Tony Blair with the category "American" than Obama.[80] It is no surprise that "the 'core essence' of American identity is defined (at least implicitly) in terms of cultural homogeneity and something close to nativistic, ethnic construal of what it means to be American. Clearly, this construal can be exploited by leaders who see political advantage in mobilizing nationalistic sentiments in the name of patriotism."[81]

Additionally, people also harbor an implicit bias against Muslims and in favor of Christians[82] and for white over Arab-Muslim.[83] They also find it easier to associate American names with pleasant words and foreign names—for example, Surinamese ones—with unpleasant words than they to make reverse pairings. This is even among individuals who lack experience with Surinamese names.[84] In essence, people tend to display not only an implicit bias for in-group and high status groups versus out-group low status groups, respectively, but they also implicitly relegate blacks beyond the bounds of authentic Americanness. Thus, whether it was Obama's political adversaries or those, generally, on the Right—especially commentators such as Rush Limbaugh, Sean Hannity, and Bill O'Reilly—the use of Obama's "otherness" spells danger for Obama. Implicit perception of American cues increases individuals' access to aggressive constructs in memory, aggressive and negative judgments of others, and aggressive behavior following mild provocation.[85]

ASSASSINATION THREATS: THE RESULT, BUT NOT THE GOAL

Media coverage of the Jeremiah Wright issue and, to a lesser extent, that of Minister Farrakhan was not an attempt by news organizations to do any harm to Obama. In all likelihood, it was simply a sensational story with which they ran in an effort to attract viewers. Similarly, the Clinton and McCain-Palin campaigns' attacks on Obama's cultural, national, and religious identities were an effort to galvanize their respective bases and peel away some of Obama's supporters. The media and the respective campaigns' approaches were fair in light of their goals.

The advertisement that many claim went too far was the August 2008 advertisement that associated Barack Obama with Britney Spears and Paris Hilton. The ad was ostensibly intended to attack candidate Obama as a mere celebrity, just like Spears and Hilton. Of course, the ad did not choose a random pair of disliked celebrities; it chose two young, white, blonde women. As such, it was reminiscent of the 2006 advertisements run against a black candidate for Senate, Harold Ford in Tennessee, that featured an attractive white blonde woman saying, "Harold, call me," and blowing a kiss.

Whatever else their purposes, these efforts play on long-standing hatred and anger that many in the white community direct against sexual contact between black men and white women. Such contact was a sure path to lynching in the Old South, and it remained illegal in many states until the late 1960s. The August ad was a great success for Senator McCain, as he closed the gap in the polls with Senator Obama during this month. But it also fanned racial tensions. It might be a coincidence that the two most serious threats against candidate Obama occurred in the wake of this ad (the Democratic convention was the same month, of course, which might well have had more to do with the timing of these threats). Still, an ad like that certainly raises concerns.

To the McCain-Palin campaign's credit, they did not pursue the kind of overt race baiting found in the Spears-Hilton ad any further. Nor did they raise the issue of Jeremiah Wright.[86] Some members of his own staff, it has been reported, criticized Senator McCain for not doing so. But the McCain-Palin campaign did continue to try to link Barack Obama with the idea of terrorism, perhaps playing on the easy associations many white Americans carry between black men and violence.

Whether these efforts can be thought of as fair game in a tough campaign, they have the potential for unintended consequence. Priming Americans to think of Obama as not American (and possibly Arab), Muslim (in a post-9/11 era), and a militant black person would likely lead some to take the bait. Senator McCain was confronted with just such a person, in public—how many more were there who did not appear on TV? Especially susceptible to such messages may be psychotic individuals who will come to feel that they are being patriotic by assassinating Obama.

Such concerns are analogous to those that violent pornography raises. Men who watch violent sexual imagery for their own entertainment also end up being affected by it to some extent. Watching such imagery tends to facilitate the beliefs that women enjoy nonconsensual sexual encounters. Most would still never act on such beliefs, but a small number have their attitudes pushed hard enough that it affects their behavior. Those who disseminate violent sexual content do so for monetary gain, but it has the unintended effect of changing behavior in a small but violent group.[87]

Of greater concern than the effect on the attitudes of the mentally ill, however, is the effect that this campaign might have had on more ordinary but implicitly antiblack Americans. They might have been influenced by such priming, and though not inclined to plot against Obama's life, will share enough in their belief system with right-wing extremists.[88] In effect, the priming techniques create unsavory conversations among small groups, in which a few highly militant individuals might come to feel that their hatred (and fear) of Obama is widely shared. Those who would threaten President Obama, or any successful black American, because of his or her race no longer have the support of the community and law enforcement, as they did in decades past. But enough unsavory conversations with ordinary, implicitly antiblack people might foster the mistaken belief that they have such social support. Furthermore, rhetoric that focuses on Obama's otherness or "blackness" might keep implicitly antiblack Americans, not themselves inclined toward violence, from reporting plots against President Obama.

In effect, rhetoric about Obama meant to target the intuitive psychological processes and create negative imagery might have fanned the flames of hatred among those who explicitly hate Obama because of his race. This might have created a climate where plans for violence against him can find encouragement. We obviously hope nothing more than threats come of this climate. But it is certainly wrong to conclude that the threats against President Obama will be the same as the inevitable garden variety ones that arise against any president, since there will be a racial undercurrent to them. But it is also wrong to call such threats a modern variation on lynching. Racism persists, but in a different form. What trajectory these implicit attitudes will take is unknown. Once out of office, President Obama and his family may be safe from physical harm related to implicit, antiblack bias. But from this vantage point, we cannot comfortably say they will. And in light of such uncertainty a legal, not psychological, issue remains—whether lawmakers will grant President Obama life-term Secret Service protection. Given the evidence before us, such efforts would be prudent.

NOTES

1. Gregory S. Parks and Jeffrey J. Rachlinski, "Implicit Race Bias and the 2008 Presidential Election: Much Ado About Nothing?" *University of Pennsylvania Law Review PENNumbra* 157 (2009): 210–26; Gregory S. Parks and Quinetta M. Roberson, "'Eighteen Million Cracks': Gender's Role in the 2008 Presidential Election," *Journal of Gender, Race, and Justice* (forthcoming); Gregory S. Parks and Quinetta M. Roberson, "Michelle Obama: A Contemporary Analysis of Race and Gender Discrimination through the Lens of Title VII," *Hastings Women's Law Journal* 20 (2009): 3–44.

2. Nedra Pickler, "Racial Slur Triggers Early Protection for Obama: He Called on Secret Service to Monitor Big Crowds," *Grand Rapids Press*, May 4, 2007.

3. Ibid.; Shamus Toomey, "'A Lot to Do with Race': Durbin Says Obama Needs Secret Service in Part Because He's Black," *Chicago Sun-Times*, May 5, 2007.

4. Lynn Sweet, "Michelle Obama to Play Bigger Role in Campaign," *Chicago Sun-Times*, March 12, 2007.

5. Jim Galloway and Bob Kemper, "Blog: Political Insider: 'America Is Readier to Elect a White Woman Than It Is an African-American Man,'" *Atlanta Journal-Constitution*, October 15, 2007.

6. Katherine Q. Seelye, "Obama, Civil Rights and South Carolina," *New York Times*, November 3, 2007.

7. Curt Anderson, "Fla. Man Held on Charge of Threatening Obama," *Pittsburgh Post-Gazette*, August 8, 2008.

8. Dave McKinney et al., "A Plot Targeting Obama? 3 in Custody May Be Tied to Supremacists, Said to Talk of Stadium Shooting," *Chicago Sun-Times*, August 26, 2008.

9. Angela Rozas and John McCormick, "Man Arrested a Block from Obama's Home: Bulletproof Vest, Gun Found in Car, Police Say," *Chicago Tribune*, September 24, 2008.

10. Kevin Johnson, "2 Men Accused of Planning Massacre, Targeting Obama," *USA Today*, October 28, 2008.

11. Gregory Mitchell, "Racial Incidents and Threats Against Obama Soar: Here Is a Chronicle," *The Huffington Post*, November 15, 2008.

12. Associated Press, "Obama Election Spurs Race Threats, Crimes: From California to Maine, 'Hundreds' of Incidents Reveal Racism in America," November 15, 2008; Patrik Johnsson, "After Obama's Win, White Backlash Festers in US: The Election of a Black President Triggered at Least 200 Hate-Related Incidents, a Watchdog Group Finds," *Christian Science Monitor*, November 17, 2008; Mitchell, "Racial Incidents and Threats"; Eileen Sullivan, "Obama Faces More Personal Threats than Other Presidents-Elect," *The Huffington Post*, November 14, 2008.

13. Peter Boylan, "Man Held in Obama Threats," *Honolulu Advertiser*, December 10, 2008.
14. Shaila Dewan, "Obama's Wife Evokes Dangers of Campaign," *New York Times*, January 15, 2008.
15. Timothy D. Wilson and Richard E. Nisbett, "The Accuracy of Verbal Reports about the Effects of Stimuli on Evaluations and Behavior," *Social Psychology* 41 (1978): 118–31.
16. Ibid.
17. Chris Guthrie et al., "Blinking on the Bench: How Judges Decide Cases," *Cornell Law Review* 93 (2007): 1–43.
18. Drew Westen, *The Political Brain: The Role of Emotion in Deciding the Fate of the Nation* (New York: PublicAffairs, 2007).
19. William G. Christ, "Voter Preference and Emotion: Using Emotional Response to Classify Decided and Undecided Voters," *Journal of Applied Social Psychology* 15 (1985): 237–54.
20. Ted Brader, "Striking a Responsive Chord: How Political Ads Motivate and Persuade Voters by Appealing to Emotions," *American Journal of Political Science* 49 (2005): 388–405.
21. George Marcus and Michael Mackuen, "Anxiety, Enthusiasm, and the Vote: The Emotional Underpinnings of Learning and Involvement during Presidential Campaigns," *American Political Science Review* 87 (1993): 672–85.
22. James N. Druckman, "Priming the Vote: Campaign Effects in a U.S. Senate Election," *Political Psychology* 25 (2004): 577–94.
23. Jennifer Jerit, "Survival of the Fittest: Rhetoric During the Course of an Election Campaign," *Political Psychology* 25 (2004): 563–75.
24. Inna Burdein et al., "Experiments on the Automaticity of Political Beliefs and Attitudes," *Political Psychology* 27 (2006): 359–71; Malte Friese et al., "Predicting Voting Behavior with Implicit Attitude Measures: The 2002 German Parliamentary Election," *Experimental Psychology* 54 (2007): 247–55; Westen, *The Political Brain*.
25. Cindy D. Kam, "Implicit Attitudes, Explicit Choices: When Subliminal Priming Predicts Candidate Preference," *Political Behavior* 29 (2007): 343–67.
26. Anthony G. Greenwald and Linda Hamilton Krieger, "Implicit Bias: Scientific Foundations," *California Law Review* 94 (2006): 945–67.
27. Anthony G. Greenwald and Mahzarin R. Banaji, "Implicit Social Cognition: Attitudes, Self-Esteem, and Stereotypes," *Psychology Review* 102 (1995): 4–27; Brian A. Noesk et al., "The Implicit Association Test at Age 7: A Methodological and Conceptual Review," in *Social Psychology and the Unconscious: The Automaticity of Higher Mental Processes*, ed. John A. Bargh (New York: Psychology Press, 2006), 265–92.
28. Brian A. Nosek et al., "Harvesting Implicit Group Attitudes and Beliefs from a Demonstration Website," *Group Dynamics: Theory, Research and Practice* 6 (2002): 101–15; Kristin A. Lane et al., "Implicit Social Cognition and Law," *Annual Review of Law and Social Science* 3 (2007): 427–51 (reviewing evidence that the implicit social cognition predicts behavior).
29. Greenwald and Krieger, "Implicit Bias."
30. Hal R. Arkes and Philip E. Tetlock, "Attributions of Implicit Prejudice, or 'Would Jesse Jackson Fail the IAT?'" *Psychological Inquiry* 15 (2004): 257–78.
31. Greenwald and Krieger, "Implicit Bias"; Kristin A. Lane et al., "Understanding and Using the Implicit Association Test: IV: What We Know So Far About the Method," in *Implicit Measures of Attitudes*, ed. Bernd Wittenbrink and Norbert Schwarz (New York: Guilford, 2007), 59–102.
32. Lane et al., "Implicit Social Cognition and Law."
33. Andrew Scott Baron and Mahzarin S. Banaji, "The Development of Implicit Attitudes: Evidence of Race Evaluations from Ages 6 and 10 and Adulthood," *Psychological Science*

17 (2006): 53–58 (indicating that whereas seemingly egalitarian views about race emerge over time, implicit racial attitudes stay the same).

34. Do-Yeong Kim, "Voluntary Controllability of the Implicit Association Test (IAT)," *Social Psychology Quarterly* 66 (2003): 83–96.

35. Kevin N. Ochsner and Matthew D. Lieberman, "The Emergence of Social Cognitive Neuroscience," *American Psychologist* 56 (2001): 717–34.

36. Elizabeth A. Phelps et al., "Performance on Indirect Measures of Race Evaluation Predicts Amygdala Activation," *Journal of Cognitive Neuroscience* 12 (2000): 729–38.

37. William A. Cunningham et al., "Separable Neural Components in the Processing of Black and White Faces," *Psychological Science* 15 (2004): 806–13.

38. Ibid.

39. B. Keith Payne, "Prejudice and Perception: The Role of Automatic and Controlled Processes in Misperceiving a Weapon," *Journal of Personality and Social Psychology* 81 (2001): 181–92.

40. Samuel L. Gaertner and John P. McLaughlin, "Racial Stereotypes: Associations and Ascriptions of Positive and Negative Characteristics," *Social Psychology Quarterly* 46 (1983): 23–30.

41. John F. Dovidio et al., "On the Nature of Prejudice: Automatic and Controlled Processes," *Journal of Experimental and Social Psychology* 71 (1996): 510–40.

42. John A. Bargh et al., "Automaticity of Social Behavior: Direct Effects of Trait Construct and Stereotype Activation on Action," *Journal of Personality and Social Psychology* 71 (1996): 230–44.

43. Patricia G. Devine, "Stereotypes and Prejudice: Their Automatic and Controlled Components," *Journal of Personality and Social Psychology* 56 (1989): 5–18.

44. Lane et al., "Understanding and Using the Implicit Association Test."

45. Jennifer L. Eberhardt et al., "Looking Deathworthy: Perceived Stereotypicality of Black Defendants Predicts Capital-Sentencing Outcomes," *Psychological Science* 17 (2006): 363–86.

46. Angela Onwuachi-Willig, "The Admission of Legacy Blacks," *Vanderbilt Law Review* 60 (2007): 1141–1231; Angela Onwuachi-Willig, "Volunteer Discrimination," *Davis Law Review* 40 (2007): 1895–1934.

47. David Remnick, "The Joshua Generation: Race and the Campaign of Barack Obama," *New Yorker*, November 17, 2008.

48. Margaret Ramirez and Mike Dorning, "Farrakhan Praises Obama," *Chicago Tribune*, February 25, 2008.

49. Steven Thomma, "Pivotal Debate a Crackling Exchange," *Miami Herald*, February 27, 2008.

50. Nilanjana Dasgupta and Anthony G. Greenwald, "On the Malleability of Automatic Attitudes: Combating Automatic Prejudice with Images of Admired and Disliked Individuals," *Journal of Personality and Social Psychology* 81(2001): 800–14.

51. Laurie A. Rudman and Matthew R. Lee, "Implicit and Explicit Consequences of Exposure to Violent and Misogynous Rap Music," *Group Processes & Intergroup Relations* 5 (2002): 133–50.

52. Travis L. Dixon, "Psychological Reactions to Crime News Portrayals of Black Criminals: Understanding the Moderating Roles of Prior News Viewing and Stereotype Endorsement," *Communication Monographs* 73 (2006): 162–87 (viewers support death sentences for black criminals).

53. Brian P. Meier et al., "Turning the Other Cheek: Agreeableness and the Regulation of Aggression-Related Primes," *Psychological Science* 17 (2006): 136–42.

54. Gian Vittorio et al., "Personality Profiles and Political Parties," *Political Psychology* 29 (1999): 175–97.

55. Greenwald and Krieger, "Implicit Bias."

56. Inna Burdein, "Principled Conservatives or Covert Racists: Disentangling Racism and Ideology through Implicit Measures" (PhD diss., State University of New York, Stony Brook, 2007).

57. Anthony Giddens, *The Third Way: The Renewal of Social Democracy* (Malden, MA: Polity, 1998).

58. Greenwald and Krieger, "Implicit Bias."

59. Laurie A. Rudman and Richard D. Ashmore, "Discrimination and the Implicit Association Test," *Group Process and Intergroup Relations* 10 (2007): 359–72.

60. "Sit Delete: Email Lies about Obama Are Breeding Ground for Uncritical Thinking," *Houston Chronicle*, February 29, 2008.

61. Alberta Phillips, "Clintons Open Deep Wounds with Blacks," *Seattle Post-Intelligencer*, March 11, 2008.

62. William Safire, "Gaffe," *New York Times Magazine*, June 29, 2008.

63. Daphne Retter and Leonard Greene, "Obama Invokes RFK, Ignores Rival's Gaffe in Speech," *New York Post*, May 26, 2008.

64. Kathleen Parker, "Hard to Stomach All the Ugliness," *Chicago Tribune*, October 22, 2008.

65. Michael Lou, "A Host Disparages Obama, and McCain Quickly Apologizes," *New York Times*, February 27, 2008.

66. Parker, "Hard to Stomach All the Ugliness."

67. Frank Rich, "The Terrorist Barack Hussein Obama," *New York Times*, October 12, 2008.

68. Parker, "Hard to Stomach All the Ugliness"; Pavallan S. Mohan, "McCain Relying on Fear-Based Politics," *Seattle Post-Intelligencer*, October 27, 2008.

69. Rich, "The Terrorist Barack Hussein Obama."

70. Ibid.

71. Frank Schaeffer, "McCain's Attacks Fuel Dangerous Hatred," *Baltimore Sun*, October 10, 2008.

72. Alec MacGillis, "Obama Faces Test in Asserting His Own Brand of Patriotism," *Washington Post*, May 4, 2008.

73. Jeff Zleny, "The Politician and the Absent American Flag Pin," *New York Times*, October 5, 2007.

74. Ibid.; MacGillis, "Obama Faces Test."

75. Thierry Devos and Mahzarin R. Banaji, "American = White," *Journal of Personality and Social Psychology* 88 (2005): 447–66.

76. Ibid.

77. Ibid.

78. Melissa J. Ferguson et al., "On the Automaticity of Nationalist Ideologies" (paper presented at the Society for Personality and Social Psychology Conference Symposium: Priming Ideology: Demonstrating the Malleability of Political Ideology, Albuquerque, New Mexico, February 2008).

79. Ibid.; Shanette C. Porter et al., "The American Flag Increases Prejudice Toward African-Americans" (unpublished manuscript) (on file with author).

80. Thierry Devos et al., "Is Barack Obama American Enough to be the Next President? The Role of Racial and National Identity in American Politics," available at http://www-rohan.sdsu.edu/~tdevos/thd/Devos_spsp2008.pdf.

81. Qiong Li and Marilynn B. Brewer, "What Does It Mean to Be American? Patriotism, Nationalism, and American Identity after 9/11," *Political Psychology* 25 (2004): 727–39.

82. Wade C. Rowatt et al., "Patterns and Personality Correlates of Implicit and Explicit Attitudes toward Christians and Muslims," *Journal for the Scientific Study of Religion* 44 (2005): 29–43.
83. Jaihyun Park et al., "Implicit Attitudes toward Arab-Muslims and the Moderating Effects of Social Information," *Basic and Applied Social Psychology* 29 (2007): 35–45.
84. Leslie Ashburn-Nardo et al., "Implicit Associations as the Seeds of Intergroup Bias: How Easily Do They Take Root," *Journal of Personality and Social Psychology* 81 (2001): 789–99.
85. Melissa J. Fergusson and Ran R. Hassin, "On the Automatic Association between America and Aggression for News Watchers," *Personality and Social Psychology Bulletin* 33 (2007): 1632–37.
86. "McCain Finds Old Self in Loss," *Columbia Daily Tribune*, November 9, 2008.
87. Neil M. Malamuth and Edward Donnerstein, *Pornography and Sexual Aggression* (St. Louis: Academic Press, 1986).
88. Brian Lickel et al., "A Case of Collective Responsibility: Who Else Was to Blame for the Columbine High School Shootings," *Personality and Social Psychology Bulletin* 29 (2003): 194–204.

THE STRUGGLE CONTINUES

COMBATING VOTING DISCRIMINATION IN THE OBAMA ERA

KRISTEN CLARKE

INTRODUCTION

WHILE SOME COMMENTATORS HAVE POINTED TO BARACK OBAMA'S PRESIDENTIAL VICTORY as evidence suggesting that our nation has overcome the problem of race in America,[1] the 2008 election yields significant evidence showing quite the opposite. Close and careful analysis of those voting patterns that emerged during the 2008 presidential election reveals striking evidence about the enduring legacy of racism and persisting levels of vote discrimination in a number of communities around the country. Indeed, voting patterns that emerged from the Deep South states of Louisiana, Alabama, Mississippi, Georgia, and South Carolina suggest that Barack Obama's status as an African American candidate played a strong role in shaping candidate choice at the polls during the 2008 election as these were the very states where Obama yielded the lowest levels of support among white voters. These patterns also suggest that racial discrimination remains particularly entrenched and intractable in this region of the country. Moreover, this political reality complicates the story that a number of commentators have offered suggesting that Obama's victory marks the beginning of a "postracial" era in our country.[2]

Indeed, the 2008 presidential election presents a number of complexities for those concerned about issues that lie at the intersection of race and politics. Moreover, the election also poses significant questions for those who seek to enforce the guarantees

The author wishes to thank Dr. Manning Marable, Kareem Crayton, Nathaniel Persily, John Payton, Pamela Karlan, Samuel Spital, Laughlin McDonald, Leslie Proll, Dale Ho, Desiree Pipkins, and attendees at the University of Maryland Law School's October 2008 Election Law Symposium for feedback and comments on earlier drafts and presentations of this chapter.

and realize the full promises of the Voting Rights Act of 1965—one of our nation's most successful federal civil rights laws.[3] In particular, this election raises questions about the way to best analyze and wrestle with ongoing problems of voting discrimination at a time when many may be inclined to discount or discredit evidence that such problems persist given the election of a minority candidate to our nation's highest office. Thus, this chapter provides careful analysis of voting patterns that emerged during the 2008 presidential contest and presents a view on the probative value that this election should have in shaping discussion about contemporary voting discrimination. These issues are of particular consequence for political scientists and litigants seeking to measure racially polarized voting, one of the critical pieces of evidence that must be presented in the kinds of cases most frequently brought to enforce the antidiscrimination provisions of the Voting Rights Act.[4] Success in voting rights cases is generally tied to the ability of litigants to demonstrate a pattern of racially polarized voting in a particular jurisdiction: a pattern in which nonminority voters vote as a block and cast ballots in favor of one particular candidate resulting in the defeat of the minority voters' candidate of choice.

In this chapter, I urge resistance to any effort to offer generalized presumptions and conclusions about Obama's overall victory in the 2008 presidential election. Indeed, close analysis of the 2008 presidential election outcome reveals a mixed pattern of racially polarized voting in some jurisdictions and significant cross-racial coalition building in others. Specifically, while exit polling results from the November 2008 general election reveal stark racial polarization in the Deep South states of Louisiana, Mississippi, Alabama, Georgia, and South Carolina, there are notable and encouragingly high levels of white crossover voting in the New England states of Vermont, Massachusetts, Rhode Island, and Maine. While Obama's victory most certainly represents a sign of significant racial progress in our nation's long struggle to achieve real political equality, close and careful analysis of the 2008 presidential election makes clear that many communities remain far from the postracial era that various commentators have begun to ascribe to this unique moment in our political history.

The first part of this chapter focuses on the important role that the Voting Rights Act has played in dealing with ongoing problems of voting discrimination in our country while highlighting the overall significance of racially polarized voting generally. Given the important role that evidence of racially polarized voting plays in helping determine whether voting discrimination persists in a particular community, this section outlines key questions raised in the wake of Barack Obama's presidential victory. This chapter also examines and analyzes the role that race played in shaping voting patterns in the 2008 presidential election cycle based on available results from comprehensive exit polling conducted during the primary and general elections. This data reveals that there were clearly a number of areas where Obama did not obtain support among white voters and others where his level of support among white voters was notably high. In addition, this chapter highlights a number of unique features about presidential elections that distinguish these contests from other elected offices at the local and state levels. These distinguishing features suggest that the 2008 presidential election could be of limited value in efforts to consider how most minority candidates fare in American electoral politics and in assessments of ongoing voting discrimination. Finally, this chapter concludes by providing analysis of the role of partisanship in efforts to understand the influence of race on voting patterns and considers the question of whether primary or general elections carry more probative value and weight.

THE ROLE OF THE VOTING RIGHTS ACT IN COMBATING CONTEMPORARY VOTING DISCRIMINATION

No federal law has proven more successful in addressing ongoing racial discrimination in the context of voting than the Voting Rights Act. The act is frequently credited as one of the most effective federal civil rights statutes passed by Congress because its strong antidiscrimination provisions have provided tools for challenging those barriers that deny or dilute minority voters' ability to access the ballot box. Enforcement under the act has also led to significant increases in rates of minority voter participation and minority electoral success.[5] Indeed, the Voting Rights Act, in part, created the circumstances and helped level the playing field in a way that opened the door to Obama's 2008 presidential victory. By providing a means to contest those practices that "minimize or cancel out the voting strength and political effectiveness of minority groups,"[6] the Voting Rights Act has helped our nation move closer to realizing the goal of political equality.

One of the most frequently used antidiscrimination provisions of the Voting Rights Act—the Section 2 vote dilution provision—has helped ensure that minority voters are able to enjoy the same opportunity to participate in the political process as non-minorities. This provision plays a powerful role in combating present-day discrimination by providing a tool for challenging and contesting practices or procedures that deny minority voters an equal opportunity to participate in the political process and elect candidates of their choice.[7] Vote dilution claims generally focus on a number of contextual questions, looking to see, among other things, whether white voters typically vote as a bloc to defeat minority voters' candidate of choice. Dilution claims might also focus on the way that district lines are drawn in a particular community, looking to see if those lines are drawn in such a way as to "pack" or "fracture" cohesive groups of minority voters. These are the kind of voting rights cases in which litigants must typically present evidence of racially polarized voting to support their claim. The significance of polarized voting, particularly in a post-Obama era, is thus the underlying focus of this chapter.

The Supreme Court set forth the prevailing and key legal standard for adjudicating Section 2 claims in a case captioned *Thornburg v. Gingles*.[8] The *Gingles* court outlined a three-pronged inquiry to help determine liability under Section 2. This inquiry looks to whether (1) the minority community is sufficiently large and geographically compact to constitute a majority in a single member district; (2) the minority group is politically cohesive; and (3) the majority generally votes as a bloc to defeat the minority group's candidate of choice.[9] The purpose underlying the inquiry is to determine whether some contested practice or procedure operates within an environment in which minority voters are politically cohesive, in which there is evidence of discriminatory voting behavior on the part of whites and in which the resulting discrimination can be remedied. Satisfaction of the three *Gingles* factors serves as strong evidence that a jurisdiction likely employs some practice or procedure that is discriminatory in purpose or effect and is likely indicative that there is a way to modify the system to provide a more fair and equal opportunity for minority voters to participate in the political process.[10] Political scientists play a key role in helping resolve these questions for courts.

One of the critical points underscored by the Supreme Court in the *Gingles* case is that liability determinations are "peculiarly dependent upon the facts of each case"[11] and require "an intensely local appraisal of the design and impact" of the contested electoral mechanisms.[12] This long-standing precedent underscores the argument set forth in this chapter which is that Obama's victory alone should not preclude inquiries into the potential existence of voting discrimination in a community or dispose of future voting rights claims that require a demonstration of racially polarized voting. Analysts, commentators, scholars and courts alike must continue to make careful, case-by-case assessments to determine whether vote dilution or discrimination persists even in the wake of the remarkable outcome of the 2008 presidential election. To date, many have been apt to dismiss the notion that voting discrimination persists merely because an African American now occupies the White House.

Both the second and third *Gingles* factors highlight the importance of looking to see whether voting is racially polarized in a particular jurisdiction. Under the second *Gingles* factor, analysis of the preferences of minority voters is conducted alongside a determination about the preferences of non-minority voters to determine whether minority voters are a politically cohesive unit. Ultimately, the second *Gingles* factor is deemed satisfied if the evidence demonstrates that minority voters tend to vote consistently for some clear candidate of choice.[13] In the 2008 presidential election cycle, the strong support levels for Obama, which ranged from 90 percent in Indiana to 99 percent in Delaware, are certainly strong evidence of political cohesion among Black voters and evidence that Obama was clearly the candidate of choice among them.

However, the focus here lies on the third *Gingles* prong, as this chapter endeavors to analyze the role of the 2008 presidential election in determining whether racially polarized voting and voting discrimination generally persists. This question can be answered, in large part, by determining whether white voters vote as a bloc to defeat minority voters' candidate of choice. The underlying purpose of this inquiry is to determine whether the contested practice or procedure interacts with high levels of racially polarized voting in the jurisdiction at issue to make it particularly difficult for minority voters to participate equally in the political process. To that end, the inquiry is focused on determining whether there is some consistent relationship and significant correlation between a voter's race and voting preference in elections, leading to non-minority voters generally being able to vote as a bloc to defeat minority voters' preferred candidates.

The question of whether racially polarized voting exists in a given jurisdiction is best answered by statistical analysis of election data to determine whether non-minority voters in some particular area or set piece of geography vote differently from minority voters. Political scientists and statisticians are generally relied upon to measure the level of racial polarization in a contested jurisdiction, while courts make the ultimate determination as to whether the level of polarization is of legal significance. Comparing precincts or districts containing high percentages of non-minority voters with those precincts or districts containing high percentages of minority voters—a process called homogenous precinct analysis—is one particularly useful way of analyzing racial voting patterns.[14] Ecological regression analysis, which determines the correlation between race and voting preference by examining voting patterns in voting precincts regardless of their particular racial composition, is another prevailing methodology.[15] Comprehensive exit polling conducted as voters leave polling sites has also proven to be a reliable indicator of voting patterns in a jurisdiction,[16] although experts retained to present evidence of racial polarization in voting rights litigation often use other methodologies. Historically, exit poll data (including that referenced in the second part of this chapter) has proven to be an extremely insightful and comprehensive assessment of voting patterns that emerge in presidential elections, as extensive exit polling is very rarely conducted for local or state contests.

Beyond deciding which methodology to employ, another key question concerns which set of elections to analyze in determining whether racially polarized voting exists in a particular community. Generally, elections for the office or jurisdiction that is the focus of the analysis or the subject of the litigation ("endogenous elections") prove to be the most probative starting point for launching an inquiry into racially polarized voting.[17] Data from other contests ("exogenous elections") might also be considered. In focusing on the question of voting discrimination at the local or state level, the results from a presidential primary or general election would almost always constitute exogenous election data.

While courts typically consider data from endogenous elections to be the most valuable in analyzing the voting patterns of the jurisdiction at issue, courts are split on the value of looking at exogenous election data such as data from presidential contests.[18] Some courts deem contests between a minority and a non-minority candidate to be the most probative evidence of racially polarized voting,[19] which may require plaintiffs to turn to exogenous elections to find such a contest. However, history has shown that there may be few examples of minority candidates competing on a local level against non-minority candidates in those jurisdictions in which the most potentially attractive and viable minority candidates (those with significant experience and leadership) are discouraged from running because of the futility of seeking election in a jurisdiction that conducts at-large elections or has district configurations that pack or fracture minority voters. Thus, depending on the jurisdiction in question, exogenous elections may offer the sole source of evidence regarding the racial voting patterns that emerge in minority versus non-minority contests.[20] With the 2008 presidential election now behind us, political scientists and future Section 2 litigants will always have, at minimum, one recent example of a minority versus non-minority contest to point to when no such endogenous election exists. Indeed, Jesse Jackson's presidential primary runs in 1984 and 1988 were occasionally used by experts to demonstrate racially polarized voting. Where prevailing standards look to minority versus non-minority contests for evidence of racially polarized voting and where the 2008 presidential contest is the only such election available for consideration, such factors could weigh in favor of careful analysis of the election results to determine what weight they should carry. However, even under these circumstances, an Obama victory, without more, should not defeat a Section 2 claim.

PRELIMINARY EVIDENCE FROM THE 2008
ELECTION CYCLE ILLUSTRATING PERSISTING
VOTING DISCRIMINATION IN SOME STATES

Comprehensive exit polling data from the primary and general elections during the 2008 presidential election provide some preliminary insights into racial voting patterns. Exit poll data are generally considered very reliable evidence regarding racial bloc voting but are traditionally only available during presidential elections.[21] These poll numbers reveal stark differences in the voting preferences exhibited by black and white voters in a number of jurisdictions, particularly in the Deep South. In particular, as shown in Table 17.1, analysis of voting patterns in those states stretching between Louisiana and Georgia reveals exceptionally high levels of political cohesion among African Americans in support of Obama, standing in stark contrast to bloc voting for John McCain by white voters. Notably, many of these states are subject to the special Section 5 preclearance provision of the Voting Rights Act, which applies to a select number of jurisdictions that Congress determined to have very long and entrenched histories of voting discrimination.[22] The preclearance provision, the subject of a constitutional challenge recently heard by the U.S. Supreme Court in *Northwest Austin Municipal Utility District Number One v. Holder*, requires select jurisdictions to obtain federal approval before implementing new voting changes.[23] Federal approval is contingent upon the jurisdiction's showing that the proposed voting change was not adopted with a discriminatory purpose and will not have a "retrogressive" or discriminatory effect. Indeed, the five states in which Obama attracted the lowest level of crossover support from white voters—Louisiana, Alabama, Mississippi, Georgia, and South Carolina—are all fully covered under this special Section 5 preclearance provision of the Voting Rights Act. In addition, these five states also have relatively high percentages of African Americans. This combination of facts reinforces Congress's judgment and finding that the problem of voting discrimination continues to be most entrenched in these particular states. Indeed, in these states, it is more likely that the results from the 2008 presidential election will prove consistent with existing levels of racially polarized voting, which historically have been particularly severe in these regions of the country.

Moreover, political scientists generally employ the term landslide to describe those elections in which a candidate secures around or more than 60 percent of the vote.[24] Thus, most political scientists interpreting white voting preferences in this election would likely conclude that McCain defeated Obama by landslide proportions in every single one of the fully covered Section 5 states. These landslide victories even took place in states in which white Democrats have recently been elected to statewide office, further illustrating the strong influence of race (over partisanship) on white voters' candidate preferences in these regions of the country. Further, not only is white crossover support for Obama minimal, at best, in the Section 5 covered states, the final results reveal that Obama lost outright in every one of these states. Indeed, the election outcome in the fully covered Section 5 states reflects the very definition of racially polarized voting, which is a term that describes those jurisdictions in which white voters voted sufficiently as a bloc to defeat minority voters' candidate of choice.

Table 17.1.   Support for Barack Obama in states fully covered under Section 5 of the Voting Rights Act in the 2008 general election

Section 5 covered state	% of white vote for Obama	% of black vote for Obama
Alabama	10	98
Mississippi	11	98
Lousiana	14	94
Georgia	23	98
South Carolina	26	96
Virginia	39	92
Texas	26	98
Alaska	33	—
Arizona	40	—

As seen above, the exit polling results of those states that are fully covered by Section 5 of the Voting Rights Act are indicative of significant voting discrimination in these particular regions of the country. Despite the stark levels of polarized voting revealed by exit polling results from the Deep South states, it remains clear that there are no generalized assumptions that can be drawn regarding the level of racially polarized voting even in the face of Obama's overall victory in the 2008 election.[25] In two of the five states that are partially covered under the Section 5 preclearance provision, California and New York, about 52 percent of white voters supported Obama. However, in the partially covered state of North Carolina, Obama lost by landslide proportions among white voters securing only a 35 percent share of their votes.[26] While cursory examination of these results would suggest that racially polarized voting may not be deeply entrenched in the partially covered states of California and New York, nothing conclusory can be drawn from those numbers as voting discrimination against minority voters persists in all three of these states. Indeed, California and New York have been the sites of significant voting rights struggles that includes litigation, complaints of voter intimidation, and discrimination based on both racial and language minority status. Therefore, regardless of Obama's overall success in a particular state, political scientists, analysts and courts must continue to conduct very careful and localized analyses to help determine whether voting discrimination persists in a particular community.[27]

Available exit polling data reveals some other notable patterns. While Obama was clearly the preferred candidate of choice among African Americans, Obama enjoyed support from a majority of white voters in only eighteen of the fifty states. Political cohesion among African Americans appears unquestionably high, with over 95 percent of African Americans supporting Obama in most states in which reliable data was available. These patterns are demonstrated in Table 17.2.

In some instances, courts might reject a minority voting rights claim where the evidence suggests that partisanship, not race, was the preliminary factor shaping voting preferences.[28] Indeed, some might attribute Obama's victory to widespread

Table 17.2.   Racially polarized voting in the 2008 general election

State	% of white vote for Obama	% of black vote for Obama
Alabama	10	98
Alaska	33	—
Arizona	40	—
Arkansas	30	95
California	52	94
Colorado	50	—
Connecticut	51	93
Delaware	53	99
Florida	42	96
Georgia	23	98
Hawaii	70	—
Idaho	33	—
Illinois	51	96
Indiana	45	90
Iowa	51	93
Kansas	40	—
Kentucky	36	90
Louisiana	14	94
Maine	58	—
Maryland	47	94
Massachusetts	59	—
Michigan	51	97
Minnesota	53	—
Mississippi	11	98
Missouri	42	93
Montana	45	—
Nebraska	39	—
Nevada	45	94
New Hampshire	54	—
New Jersey	49	92
New Mexico	42	—
New York	52	100
North Carolina	35	95
North Dakota	42	—
Ohio	46	97
Oklahoma	29	—
Oregon	57	—

Table 17.2. (*continued*)

State	% of white vote for Obama	% of black vote for Obama
Pennsylvania	48	95
Rhode Island	58	—
South Carolina	26	96
South Dakota	41	—
Tennessee	34	94
Texas	26	98
Utah	31	—
Vermont	68	—
Virginia	39	92
Washington	55	—
West Virginia	41	—
Wisconsin	54	91
Wyoming	32	—

disaffection with the Republican Party and a national shift in the political tide that was the direct result of poor economic conditions and a protracted war in Iraq and Afghanistan, among other things. Some claim that this deep-seated disaffection, reflected by historically low approval ratings for George W. Bush, created an opening for a Democratic candidate and that Obama's candidacy ultimately benefited from these unique factors. Despite these claims, analysis of the 2008 presidential primary exit polling results reveals that the vast majority of white voters extended their support to Hilary Clinton. This intraparty analysis neutralizes some of the arguments regarding the role of partisanship and provides another way to assess the influence of race during the 2008 election cycle. Indeed, a majority of white voters extended their support to Clinton during the Democratic primaries, with a majority voting for Obama only in his home state of Illinois and in Wisconsin, Virginia, Vermont, Utah, Oregon, and New Mexico. Obama's losses in the primary would be considered of landslide proportions among white voters in twenty-four of the thirty-six states in which exit polling data is available. Voting patterns that emerged during the 2008 presidential primary are reflected in Table 17.3.

In addition, the 2004 election also reveals that, in some states, white voters supported former Democratic presidential candidate John Kerry at far higher percentages than they supported Obama in the 2008 primary. Although this evidence is not entirely dispositive, it does suggest that race played a far greater role in shaping voting preferences than partisanship in many places. Indeed, an analysis of exit polling data reveals that there were notable declines in white voter support for the Democratic presidential nominee between 2004 and 2008—declining from 19 percent to 10 percent in Alabama, 14 percent to 11 percent in Mississippi; and 24 percent to 14 percent in Louisiana.[29] Indeed, the fact that Obama performed worse than Kerry among white voters in a number of states, particularly in the Deep South, at a time period

Table 17.3.   Voting patterns in the 2008 Democratic presidential primary election

State	% of white vote for Obama	% of black vote for Obama
Alabama	25	84
Alaska	—	—
Arizona	38	79
Arkansas	16	74
California	45	78
Colorado	—	—
Connecticut	48	74
Delaware	40	86
Florida	23	73
Georgia	43	88
Hawaii	—	—
Idaho	—	—
Illinois	57	93
Indiana	40	89
Iowa	33	72
Kansas	—	—
Kentucky	23	90
Louisiana	30	86
Maine	—	—
Maryland	42	84
Massachusetts	40	66
Michigan	—	—
Minnesota	—	—
Mississippi	26	92
Missouri	39	84
Montana	—	—
Nebraska	—	—
Nevada	34	83
New Hampshire	36	—
New Jersey	31	82
New Mexico	55	—
New York	37	61
North Carolina	37	91
North Dakota	—	—
Ohio	34	87
Oklahoma	29	—
Oregon	57	—

Table 17.3. (*continued*)

State	% of white vote for Obama	% of black vote for Obama
Pennsylvania	37	90
Rhode Island	37	—
South Carolina	24	78
South Dakota	—	—
Tennessee	26	77
Texas	44	84
Utah	55	—
Vermont	60	—
Virginia	52	90
Washington	—	—
West Virginia	23	—
Wisconsin	54	91
Wyoming	—	—

marked by a historically unpopular presidency,[30] is strong evidence that race likely played a significant role in shaping preference in these states.

Finally, it is worth noting that Obama had mixed success between the primary and general elections when examined on a state-by-state basis. Such an analysis reveals that Obama won the Democratic primary but then lost the general election in fourteen states;[31] lost the primary but won the general election in twelve states[32]; and lost both the primary and the general election in an additional and separate eight states.[33] Indeed, the rules controlling the way in which the primary elections were conducted had a notable impact and helped propel Obama forward to the general election. Interestingly, there are sixteen states in which Obama was successful during both the primary and general elections,[34] and only two of these are states that are subject to Section 5 of the Voting Rights Act, including North Carolina, and Virginia.

THE UNIQUE NATURE OF PRESIDENTIAL CONTESTS: DETERMINING THE PROBATIVE VALUE OF PRESIDENTIAL ELECTION ANALYSIS

Preliminary analysis of the 2008 election results certainly underscores high levels of racially polarized voting in the Deep South—which includes a significant number of places subject to the special Section 5 preclearance provision of the Voting Rights Act. With unquestionably high levels of polarized voting established in the covered jurisdictions, the central question then turns to the role of the 2008 presidential election in any analysis of voting discrimination or in any Section 2 claim that may be brought in those jurisdictions beyond the Deep South where Obama sustained enough white crossover support to help him carry the state. In this section, I argue that there are a number of distinguishing and unique features about the office and experience of running for presidency that significantly distinguish it from other local and state elected positions. Indeed, these unique features illustrate the exceptionalism characterizing the office of the presidency and provide additional bases for continuing to conduct case-by-case analysis and localized assessments to help determine whether voting discrimination persists in a particular community.

In many contexts, presidential contests may not prove to be the best metric of racially polarized voting at the local level, because these elections are unique in form and conduct, and are easily distinguishable from other kinds of positions or offices. Thus, depending on the particular jurisdiction or voting practice at issue, results from any presidential contest, and especially this most recent one, may not, by themselves, provide the most probative evidence of local voting patterns.

In certain instances, Obama's electoral success may stand in stark contrast to an otherwise consistent pattern of racially polarized voting. In such instances, evidence of Obama's electoral success could be deemed aberrational or inconsistent with prevailing voting patterns.[35] In certain communities, Obama's success may contrast significantly with the fates and experiences of other minority candidates who have run unsuccessfully in a particular local jurisdiction. In those instances, the singular evidence of minority electoral success in the 2008 presidential election should not negate the ability of a political scientist or other expert to demonstrate racially polarized voting. On the other hand, in those regions of the country where Obama was unsuccessful, it may be that the data confirms and further reinforces existing patterns of racially polarized voting. This evidence alone may not be enough to satisfy legal requirements in the context of litigation, but it may help tilt the scales where other endogenous or other local contests reveal the existence of racially polarized voting. In the remainder of this section, I will consider other aspects of the 2008 presidential election that may require further consideration and analysis by political scientists and that may make it more difficult for those seeking to use Obama's victory to prove or disprove the existence of voting discrimination in a community.

SPECIAL CIRCUMSTANCES: WHERE OBAMA'S VICTORY STANDS AS AN EXCEPTION TO THE RULE FOR THE FATE OF OTHER MINORITY CANDIDATES

Since Obama's 2008 victory, there appears to have been a notable increase in the number of minoirty candidates vying for elected office in majority white communities. In June 2009, James Young, earned a unique place in history after being elected as the first black mayor of Philadelphia, Mississippi—a town that became infamous after Ku Klux Klan members brutally murdered three civil rights workers (Cheney, Goodman, and Schwerner) in 1964. The town's population is 55 percent white. However, examples of such victories remain few and far between. In certain instances, courts may dismiss these kind of isolated victories as attributable to "special circumstances." Examples of the kind of facts that may be recognized as special circumstances include the absence of an opponent, a candidate's incumbency status, or the utilization of bullet or straight-ticket voting.[36] Of course, incumbency could play no role in any interpretation of Obama's victory, because no incumbent ran in the race.[37] However, in certain instances, one might view Obama's exceptional name recognition, attributable largely to his then-status as the sole black member of the U.S. Senate, as a special circumstance making his success more unusual than the kind of success that a typical minority candidate would likely achieve in a local or state contest in the relevant jurisdiction.[38] However, courts may express skepticism toward this contention as every presidential candidate arguably enjoys some level of stature and public name recognition—prerequisites that are debatably necessary in order to mount a viable bid for the office of presidency.

Another factor that might be given some consideration as a special circumstance is Obama's status as a biracial candidate, with a father of African descent and a white mother from Kansas.[39] Imagery from the 2008 election cycle included various photos of Obama and members of his family on his mother's side, and this fact may have made some white voters more inclined to support him.[40] Moreover, the fact that Obama's father was from outside America and that Obama was raised in Hawaii may also have served as points of demarcation that made some white voters more comfortable and willing to support him while less willing to support minority candidates generally. However, there is no known empirical study that has assessed how white voters perceived Obama or that has looked to see how many white voters supported Obama because they did not view him as a traditional Black candidate.

BALLOT DROP-OFF

Comparing voting patterns in presidential contests with patterns that emerge in local and state contests may also be complicated by what political scientists call "ballot drop-off" (also referred to as "voter drop-off"), a phenomenon in which voters vote for the most prestigious offices at the top of the ballot but not for those offices appearing lower on the ballot.[41] History has shown that presidential and gubernatorial elections draw the highest levels of voter turnout.[42] These special factors provide yet other reasons why the presidential election may not be the best gauge of racially polarized voting in a particular jurisdiction. Significant population differences between those who participated in the 2008 presidential election and those who participate in the particular local or state contests may further complicate efforts to draw conclusions about Obama's victory in any analysis of racially polarized voting.

THE IMPACT OF A PRESIDENTIAL RUNNING MATE

In addition to considering any special circumstances that may explain Obama's performance as a minority candidate, any empirical analysis of the 2008 presidential race might also take into account the impact of the vice presidential candidate on the level of public support that Obama received in the November general election. Some scholars and analysts have expressed skepticism about whether the naming of a vice presidential nominee affects the prospects of a presidential contender.[43] The general view is that voters cast their ballots for presidential candidates giving little attention to that candidate's choice of a vice presidential running mate. However, the 2008 presidential election presents the first opportunity to gauge the influence that a non-minority vice presidential candidate can have on a minority presidential candidate's prospects for success. Thus any analysis of Obama's success should attempt to measure the impact that Joe Biden had on Obama's ability to attract white crossover support. Indeed, no typical minority candidate running for a city council, a school board, a state legislature, or the U.S. Senate or House of Representatives has the opportunity to run alongside a running mate who might help that candidate attract a broader level of public support.[44]

NATIONAL FUND-RAISING DURING PRESIDENTIAL ELECTIONS

The ability to fund-raise on a national stage is most certainly another feature that distinguishes the experience of presidential candidates from those seeking election to local and states bodies. Federal Election Commission Chairman Michael E. Toner indicated that viable, major party presidential candidates would have needed to raise at least $100 million by the end of 2007.[45] Final estimates revealed that Obama raised nearly 750 million dollars during the course of the 2008 election cycle, after being the first major party candidate to bypass public financing.[46] Presidential candidates work to meet these substantial campaign finance expectations by fund-raising around the country, strategically focusing on those areas where they may have a loyal and wealthy support base. In the 2008 election, Obama was able to strategically focus on and fund-raise among existing supporters around the country. However, most candidates running for small, local, and state positions are not able to turn to or rely on outside sources of funding, or strategically fund-raise among non-minority voters in other parts of the country that might be willing to extend crossover support. Overall, there is far less national interest in local and state positions, which further suggests the importance of conducting very localized analyses into the existence of racially polarized voting.

DETERMINING THE PROBATIVE VALUE OF PRESIDENTIAL PRIMARIES VIS-À-VIS THE GENERAL ELECTION

In any analysis of the 2008 presidential election, one must also decide the relative significance to be given to the primary and general elections. This balancing test will vary, given factors such as the nature of partisanship in each jurisdiction and the design of the ballot. A discussion of some of these factors and how they should inform particularized findings regarding racial polarization follows.

DNC PROPORTIONAL REPRESENTATION RULES AND COMPLEX DEMOCRATIC PRIMARY SYSTEM

Many of the Democratic presidential primary contests that ultimately produced an Obama victory were conducted in ways that were very atypical of elections generally, with caucuses in some states and Democratic National Committee (DNC) proportional representation rules in effect throughout the country. Under DNC rules, the Democratic presidential candidate was selected through a rather complex series of primaries and caucuses culminating in the 2008 Democratic National Convention in late August.[47] Democratic candidates campaigned for the nomination in a series of primary elections and caucus events through which the delegates were selected. The results from these primaries and caucuses determined the number of pledged delegates committed to vote for each candidate at the Democratic National Convention.[48] In some states, voters selected their delegates for the Democratic National Convention by caucus—where votes are cast by voice in public.[49]

Ultimately, DNC proportional representation rules resulted in tremendous variance in the weighting of votes that determined how delegates were selected and distributed for purposes of participating in the National Convention.[50] The complex rules and mechanisms governing the selection of a Democratic presidential candidate are unlike the relatively simple direct voting methods used to elect candidates for the vast majority of other local and state offices. These facts would also seem to complicate use of traditional methodologies to measure racially polarized voting during the presidential primaries, and provide yet another reason to give the 2008 presidential election less probative value in any localized analysis of racially polarized voting. However, the complexity of the system for selecting a candidate may not necessarily warrant altogether discounting presidential primary results, but rather may warrant more weight being placed on exit polling data in assessing the existence of racially polarized voting.

CLOSED PRIMARIES

Further, a number of states conduct closed primary elections. Closed primaries restrict voters from voting for candidates outside their party of registration and thereby eliminate the likelihood that white voters in a jurisdiction (whether majority black or majority white) would cross party lines to support a candidate from another party. Thus, closed primaries decrease the significance of partisanship by essentially neutralizing this as a factor in a voter's selection of a candidate. Courts may be inclined to place greater significance on the racially polarized voting analysis yielded from closed primary states.[51]

Again, only a careful, case-by-case inquiry can help determine what probative value, if any, the 2008 presidential election should have in any future analyses of racially polarized voting. A fact-intensive inquiry is particularly necessary because, in certain instances, the presidential primary and presidential general elections may have been conducted under very different factual circumstances. For example, in states that conduct closed primary contests, where the impact of partisanship may be deemed somewhat neutralized, racial bloc voting patterns in the primaries may be particularly probative. However, in closed primary states where minority voters disproportionately comprise the electorate of a particular party, the general election may present a better opportunity to gauge racial voting patterns among non-minority voters.[52] In short, it is clear that there are no obvious rules shaping the role that 2008 presidential election data should have on assessments of racially polarized voting, and political scientists will need to scrutinize Obama's November 2008 victory carefully to determine what role partisanship played vis-à-vis race in shaping voters' choices.

CONCLUSION: DISCUSSING CONTEMPORARY VOTING DISCRIMINATION BEYOND THE CONTEXT OF THE 2008 ELECTION

What did Barack Obama's decisive victory in the 2008 election have to say about ongoing voting discrimination and racial polarization in American politics today? While some have argued that this election has moved the entire country beyond race, that conclusion seems to be the result of mere wishful thinking as careful analysis yields a very different result. Indeed, race proved to be a factor throughout the 2008 presidential election cycle—at times sparking interesting debate and hopeful discussion about our nation's long struggle to achieve racial progress, and at other times serving as a stinging reminder of both the enduring legacy of racism and ongoing problems of voting discrimination. The starkest evidence of ongoing discrimination was perhaps yielded by significant examples of racial appeals throughout the campaign led largely by white supremacist organizations and other individuals seeking to use race as a divisive wedge. However, these racial appeals were also accompanied by significant empirical data showing that voting remains deeply polarized in a number of communities across the country.

Alongside the victory of the nation's first African American president stands significant evidence that both racial polarization and voting discrimination persist in many jurisdictions. The weight of this evidence, which includes judicial findings, scholarly studies, expert analyses, exit polls, and personal testimonies, is not trumped by the outcome of the 2008 presidential election cycle alone. While this most recent presidential election suggests that, in some areas of the country, discriminatory voting patterns may not be as entrenched as in others, there is a much longer record of evidence that voting discrimination continues to stand as a significant barrier to equal political participation. I conclude that Obama's historic 2008 victory in the presidential election should neither cease the long struggle to achieve real political equality nor serve as a basis for precluding litigants from demonstrating the extent to which racially polarized voting may persist in future voting rights litigation.

NOTES

1. See, for example, Abigail Thernstrom and Stephan Thernstrom, op-ed., "Racial Gerrymandering Is Unnecessary," *Wall Street Journal*, November 11, 2008 (suggesting that an Obama victory means that "the doors of electoral opportunity in America are open to all" and arguing that "the Voting Rights Act should therefore be reconsidered").
2. See, for example, Michael Crowley, "Post-Racial," *The New Republic*, March 12, 2008; Shelby Steele, "Obama's Post-Racial Promise," *Los Angeles Times*, November 5, 2008 (characterizing Obama as a postracial candidate and pointing to an interview with former Klansman David Duke, who found little difference between Hillary Clinton and Barack Obama); see Abigail Thernstrom and Stephan Thernstrom, op-ed., "Taking Race Out of the Race," *Los Angeles Times*, March 2, 2008.
3. 42 U.S.C. § 1973(a) (2006).
4. See, for example, *Bone Shirt v. Hazeltine*, 336 F. Supp. 2d 976, 1010 (D.S.D. 2004) (noting that racially polarized voting was ordinarily the "keystone of a vote dilution case").
5. J. Morgan Kousser, Colorblind Injustice: Minority Voting Rights and the Undoing of the Second Reconstruction 53 (1999) (describing the relatedness of the purposes of the Voting Rights Act and the Fourteenth and Fifteenth Amendments); Alexander Keyssar, The Right to Vote: The Contested History of Democracy in the United States (2000) (chronicling the legal and political history surrounding the struggle for suffrage rights among African Americans and other groups).
6. *Reno v. Bossier Parish Sch. Bd.*, 520 U.S. 471, 479 (1997) (quoting S. Rep. NO. 97417, at 28).
7. S. Rep. NO. 97–417, at 30 (1982) (Senate report on the Voting Rights Act amendments of 1982).

8. 478 U.S. 30 (1986). In 1982, Congress amended Section 2 to implement a discriminatory results standard that eliminated the requirement that litigants provide proof of purposeful discrimination. See Voting Rights Act Amendments of 1982, Pub. L. No. 97–205, § 3, 96 Stat. 131, 134 (codified at 42 U.S.C. § 1973a [2000]).

9. *Gingles*, 478 U.S. at 50–51.

10. The Supreme Court recently ruled in the case of *Bartlett v. Strickland* (07–689) that the Voting Rights Act only requires districts that are at least 50 percent minority in composition.

11. Rogers, at 621, quoting *Nevett v. Sides*, 571 F.2d 209, 224 (CA5 1978),

12. 458 U.S. at 458 U. S. 622.

13. *Mallory v. Ohio*, 38 F. Supp. 2d 525, 537 (E.D. Ohio 1997); Allan J. Lichtman and J. Gerald Hebert, "*A General Theory of Vote Dilution*," *La Raza Law Journal* 6 (1993): 1, 5.

14. Bernard Grofman, "*A Primer on Racial Bloc Voting Analysis*," in *The Real Y2K Problem: Census 2000 Data and Redistricting Technology*, ed. Nathaniel Persily (2000), 43.

15. Ibid.; Bernard Grofman, "Multivariate Methods and the Analysis of Racially Polarized Voting: Pitfalls in the Use of Social Science by the Courts," *Social Science Quarterly* 72 (1991): 826.

16. See *Cottier v. City of Martin*, 445 F.3d 1113, 1120 (8th Cir. 2006) (crediting findings of exit poll in concluding that plaintiffs satisfied their burden of showing racially polarized voting*); Harvell v. Blytheville Sch. Dist.*, 71 F.3d 1382, 1386 (8th Cir. 1995) (considering evidence including statistical analysis, exit polling, and lay testimony); *Hall v. Holder*, 955 F.2d 1563, 1571 (11th Cir. 1992) (finding strong correlation between results of regression analysis and exit polling figures and crediting findings of exit poll data in determining that jurisdiction experienced racially polarized voting), *rev'd on other grounds*, 114 S. Ct. 2581 (1994); *Romero v. City of Pomona*, 883 F.2d 1418, 1426–27 (9th Cir. 1989) (crediting findings from exit poll from city council primary election in concluding that third *Gingles* precondition was not satisfied); *Chisom v. Roemer*, No. 86–4057, 1989 U.S. Dist. LEXIS 10816, at 14–15 (E.D. La. September 13, 1989) ("In analyzing statistical data, the Court finds that the best available data for estimating the voting behavior of various groups in the electorate would come from exit polls . . . but such evidence is not available."), *remanded*, 917 F.2d 187 (5th Cir. 1990), *rev'd on other grounds*, 501 U.S. 380 (1991).

17. See *Cane v. Worcester County*, 840 F. Supp. 1081, 1088 n.6 (D. Md. 1994) (stating that "endogenous elections include voting patterns in elections for offices the plaintiffs challenge in their § 2 suit").

18. See *Bone Shirt v. Hazeltine*, 461 F.3d 1011, 1021 (8th Cir. 2006) (noting that "although they are not as probative as endogenous elections, exogenous elections hold some probative value"); *Johnson v. Hamrick*, 155 F. Supp. 2d 1355, 1375 (N.D. Ga. 2001) (allowing both exogenous and endogenous elections as evidence).

19. See, for example, *Jenkins v. Red Clay Consol. Sch. Dist. Bd. of Educ.*, 4 F.3d 1103, 1128 (3rd Cir. 1993) (finding that white vs. white elections are less probative for the third *Gingles* prong); *League of United Latin Am. Citizens, Council No. 4344 v. Clements*, 999 F.2d 831, 864 (5th Cir. 1993) (finding that white vs. white elections are less probative); *Westwego Citizens for Better Gov't v. Westwego*, 872 F.2d 1201, 1208 n.7 (5th Cir. 1989) ("The evidence most probative of racially polarized voting must be drawn from elections including both black and white candidates."); *City of Carrolton Branch of the NAACP v. Stallings*, 829 F.2d 1547, 1559 (11th Cir. 1987). See also *Southern Christian Leadership Conference of Ala. v. Sessions*, 56 F.3d 1281, 1303–04 (11th Cir. 1995), *cert. denied*, 516 U.S. 1045 (1996); *Nipper v. Smith*, 39 F.3d 1494, 1541 (11th Cir. 1994) (Tjoflat, C. J., joined by Anderson, J.) (finding that the most probative white vs. white elections are ones "in which the candidate of choice of black voters differed from the candidate of choice of white voters").

20. See, for example, *Westwego Citizens*, 872 F.2d at 1209 (finding that, in a case with no available endogenous interracial elections, exogenous election data may be used to help prove racial voting patterns); *Citizens for a Better Gretna v. Gretna*, 834 F.2d 496, 502 (5th Cir. 1987) (allowing use of exogenous elections to make a showing for the third prong of the *Gingles* test).

21. See Warren J. Mitofsky, "A Short History of Exit Polls," in *Polling and Presidential Election Coverage* (Paul J. Lavrakas & Jack K. Holley eds., 1991): 83–99.

22. *South Carolina v. Katzenbach*, 383 U.S. 301, 309–15 (1966) (citing H.R. Rep. NO. 89–439, at 8–16 [1965]; S. Rep. No. 89–162, pt. 3, at 3–16 [1965]). Congress selected these jurisdictions by designing a coverage formula (based in part on turnout figures from presidential elections in 1964, 1968, and 1972, and on the presence of a prohibited device such as a literacy test), which effectively serves as a proxy for identifying jurisdictions with the longest and most egregious histories of entrenched voting discrimination. 42 U.S.C. §1973b(b) (2000).

23. Jurisdictions can obtain Section 5 preclearance administratively by submitting the change to the attorney general of the U.S. Department of Justice or judicially by means of a Section 5 declaratory judgment action filed in the U.S. District Court for the District of Columbia. Until the voting change is precleared, the change is deemed legally unenforceable. *See South Carolina v. United States*, 589 F. Supp. 757 (D.D.C. 1984) (the District Court for the District of Columbia can enjoin any attempt to implement the change prior to granting of a declaratory judgment of preclearance). Changes that are retrogressive are ones that worsen the position of minority voters.

24. See Allan J. Lichtman and J. Gerald Herbert, *"A General Theory of Vote Dilution,"* *La Raza Law Journal* 6 (1993): 1, 5. (observing the sixty-percent "landslide standard" for elections).

25. Cf. *Houston v. Lafayette County*, 56 F.3d 606, 612 (5th Cir. 1995) (holding that the district court should have focused evidence of racially polarized voting on particularized findings instead of broad evidence); *Clark v. Calhoun County*, 21 F.3d 92, 93 (5th Cir. 1994) (remanding because of the district court's lack of particularized findings regarding racially polarized voting); *Teague v. Attala County*, 17 F.3d 796, 798 (5th Cir. 1994) (holding that the lower court should have evaluated statistical evidence about racially polarized voting more comprehensively).

26. A county-by-county analysis of the vote in North Carolina reveals that Obama received 50 percent or more of the overall vote in twenty-two of the state's thirty-eight covered counties. Losses in the noncovered counties were relatively deeper, perhaps illustrating the success of the Voting Rights Act in bringing about greater potential for multiracial coalitions.

27. See *Johnson v. De Grandy*, 512 U.S. 997, 1011 (1994) (recognizing that the "ultimate conclusions about equality or inequality of opportunity were intended by Congress to be judgments resting on comprehensive, not limited, canvassing of relevant facts").

28. See Charleston County Litig. (SC), 365 F.3d 341, 353 (4th Cir. 2004) (holding that it was not clearly erroneous for the district court to conclude that "even controlling for partisanship in Council elections, race still appears to play a role in the voting patterns of white and minority voters in Charleston County"); *Reed v. Town of Babylon*, 914 F. Supp. 843, 877 (E.D.N.Y. 1996) (stating that losses attributable to partisanship voting rather than racial bias would not constitute legally significant bloc voting).

29. See 2004 exit polls and election results, http://www.cnn.com/ELECTION/2004/pages/results/president.

30. Susan Page, "Disapproval of Bush Breaks Record," *USA Today*, April 22, 2008 (noting results of a 2008 Gallup Poll that revealed 69 percent of Americans disapproved of the job Bush was doing and noting that the disapproval rating set a new high for any president

since Franklin Roosevelt, and also observing that the previous record of 67 percent was reached by Harry Truman in January 1952, when the United States was enmeshed in the Korean War).

31. Those states include Alabama, Alaska, Georgia, Idaho, Kansas, Louisiana, Nebraska, Missouri, North Dakota, Montana, Mississippi, South Carolina, Utah, and Wyoming.

32. Those states include California, Florida, Indiana, Massachusetts, Michigan, Nevada, New Hampshire, New Jersey, New Mexico, New York, Pennsylvania, and Rhode Island.

33. The eight states where Obama lost the primary and general elections include Arizona, Arkansas, Kentucky, Oklahoma, South Dakota, Tennessee, Texas, and West Virginia.

34. Those states in which Obama was successful both in the primary and general elections include Colorado, Connecticut, Delaware, Hawaii, Illinois, Iowa, Maine, Maryland, Minnesota, North Carolina, Oregon, Virginia, Vermont, Washington, Washington, D.C., and Wisconsin.

35. Cf., for example, *Magnolia Bar Ass'n, Inc. v. Lee*, 994 F.2d 1143, 1149 (5th Cir. 1993) (finding that it is "entirely reasonable to permit [a] district court to examine the election results offered by both sides, as well as the circumstances surrounding those elections . . . [to determine] which elections are aberrational").

36. See *Gingles*, 478 U.S. at 57 (success of a minority candidate in a particular election does not necessarily prove that the district did not experience polarized voting in that election; special circumstances, such as the absence of an opponent, incumbency, or the utilization of bullet voting, may explain minority electoral success in a polarized contest). But see *Bradley v. Work*, 916 F. Supp. 1446, 1469 (S.D. Ind. 1996) (refusing to find special circumstances based on "bare conclusory assertions that [black candidate] was elected as part of a political deal," without any explanation of the relevance of the "deal").

37. Indeed, another factor that made this presidential election historic was that it was the first in forty years in which neither the sitting president's nor sitting vice president's name appeared on the ballot. For more discussion regarding courts' treatment of incumbency as a special circumstance, see *Anthony v. Michigan*, 35 F. Supp. 2d 989, 1006 (E.D. Mich. 1999) (providing limited examples of successful, nonincumbent African American candidates who were considered subject to "unique circumstances" but not "special circumstances"); *Clarke v. City of Cincinnati*, 40 F.3d 807, 813 (6th Cir. 1994) (finding that "incumbency plays a significant role in the vast majority of American elections" and "to qualify as a 'special' circumstance . . . incumbency must play an unusually important role in the election at issue").

38. Cf. *Brown v. Bd. of Comm'rs of Chattanooga, Tenn.*, 722 F. Supp. 380, 394 (E.D. Tenn. 1989) (recognizing that most African Americans in Chattanooga could not achieve the success of a certain black candidate).

39. Barack Obama, *Dreams From My Father: A Story of Race and Inheritance* (1995; New York: Three Rivers, 2004) (describing both his African lineage on his paternal side his maternal lineage which traces back from Hawaii to a small town in Kansas); Colm Tóibín, "James Baldwin & Barack Obama," *New York Review of Books*, October 23, 2008 ("When Obama was a child, he wrote, 'my father . . . was black as pitch, my mother white as milk.'").

40. See Chris Edley, Keynote address, *Stanford Journal of Civil Rights & Civil Liberties* 4 (2008):151 (describing problem he labels as "racial exhaustion" in the American public and linking Barack Obama's appeal among many white voters to the fact that Obama does not talk much about race which produces a certain comfort level with his candidacy); see also Amos N. Jones, "Black Like Obama: What the Junior Illinois Senator's Appearance on the National Scene Reveals about Race in America, and Where We Should Go from Here," *Thurgood Marshall Law Review*, 31 (2005): 79–80; "The Identity Card," *Time*,

November 30, 2007 (noting that there were constant reminders of Obama's biracial identity throughout the election cycle and observing that Obama's interracial background puts him at cross-purposes and gives him a racelessness that is politically appealing to whites), available at http://www.time.com/time/magazine/chapter/0,9171,1689619–2,00.html.

41. Thomas E. Cronin, *Direct Democracy: The Politics of Initiative, Referendum and Recall* (1989), 66–67. (explaining that while "voter falloff is typical, voter 'turnon' occurs when controversial and highly visible issues are placed on the ballot "and also discussing studies that show a 5 percent to 15 percent drop-off in voter participation, which means that voters come to the polls but fail to vote on candidates or issues at the bottom of the ballot). See also R. Darcy and Anne Schneider, "Confusing Ballots, Roll-Off, and the Black Vote," *Western Political Quarterly*, 42 (1989): 347–48.

42. Richard Briffault, "Distrust of Democracy," 63 *Texas Law Review, 63* (1985): 1358–59 (observing that the candidate contests with the highest turnouts are presidential and gubernatorial elections); see Harold W. Stanley and Richard G. Niemi, *Vital Statistics on American Politics*, 2001–2002 (Congressional Quarterly Press, 2001): 13 tbl.1–1 (observing that since 1980, voter turnout in presidential election years has hovered above 50 percent, while during the same period voter turnout in nonpresidential election years (i.e., years in which elections for state offices share the ballot only with federal congressional or senatorial races) has on only one occasion been as high as 40 percent and typically hovers in the mid-30 percent range).

43. See, for example, Howard M. Wasserman, "The Trouble with Shadow Government," *Emory Law Journal* 52 (2003): 281, 314. (arguing that "voters cannot cast a separate vote for vice president, and it is unlikely that the vice presidential candidate's presence will affect the decision to vote for the presidential candidate at the head of the ticket"); David W. Romero, "Requiem for a Lightweight: Vice Presidential Candidate Evaluations and the Presidential Vote," *Presidential Studies Quarterly* 31 (2001): 454, 462. (finding that vice presidential nominees have little impact on voters' choice in their presidential vote); Nelson Polsby, "A Safe Choice, But Edwards Is on the Sidelines," *Financial Times* (UK), July 8, 2004 (concluding that "US public opinion surveys and exit polls have pretty much established that the identity of a vice-presidential candidate has little or no effect on the outcome of a US presidential election").

44. Some might equate the impact of a vice presidential candidate on the prospects of a presidential candidate to the impact that endorsements generally have on any candidate for elective office. However, vice presidential candidates would appear to have more significance and impact than endorsements, in that the vice presidential candidate exercises actual power and responsibility during the course of a president's term in office. See, generally, U.S. Constitution, Article II, Section 1, clause 6 ("In Case of the Removal of the President from Office, or of his Death, Resignation, or Inability to discharge the Powers and Duties of the said Office, the Same shall devolve on the Vice President, and the Congress may by Law provide for the Case of Removal, Death, Resignation or Inability, both of the President and Vice President, declaring what Officer shall then act as President, and such Officer shall act accordingly, until the Disability be removed, or a President shall be elected."); Richard D. Friedman, "Some Modest Proposals on the Vice-Presidency," *Michigan Law Review*, 86 (1988): 1703.

45. David D. Kirkpatrick, "Death Knell May Be Near for Public Election Funds," *New York Times*, January 23, 2007 (Toner observed that "top-tier candidates are going to have to raise $100 million by the end of 2007 to be a serious candidate," which essentially amounted to what he described as "a $100 million entry fee.").

46. Michael Luo, "Obama Hauls in Record $750 Million for Campaign," *New York Times*, December 4, 2008.

47. In order to secure the nomination at the convention, the candidate had to receive at least 2,117 votes from delegates (a simple majority of the total 4,233 delegate votes). Delegates, not voters themselves, decided the nomination at the Democratic National Convention. Ultimately, delegates from forty-eight U.S. states, the District of Columbia, and Puerto Rico had a single vote each, while delegates from the protectorates and from Florida and Michigan had one-half vote each. See, Democratic National Committee, delegate selection rules for the 2008 Democratic National Convention (2006), available at http://www .demconvention.com/a/2007/03/delegate_select.html.

48. Ibid. Pledged delegates were allocated according to two main criteria: (1) the proportion of votes each state gave to the Democratic candidate in the last three presidential elections and (2) the percentage of votes each state has in the Electoral College. In addition to delegates, each state was allotted some number of superdelegates who were free to vote for any candidate of their choice at the convention.

49. Some political scientists braced themselves for what has come to be known as the Bradley effect—a phenomenon where white voters' actual levels of support for black candidates, once they go behind the curtain to cast a secret ballot, prove far lower than the levels of support they reported to pollsters. To date, there has been little evidence that the Bradley effect materialized during the 2008 election cycle, as there was general consistency between the results of preelection polls and Election Day outcomes.

50. See Richard Hasen, "'Too Plain for Argument?' The Uncertain Congressional Power to Require Parties to Choose Presidential Nominees Through Direct and Equal Primaries," 102 *Northwestern University Law Rev.* 102 (2008): 2009–10 (observing that the hotly contested 2008 presidential primary election for the Democratic Party nomination would likely to lead to future calls for reform because of critics' arguments that the caucus system used in some states is unfair and poorly administered; that the unequal weighting of votes for purposes of delegate selection violates democratic principles; and that the fate of the Democratic Party presidential nomination should not turn on the votes of unelected "superdelegates"); William G. Mayer and Andrew E. Busch, "Can the Federal Government Reform the Presidential Nomination Process," 3 *Election Law Journal* (2004): 613–14.

51. Further complicating this analysis is the fact that in some states, including Oklahoma, Arkansas, Louisiana, and Tennessee, many more voters voted Republican in the 2008 general election than in 2004, indicating that Democrats may have crossed party lines in these states at exceptionally high rates. One explanation for this may be particularly acute racial polarization in these jurisdictions, where white voters were unwilling to extend support to Obama during the general election, perhaps because of race. See Shan Carter et al., "Electoral Shifts," *New York Times*, November 5, 2008, http://www.nytimes.com/ interactive/2008/11/05/us/politics/20081104_ELECTION_RECAP.html.

52. In a number of states in the South, African Americans make up nearly half of registered Democratic voters. Juan Williams, op-ed., "The Race Issue Isn't Going Away," *Wall Street Journal*, August 4, 2008.

About the Editors and Contributors

The editor of Palgrave Macmillan's Critical Black Studies Series, **Manning Marable** has been one of America's most prominent progressive intellectuals for over three decades.

Marable is the M. Moran Weston and Black Alumni Professor of African American Studies and professor of public affairs, political science, and history at Columbia University. For ten years he was the founding director of the Institute for Research in African American Studies at Columbia, from 1993 to 2003. Under his leadership, the Institute became one of the nation's most respected African American Studies programs in the country.

Since receiving his PhD in American history at the University of Maryland–College Park in 1976, Marable has been a major architect of outstanding African American Studies and interdisciplinary studies university programs. In the early 1980s, he reestablished Fisk University's historic Race Relations Institute, founded originally in 1944 by sociologist Charles S. Johnson. From 1983 to 1986, Marable was founding director of Colgate University's Africana and Latin American Studies Program.

At Columbia University in 2002, Marable established the Center for Contemporary Black History (CCBH), an innovative research, publications, and new media resources center. CCBH produces the leading African American Studies academic journal in the country, *Souls: A Critical Journal of Black Politics, Culture and Society*. Under Marable's editorial direction, *Souls* is published by Taylor and Francis.

A prolific author since 1975, Marable has produced fifteen books, thirteen edited volumes, and over four hundred articles in academic journals, edited volumes, encyclopedias, and related publications. Some of Marable's major works include *How Capitalism Underdeveloped Black America* (1983); *Beyond Black and White* (1995); *Black Leadership* (1998); *The Great Wells of Democracy: The Meaning of Race in American Life* (2002); *The Autobiography of Medgar Evers* (coedited with Myrtle Evers Williams, 2005); *Living Black History: How Reimagining the African-American Past Can Remake America's Racial Future* (2006); and *Race, Reform and Rebellion: The Second Reconstruction and Beyond in Black America, 1945–2006* (2007).

Kristen Clarke is a civil rights attorney based in Washington, D.C., and is recognized as an expert on voting rights and election-related matters. Currently, she serves as the codirector of the Political Participation Group at the NAACP Legal Defense and Educational Fund (LDF) where she oversees and coordinates the organization's legal program in the areas of voting rights, including redistricting and federal voting rights enforcement. Ms. Clarke has provided testimony to Congress regarding election reform and other voting rights matters and recently helped defend the Voting Rights Act against a constitutional challenge in one of the most important civil rights cases to come before the Supreme Court in years. Prior to joining LDF, Ms. Clarke worked for several years in the Civil Rights Division of the U.S. Department of Justice.

Ms. Clarke writes and comments frequently on issues concerning race, law, and democracy. Her scholarly work has appeared in a number of leading journals and publications including the *Harvard Civil Rights and Civil Liberties Law Review*, *Harvard Law and Policy Review*, *Houston Law Review*, *Howard Law Journal*, and *America Votes!: A Guide to Modern Election Law and Voting Rights*, among others. Along with Dr. Manning Marable, she also served as coeditor of *Seeking Higher Ground: The Hurricane Katrina Crisis, Race, and Public Policy Reader*. She received her AB from Harvard University and her JD from Columbia Law School.

David A. Bositis is a senior research associate at the Joint Center for Political and Economic Studies in Washington, D.C. He is the author of several books and studies, including *Diverging Generations: The Transformation of African American Policy Views (2001)*.

Kareem U. Crayton is an associate professor of law and political science at the University of Southern California. He holds a PhD in Political Science and JD from Stanford University. His research addresses questions on race and electoral politics, particularly on policies designed to encourage and maintain the political representation of racial minority groups. He is the author of publications including *What's New About the New South?* (2000), which examines the effects of the 1965 Voting Rights Act on the redistricting politics of the American South in the 1990s.

Grant Farred is a professor of Africana Studies and English at Cornell University. He is author of works such as "What's My Name? Black Vernacular Intellectuals," "Long Distance Love: A Passion for Football," and "Phantom Calls: Race and the Globalization of the NBA." He has served as General Editor of the *South Atlantic Quarterly* since 2002.

Bill Fletcher, Jr., is the executive editor of BlackCommentator.com, a Senior Scholar with the Institute for Policy Studies, and immediate past president of TransAfrica Forum. The author of numerous articles, he is a long-time labor and global justice activist and was deeply involved in the 1984 and 1988 Jackson campaigns. He is the coauthor, with Dr. Fernando Gapasin, of *Solidarity Divided* (University of California Press, 2008), which analyzes the crisis in organized labor in the United States.

Carly Fraser is a master's candidate in American Studies at Columbia University's Graduate School of Arts and Sciences. Her research focuses on African American history. She works in the college editorial department at an independent publishing house in New York City. She is also an assistant editor at W. W. Norton & Company.

Danny Glover is a long-time human rights activist and internationally recognized actor. He has been a spokesperson for many causes including anemia, HIV/AIDS, Haitian sovereignty, and global justice.

Fredrick C. Harris is Professor of Political Science and Director of the Center on African-American Politics and Society at Columbia University. He is the author of the forthcoming book tentatively titled *The Price of the Ticket: Barack Obama and the Rise and Decline of Black Politics,* to be published by Oxford University Press.

Rickey Hill is a professor of political science and dean of Graduate Studies at Mississippi Valley State University. Over the past thirty years, Hill has taught on the political science faculties at Fisk University, Tennessee State University, Tougaloo College, South Carolina State University, University of South Carolina, DePauw University, and Williams College. His specialty areas are black politics, political theory, and the politics of black public intellectuals. Hill has published thirteen book chapters and more than twenty journal and general articles. His semnial essay, "The Contemporary Black Predicament: Crisis and Political Obligations," is in its third printing in Franklin D. Jones and Michael O. Adams, *Readings in American Political Issues* (Dubuque: Kendall/Hunt, 1987, 2004, 2007), and is widely used in colleges and universities throughout the United States.

Gerald Horne is a Moores Professor of history and African American Studies and the University of Houston and has published two dozen books, including *Fire This Time: The Watts Uprising and the 1960s.*

Malaika Horne, PhD, is director of the Executive Leadership Institute/College of Business at the University of Missouri–St. Louis. Dr. Horne is Curator Emeritus of the University of Missouri System, serving as president in 1997.

Derek S. Hyra is an associate professor of urban affairs and planning at Virginia Tech. He is the author of *The New Urban Renewal: The Economic Transformation of Harlem and Bronzeville* (University of Chicago Press, 2008). He received his PhD from the University of Chicago and is a former Resident Fellow of the W. E. B. Du Bois Institute at Harvard University.

Sherrilyn A. Ifill is a professor at law at the University of Maryland School of Law in Baltimore. For over twenty years she has served as a litigator and consultant on voting rights cases. She is the author of numerous articles about racism and racial violence, judicial decision making, voting, and political participation. Her book *On the Courthouse Lawn: Confronting the Legacy of Lynching in the 21st Century* was a finalist for the 2008 Hurston/Wright book award for nonfiction. She received a BA from Vassar College in 1984 and a Juris Doctor degree from the New York University School of Law in 1987.

Joy James is John B. and John T. McCoy Presidential Professor of the Humanities and college professor in political science at Williams College. James is also a Senior Research Fellow at the John Warfield Center for African and African American Studies at the University of Texas, Austin.

Keesha M. Middlemass is an assistant professor of political science at Rutgers University–Newark. Middlemass's scholarship is grounded in social science research and explores the intersectionality of institutions, voting behavior, politics, race, and public policy, and she has published in a variety of venues on these same topics.

Gregory S. Parks, JD, PhD, is a law clerk to a federal appeals court judge in the Washington, D.C., area. His work has appeared in the *Cornell Journal of Law and*

Public Policy, Hastings Women's Law Journal, Journal of Criminal Law and Criminology, and the *University of Pennsylvania Law Review PENNumbra*. Dr. Parks is the editor of six books, including *Black Greek-letter Organizations in the 21st Century: Our Fight Has Just Begun* (2008) and *Critical Race Realism: Intersections of Psychology, Race, and Law* (2008).

Jeffrey J. Rachlinski holds a JD and a PhD in psychology from Stanford University and is a professor of law at Cornell Law School.

Ryan Reft holds a BA from the University of Chicago (History, 1998) and master's degrees from NYU (Social Studies, 2001) and Columbia University (American Studies, 2007). He taught history and English in New York City public high schools for nine years. Currently, he is a twentieth-century urban history doctoral candidate at the University of California–San Diego.

Mark Sawyer is currently an associate professor of African American Studies and political science at UCLA and the director of the Center for the Study of Race, Ethnicity, and Politics. He received his PhD in political sScience from the University of Chicago in December of 1999. His book titled *Racial Politics in Post Revolutionary Cuba* (Cambridge University Press, 2006) received the Du Bois Award for the best book by the National Conference of Black Political Scientists and the Ralph Bunche Award from the American Political Science Association.

Robert C. Smith is a professor of political science at San Francisco State University. He is General Editor of the State University of New York (SUNY) Press Africa American Studies Series and associate editor of the *National Political Science Review*. He is author or coauthor of scores of articles and essays and ten books. Among the books are *Race, Class and Culture* (1992); *Racism in the Post–Civil Rights Era* (1995); *We Have No Leaders* (1996); *African American Leadership* (1999); *Contemporary Controversies and the American Racial Divide* (2000); *American Politics and the African American Quest for Universal Freedom* (2009); and the forthcoming *Conservatism and Racism and Why in America They Are the Same* (SUNY, 2009).

Index

Reason for not voting	1997 50+ years Total %	2000 18–35 years Total %	2000 18–35 years Nonvoters %
Neither candidate is worth supporting	7.8	22.2	41.7
Politicians don't keep their campaign promises	6.5	30.3	56.1
Your one vote won't make any different to the outcome	0	17.0	31.4
Not voting is a way to show dissatisfaction with the system	1.2	18.3	33.8
Don't know enough about the candidates	5.7	25.7	47.5
(N =)	245	750	408

9 780230 620506